FORMS and FUNCTIONS
of TWENTIETH-CENTURY
ARCHITECTURE

IN FOUR VOLUMES

VOLUME II

The Principles of Composition

FORMS and FUNCTIONS of TWENTIETH-CENTURY ARCHITECTURE

Edited by TALBOT HAMLIN, *F.A.I.A.*

With an Introduction by Leopold Arnaud, F.A.I.A.

VOLUME II

The Principles of Composition

BY THE EDITOR, WITH A CHAPTER ON COLOR
BY JULIAN E. GARNSEY

Prepared under the auspices of the
School of Architecture of Columbia University

New York COLUMBIA UNIVERSITY PRESS *1952*

Acknowledgments

FOR AID in the preparation of this volume the editor wishes to make grateful acknowledgments to:

Dean Leopold Arnaud, of the School of Architecture of Columbia University, for a critical reading of the entire volume;

Dean Joseph Hudnut, of the Graduate School of Design, Harvard University, for permission to make use of the outlines in architectural theory prepared by him while he was Dean of the School of Architecture of Columbia University;

Professor William H. Hayes, of the School of Architecture of Columbia University, for a critical reading of the chapters on architectural design and structural methods and for many important suggestions;

Professor Eugene Raskin, of the School of Architecture of Columbia University, for valuable assistance and a critical reading of the chapter on architectural design and building materials;

Payson & Clarke, Ltd., for permission to make extensive quotations from Le Corbusier's *Towards a New Architecture*, translated by Frederick Etchells;

Several museums, foundations, institutes, and historical societies for assistance in obtaining illustrations, notably the American Institute of Steel Construction, the Buhl Foundation at Pittsburgh, the Essex Institute in Salem, Massachusetts, the Metropolitan Museum of Art in New York, the Museum of the City of New York, and the Museum of Modern Art in New York;

The American Swedish News Exchange, the British Information Services, and the Netherlands Information Bureau for many illustrations;

The New York City Parks Department, the Triborough Bridge and Tunnel Authority in New York, the Graphics Material Section of the Tennessee Valley Authority, and the St. Louis City Planning Commission for various illustrations;

Numerous publishers who have kindly permitted the reproduction of illustrations from their books and periodicals, the detailed credits for which will be found in the List of Illustrations; and

Many architects, architectural photographers, and commercial firms who have furnished illustration copy; the complete credits for these are given in the List of Illustrations.

THE EDITOR

Contents

CONTENTS

Illustrations

The Principles of Composition

JULIAN ELLSWORTH GARNSEY, author of the chapter "Color in Architecture," is a professional color consultant for architecture and industry. His clients have included the Metropolitan Life Insurance Company, the Socony-Vacuum Oil Company, the *Oregon Journal*, the Los Angeles Public Library, the Dallas Centennial Exposition, and the New York World's Fair of 1939–40. He has lectured widely at universities and architectural schools and before professional societies and institutes.

I

Architectural Aesthetics
An Introduction

MARCUS VITRUVIUS POLLIO, the earliest architectural writer whose entire work has come down to us, writing at the time of Augustus, stated that architecture had a triple basis: in its works it sought for convenience, for solid and lasting strength, and for beauty (Fig. 1). The critic of today would put it as the search for perfect functioning, for good construction, and for sensitive and imaginative creative design. From the time of Vitruvius down to our own, these three different factors have remained as essential elements in good architecture, although different periods have given differing relative weights to them. The thirteenth-century sketchbook of Villard de Honnecourt (Figs. 3, 4, 12) shows an eager interest in both structure and appearance, and the plans of medieval houses, big and little—especially of the town houses—reveal in many ways a careful consideration of convenience, as convenience was then considered. Monastery, church, and cathedral design was marked by the most careful construction, and the aesthetic character of it all is obvious. Apparently medieval architects gave equal stress to all three approaches. In the Renaissance period, and increasingly through the later sixteenth and seventeenth centuries, aesthetic form came to occupy the chief position, until the academic writers of Louis XIV France—men like François Blondel (Fig. 5) and Claude Perrault (Fig. 6)—seem, at least in their books, to be interested almost solely in questions of proportion, detail, and façade design. They realized, of course, that buildings were built to serve a purpose and that construction must be solid; but their chief interest lay in matters of aesthetic theory.

In the eighteenth century there was a reaction against this one-sided view. The rationalistic temper of the age and the development of the concept of the small convenient house alike forced attention on matters of convenience and of efficient and compact planning. New materials and new ways of utilizing

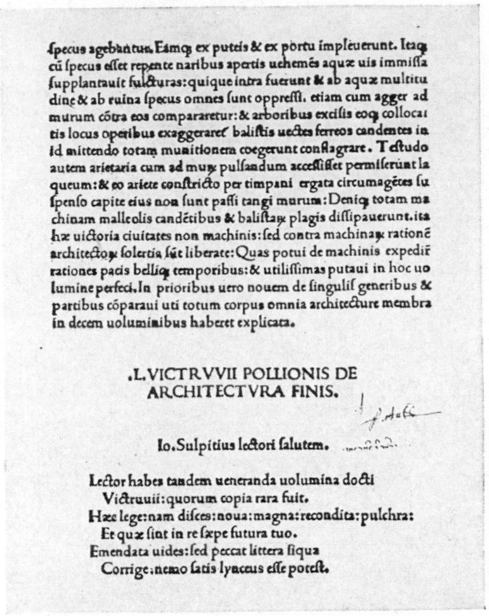

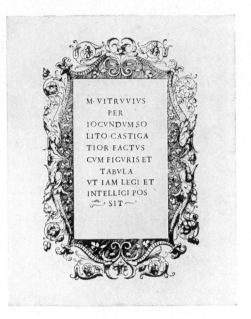

ſpecus agebantur. Eamq; ex puteis & ex portu impleuerunt. Itaq;
cũ ſpecus eſſet repente naribus apertis uehemẽs aquæ uis immiſſa
ſupplantauit fulcturas: quique intra fuerunt & ab aquæ multitu
dine & ab ruina ſpecus omnes ſunt oppreſſi. etiam cum agger ad
murum cõtra eos compararetur: & arboribus excilis eoq; collocai
tis locus operibus exaggeraret balistis uectes ferreos candentes in
id mittendo totam munitionem coegerunt conflagrare. Teſtudo
autem arietaria cum ad murꝝ pulſandum acceſſiſſet permiſerũt la
queum: & eo ariete conſtricto per timpani ergata circumagẽtes ſu
ſpenſo capite eius non ſunt paſſi tangi murum: Deniq; totam ma
chinam malleolis candẽtibus & baliſtaꝝ plagis diſſipauerunt. ita
hæ uictoria ciuitates non machinis: ſed contra machinaꝝ rationẽ
architectoꝝ ſolertia ſũt liberate: Quas potui de machinis expedirẽ
rationes pacis belliq; temporibus: & utiliſſimas putaui in hoc uo
lumine perfeci. In prioribus uero nouem de ſingulis generibus &
partibus cõparaui uti totum corpus omnia architecture membra
in decem uoluminibus haberet explicata.

.L. VICTRVVII POLLIONIS DE
ARCHITECTVRA FINIS.

Io. Sulpitius lectori ſalutem.

Lector habes tandem ueneranda uolumina docti
Victruuii: quorum copia rara fuit.
Hæc lege: nam diſces: noua: magna: recondita: pulchra:
Et quæ ſint in re ſæpe futura tuo.
Emendata uides: ſed peccat littera ſiqua
Corrige: nemo ſatis lynceus eſſe poteſt.

M· VITRVVIVS
PER
IOCVNDVM SO
LITO CASTIGA
TIOR FACTVS
CVM FIGVRIS ET
TABVLA
VT IAM LEGI ET
INTELLIGI POS
SIT

FIGURE 1 (LEFT). FINAL PAGE AND COLOPHON OF THE FIRST PRINTED EDITION OF VITRUVIUS, ROME, 1486

The verse reads in part: "Reader, now you have the revered volumes of the learned Vitruvius, copies of which have been rare. Read these; you will learn great, new, learned, and beautiful things. . . ." Courtesy Avery Library

FIGURE 2 (RIGHT). TITLE PAGE OF THE FIRST PRINTED ILLUSTRATED EDITION OF VITRUVIUS, VENICE, 1511

The illustrations are by the architect Fra Giocondo. The title page reads in part: ". . . with illustrations and an index, so that now it can be read and understood." Courtesy Avery Library

old materials were coming into use, and economy of construction was becoming an ever more insistent demand. The science of construction accordingly received a new impetus; the old Vitruvian balance between use, structure, and beauty reasserted itself. Jacques François Blondel's *Cours d'architecture*, completed by Pierre Patte and issued between 1771 and 1774, is a remarkably thorough analysis of the problems of efficient planning and of building materials and construction methods—as well as a treatise on aesthetic design and detail. The curriculum of the school which this, the later, Blondel conducted shows an extraordinarily broad approach to architecture, quite "modern" in type. In England, Isaac Ware's *Complete Body of Architecture*, 1756, shows a similar broad and rational attitude; for him the "complete body" comprises building

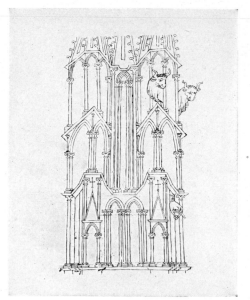 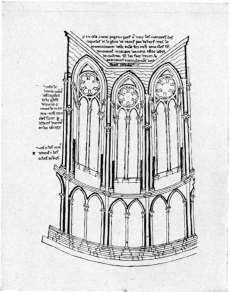

FIGURE 3 (LEFT). CATHEDRAL TOWER, LAON, FRANCE, AS DRAWN BY VILLARD DE HONNECOURT

This sketch by a thirteenth-century architect shows his attempt to portray the projecting and receding planes of the tower of Laon Cathedral by means of a crude perspective.

From *Facsimile of the Sketch-book of Wilars de Honecort*, London, 1859

FIGURE 4 (RIGHT). CHOIR CHAPELS OF THE CATHEDRAL, RHEIMS, FRANCE, AS SKETCHED BY VILLARD DE HONNECOURT

Here is evidence of Villard de Honnecourt's interest in the architecture of his own day; from Rheims Cathedral he received many inspirations for his designs.

From *Facsimile of the Sketch-book of Wilars de Honecort*, London, 1859

materials, construction, economy and efficiency of planning, as well as the creation of beautiful façades and interiors.

There was no unanimity on this question during the nineteenth century. Rationalism continued to dominate during its earlier years and controlled most of the architectural thinking of the Classic Revival architects. Later, style controversy was paralleled by critical confusion. To Ruskin, in the early period when he wrote *The Seven Lamps of Architecture*, 1849, the great element which distinguished architecture from mere building was ornament; there is an almost complete absence in his writings of any consideration of construction or of convenient planning (Figs. 10, 11). Viollet-le-Duc, on the other hand, returned to the Vitruvian triad but gave perhaps the highest place to construc-

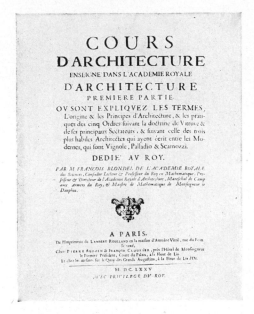

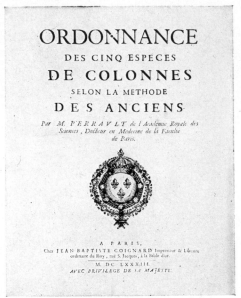

FIGURE 5 (LEFT). TITLE PAGE OF FRANÇOIS BLONDEL'S *Cours d'architecture enseigné dans l'Académie royale d'Architecture*, PARIS, 1675

This book contains the official architectural doctrine of the Louis XIV period, as taught at the Royal Academy of Architecture. It stresses absolute proportion as the chief means to aesthetic effect. *Courtesy Avery Library*

FIGURE 6 (RIGHT). TITLE PAGE OF CLAUDE PERRAULT'S *Ordonnance des cinq espèces de colonnes . . .* PARIS, 1683

This work by the physician-architect who designed the east front of the Louvre, supporting freedom in design, is the protest of a scientific mind against the doctrinaire theories of the Royal Academy. *Courtesy Avery Library*

tion, for to him good architecture is *always* based on good construction, and its aesthetic forms are structurally determined.

But the architects of the last third of the century turned increasingly toward a primary interest in aesthetic design. The most thoughtful gave great importance to convenience in planning, and direct and logical planning marks all the best works of the time; in fact, the architects of the nineteenth century made perhaps their greatest contribution in their imaginative solutions of the difficult planning problems offered by the complex buildings which an industrial civilization required. Nevertheless, the critical atmosphere was one of aesthetic and stylistic preoccupation. It could hardly be otherwise in an era of free eclecticism. Where a building had to be in some recognizable "style"—classic, Gothic, English, French, Italian, Spanish, Colonial, or what not—the

FIGURE 7 (LEFT). TITLE PAGE OF C. E. BRISEUX'S *Traité du beau . . .* **PARIS, 1752**

This superb volume, entirely engraved and one of the most lavish architectural books ever published, was written in support of the theory of absolute proportions as the sole source of true beauty.   Courtesy Avery Library

FIGURE 8 (RIGHT). TITLE PAGE OF GERMAIN BOFFRAND'S *Livre d'architecture . . .* **PARIS, 1745**

The author aims to define good taste in architecture in terms of fitness, utility, healthfulness, and common sense, as well as pure form.   Courtesy Avery Library

choice of style for any given building became the major design question, and architects and architectural critics were much exercised about it. Much critical writing was devoted to propaganda for one style or the other, and the importance of this question more and more led to an undue emphasis on mere superficial appearance.

It was perhaps this which caused the extreme reaction toward rationalism which characterized the birth of the so-called International Style. Thus, certain critics of the recent past have questioned the validity of a search for beauty as a conscious architectural aim. They have not denied the fact of architectural beauty, but they have considered it to be merely the by-product of good functional and structural design; they have claimed that a conscious search for beauty, by directing the architect's attention to "non-essentials," can lead only

FIGURE 9 (LEFT). TITLE PAGE OF THE FIRST EDITION OF ANDREA PALLADIO'S
I Quattro Libri dell' Architettura . . . VENICE, 1581

Palladio's influential work endeavored to reinstate classic dignity and common sense at a time when architectural fashions were turning toward an arbitrary license in detail.

Courtesy Avery Library

FIGURE 10 (RIGHT). TITLE PAGE OF THE FIRST EDITION OF *The Seven Lamps of Architecture*, LONDON, 1849

From the first architectural writing of one of the most influential and inspiring of nineteenth-century critics.   Courtesy New York Public Library

to sentimental or untrue design and will merely fog the clarity and produce confusion.

Yet this attitude contradicts the experience of ages. We can gather from the references Vitruvius makes to Greek architectural writings that Greek architects, at least, were almost always primarily interested in the beauty of the structures they designed. Even without this evidence the buildings themselves would tell us—in their record, for instance, of constant delicate change and refinement in the development of the Doric order. For Rome, Vitruvius is himself the witness. And from what we know of medieval architecture we must reach the same conclusion there; Villard de Honnecourt's sketchbook is obviously the work of a man constantly excited by natural as well as architectural beauty, the work of one devoted to seeing that his own creations were no less visually satisfactory than the Rheims and Laon he so lovingly sketched. The

FIGURE 11 (LEFT). AN ILLUSTRATION FROM *The Seven Lamps of Architecture*, DRAWN BY ITS AUTHOR

Ruskin, although not an architect, was a delineator of extraordinary skill and accuracy.

Courtesy New York Public Library

FIGURE 12 (RIGHT). FIGURE SKETCHES BY VILLARD DE HONNECOURT

A series of drawings which illustrate the artist's attempt to reduce many different kinds of shapes to basic geometric forms.

From *Facsimile of the Sketch-book of Wilars de Honecort*, London, 1859

famous conference of architects called from all over Europe to debate the question of whether Milan Cathedral should be completed *ad triangulam* or *ad quadratum* reveals a deep interest in abstract form. From the Renaissance on, the story of the architect's search for beauty is too well known to need further note, and such great precursors and founders of our contemporary architecture as Otto Wagner, Louis Sullivan, Le Corbusier, and Frank Lloyd Wright have all been unanimous in their feeling that the creation of beauty was the architect's highest function.

But there is still another reason why a search for beauty is architecturally important. It is a matter of mere common-sense logic, and it is inherent in the answer to the simple question: Do people like visual experiences that are ordered or confused, attractive or repellent? Any building or group of buildings creates or modifies a visual experience; it cannot fail to do so, and if the building is a large one the visual experience it creates is correspondingly important. It is obvious that the mental health, happiness, and satisfaction of those who come in visual contact with the building will be increased if the visual experience it creates is itself ordered and satisfactory. Therefore the search for this quality—roughly termed beauty—is an essential part of responsible architectural design.

In the final analysis, it always seems to be this aesthetic criterion which determines the greatness of a building. There were hundreds of Greek temples, scattered over the Mediterranean world, almost identical in general plan conception; undoubtedly each was as good a functional answer to the program as the next. Yet, of them all, the judgment of generations has picked out but two as supreme—the Temple of Zeus at Olympia and the Parthenon at Athens—and picked them out on what seems to be a purely aesthetic basis. In plan, there are many French cathedrals of similar type; they all "worked," as the expression is. But in those we love and admire there is something more than mere "working," something more than the mere superb solution of a complicated program; there is the quality that we can only call beauty.

Moreover, pure materialistic functionalism can never create entirely satisfactory structures, for there are many problems to which pure physical functionalism can give no certain answer—questions like "How big is a room?" "How tall should a door be?" "How wide must this corridor be made?" To questions like these, functional analysis can answer only with minima; it can say "Such a room, for such a purpose, can*not* be smaller than so and so"; "A door must be *at least* so wide"; "This corridor must not be *narrower* than so and so." And an architecture—a world—built only on minima is unthinkable; the human spirit has its demands, too, and among them is its demand for space in which to stretch itself, to enlarge itself, to enjoy. To questions such as those set forth above, functionalism has no complete answer; yet the architect must answer them in every structure he designs. What criteria shall he use? Imagination and the desire to create beautiful spaces and beautiful structures must apparently control in many of these matters.

Thus it follows that the conscious search for beauty in buildings becomes an inevitable part of the architect's task. To search for beauty intelligently, one must know something of what beauty is, and there is hardly any question about which there are more different opinions. The study of beauty as a quality is the domain of aesthetics—a study partly scientific, partly metaphysical. It is not the aim of this work to be a complete guide to this baffling field of knowledge. Yet perhaps a brief summary of the major aesthetic theories will not be out of place.

The first great class of aesthetic theories comprises those which consider beauty as the primary result of special formal relationships—of such things as height, width, size, or color. Beauty either resides in, or is caused by, the form itself or the perception of it. The sense of beauty is a direct emotion produced by the form, irrespective of its meaning or of any other extraneous conceptions. To Plato forms were beautiful in the proportion that they resembled, recalled, or pointed toward an "ideal form" which, existing only in the ideal world, contained within itself all the various accidental forms of our imperfect worldly actuality. Deeply felt beauty produced both pleasure and pain, but a sort of pleasant pain: the pain comes from our realization of the imperfection of the actual, our sense of removal from or distance from this ideal world toward which we yearn; the pleasure comes from the almost unconscious recognition in the beautiful object of the perfection of the ideal itself. In fact, this theory of the autonomy of forms *per se* almost demands the concept of an ideal absolute toward which beautiful forms converge; it is a theory that leads almost inevitably into mysticism and metaphysics.

In architectural criticism, this type of thinking has given rise to concepts of the supremacy of proportion in design and has searched for the secret of architectural beauty in the mathematical relationships of heights, widths, thicknesses, lengths. It has produced a vast literature in which the secret of the beauty of buildings is sought in triangles, circles, five-pointed stars, the Golden Section (extreme and mean ratio), root-five rectangles, modules, arithmetical ratios, and so on; its most noted recent expression is Jay Hambidge's theory of dynamic symmetry, based essentially on the relation of the diagonals of rectangles to their sides.

The second type of aesthetic thinking is based on the concept that the beauty of a work of art depends primarily on what it expresses and that form is beautiful just in so far as it is expressive. To Hegel, for instance, that is most beautiful which expresses the noblest thought in the most perfect manner. Schopenhauer feels that art gains its value through its externalization of the basic and inevitable struggle between will (desire, force) and idea (mass, material)—a struggle which underlies all of life and all of nature. In architecture, to which he devotes a long and carefully analytic section, he sees the greatest beauty as the result of the most perfect expression of the struggle between the force of gravity and the strength of materials. This concept is of special architectural importance because Schopenhauer, first among architectural critics, sees the expression of structure as basic in architectural beauty. Other critics of this same general "expressionist" school base the beauty of art on its expression of ethical ideals or religious doctrines or dogmas; to Ruskin, for instance, the beauty and worthwhileness of buildings come from their expression of the works and thoughts of the Deity, and for Pugin beautiful buildings can be erected by Christian nations only if they are erected in accordance with the Gothic ideals, for the Gothic style was to him the Christian style *par excellence*. Many critics of more recent times find one of the chief bases for architectural beauty to be the expression of function or purpose in a building.

Both these classes of critics—the formalists and the expressionists—lay their chief emphasis on the work of art itself. Yet one of the most important achievements of nineteenth-century science was the creation of the science of psychology, the study of how men's brains and nervous systems actually work. It was obvious that there were many objects of art which pleased some and displeased others; as soon as the importance of the individual reaction was grasped, it became clear that the sense of beauty was a psychological fact and that perhaps the best way of clarifying the deeply controversial question of what constituted beauty was by studying the reaction rather than the object— thus developing a theory of beauty on psychological rather than on merely external or basically metaphysical grounds.

Psychological theories of art have been legion. They have varied as psychology has varied; as it has split into two often warring camps—the experimental and physiological psychologists and the analytic psychologists—just so has psychological aesthetics split. It varies from the ideas of those theorists who find the sole cause of beauty in simple and easy eye movements to the theories of those who, like the psychoanalysts, find the secret of beauty in the connections which exist between the object called beautiful and the early, intense— and often "forgotten," or buried—universal infant experiences.

Somewhere between these two extremes lie two of the most important of psychological theories—the theory of *Einfühlung* and the Gestalt-psychology concept. According to the first of these theories, a work of art is powerful when the observer feels himself into it—lives, as it were, in its life. Beauty is the result of feeling one's self into a thing pleasantly; in architecture it comes from the observer's feeling himself actually doing the work the building does, simply, easily, and gracefully—hence the pleasure in the appearance of strength in a building, the repose in long horizontal lines, the serenity in effortless simplicity, and so on. This school of architectural aesthetics is growing in influence. The second of the theories mentioned is based on the general theory of Gestalt psychology that every conscious experience or perception is a complex happening. Thus the sense of beauty is no simple, separate emotion, which can be abstracted from all other emotions and studied alone. It is, instead, a constellation of feelings, associations, memories, motor impulses, perceptions, and so on, which reverberates through the entire being. No one element in it can be abstracted without destroying the whole. The work of art owes the power of its beauty to this great mass of differing reactions; beauty comes from the relaxation of tensions upon many levels. The chief importance of this theory for architecture lies in the fact that, almost alone among aesthetic theories, it finds a place for the associations which the sight of any building arouses.

The aesthetics of buildings has many special elements which are of peculiar interest to the architect. Architecture is usually considered one of the arts of sight, and it has become the convention of aestheticians to consider all the arts of sight as though they were based on the perception of the work of art from *one* point of view and at only *one* moment. This, of course, is a pure convention. Even a simple picture requires an examination over a certain period of time for any adequate appreciation. In architecture this time element becomes of major importance. A building is never merely a façade. It is a complex organization of exterior and interior forms, and in the great architectural monument every element in this complexity takes its part in the entire artistic experience. Thorough appreciation of a complex structure will require not only minutes or hours but sometimes days or weeks.

The great building is nevertheless one artistic whole; everything that is experienced by the observer in connection with it becomes part of the massive artistic experience which a great building produces. Its beauty grows on one gradually. As one approaches it, walks around it, comes to its main entrance, and enters, the harmonious power or the graceful repose of the building becomes increasingly evident. One enters, passes through whatever interior spaces there may be. He sees changing views—piers or walls at changing distances; openings, floors, and ceilings; masses of color; changes of light and dark—all in the order which the designer has ordained. Yet this complex and changing experience is part of the aesthetic quality of the building, and the order in which the experiences come is an integral part of the building's design. Suspense, contrast, climax—these all enter in, and thus the time element in architectural de-

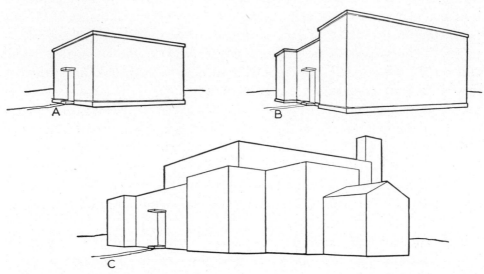

FIGURE 13. INSTINCTIVE ALLOWANCE FOR PERSPECTIVE

A and B appear as symmetrical buildings despite perspective distortion. In C, however, because
of the complexity of the whole, the symmetry of the front is less instantly grasped.

sign becomes as definite and natural a feature as the time element in musical
composition.

Another peculiar quality of architectural aesthetics arises from the fact that
the observer of a building frequently makes instinctive allowances for the distortions and seeming changes in the effect of equal dimensions when seen from
different points of view. For instance, in a simple rectangular building, the
chief front of which is symmetrically composed, a sense of that symmetrical
composition is strong even if the building is approached from the corner and
the architectural perspective view of it is anything but symmetrical (Fig. 13).
This matter of the instinctive allowance for perspective will also hold true in
many matters of height dimension.

Yet there are limits to this instinctive adjustment for perspective distortion.
When a building becomes too large or too complex, the eye becomes confused
and tends to see dimensions as they are altered by perspective, and the imagination fails to make the requisite allowances. This is especially true in matters of
height, where the eye is often fooled. Spires and vertical elements, in order to
look well, almost always have to be designed markedly higher than the elevation or even a perspective drawing would seem to require (Fig. 16). It is one
of the marks of the sensitive and imaginative designer to be able to judge the

FIGURE 14. THESEUM, ATHENS. VIEW FROM THE CORNER

Seen from any angle the Greek temple displays its form so simply that its symmetry is always obvious.
                                                                    Courtesy Ware Library

FIGURE 15. POST OFFICE, NEW YORK. VIEW FROM THE NORTHEAST

McKim, Mead & White, architects

This building is so designed that there can be no doubt in the mind of the observer as to which side is the front. Although the corner view is unsymmetrical, the composition is readily accepted as symmetrical.   From *A Monograph of the Work of McKim, Mead & White*

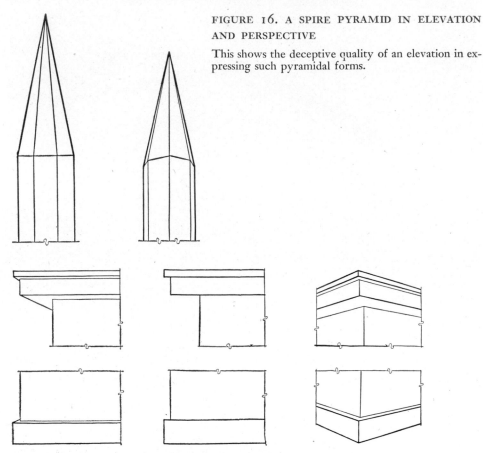

FIGURE 16. A SPIRE PYRAMID IN ELEVATION
AND PERSPECTIVE

This shows the deceptive quality of an elevation in expressing such pyramidal forms.

FIGURE 17. DIFFERING PROJECTIONS OF A SIMPLE PROJECTING WALL CAP AND
BASE

LEFT: Perspective of a corner from a point in front; CENTER: A true elevation; RIGHT: Perspective
from the corner.

Any three-dimensional object varies in its visual aspect according to the point of view.

probable amount of the allowance which the average observer will make and
to design accordingly.

The importance to the architect of what one might call the instinctive perspective imagination is enormous. Buildings exist as three-dimensional entities,
and no drawings or photographs can represent them perfectly. There is hardly
an architectural form of which this is not true. Let us consider, for example,
the simplest element which projects from the face of a building—a gutter or a
base. If this runs around a 90-degree corner, it will appear from almost any
point of view to be different from what the elevation shows. If it is seen from

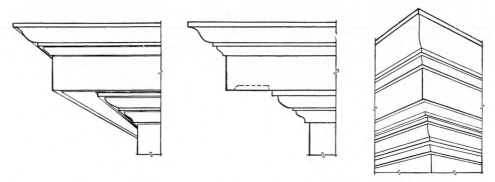

FIGURE 18. A SIMPLE CLASSIC CORNICE IN PERSPECTIVE AND ELEVATION

LEFT: Its appearance as seen from in front; CENTER: A true elevation; RIGHT: Its appearance as seen from the corner.

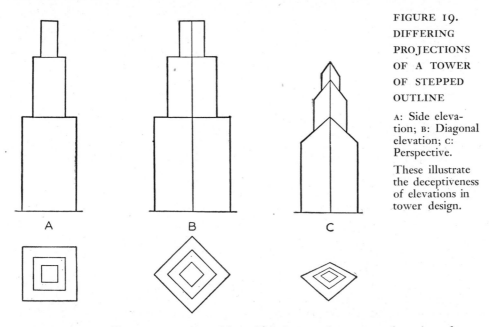

FIGURE 19. DIFFERING PROJECTIONS OF A TOWER OF STEPPED OUTLINE

A: Side elevation; B: Diagonal elevation; C: Perspective.

These illustrate the deceptiveness of elevations in tower design.

the corner, it will appear as one thing; if it is seen in an angular view from a position along one side, it will appear as something quite different (Fig. 17). If there are moldings, as in a classic cornice, the whole profile of the molding at the corner will vary according to the point of view (Fig. 18). In any rectangular prismatic form, changes of projection will usually seem greater than a right section or geometrical elevation would indicate (Figs. 16–18, 20). This is of the greatest importance in the design of rectangular or square piers in interiors or porticos, in the design of cornices or projecting roof eaves, and in the design

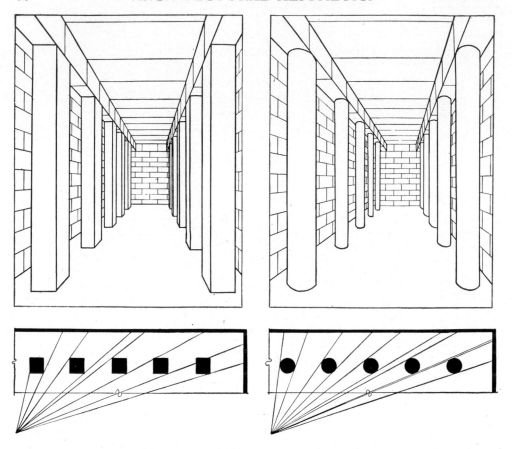

FIGURE 20. SQUARE AND CIRCULAR PIERS

Perspective and part plans, showing how, from any one point of view, pier shapes determine the visual aspect and the feeling of openness or constriction. In direct-line elevation these two schemes would be identical.

of square towers with breaks, like many Baroque or Colonial towers (Fig. 19). In such elements an architect must always consider the increased width which diagonal views produce and must make the requisite allowances, whether or not he makes a drawing to show the diagonal elevation or diagonal perspective.

Of course, the varying apparent widths of the sides and ends of whole buildings or projecting wings or pavilions are also important design factors in the experience of one walking by or around them. These are so obvious that any sensitive designer is likely to consider them; instinctively he will imagine the effect as he determines the plan and the elevation. Yet if he is wise he will check his imagination by a series of small sketch perspectives.

There is one more general fact to be noticed in connection with this vast

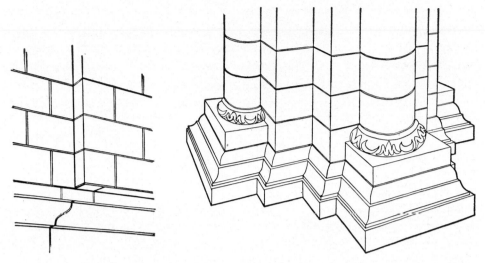

FIGURE 21 (LEFT). A PANELED STONE WALL

The stone joints, seen in perspective, emphasize the break in surface at the panel; similarly, the existence of the panel emphasizes the stone joints by breaking their joint line.

FIGURE 22 (RIGHT). BASE OF THE NAVE PIERS, VÉZELAY, FRANCE

Horizontal lines, seen in perspective, stress and express the plan quality.

Redrawn from Viollet-le-Duc, *Dictionnaire raisonné* . . .

subject of architecture as a three-dimensional art, and that is the mutual effect of the horizontal lines of stone joints, moldings, or faces carried around a break in plan and of the break itself. When seen in perspective, at any level either above or below eye height, such a horizontal motif will have its visual continuity destroyed at any angle or break in the plan. This sudden change of direction, this loss of continuousness, often will strongly accent the vertical corner and give it importance. Similarly, the existence of any corner, by breaking the apparent continuity of horizontal lines, will in its turn emphasize them. It is probably for this reason that eighteenth-century architects often liked to use slightly recessed panels in stone walls (Fig. 21), and it is certainly one reason for the complex plans of Romanesque clustered piers (Fig. 22).

It will be seen that all these observations will be true whatever the basic theory of architectural aesthetics we adopt. They are qualities inherent in the very nature of buildings. We can, therefore, with a clear mind examine buildings with the purpose of discovering the attributes characteristic of those structures which almost all ages have found beautiful, and we can thus develop, not a series of rules or even laws of design, but rather a series of general principles which can be applied in many different ways. In that way we can discover much about the basic qualities apparently necessary to architectural beauty. Such an examination, both of buildings and of much of the writing about them, reveals a group of dominant characteristics so important that they deserve a full discussion. Those attributes are as follows: unity, balance, proportion, scale, rhythm, climax, and designed sequence. It will be the purpose of the following chapters to study these qualities in buildings and the principles of design which may be deduced from them.

SUGGESTED ADDITIONAL READING FOR CHAPTER I

THE BOOK LISTS which follow this and succeeding chapters do not form a complete bibliography. They are rather a somewhat arbitrary selection of references chosen to assist the reader in a more detailed study of the subject. Because the books suggested do not always support the opinions stated in the text, they may help the reader to achieve an unbiased judgment in controversial questions.

BOOKS DEALING WITH AESTHETICS IN GENERAL

Ackhoff, Russell L., "Aesthetics of Twentieth-Century Architecture," lecture delivered at the Annual Convention of the American Institute of Architects, Salt Lake City, Utah, June 22, 1948.

Allen, Beverly Sprague, *Tides in English Taste (1619–1800)*, 2 vols. (Cambridge, Mass.: Harvard University Press, 1937).

Aristotle, *The Poetics*, any good edition.

Birkhoff, George David, *Aesthetic Measure* (Cambridge, Mass.: Harvard University Press, 1933).

Dewey, John, *Art as Experience* (New York: Minton, Balch [c1934]).

Edman, Irwin, *Arts and the Man* . . . (New York: Norton [c1939]).

—— *The World, the Arts, and the Artist* (New York: Norton [c1928]).

Greene, Theodore Meyer, *The Arts and the Art of Criticism* (Princeton: Princeton University Press, 1940).

Hammond, William Alexander, *A Bibliography of Aesthetics and of the Philosophy of the Fine Arts from 1900 to 1932* . . . (New York: Longmans, Green [1933]).

Listowell, Earl of (William Francis Hare), *A Critical History of Modern Aesthetics* (London: Allen & Unwin [1933]).

Parker, De Witt Henry, *The Analysis of Art* (New Haven: Yale University Press, 1926).

Plato, *Symposium, Crito, Phaedrus*, any good edition.

Raymond, George Lansing, *The Essentials of Aesthetics in Music, Poetry, Painting, Sculpture and Architecture*, 3rd ed. rev. (New York: Putnam's [c1921]).

—— *Proportion and Harmony of Line and Color in Painting, Sculpture, and Architecture* . . . 2nd ed. (New York: Putnam's, 1909).

Schopenhauer, Arthur, *The World as Will and Idea*, Book III and appendix to Book III, any good edition.

BOOKS DEALING CHIEFLY WITH THE AESTHETICS OF ARCHITECTURE

Blondel, François, *Cours d'architecture enseigné dans l'Académie royale d'Architecture*, 3 vols. (Paris: Vol. I, Lambert Roulland; Vols. II and III, Chez l'auteur et Nicolas Langlois, 1675–83).

Boffrand, Germain, *Livre d'architecture* . . . (Paris: Cavelier père, 1745).

Borissavliévitch, Miloutine, *Les Théories de l'architecture; essai critique* . . . (Paris: Payot, 1926).

Cram, Ralph Adams, *Convictions and Controversies* (Boston: Marshall Jones [c1935]).

Fry, Maxwell, *Fine Building* (London: Faber and Faber [1944]). An essay in the criticism of architecture from a contemporary viewpoint.

Hamlin, Talbot [Faulkner], *Architecture, an Art for All Men* (New York: Columbia University Press, 1947).

—— "Theories of Architecture, 19th and 20th Centuries," 1935, mimeographed manuscript in Avery Library, Columbia University.

Hitchcock, Henry Russell, and Philip C. Johnson, *The International Style* (New York: Museum of Modern Art, 1931).

Le Corbusier (Charles Édouard Jeanneret), *New World of Space* (New York: Reynal & Hitchcock, 1948).

—— *Vers une Architecture* (Paris: Crès, 1923); English ed., *Towards a New Architecture*, translated by Frederick Etchells (New York: Payson & Clarke [1927]).

Lundberg, Erik, *Arkitekturens Formsprak* (Stockholm: Nordisk Rotogravyr [1945]).

Pugin, Augustus W. N., *An Apology for the Revival of Christian Architecture in England* (London: Weale, 1843).

—— *The True Principles of Pointed or Christian Architecture* . . . (London: Weale, 1841).

Ruskin, John, *The Seven Lamps of Architecture*, 1st American ed. (New York: Wiley, 1849).

—— *The Stones of Venice* (New York [Lovell], 1851).

Scott, Geoffrey, *The Architecture of Humanism* . . . (Boston: Houghton Mifflin, 1914).

Taut, Bruno, *Modern Architecture* (London: Studio [1929]). One of the best introductions to the ideals of contemporary building; imaginative, restrained, and soundly critical.

Viollet-le-Duc, Eugène Emmanuel, *Entretiens sur l'architecture*, 2 vols. (Paris: Morel, 1863–72); translated as *Discourses on Architecture* . . . with an introductory essay by Henry Van Brunt, 2 vols. (Boston: Osgood, 1875–81).

Wright, Frank Lloyd, *Frank Lloyd Wright on Architecture; Selected Writings 1894–1940*, edited with an introduction by Frederick Gutheim (New York: Duell, Sloan & Pearce, 1941).

—— *Modern Architecture; being the Kahn Lectures for 1930*, Princeton Monographs in Art and Archeology (Princeton: Princeton University Press, 1931).

2

Unity

I T HAS LONG been accepted as a critical principle that any artistic experience must have unity. Aristotle based the greater part of his *Poetics* on the idea that in any work of literature unity was the one great desideratum, and this seems to hold true of all the arts. A supposed work of art which is so unsystematic and complicated that all its parts seem separate and unrelated, conflicting and contradictory, hardly deserves to be called a work of art. It has also been commonly accepted that the greatness of a work of art depends in no small measure on the number of different elements on which the artist has imposed unity, or, in other words, the greatest art is that in which the greatest variety has been transmuted into the greatest unity.

In architecture it is seldom necessary to worry about variety—about the number of differing elements which must be composed into a single whole. The very conditions of building make variety essential. When a building is designed to fulfill complex purposes, the resulting complexity of the building itself is bound to develop variety in its form, and even when it is planned for simple purposes there may be need for a multitude of varying structural elements. One of the architect's chief tasks, therefore, is to impose a compelling unity upon that necessary variety.

This problem is rendered all the more pressing in architecture by the fact, already stressed, that architecture is not simply the design of one single aspect of the exterior of a building; it entails the welding together of all possible exterior views of a structure with all possible interior views into one unified artistic creation. In architectural terms this may be stated as the principle that all good buildings must have unity of plan, elevation, and section. In other words, a building must be so arranged in plan and so studied in the shape and volume of its interior spaces—and must have its exterior composition so conceived and detailed—that all will form a harmonious whole. It may be well, therefore, to consider some of the ways in which unity may be achieved.

The first and simplest type of architectural unity is that which we may call

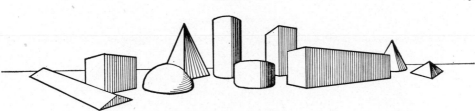

FIGURE 23. THE BASIC ARCHITECTURAL FORMS

Triangular prism, cube, hemisphere, pyramid, cylinder, low cylinder, vertical parallelepiped, horizontal parallelepiped, cone, low pyramid.

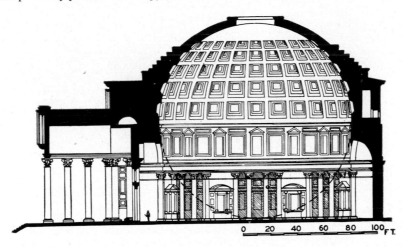

FIGURE 24. PANTHEON, ROME. SECTION

Unity given by the enclosing shape and the fact that a circumscribed sphere of the diameter of the dome would be framed by the height.

the unity of simple geometrical form. Any simple, easily recognizable geometrical form has a necessary unity that is instantly felt. Thus pyramids, cubes, spheres, cones, and cylinders are all felt to be unified wholes, and buildings which fall into such shapes will naturally have unity in so far as one of those geometric shapes controls the appearance (Fig. 23). One of the great reasons for the emotional power of the Egyptian tomb pyramids lies in this compelling geometry. Similarly, it is probably true that part of the success of the interior of the Roman Pantheon is due to the fact that a sphere may be exactly inscribed within it (Fig. 24). The Colosseum and the curved walls of Roman theaters and amphitheaters are similarly effective because of the basic geometry of their cylindrical form and because all the elements seem somehow designed to emphasize that quality (see Figs. 25, 26). The Greek temple is also a basically simple geometric form (Fig. 30). It is interesting to see how the Greeks empha-

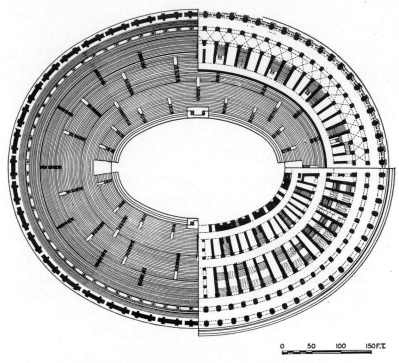

0   50   100   150 F.T.

FIGURE 25. COLOSSEUM, ROME. PLANS AT VARYING LEVELS

Unity given by the subordination of all forms to the basic oval of the plan. Seats, corridors, arena, and exterior follow this line; all other structural features are radials and normal to it.

sized the feeling of unity in their temples by the slight inclination of the columns inwards and by varying the intercolumniations. Many small gabled houses and barns are similar in their controlling shapes (Fig. 31).

It is seldom, however, that buildings can be so simply organized; even in structures where that type of geometrical simplicity cannot be imposed, it is still necessary to produce unity. The two chief ways of doing this are: first, through subordination of all minor elements to some major element; and, second, through harmony of shape and detail in all the elements which go to make up a building. Unity through subordination is itself of several types. In certain buildings, as, for instance, in the case of the Colosseum mentioned above, everything can be subordinated to the general shape of the whole. More common, however, is the subordination of all the smaller portions to some major and dominating element such as a dome or a pavilion. This subordination can be one of mere mass or size. Thus in Figure 32 the two smaller side wings are obviously subordinated to the wider and higher central block. This is a common type of satisfactory architectural composition and accounts for such

FIGURE 26. COLOSSEUM, ROME. GENERAL VIEW

Every line in the exterior design accents the basic form.   Courtesy Ware Library

FIGURE 27. OHIO STATE CAPITOL, COLUMBUS

Henry Walters and others, architects

Complex requirements have been integrated into a single rectangular shape of great power and scale.   Courtesy J. M. Howells and Metropolitan Museum of Art

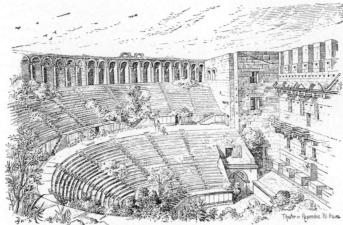

FIGURE 28. ROMAN THEATER, ASPENDOS, ASIA MINOR

The powerful unifying character of definite geometrical form is well illustrated in this view of a Roman theater; the concentric circular lines of the seats bind the whole strongly together.

FIGURE 29. LITTLE THEATER, POMPEII, ITALY. INTERIOR

The concentric lines of the seats produce a sharply focused unity.

Courtesy Ware Library

well-known examples as the Colonial house, Mount Airy, in Virginia, the river front of the Chambre des Députés in Paris, and many other symmetrical structures. The radio station at Kottwyk in the Netherlands, by Luthman, is another more recent example (Fig. 33). It is interesting here to note how the architect has striven to cut away the apparent weight of the side wings by the use of corner windows to break the outline; he has gone to great lengths to give a sense of direction from outwards in toward the center by means of railings and terrace walls, all with the definite purpose of emphasizing the importance of the great central tower to which the whole is subordinated.

The tower of this Kottwyk radio station is further distinguished by being not only the most massive but also the highest portion of the building. In fact,

FIGURE 30. TEMPLE OF NEPTUNE, PAESTUM, ITALY

Unity of simple geometric form.

Courtesy Ware Library

FIGURE 31. A BARN

Unity of simple geometric shape.

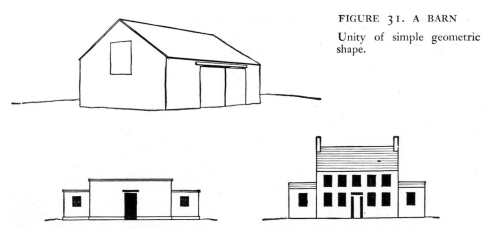

FIGURE 32. UNITY ACHIEVED BY THE SUBORDINATION OF MINOR WINGS TO A CENTRAL AND LARGER BLOCK

subordination of low elements to high elements is one of the surest ways of obtaining architectural unity. If one takes two rectangular prismatic masses of equal size and places them together, with one standing on its end and the other on its side, the taller of the two—the one on its end—will instantly dominate the other (Fig. 34). It will be seen, then, that in any composition of this type it is much easier to subordinate the lower element to the higher than the higher element to the lower.

FIGURE 33. KOTTWYK RADIO STATION, THE NETHERLANDS

Jules Luthman, architect

Unity achieved by the subordination of the wings to the central tower and emphasized by the careful design of all the architectural elements.

Courtesy School of Architecture, Columbia University

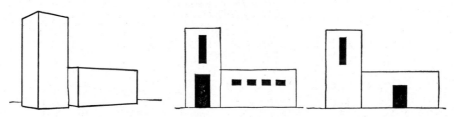

FIGURE 34. SUBORDINATION OF WIDTH TO HEIGHT

The two parallelepipeds are of equal dimensions. It is obviously easier to subordinate the horizontal to the vertical than the reverse. This is the secret of the pleasant composition of many small churches.

Many examples may be cited which will illustrate that principle. In the Stockholm Town Hall, a large and elaborate building with various parts of differing appearance and detail, extraordinary unity is given by the great corner tower. This has been so placed on the site that its reflection in the harbor water still more emphasizes the height quality and thus helps to establish the powerful unity of the building. Even when seen from the side, with the lower portions in

FIGURE 35. STOCKHOLM TOWN HALL. VIEW FROM ACROSS THE HARBOR

The vertical mass of the corner tower dominates and gives unity to the entire complex structure.

Ragnar Ostberg, architect

Courtesy American Swedish News Exchange

FIGURE 36. CATHEDRAL, AMIENS, FRANCE. VIEW FROM OVER THE CITY ROOFS

By sheer dominance of height and bulk the cathedral often confers unity on many a European town.

Courtesy Ware Library

FIGURE 37. TRINITY CHURCH, BOSTON, MASSACHUSETTS.

VIEW FROM THE REAR

H. H. Richardson, architect

Unity achieved by the dominance of the central tower.

From Mrs. Schuyler Van Rensselaer, *Henry Hobson Richardson and His Works*

the foreground, the same sense of unity through the dominance of the tower is felt. This tower, a superb piece of sensitive design, also serves through its dominating height to convey a sense of basic unity to the entire portion of the city in which it stands. And the same unifying quality of height may be seen in the way in which a cathedral like Amiens dominates the entire city. One reason, in fact, for the restless confusion of many modern towns and cities lies in the absence of any similar dominating element. When great height is combined with great mass, an even more powerful impression is produced and the subordination of many smaller elements becomes easier. That is the reason for the tremendous feeling of unity conveyed by churches with a large central crossing tower; Trinity Church in Boston is an outstanding example. It is interesting to realize that Richardson's winning competition drawing for the church had no such dominating central motif, but as the architect studied the problem he came to realize how indispensable it was. Once he had decided on a central tower, he went to great lengths to emphasize its dominance. (See Figs. 35–37.)

When Thomas U. Walter added the two great House and Senate wings to the United States Capitol in the decade before the Civil War, he realized at once that the old dome was not sufficiently powerful to dominate the new and larger building and therefore added the present great cast-iron dome with

FIGURE 38. ARCH OF THE CAR-
ROUSEL, PARIS

Percier & Fontaine, architects

The small arched passages at each
side accent the central passage and
increase its apparent size.

Courtesy Avery Library

FIGURE 39. CATHEDRAL, CAN-
TERBURY, ENGLAND

The large central tower, the effect
of which is enhanced by the two
front towers, somewhat similar but
smaller, confers unity on the entire
structure.

Courtesy Avery Library

its high colonnaded drum. This not only unifies the complex structure which
it crowns but also, through its size, its hilltop position, and the great avenues
which radiate from it, serves to tie together large sections of the city of Washington.

One method of emphasizing the dominance of any architectural element is by
flanking it with other elements that are similar in general shape but markedly
smaller in dimension. Thus, in such a triumphal arch as the Arch of the Car-
rousel in Paris (Fig. 38), the apparent size of the central passage is emphasized
by the smaller pedestrian passages on either side. Similarly, in Canterbury

FIGURE 40. CATHEDRAL, LINCOLN, ENGLAND. EXTERIOR VIEW OF CROSSING

A tall central crossing tower unifies nave and transept.   Courtesy Ware Library

Cathedral and many other churches the dominance of the central tower is assisted by the fact that the two smaller western towers are generally similar to it in shape if not in size (see Figs. 39, 40). Another method of assisting the dominance of any motif is by enframing it with smaller but definitely vertical accents. These seem to stop the eye at each side and direct it toward the center of the space between. The Karlskirche in Vienna, for example, owes much of its superbly unified effect to the twin columns which so daringly flank the entrance pavilion, for without them the complex architecture of the front would overbalance the composition. Gate posts and vertical trees will often give the same accent on a door or any feature between and behind them.

Another major method of obtaining the dominance of a feature is through the interest inherent in the form of the feature itself. Thus, as we have seen, high forms command the attention more quickly than low ones; in addition, curved elements are more compelling than straight ones; and elements that suggest motion, like doorways, gates, steps, and stairs, are more interesting

FIGURE 42. DOMINANCE OF THE CURVED OVER THE STRAIGHT SURFACE

Although the sphere is much smaller in content than the cube, it is more attention-calling. The
combination of the two furnishes a striking unity because of the dominance of the domelike
hemisphere.

than those which imply only static attitudes. That is one reason why architects
have frequently used staircases of far larger size than are actually needed; they
realize that such stairs will have a tremendous interest-giving quality. Numerous buildings of the Moslem world and many more of Renaissance Spain owe

FIGURE 43. FRAUENKIRCHE, DRESDEN, GERMANY

Georg Bähr, architect

An illustration of the dominance of the dome form and the subordination of all other elements in the building to it.

Courtesy Ware Library

their unity and their power to the extreme importance given to the doorway or gate (Fig. 41).

The dome form is perhaps the best example of the dominating interest inherent in curved forms. If a cube and a sphere of the same width and diameter, respectively, are placed side by side, the eye will usually go at once to the sphere, although its mass is markedly less than that of the cube (Fig. 42). This will explain the power of the dome form as a producer of unity in buildings. Byzantine churches, the mosques of Turkey, many Renaissance and Baroque churches, and in more recent times such buildings as the Low Library at Columbia University and the Chicago planetarium reveal the truth of the fact, for they owe much of their effect to the interest of their crowning domes (see Figs. 43–45, 47).

A second quality that contributes unity to a building is harmony in the shapes used. If, for instance, all the windows in a structure are alike or, in the geometric sense, similar—that is, if they have an identical ratio of height and width

FIGURE 44. KARLSKIRCHE, VIENNA
Johann B. Fischer von Erlach, architect
Note how the flanking columns accent the dome.   Courtesy Metropolitan Museum of Art

FIGURE 45. LOW LIBRARY, COLUMBIA UNIVERSITY, NEW YORK
McKim, Mead & White, architects
An excellent example of the power of the dome form.
          Photograph W. L. Bogert, courtesy Columbiana Collection, Columbia University

FIGURE 46. FARNESE PALACE, ROME. ELEVATION
Unity given by the repetition of harmonious elements.

—there will be a perfect harmony between them which will assist in the sense
of unity such a building possesses. If, in addition, the spaces between the openings are equal, a still greater sense of unity will be developed; that is one of the
reasons why many simple Italian Renaissance palaces are architecturally so
satisfactory (Fig. 46). This type of unity, through harmony, has vast implications. Many towns owe the pleasant unity which makes them lovely to the
basic shape harmony of the buildings of which they are composed. Nuremberg
and Hildesheim, before the Second World War, like many towns of Normandy
and some of our own early New England villages, revealed this quality to a
marked degree; similarly, any view from a height over Istanbul has great basic
unity through the harmony furnished by the recurrent domes which roof the
bazaars, the baths, and the courtyard arcades of the mosques.

Harmony of shape and size can carry through into the smallest details of a
structure, and this is one of the surest methods of making the inside and the
outside of a building integral parts of the same composition. Thus the persistence inside a building of the dimensions one sees from the outside will create
an inevitable unity between the exterior and the interior. This may easily be
seen in the Gothic cathedrals and in many of the reinforced concrete buildings designed by the Perret brothers in France, and it is an outstanding quality

FIGURE 47. MOSQUE OF SULEIMAN, ISTANBUL, TURKEY

Domes, half domes, and related forms give a sense of unity not only to the mosque itself but also to many portions of the entire city.   Courtesy Ware Library

in Frank Lloyd Wright's Larkin factory administration building in Buffalo (Figs. 48, 49). The interior of St. Peter's in Rome (Fig. 50) illustrates to an amazing degree the unity made possible by a combination of almost all these methods—through the similarity of the arch shapes, the subordination of smaller arches to larger ones, and the subordination of all the interior volumes to the great central dome.

Closely related to the unity achieved by harmony of shape is that which results from harmony of color. In this respect architecture is most fortunate, because integral color can be obtained by the correct choice of building materials. Frequently where unity and harmony can be obtained in no other way—as, for instance, in building a new and modern structure in the middle of an old college campus or of an old and distinguished town—the use of similar materials will often produce a powerful unity despite marked differences of style in the old and the new structures. That is often true in the case of twentieth-century buildings in old Dutch cities, where similar uses of burned-clay prod-

FIGURE 48. ADMINISTRATION
BUILDING, LARKIN SOAP COM-
PANY, BUFFALO, NEW YORK.
EXTERIOR

Frank Lloyd Wright, architect

Unity achieved by harmony of
proportions; these derive directly
from the creative development of
the structural system.

Courtesy Museum of Modern Art

FIGURE 49. ADMINISTRATION
BUILDING, LARKIN SOAP COM-
PANY, BUFFALO, NEW YORK.
INTERIOR

Frank Lloyd Wright, architect

Imaginative interior expression of
the structural system creates a compelling unity of interior and exterior.

Courtesy Museum of Modern Art

FIGURE 50. ST. PETER'S, ROME. VIEW IN THE CROSSING
Bramante and Michelangelo, architects
Unity gained by the repeated use of the arch form integrated in a classic framework.

Courtesy Ware Library

ucts and of glass in the past and the present give rise to pleasant unity and harmony, although the old buildings are Baroque and the newer ones of developed contemporary design.

Contrast in the colors of building materials can also be used to produce a dramatic unity, provided the contrasts are accents only and do not lead to a conflict of interest between the contrasting colors or materials. Thus many buildings of many periods have used combinations of brick and stone, of marble and mosaic, or of plaster and wood. In the successful examples it will always be found that one color or one material predominates strongly and that the contrasting color or material serves only to accent it; seldom if ever is there an equal balance.

Another kind of harmony is necessary to give unity to buildings—harmony of expression. This means that all the parts of a building must "say" related or similar things. One type of expressive harmony resides in the expression of structure. If structure is expressed as a dominant feature, harmony will arise if the same kind of structural system is used for the entire building. That, of course, is the case in almost all Gothic churches and in much contemporary architecture; on the other hand, it is one reason for the lack of success of many eclectic buildings. The works of Frank Lloyd Wright, of the Perret brothers, of Le Corbusier, of Ludwig Mies van der Rohe, and of Eric Mendelsohn are all worthy of study as structural expressions.

Another type of expressive harmony lies in the expression of function or purpose. Every building or group of buildings is obviously designed to fill some basic human need. It usually houses some definite class of human activities. Thus a school group shelters some portion of the educational process, factories enclose production machinery, office buildings serve commercial and professional activities, and so on. Each type of human activity will require spaces of an appropriate kind, and the spaces for each type are naturally different, not only in size but in the amount of light and air required, the ease of public approach, the arrangements for delivery of goods, and so forth. These differences in turn will develop different types of exterior aspect and interior effect.

By unity of functional expression is meant unity in the aspect of buildings with regard to such special functional requirements. If the program for any given building is carefully and sensitively carried out in the architect's design, unity of functional expression will often result. If, however, an attempt is made to surround the functional elements with exteriors developed originally for some other type of activity or designed primarily in accordance with some historical style, unity of functional expression will almost necessarily suffer. There will be many places in such a building where the specialized requirements of the problem will force themselves into view and produce a basic conflict with other portions of the building where function does not necessarily control shapes and sizes. For example, in the Ford museum in Dearborn, Michigan, the façade is based on Independence Hall in Philadelphia; the rear portions, on the other hand, are of a simple industrial construction type with large glass areas set in steel frames (Fig. 204). The resultant effect, of course, is one of complete conflict both outside and in. Unity is lost entirely, and architectural beauty disappears with it.

But unity of functional expression entails more than the mere automatic or mechanical following of functional requirements. There is also a controlling spirit, as it were, to each architectural problem. This is an intangible matter of sensitive imagination. What is called the character of a building will frequently be set by the function which the structure serves; it is obvious, for example, that an architect will not design an amusement park with the same kind of expressive quality as that of a church, or a house for quiet living with the same atmosphere as that of a theater or an industrial building. Unity of functional expression, therefore, demands some knowledge of the emotional connotations natural to any type of problem, as well as the ability to express that emotional quality in the design of the building (see Figs. 49, 173, 278).

A lack of unity is one of the most common faults in executed buildings. There are two chief causes for this: first, lack of proper subordination of less important elements to some major element; and, second, lack of harmony in the shapes of individual portions of a building (Fig. 54). The first is probably the more common fault. And there are many kinds of architectural problems in which at first it seems almost impossible to obtain this primary kind of unity. If, for instance, a program calls for a group of two buildings of almost equal size and importance, a conflict of interest between them seems at first glance inevitable. That dilemma can be solved in various ways. One is by combining the two buildings into a single structure by means of a common vestibule, portico, or entrance rotunda. Another is by placing, at some well-selected place between them, a third object which, though perhaps purely decorative, will serve as a major element and thus subordinate the buildings themselves. In rare cases the view between the buildings can be made the climax and the buildings be rendered so quiet and unassuming that the view itself becomes a major and unifying element.

An example of the second method can be seen in the municipal group at Springfield, Massachusetts, where the competition program called for two buildings of almost identical size (Fig. 51). In the winning design, the architects, Pell and Corbett, realizing that it was impossible to make an architectural composition of the buildings, frankly added a third motif between them, a high clock tower. When working drawings were being made, the size of this tower was still further increased over that shown in the competition drawings; the executed group proves the value of this larger tower in the powerful sense of repose and unity which the group possesses.

If a composition contains two masses which are of almost equal weight, and if in addition there is a basic lack of harmony between the shapes of the two

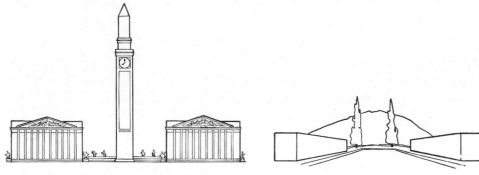

FIGURE 51. UNITY AND DUALITY

Unity conferred on a duality by the insertion of a dominating element. The example on the left is based on the Springfield, Massachusetts, Civic Center, by Pell and Corbett; unity is conferred upon the two equal buildings by the memorial tower. In the example at the right, a view of a mountain, emphasized by enframing trees, acts as the unifying element.

FIGURE 52. MONU-
MENTAL CHURCH AND
TOMB OF CANOVA,
POSSAGNO, ITALY

G. A. Selva, architect

Complete lack of unity resulting from two conflicting motifs of equal power.

From G. Pauli, *Die
Kunst des Klassizismus
und der Romantik*

masses, still greater confusion arises. That accounts for the extreme difficulty of combining a pedimented porch with a circular domed building. The Tomb of Canova at Possagno reveals the basic inconsistency inherent in such an attempt (Fig. 52). The huge Greek Doric portico and the circular walls and dome of the tomb proper form a whole that is ugly from almost any point of view. The dome is too heavy for the porch, and the porch is too large and rich for the dome. No beauty of detail, no richness of material, no perfection of execution can surmount this basic composition error. A more recent example of the same difficulty may be seen in the Jefferson Memorial in Washington.

FIGURE 53. SAN FRANCESCO DI PAOLA, NAPLES, ITALY

P. Bianchi, architect

Unity achieved by the subordination of the portico to the dome and by the judicious design of the minor elements.   Courtesy Ware Library

Here an attempt was made to unify the two motifs by carrying the colonnade of the porch around the domed mass, but even this daring is unavailing. Moreover, the circular colonnade destroys completely the sense of power which a dome of that size should have; the result is necessarily inconclusive and nonstructural in appearance.

The case of the Pantheon in Rome is somewhat different. The Roman architect was skillful enough to realize at once the difficulty of his problem, and he solved it in two ways: first, by interposing a rectangular mass between the circular wall and the portico; and, second, by designing the dome in such a way that from any position close to the building it completely disappears. From the front the rectangular mass helps to conceal the dome so that the porch becomes dominant; from any other point of view the circular wall and the dome are the dominant elements. Another successful attempt at combining a pedimented portico and a dome may be seen in the church of San Francesco di Paola at Naples (Fig. 53). Here the architect has brilliantly contrived to have the dome dominate from every point of view by keeping the portico relatively small and by emphasizing the dome form through the use of small domes on each side and through the basic curved plane of the flanking colonnade.

The problem of unity is a particularly pressing one; the present emphasis on

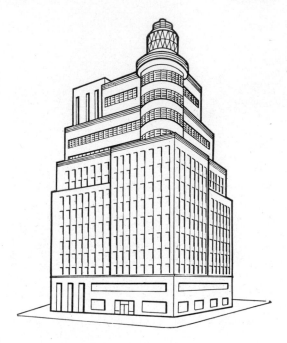

FIGURE 54. PERSPECTIVE OF A
PROPOSED OFFICE BUILDING FOR
A SHORE SITE

Complete lack of unity: no subordination, no harmony, lines in conflict; the
result is incoherence.

functional planning frequently results in plans of great complexity, with many
separate elements of approximately similar sizes. The tendency toward making
window sizes dependent primarily on the amount of light required by each
interior space often develops windows of widely varying area, and the use of
free rhythms in window spacings sometimes produces apparent confusion. Yet
it is inconceivable for the thinking architect to attempt to turn back the clock
and return to the days of an artificially imposed pattern. He must, therefore,
strive with all the more effort to compose and arrange his building so that these
difficulties will be resolved and so that, by the careful subordination of minor
elements, the intensive study of geometric spaces, and the most careful and
harmonious arrangement of openings, true architectural unity will result.

SUGGESTED ADDITIONAL READING FOR CHAPTER 2

Aristotle, *The Poetics*, any good edition.
Butler, Arthur Stanley George, *The Substance of Architecture*, with a foreword
    by Sir Edwin Lutyens (New York: MacVeagh, 1927), pp. 309 f.
Greeley, William Roger, *The Essence of Architecture* (New York: Van Nostrand
    [c1927]), Chap. 9.

Greene, Theodore Meyer, *The Arts and the Art of Criticism* (Princeton: Princeton University Press, 1940), pp. 402 ff.

Hamlin, Talbot [Faulkner], *Architecture, an Art for All Men* (New York: Columbia University Press, 1947), pp. 61–71.

Raymond, George Lansing, *The Essentials of Aesthetics in Music, Poetry, Painting, Sculpture, and Architecture*, 3rd ed. rev. (New York: Putnam's [c1921]).

3

Balance

I N THE VISUAL ARTS, balance is a quality that is present in any object in which the visual interest of the two portions on either side of the center of balance, or center of interest, is equal. The aesthetic pleasure which results from balance seems to have something to do with the quality of the eye motion as the eye "scans" the whole (as a line of poetry is scanned). If the eye, passing from side to side, finds equal attraction in both left and right halves, the attention seems to swing like a pendulum and comes to rest at last at a point midway between the two extremes. If this center of balance is strongly marked so that the eye rests upon it satisfied, an instant feeling of well-being and of repose is produced in the observer.

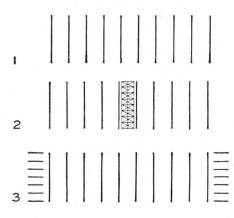

FIGURE 55. BALANCE AND ACCENT ON CENTER OF BALANCE

(1) This is numerically balanced because symmetrical on either side of the center space, but the balance is illegible; the result is a mere series.

(2) The balance in the same series of vertical lines is rendered legible by accenting the center.

(3) The balance is rendered legible by strong stops at the ends of the series, thus implying a center of balance between.

From this it follows that the well-balanced work of art must have some kind of emphasis on the center of balance; in other words, the balance, to be completely satisfactory, must be legible. If, for instance, one places vertical lines at equal distances from each other in any series of indeterminate length, some kind of balance will be present because of the systematic arrangement (Fig. 55–1). Yet such a series will seem indeterminate and indefinite, and the effect will be one of either monotony or restlessness because there is no point on which

FIGURE 56. PARTHENON, ATHENS. RESTORED MODEL

The center of balance is accented by the peak of the pediment, the column spacing, and the arrangement of the sculpture.   Courtesy Metropolitan Museum of Art

the eye can rest. If, however, we add a note or accent of interest at the center of such a group of lines, that accent on the center of interest, or the center of balance, will at once cause a pleasant sensation of satisfaction and repose (Fig. 55-2). This shows the importance of accenting the center of balance even in the simplest of compositions.

We can produce something of the same effect in a different way. If, for example, we oppose to the vertical lines some strongly marked closing motif at each end of the series, the sense of balance is again emphasized. The eye's wandering over the composition is definitely stopped at each end, and the center of balance halfway between the ends is thereby felt though not expressed (Fig. 55-3).

In building, the quality of architectural balance is of the greatest importance. It is made more complicated by the problems of three-dimensional vision noted in Chapter 1; but fortunately, in simple buildings at least, the average eye will make allowances for the visual distortions resulting from perspective vision. We are, accordingly, free to consider these principles of balance largely through studies made in pure elevation.

The simplest type of balance is that usually termed symmetry; in this type

FIGURE 57. WADSWORTH
HOUSE, DANVERS, MASSACHU-
SETTS

A typical Colonial house balanced on both front and end, with the accent on the line of balance furnished by the pedimented doors, the curve-headed dormer, and the upper gable and chimney at the end.

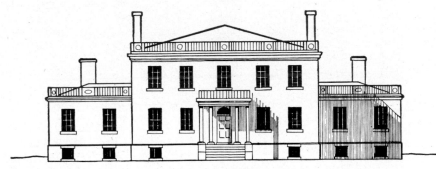

FIGURE 58. CLERMONT, THE LIVINGSTON MANOR HOUSE, TIVOLI, NEW YORK
A composition of central mass and side wings, with porch accenting the center of balance.

FIGURE 59. LADY PEPPERRELL
HOUSE, KITTERY, MAINE

Symmetrical balance: central pavilion and side wings.

From J. M. Howells, *The Architectural Heritage of the Piscataqua*

the two sides of a building on either side of a central axis are identical. Here, provided the center of balance is accented in some subtle way, a reposeful balance will immediately be perceived. Such an accent can be produced in many ways. The more complex the building, the more definite must this emphasis on the center be made in order to avoid confusion and eye wandering. Yet even in simple buildings great architects have frequently taken the most

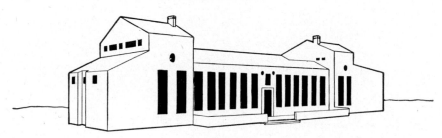

FIGURE 60. LIBERAL ARTS BUILDING, UNIVERSITY OF COLORADO, BOULDER

Charles Z. Klauder, architect

An unconventional composition of balance emphasized by strong end wings and an accented door.

careful pains to accent the balance center. In a Greek temple such as the Parthenon (Fig. 56), for instance, many things contribute to the beauty of the front. The pediment gable apex accents the center line strongly. The dark note of the entrance door, as seen in the shadowed porch, is on the center line. The end intercolumniations are narrower than those in the center, thus forming a subtle close to the series of columns. Moreover, with the same purpose, the outer columns are inclined slightly inwards, as though to direct the eye almost unconsciously toward the center of the front. The ostensibly horizontal lines have a slight curvature. All these factors not only give great life to the façade but subtly help to accent the center of balance of the composition. In a simpler way, any gabled roof on a barn or a house will give a balanced end elevation, provided other elements do not interfere (Fig. 57).

In the case of more complex symmetrical buildings, the way in which the center of balance is accented will often determine a large part of the exterior design. A number of typical schemes deserve to be noted. One scheme consists of a projecting center element with smaller and lower receding wings at the sides (Fig. 58). This type is illustrated in many Georgian houses, libraries, and other similar types of structure (Fig. 59).

In another scheme there are two projecting end pavilions or masses with a connecting element between them (Fig. 60). This second type of balance may be seen in such buildings as the New York Post Office, where the connecting link is a long colonnade; the Vendramini Palace in Venice, where the emphasis on the end pavilions is very slight; and the chief fronts of such cathedrals as Notre Dame in Paris, with its powerful twin towers (Figs. 61–63). The danger inherent in this type lies in the possibility that the interest provided by the end wings may become so strong as to overbalance the composition. Fine discrimination is needed to avoid this danger. In churches with twin towers a powerful

FIGURE 61. VENDRAMINI PALACE, VENICE, ITALY
Pietro Lombardo, architect
Symmetrical balance: end pavilions and central link.   Courtesy Ware Library

accent on the center of balance between them is needed—such, for example, as that given by the rose windows and the great portals of the cathedrals in Paris, Amiens, and Rheims.

A third scheme consists of a combination of the two preceding types of balance (Fig. 64). It is found in buildings with projecting center pavilions, accented end pavilions, and less important connecting links between them. It is admirably shown in many large French Renaissance buildings, in the United States Capitol, and in the Pennsylvania Railroad stations in New York and Washington (Figs. 65, 66). This is almost the maximum of complexity that the human eye will take in at one time.

Architects have often tried to achieve more complex compositions, nearly always with complete failure. The National Gallery in London (Fig. 67) is an example; its repeated end pavilions, three on each side, the stretches of inconclusive wall between them, and the unimportant portico at the center all combine to produce only a sense of confusion and frustration. Apparently the

FIGURE 62 (LEFT). NOTRE DAME CATHEDRAL, PARIS. ELEVATION

Powerful balance achieved by the corner towers, with the center accented by the rose window, the largest of the three doors, and the flèche over the crossing.

FIGURE 63 (RIGHT). NOTRE DAME CATHEDRAL, PARIS. FAÇADE

Simple symmetrical balance.   Courtesy Avery Library

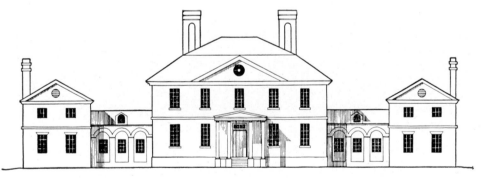

FIGURE 64. TULIP HILL, ANNE ARUNDEL COUNTY, MARYLAND

A balanced composition of the richest type: central mass, end pavilions, connecting wings; accent on center of balance through pediment and porch.

human imagination finds it difficult to relate more than five units in one composition.

The confusion in the National Gallery is not a matter of the length of the building; it results purely from the multiplicity of units. In buildings of great

FIGURE 65. UNITED STATES CAPITOL, WASHINGTON. VIEW FROM THE EAST

Thornton, Latrobe, Bulfinch, and Walter, architects

Complex symmetrical balance, with balance within each unit.   Courtesy Avery Library

FIGURE 66. UNION STATION, WASHINGTON

D. H. Burnham, architect

Complex symmetrical balance: central pavilion, end pavilions, and links.

From *The Architectural Work of Graham, Anderson, Probst & White*

FIGURE 67. NATIONAL GAL-
LERY, LONDON

Incoherence through multiplicity
of parts and a dome of insufficient
size to give the proper accent on
the line of balance. The façade has
fifteen differing sections.

FIGURE 68. HOLKHAM HALL, NORFOLK, ENGLAND. ENTRANCE FRONT
William Kent, architect
A characteristic example of the superb composition of many English eighteenth-century houses.
From Lloyd, *A History of the English House . . .*

size, forms can usually be so arranged as to fall in with one of the simpler schemes, and in large buildings each of the units may itself be a composition of considerable complexity. That is the secret of the powerful monumentality one finds in many of the great English houses, such as Holkham Hall, designed by Kent (Fig. 68). Here the end wings are larger than many single houses, yet everything in their design leads them to be considered as end units to the entire composition.

Holkham Hall also illustrates another quality frequently necessary in compositions of large scale: the gradual change in the size of the unit of composition which the eye commands as the house is approached. When one gets fairly close to the entrance, the side wings almost disappear from view and the eye rests on the body of the house, which, even without the wings, is then seen to be an architectural composition of great beauty in itself. The eighteenth-century English architects were especially brilliant in this kind of abstract design; the Horse Guards in London, also by Kent, is another excellent example (Fig. 69).

One method of accenting the center of balance has already been referred to in Chapter 2—the use of two vertical accents on either side of the center. These accents, by enframing the composition, direct the attention irresistibly to the central element. Thus two tall cedars or poplars on either side of a door will accent it forcefully (Fig. 70). Similarly, gate posts will produce the same effect, as seen in the rebuilt Governor's Palace at Williamsburg (Fig. 72).

This last example shows still another method of obtaining accent—by position. A center of balance will be more interesting in a projecting pavilion than in a plain wall, provided the projection is not so great as to destroy a sense of

FIGURE 69. THE HORSE GUARDS, LONDON

William Kent and J. Vardy, architects

ABOVE: View from the park; BELOW: View from Whitehall. Another instance of English skill in complex symmetrical composition, equally effective from a distance and from close by.

Courtesy Ware Library

continuity between the projecting and receding portions. But the exact reverse of this, the placing of the center of interest on a receding element, will produce an even stronger emphasis, as in the case of the Williamsburg example. That will explain the powerful effect of balance achieved in buildings with a fore-court and also in those, like the example cited above and many large eighteenth-

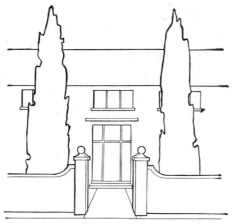

FIGURE 70 (ABOVE). BALANCE AC-
CENTED BY VERTICAL NOTES—TREES
AND GATE POSTS—ON EITHER SIDE OF
THE CENTER

FIGURE 71 (RIGHT). BAPTIST CHURCH, WICKFORD, RHODE ISLAND
Balance accented by the development of the site, by the gateway, and by the tall flanking trees.

Photograph Talbot Hamlin

FIGURE 72. GOVERNOR'S PALACE, WILLIAMSBURG, VIRGINIA. FRONT
Balance accented by its position, its walls and gate posts, its flanking buildings, and its cupola.

Photograph Richard Garrison

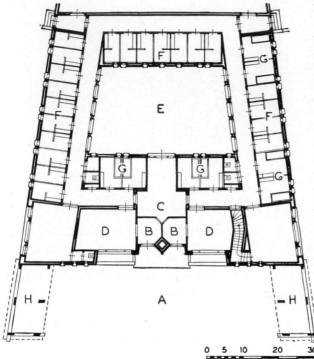

FIGURE 73. PUBLIC BATH-
HOUSE, HILVERSUM, THE
NETHERLANDS. PLAN

W. M. Dudok, architect

A: Entrance court; B: Entrance
vestibules for men and women;
C: Vestibule; D: Guardians, controls, and towels; E: Court; F:
Showers; G: Tub baths; H: Bicycle sheds.

Balance in three dimensions.
The plan, nearly symmetrical
because of the similar requirements of the men's and the
women's sides, is carefully arranged so that its masses and details, which grow naturally from
it, shall have the balance indicated in the two subsequent illustrations.

0 5 10   20   30 FT.

century houses, in which the main element is flanked by two smaller wings
projecting forward on the sides. This type of planning will be considered at
greater length in Chapter 20 on group planning.

In Chapter 1 it was pointed out that the eye would make allowances for the
effect of perspective in three-dimensional compositions. This is not merely a
matter of imagination and perception; in many cases it involves actual motion
on the part of the observer. A building must, of course, look well from all
points of view; yet many successful buildings are so designed as to suggest to
the observer a natural progress that will lead him around inevitably to the chief
front, where the main entrance is situated and where the sense of balance is
most definitely stressed.

The designer can assist this progress in many ways. Let us take, for example,
the public bath building at Hilversum, the Netherlands, designed by Dudok.
Here the building is divided into two equal parts—one for men, and one for
women—and naturally demands a symmetrical composition (Figs. 73–75). Yet
the main entrance is on the wider end of the lot. Important streets lead past
the building on both long sides. The front of the structure is symmetrical, with
the center of balance strongly accented by the chimney, the inward-turning
sense of the design of the main wall, and the projected bicycle sheds on each

FIGURE 74. PUBLIC BATHHOUSE, HILVERSUM, THE NETHERLANDS. VIEW FROM THE FRONT

W. M. Dudok, architect

Balance in three dimensions. A symmetrical composition in which every element has a strong directional sense toward the center. The bicycle sheds, the handling of the brick wall masses, the blunted ends of the upper wings with their louvered openings, the changes of level, and the design of the entrance all unite to create a balance of great power.

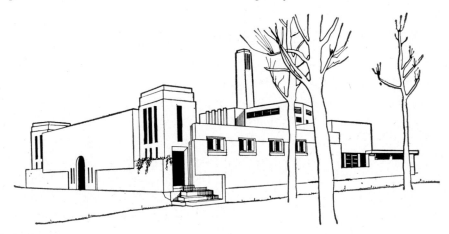

FIGURE 75. PUBLIC BATHHOUSE, HILVERSUM, THE NETHERLANDS. VIEW FROM THE REAR CORNER

W. M. Dudok, architect

Balance in three dimensions. Dynamic balance of the side. Each element toward the front is balanced by a differing element toward the rear, all designed to lead one almost unconsciously around the building toward the front.

side. All this is direct enough, with details carefully designed to produce the required accent. The subtlety of the design is more strongly shown on the sides, where we have an obviously balanced composition, symmetrical in general

FIGURE 76. THE MASS OF NOTRE DAME CATHEDRAL, PARIS, WITHOUT AND WITH
THE FLÈCHE OVER THE CROSSING

This shows the importance of the flèche in creating a secondary sense of balance in diagonal
views of the cathedral.

system but not in mass, size, or detail. The long wall of the service yard at the
rear in a way balances the stronger and shorter wall of the bicycle sheds at the
front. A high, narrow pavilion toward the rear of the main building is a perfect foil for the low, wider wing toward the front, so that the whole side elevation has a kind of balance—enough to give a preliminary satisfaction—which
is, as it were, a balance-in-motion. The tendency in every mass and line and
detail is to lead the observer from the rear to the front; his eye is directed consistently toward the more interesting details at the entrance end, and he naturally walks toward them and around the corner, where he sights the strong
façade, a suitable and sufficient climax to the whole experience. Any purely
symmetrical composition of the side elevation which lacked this dynamic
motion-suggesting quality would have made the building ordinary and banal.

The same thing is true of the composition of some of the great cathedrals,
especially Notre Dame in Paris, where the form of the twin towers inevitably
suggests, to one approaching from the side, that he go toward and around them
to the main façade. But, in a building as large as this, a feeling of restlessness
would arise if some balance were not suggested in other views than that from
the front. Without some modifying influence, the restless interest inherent in
the elaborate buttresses, gables, and pinnacles, in the strong transept end, and
in the polygonal apse might develop only confusion. In order to avoid this, the
Gothic architect has placed a tall and lavishly designed flèche at the intersection of the nave and the transept. Instantly a balance is achieved which makes
the whole extraordinarily effective from any point of view; yet the great twin
towers still remain to draw the observer around to the front. Figure 76, showing the simplified architectural mass with and without the flèche, reveals the
importance of this element.

FIGURE 77. CATHEDRAL, AMIENS, FRANCE. EAST END

The Gothic flèche as an accent on the center of balance.   Courtesy Ware Library

So far we have been dealing chiefly with symmetrical, or formal, balance. But the problem of informal, or unsymmetrical, balance is not only more complex but also of even greater importance today. Functional planning more frequently than not gives rise to plans that are unsymmetrical; moreover, our most vocal architectural critics prefer informal to formal design as a general principle. This constitutes an almost complete revolution from the eclectic attitude of the late nineteenth century. Then, as during the Renaissance, architects tended naturally to design buildings that were symmetrical; they deserted symmetry only when the requirements of the plan absolutely forced them to do so. Now the reverse is true. The mid-twentieth-century architect naturally tends to design a non-symmetrical structure unless the requirements of the problem, the site, and so forth absolutely force monumental symmetry upon him. Yet the demands for balance are as definite in unsymmetrical as in symmetrical structures, and it therefore becomes necessary to consider this problem with some care.

Informal balance, we may say, exists when there is an equality of aesthetic interest on each side of the center of balance, even though there is no equality of form. In unsymmetrical balance it is still more necessary to accent the center of balance than in a symmetrical composition, because otherwise it is much more difficult, if not impossible, for the unaided eye to discover the balance. Since, moreover, the complexity that often accompanies informality of balance leads to diffuseness and confusion unless the composition is strongly marked, a

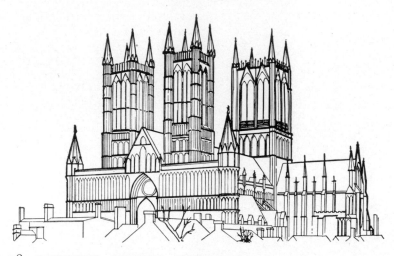

FIGURE 78. CATHEDRAL, LINCOLN, ENGLAND

This diagrammatic view shows the power of a large central tower in assisting the general balance of a cathedral mass.

powerful emphasis on the center of balance becomes all the more necessary. That, then, is the first principle of informal balance.

The second principle of informal balance has been called the leverage principle. This means that a small object of low interest far from the center of balance may be balanced by a large element of great interest close to the center of balance. The principle of leverage is felt unconsciously by many people. It is the secret of the beauty in many informally furnished rooms, as well as in many informal buildings. Let us take, for example, a simple building of L or T plan. Seen from one of the long sides, the arm which projects toward the observer will naturally form an area of greater interest than that offered by the long and unbroken arm. This is occasioned by differences in light and shade, as well as by the change of plane in the projection. In accordance with the leverage principle, the center of balance in such a building will be close to the re-entrant corner, where the projecting wing and the long body of the building come together. This point, therefore, should be chosen for accent, and it is here that the entrance can best be placed (Fig. 79, left). Such an arrangement represents a common solution in the composition of many houses and smaller public buildings.

If, instead of placing the accented entrance at that point, it is moved down the long part of the building away from the angle, the building is instantly thrown out of balance (Fig. 79, right) and nothing the architect can do will remedy the situation unless he develops a still more powerful center of interest

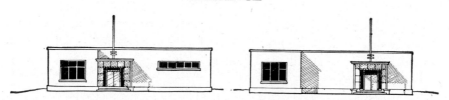

FIGURE 79. UNSYMMETRICAL BALANCE: THE LEVERAGE PRINCIPLE

LEFT: Center of balance near corner of projecting wing and main body of the building; RIGHT: Unsatisfactory and incoherent result when the porch axis does not coincide with the natural center of balance.

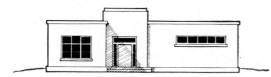

FIGURE 80. UNSYMMETRICAL BALANCE

The natural center of balance still further emphasized by the height of the entrance element.

at the true center of balance. The list of objects with their relative interest on page 32 may be helpful in determining the proper accent for the center of balance. Thus, if a tower or vertical element of some kind is placed at the center of balance, the composition will be rendered stronger, the balance more obvious (Fig. 80).

As we have insisted again and again, architecture is a three-dimensional art, and no elevation study alone will give a true picture of the building. This fact is even more important in informal than in formal structures, because the eye is less ready to make the requisite allowance for perspective distortion. In a country house, for instance, one may see the building from many different points of view, and even the approach to it may be by curving paths or roads from which it may appear at almost any angle. Yet every view of the building should show an implied, if not a definitely stated, balance, and these varying views can be thoroughly studied in advance only through perspective sketches. Even perspectives, however, may force an unnatural emphasis on certain points of view, to the disadvantage of others which may be equally important. Small-scale models are therefore often used in studying such complicated three-dimensional designs and, if rightly seen and rightly used, may be of great value to the designer, particularly in major mass relationships. But models are open to the same kind of dangers as are perspective drawings. Models are full of the delusive charm of the miniature; furthermore, they are most often viewed from a level high above them, whereas an actual building is most frequently seen from levels only slightly above the ground floor or even, if the building is on a hill, from levels far below. From such points of view the effect might be quite different from that received when looking down on the roof. What the model will show, however, is the basic system, or the regularity of system, of the composition; in addition, if it is placed high enough and the eye is brought down low enough in relation to it, it may assist enormously in the checking of a design.

If, then, neither perspective, nor elevation, nor model is a true presentation of a building, on what can the architect depend? The answer is—on his own trained, architectural, three-dimensional imagination. The experienced designer who has seen drawings become concrete facts as structures, has walked many times around buildings, and has observed both confusion and composition in executed work builds up within himself such visualizing power that he can be sure in advance that what he designs will be compositionally right. He will check his imagination by elevations, perspectives, and sometimes by models, but these will frankly be used merely as checks on his own creative sense.

Many informally designed buildings fall naturally into the class known as picturesque and have the particular kind of charm which that word connotes. Yet picturesqueness in architecture can be one of the most dangerous ideals to follow. The name itself should be a warning. That is picturesque which would look well in a picture; but a building is not a picture (or is only incidentally a picture), and between architectural beauty and picturesque beauty there is a tremendous gulf. Thus a mass of dark, dreary, and ill-designed factories with great chimneys pouring smoke across a winter sunset may be most picturesque; there may be extraordinary excitement in its color and shape, yet everything in this picture might be the worst kind of architecture. The well-designed factory minimizes smoke and is airy and full of light; the picturesque factory may be a curse on its entire neighborhood. Similarly, slums and blighted areas may be full of picturesque bits; the painter's love for the decaying mansion or the tumble-down barn is well known, yet the architect's whole effort should be toward the elimination of slums and blighted areas and deserted farms.

In fact, one might almost say that the architect should always avoid picturesqueness unless the requirements of his building and its site absolutely force it upon him. Buildings are complex enough under any circumstances. The architect's job must always be to create in them the greatest possible simplicity and repose; he should let picturesque qualities occur only as the results of this search. The "built picturesque" often achieves only the cute or the confused. Such are any number of suburban houses in which the builder—in order, as

FIGURE 81. TOWN HALL, HILVERSUM, THE NETHERLANDS
W. M. Dudok, architect
Subtle balance of vertical and horizontal lines and planes, with the tower as the fulcrum.

Courtesy Netherlands Information Bureau

he thinks, to avoid monotony—artificially complicates exteriors and produces only monotonous confusion.

The requirement of balance in architecture is not limited to exterior design. Balance is equally necessary in the interior. And the same general definitions of artistic balance that are true in the design of façades will hold true here. Architectural balance in interior design naturally is largely dependent on the plan, for the arrangement of the parts of a building as shown in the plan necessarily determines not only what the observer sees as he enters the building and passes through it but also the order in which these visual experiences come to him. Accordingly, interior balance is often spoken of as balance in plan. This definition, however, is open to misconception, for a plan is a purely abstract diagram, whereas the disposition and arrangement of visual space, which constitute interior architectural balance, are the results of concrete actualities. Interiors that are balanced in actuality will usually give rise to plans which as drawings are balanced, but there are many plan drawings that create in themselves an artificial pattern which may result in a structure that is actually confused and visually unsatisfactory. The plan, nevertheless, is the architect's chief

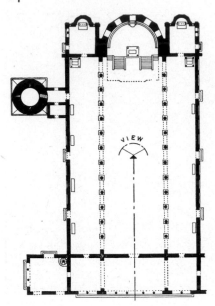

FIGURE 82. SAN APOLLINARE IN CLASSE, RA-
VENNA, ITALY. PLAN

Interior balance in plan. On the normal line of progress, shown by the dot-and-dash line, all views are
balanced and lead toward a climax at the altar.

way of studying the quality of his interior spaces, but he must always look at
plans imaginatively and never forget that they are a means to an end and not
an end in themselves.

When a person enters a building, his normal line of motion will be directly
ahead in a straight line unless something suggests or forces a change in direction.
This natural line of progress is the reality behind the architectural convention
known as the *axis*. In other words, the structure must be designed with regard
to the natural pattern of motion. The requirement of architectural balance
means, therefore, that any view from any point in this natural progress should
have visual balance, and furthermore that the center of balance should be on
that natural line of progress (Figs. 82, 83). Interior balance, like exterior balance, can be either formal or informal, either symmetrical or unsymmetrical,
and in interiors the same general rules as to the relative interest value of different kinds of form hold true that are true in exteriors. Thus a well-designed interior stair exerts a marked attractive power in an interior. Similarly, a tall
object or a high interior space will call attention to itself.

But in interior design there is another factor to be considered which is of
tremendous importance in planning—the question of the relative intensity of
the lighting. A large window commanding a wide view, for instance, will
overbalance in interest almost any other architectural element because of the
extreme contrast between the light that pours in and the darkness of the walls
on either side silhouetted against it. That is one reason why the medieval archi-

FIGURE 83. SAN APOLLINARE IN CLASSE, RAVENNA, ITALY. INTERIOR
Symmetrical interior balance.   Courtesy Avery Library

tects so frequently preferred to modulate the brilliancy of outside light by the
use of stained glass in rich colors and by intricacy of tracery.

The attractive power of the center of balance has already been referred to in
passing. The ordinary person tends unconsciously to walk toward such a center. This is the secret of much of the world's best planning, and it is as true
of the design of houses as it is of monumental public buildings. Expressing a
center of balance is one of the ways in which the architect directs a person's
footsteps in the direction in which he is supposed to go; the well-designed
building needs few directional signs. Let us take, for example, the plan of the
Propylaea and Great Temple at Baalbek (Fig. 84). In this monumental symmetrical composition the architect has achieved a group of extraordinary visual
richness, all carefully arranged to direct the visitor straight through from entrance to temple. The intercolumniations across the central axis are all slightly

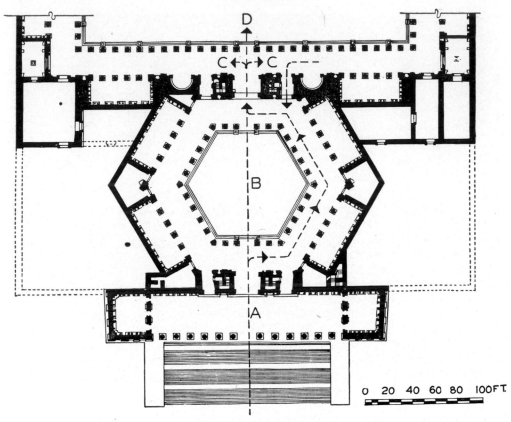

FIGURE 84. ENTRANCE COMPLEX OF THE GREAT TEMPLE AT BAALBEK, ASIA MINOR.
PLAN

A: Porch; B: Hexagonal court; C: Colonnade of great court; D: Great court.

The centers of balance of the successive views are so designed as to suggest the proper progress
through this composition. Thus the porch colonnade, like the court colonnades, has a wider
central intercolumniation and the arched entrances have wider doors in the center than at the
sides. Views from the colonnade of the hexagonal court, B, are balanced, but views across it
sidewise have a weak balance, centered on re-entrant angles; the balance on the main axis is
strong. This combination suggests a slight rest at B but eventual motion along the main axis.

wider than those on each side. The great narthex cross hall is unsymmetrical
from front to rear, and the door breaks the otherwise continuous rear wall and
forms an inviting climax at the entrance. The forecourt is hexagonal. Thus the
transverse views across it, though perfectly symmetrical and balanced, have
their center of balance in a weak re-entrant angle. In contrast to this, the great
entrance to the court is a composition of tremendous size with a strongly
marked center opening. Moreover, the hexagonal sides toward the inner-court-
yard gate, by their angle, tend to force the attention inwards toward the pas-

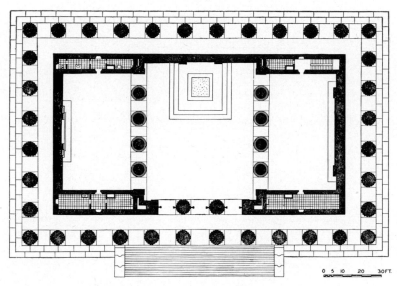

FIGURE 85. LINCOLN MEMORIAL, WASHINGTON. PLAN

Henry Bacon, architect

Strong formal balance between the two side halls. Each of these is a symmetrically balanced unit, with inscribed wall panels as the climax and the center. Yet these are less strong than the central balance between the colonnades and a point in front of the climax—the statue of Lincoln.

sage so that progress through the forecourt into the great inner court is rendered both inevitable and impressive. Many other Roman plans aim for that same quality of close relationship between visual balance and motion; they will be considered at greater length in Chapters 7 and 8. Other good examples of symmetrical, formal interior balance can be seen in any Early Christian basilica, such as San Apollinare in Classe in Ravenna (Figs. 82, 83); in monumental theaters like the Opéra in Paris; in the Nebraska State Capitol (Fig. 248), one of the most perfect of modern formal plans; and, in a smaller and simpler way, in the Lincoln Memorial in Washington, where much of the power of the effect is due to the subtle handling of transverse balance in relation to the placing of the great statue of Lincoln (Figs. 85, 86).

This quality of the attractive power of the center of balance is especially well illustrated in many informal plans that are dependent on a curved or a bending axis. Figures 87, 88, and 90 illustrate how the establishment of interesting features at one side of an axis tend to bend that axis toward them and thus bring the visitor to the place where he is supposed to go.

It will therefore be seen that formal or informal balance is at the bottom of much of the art of architectural design. Balance gives power and unity to

FIGURE 86. LINCOLN MEMORIAL, WASHINGTON. VIEW IN INTERIOR

Henry Bacon, architect

Subtle interior balance in two directions: transverse, through the two side halls; longitudinal, from entrance to statue.   Photograph Ewing Galloway

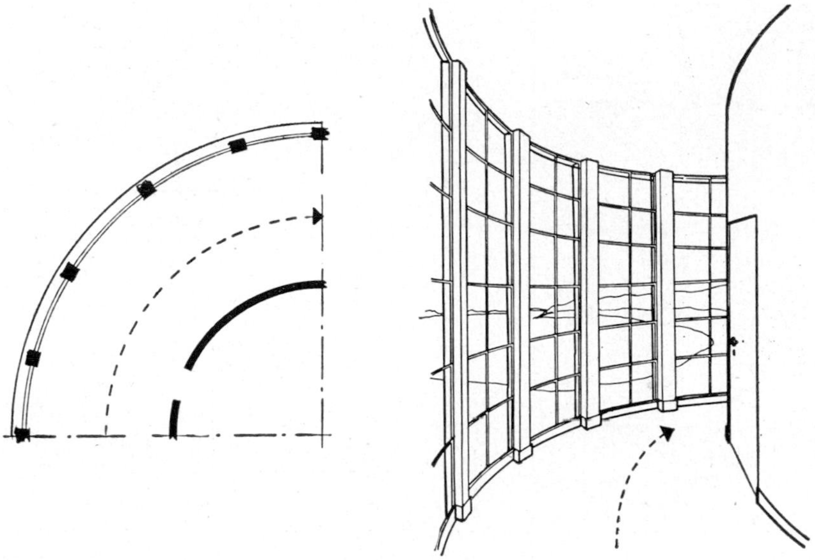

FIGURE 87. CHANGE OF DIRECTION THROUGH UNSYMMETRICAL OR DYNAMIC BALANCE

Any view around the curved passage has a powerful sense of motion because of the differing visual impressions given by the two sides.

FIGURE 88. CATHEDRAL, CHARTRES, FRANCE. VIEW IN THE AMBULATORY

Dynamic unsymmetrical balance suggesting motion through the ambulatory and around the choir.   Courtesy Ware Library

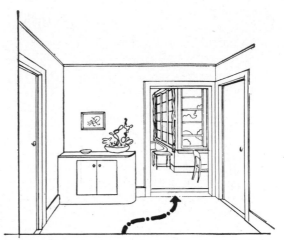

FIGURE 89 (LEFT). ST. GERMAIN-DES-PRÉS, PARIS. VIEW IN AMBULATORY
Another example of motion implied by dynamic and unsymmetrical balance.

FIGURE 90 (RIGHT). AN ENTRANCE HALL IN A HOUSE
Dynamic balance suggests approach to the living room.

exteriors. It establishes repose, it prevents restlessness and confusion, and it is at the base of much of the best planning of the world's great architectural monuments; because of its subtle power over people's natural motions, it has a functional as well as a purely aesthetic basis.

SUGGESTED ADDITIONAL READING FOR CHAPTER 3

Edwards, A. Trystan, *Style and Composition in Architecture* . . . (London: Tiranti, 1944), Chap. 4.

Greeley, William Roger, *The Essence of Architecture* (New York: Van Nostrand [c1927]), Chap. 10.

Gromort, Georges, *Essai sur la théorie de l'architecture* . . . (Paris: Vincent, Fréal, 1942).

Guadet, Julien, *Éléments et théorie de l'architecture*, 4 vols. (Paris: Aulanier, n.d.), Vol. IV, Liv. III, Chaps. 12 and 13.

Hamlin, Talbot [Faulkner], *Architecture, an Art for All Men* (New York: Columbia University Press, 1947).

Robinson, John Beverley, *Architectural Composition* . . . (New York: Van Nostrand, 1908).

Van Pelt, John Vredenburgh, *A Discussion of Composition, Especially as Applied to Architecture* (New York and London: Macmillan, 1902).

4

Proportion

ALMOST ALL architectural critics are in agreement on the importance of proportion in the art of architecture. Yet, when they attempt to become more specific with regard to what constitutes good proportion, this apparent unanimity disappears. Vitruvius, in a series of vague passages which have served to start endless controversies, does succeed in making it perfectly clear that in Greek architecture, at least, there was some definite relation between the size of the smallest parts and the size of the whole; it is usually considered that he was indicating the existence of a modular system which controlled the design of Greek temples. In the seventeenth century, François Blondel, the first professor of architecture in the French Royal Academy of Architecture, claimed that the entire beauty of architecture came from absolute and easily recognizable numerical proportions. Toward the end of the nineteenth century, Julien Guadet found the secret of good proportion in something he rather vaguely called truth or expressiveness. He says that good proportions are rational and not the products of mere instinct and that every program has its own proportions latent within it. To achieve some guide through this confusion of opinions and attitudes, we must first of all define what we mean by proportion, for it is obvious that Guadet is speaking of kinds of size relationship which are different from those that interested Blondel.

The arithmetical definition of the word states that proportion exists when two ratios are equal. In a:b::c:d, the terms a:b and c:d are the ratios. We may assume this as generally true of proportion in architecture; the problem then arises as to what a, b, c, and d may represent. In building forms, the obvious dimensions are the heights, widths, and depths of architectural members and of architectural masses. And, according to the strict mathematical concept, we may say that good proportion exists when the same ratios are found in all the major dimensions of a building and of its parts.[1]

[1] See George David Birkhoff, *Aesthetic Measure* (Cambridge, Mass.: Harvard University Press, 1933).

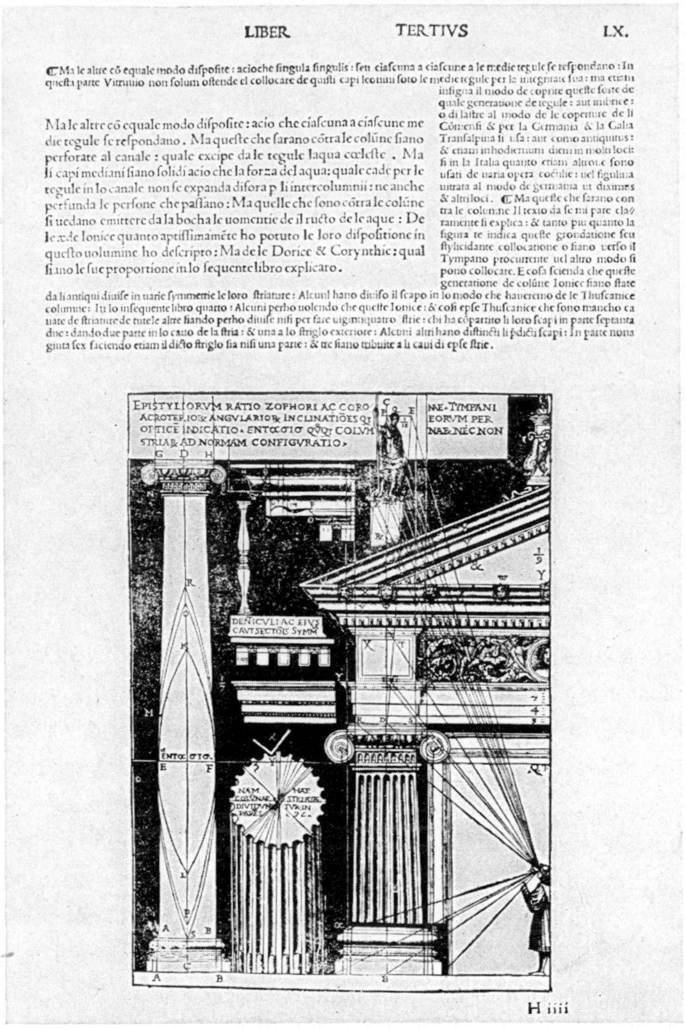

LIBER TERTIVS LX.

☞Ma le altre cō equale modo diſpoſite : acioche ſingula ſingulis : ſeu ciaſcuna a ciaſcune a le medie tegule ſe reſpondano : In queſta parte Vitruuio non ſolum oſtende el collocare de queſti capi leonini ſoto le medie tegule per la integritate ſua : ma etiam inſigna il modo de coprire queſte ſorte de quale generatione de tegule : aut imbrice : o di laitre al modo de le coperture de li Cōmenſi & per la Germania & la Galia Tranſalpina ſi uſa : aut como antiquitus : & etiam inhodiernum diem in molti loci : ſi in la Italia quanto etiam altroue ſono uſati de uaria opera coctile : uel figulina uitrata al modo de germania ut diximus & altriloci. ☞Ma queſte che ſarano contra le colunne Il texto da ſe mi pare claramente ſi explica : & tanto piu quanto la figura te indica queſte grondatione ſeu ſtylicidante collocatione o ſiano uerſo il Tympano procurrente uel altro modo ſi pono collocare. E coſa ſcienda che queſte generatione de colūne Ionice ſiano ſtate da li antiqui diuiſe in uarie ſymmetrie le loro ſtriature : Alcuni hano diuiſo il ſcapo in lo modo che hauremo de le Thuſcanice columne : In lo inſequente libro quarto : Alcuni perho uolendo che queſte Ionice : & coſi epſe Thuſcanice che ſono mancho cauate de ſtriature de tute le altre ſiando perho diuiſe niſi per fare uigintiquatro ſtrie : chi ha cōpartito li loro ſcapi in parte ſeptanta due : dando due parte in lo cauo de la ſtria : & una a lo ſtriglo exteriore : Alcuni altri hano diſtincti li pdicti ſcapi : In parte nonaginta ſex faciendo etiam il dicto ſtriglo ſia niſi una parte : & tre ſiano tribuite a li caui di epſe ſtrie.

Ma le altre cō equale modo diſpoſite : acio che ciaſcuna a ciaſcune medie tegule ſe reſpondano. Ma queſte che ſarano cōtra le colūne ſiano perforate al canale : quale excipe da le tegule laqua cœleſte. Ma li capi mediani ſiano ſolidi acio che la forza del aqua : quale cade per le tegule in lo canale non ſe expanda difora p li intercolumnii : ne anche perfunda le perſone che paſſano : Ma quelle che ſono cōtra le colūne ſi uedano emittere da la bocha le uomentie de il ructo de le aque : De le æde Ionice quanto aptiſſimamēte ho potuto le loro diſpoſitione in queſto uolumine ho deſcripto : Ma de le Dorice & Corynthic : qual ſiano le ſue proportione in lo ſequente libro explicaro.

FIGURE 91. A PAGE FROM THE EDITION OF VITRUVIUS EDITED BY CESARIANO (COMO: DA PONTE, 1521)

Text in the center, with the notes around it. The illustration deals with the effect of vertical perspective on proportion.

Courtesy Avery Library

Yet the problem of what is termed proportion in architecture is not limited to such equalities; frequently it is purely a question of the ratios themselves—the ratios, for instance, between the height and width of a door, of a window, or of the entire surface of a façade, or even between the length and width of a room. In almost any such feature there will be some ratios which give greater pleasure than others—such as those which prompt us to say, "This door has beautiful proportions and that one has ugly proportions." Is there, then, some series of absolute or ideal relationships between height and width which will

FIGURE 92. PORTE ST. DENIS,
PARIS

François Blondel, architect

A design with proportions determined on a simple arithmetical basis. Compare Figure 93.

Courtesy Avery Library

FIGURE 93. PORTE ST. DENIS,
PARIS. ELEVATION

François Blondel, architect

Arithmetical, or numerical, proportion controls all the main lines of
this design. The scales at sides and
bottom show how these divisions
were made. Thus the main gate
height is twice its width, its width
is one-third the total width, the
main cornice is one-sixth the
height, the impost level is half the
height, the pedestals are one-quar-
ter the height, and so on, to the
smallest details.

guarantee beauty in design or will be found true in the case of any object generally considered beautiful? It is this question which has caused by far the greatest amount of architectural controversy. Thus the simple modular proportion
enunciated by Blondel will determine unitary ratios (Figs. 92, 93). According
to him, only the simpler of such ratios can be appreciated by the observer and
are therefore effective—ratios such as 1:1, 1:2, 2:3, 3:4:5, and so on; more complex proportions are ineffective, and the absence of unitary proportions of any
kind produces ugliness. On the other hand, the supporters of the theory of
dynamic symmetry claim that the only really effective aesthetic ratios are in-

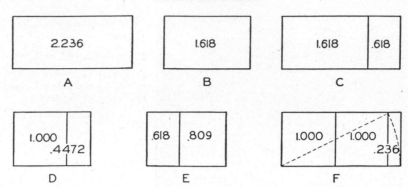

FIGURE 94. CONTROLLING RECTANGLES ACCORDING TO THE THEORY OF DYNAMIC SYMMETRY AS DEVELOPED BY JAY HAMBIDGE

A: Root-five rectangle, its long side being the $\sqrt{5}$ if its height is unity; B: Golden Section rectangle; C: Root-five rectangle, containing a Golden Section rectangle and its reciprocal; D: Root-two rectangle; E: The same, differently divided; F: Subdivision of the root-five rectangle.

In every case, these rectangles are easily determined by purely graphic means. Thus in D, the long side is the diagonal of the square, etc.

Redrawn from Hambidge, *The Parthenon* . . .

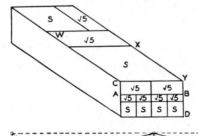

FIGURE 95. PARTHENON, ATHENS. MASS

According to Jay Hambidge, this shows the units of which the Parthenon is composed.

Redrawn from Hambidge, *The Parthenon* . . .

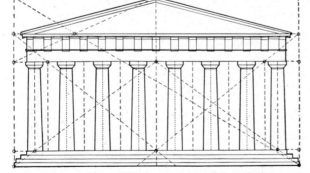

FIGURE 96. PARTHENON, ATHENS. FAÇADE

Proportions, according to Jay Hambidge; the major points determined by dynamic symmetry. Compare Figure 95.

Redrawn from Hambidge, *The Parthenon* . . .

commensurable and can only be obtained graphically; this system is based on two relationships: first, on the relationships of the sides of a square to its diagonal; and, second, on the development of related series of rectangles from a single square in such a way that the long side of each rectangle is the diagonal of the rectangle immediately preceding it. Of these various rectangles, they choose as the most important the root-five rectangle (Figs. 94–96).

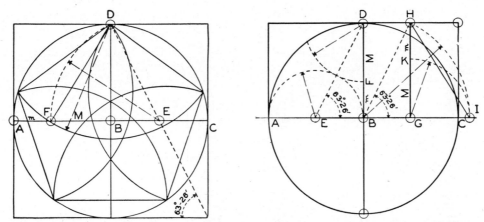

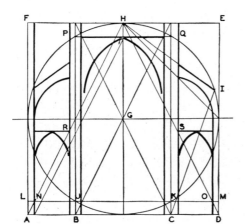

FIGURE 97. THE PENTAGON, PENTAGRAM, AND DESIGN "AD QUADRATUM," ACCORDING TO LUND

LEFT: Diagram showing how the *ad quadratum* triangle (the triangle inscribed in a square) can be used to generate a regular pentagon with a pentagram (five-pointed star) within it; this construction also achieves the Golden Section of the radius of the circle, AF and FB being in extreme and mean ratio $\left(\dfrac{AF}{FB} = \dfrac{FB}{AB} \right)$. RIGHT: Other constructions of extreme and mean ratio; in each case $\dfrac{m}{M} = \dfrac{M}{m+M}$. This also shows the use of the *ad quadratum* angle (63° – 26′) in this process.

Redrawn from Lund, *Ad Quadratum*

FIGURE 98. THE LAYOUT OF THE SECTION OF A TYPICAL GOTHIC CHURCH ON "AD QUADRATUM" PRINCIPLES, ACCORDING TO LUND

All major points are established by the intersection of *ad quadratum* divisions with important and easily determined elements. A pentagon determines the slope and height of the flying buttresses. One starts with the square ADEF, dividing its base into four equal parts to determine the width of nave and aisles. By drawing the correct *ad quadratum* diagonals, the width of walls and pier arches and the height of the side aisles (R and s) and of the main nave vault (P–Q) may all be determined.

Redrawn from Lund, *Ad Quadratum*

Lund, in his interesting book, *Ad Quadratum*, claims that the basis for the design of all Greek temples and medieval cathedrals lay in the triangle which can be inscribed in a square—in other words, a form closely related to the root-five rectangle—and also in the closely related forms of the pentagon and the pentagram, or five-pointed star, as well as in the Golden Section (Figs. 97–99). R. W. Gardner, one of the most assiduous of workers in this much-plowed field, claims that the basis of all good classic design resides in a series of squares

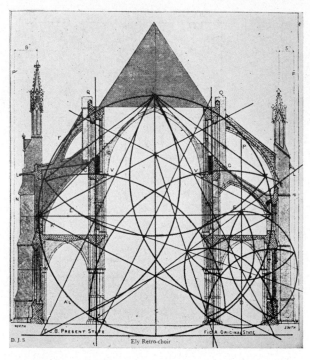

FIGURE 99. CATHEDRAL, ELY, ENGLAND. SECTION

This section shows Lund's analysis of the proportions of Ely Cathedral, based upon the pentagon, five-pointed star, and the *ad quadratum* triangle.

From Lund, *Ad Quadratum*

so related that the area of each is either double or one-half of the preceding square in the series (Figs. 100–102). Viollet-le-Duc assumes the equilateral and the 45-degree triangles as the basis of most medieval architecture (Figs. 103, 104).

That some type of directing geometrical or modular basis was used for establishing certain controlling elements in much past architecture can hardly be questioned. We have, for instance, the record of the famous conference of architects held in 1401 for the purpose of determining whether Milan Cathedral should be completed *ad triangulam* (based on the equilateral triangle) or *ad quadratum* (based on the triangle inscribed in a square). In the 1521 Italian edition of Vitruvius, a plan and sections are given showing the results obtained by the use of different triangles (Fig. 105). Moreover, there still exists a well-known manuscript by the German fifteenth-century architect Roritzer, or Roriczer, which states his method of laying out a pinnacle. This is an easy graphic method based on a modular system and on the size of squares inscribed diagonally within each other (Fig. 106). That is the only direct evidence we possess from an architect as to the use of such a system in medieval times. It is probably to be considered less in the nature of an infallible or mystical rule than as a quick method of taking care of certain details in design—a procedure

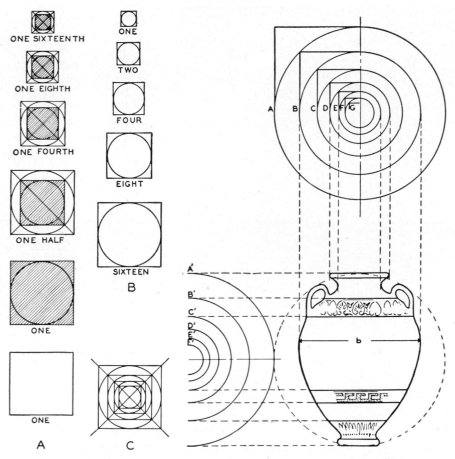

FIGURE 100 (LEFT). THE CONTROLLING SQUARES OF R. W. GARDNER

A: Related squares each one of which is one-half the preceding one in area; B: Related squares each one of which is twice the preceding one in area; C: A group of squares related according to this system showing the method of graphic determination.

Redrawn from Gardner, *A Primer of Proportion* . . .

FIGURE 101 (RIGHT). ANALYSIS OF THE DESIGN OF A GREEK VASE BY R. W. GARDNER

The basis of Gardner's aesthetic system is a series of squares, each of which is half the area of the preceding square. These may be easily constructed by inscribing each square diagonally within the preceding one. Dimensions derived from these squares establish critical points in the design. Redrawn from Gardner, *A Primer of Proportion* . . .

somewhat analogous to that employed by the classic designers in connection with the various rules for drawing the orders of architecture.

Generally speaking, the varying analyses of executed works by these supporters of different and frequently conflicting systems seem more artificially imposed than natural; often the directing or controlling points used in the

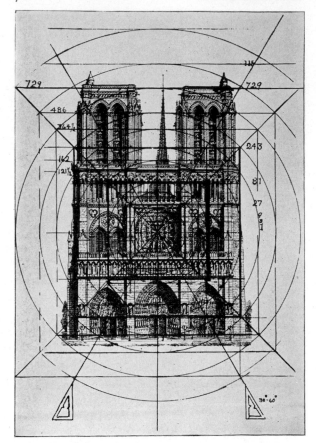

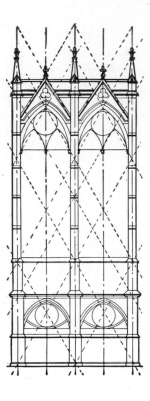

FIGURE 102 (LEFT). NOTRE DAME CATHEDRAL, PARIS. FAÇADE

This is analyzed according to two concurrent systems: one based on the equilateral triangle and the other on a series of squares so related that the area of each is double that of the next smaller one.   From Gardner, *A Primer of Proportion* . . .

FIGURE 103 (RIGHT). TWO BAYS OF STE CHAPELLE, PARIS, ACCORDING TO THE ANALYSIS OF VIOLLET-LE-DUC

This analysis bases the design on the equilateral (60°) triangle. All important controlling points are determined by such lines.   Redrawn from Viollet-le-Duc, *Dictionnaire raisonné* . . .

analyses are not the obvious points which a practical architect would determine as basic. All the systems seem to work—provided one chooses the proper points and the requisite base lines or basic dimensions. Sometimes the base line is at the floor level, sometimes at the level of the top of the base of columns, sometimes far beneath the grade. The various systems seem perhaps more like monuments to the patience of their creators than true descriptions of architectural design (see Figs. 96, 99, 102).

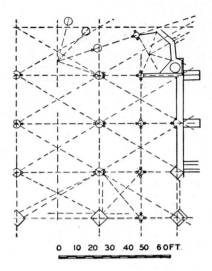

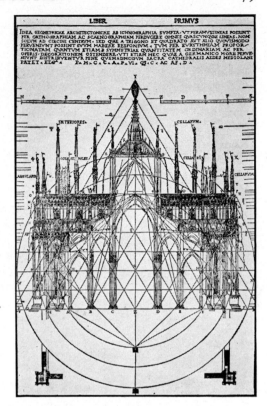

FIGURE 104 (LEFT). CHOIR OF CATHEDRAL, BEAUVAIS, FRANCE. PART PLAN

The entire plan is developed on a network of lines at 60°, forming equilateral triangles; thus the width of the aisles is less than the pier-arch spacing, and, by placing the apex of the outer triangle on the outside of the wall line, the outer aisle is determined as slightly narrower than the inner one. At the crossing (at the bottom of the plan) the piers are enlarged to take the crossing vault, hence slightly narrowing the pier-arch bay at this point.

Redrawn from Viollet-le-Duc, *Dictionnaire raisonné* . . .

FIGURE 105 (RIGHT). SECTION OF CATHEDRAL, MILAN, ITALY, FROM THE 1521 COMO VITRUVIUS

This diagram was used to illustrate the Vitruvian concept of proportion or eurhythmy. Based on the discussions held in the years immediately preceding and following the beginning of the fifteenth century, the section shows the use of *ad quadratum* triangles to establish the correct height.

If the validity of any mathematical rules for the ratios of individual elements of a building thus appears extremely questionable, it becomes necessary to broaden the scope of our examination of the problem and to consider the relationship of elements to one another. Here we may definitely return to the mathematical definition of proportion; we may accept, for instance, the facts

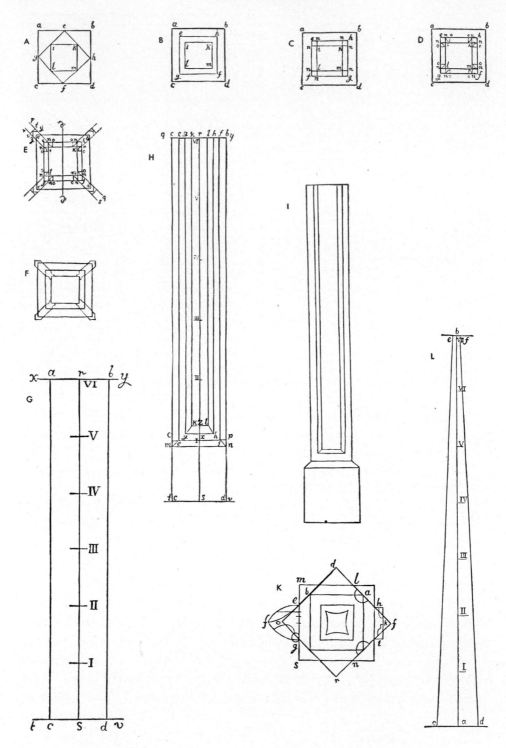

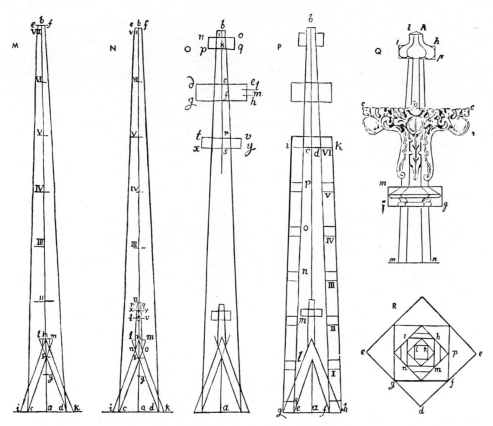

FIGURE 106 (ABOVE AND OPPOSITE). RORITZER'S SCHEME FOR DETERMINING THE
PROPORTIONS OF A PINNACLE (1486)

The late Gothic architect, Matthias Roritzer, left an illustrated manuscript describing the manner
in which the dimensions of a pinnacle were developed. The basis was the square plan of the
base, abcd, as in A. This was divided by successive diagonal inscribed squares, B. These, rotated,
established all the plan thicknesses of the pinnacle shaft, C and D. This plan and its intersections
determine the projection of the spire moldings, E and F. The height of the shaft is six times its
width, G and H. Diagram I shows the final shaft. The development of all the major elements of
the spire, with its gables, crockets, and finial, is determined in a somewhat similar way, K TO R.

From von Heideloff, *Die Bauhütte des Mittelalters in Deutschland*

that rectangles which have the same ratio of width to height will be harmonious with one another, no matter what the actual sizes may be, and that this
harmony will give a sense of pleasant proportion. Thus, if openings in a building have themselves the same ratio of height to width as does the wall in which
they are placed, there will be some sort of natural coherence between the openings and the wall (Figs. 107, 108).[2] All rectangles of identical ratios, if super-

[2] There are exceptions: in tower design, for example, the higher rectangles look better when
relatively taller than those below. This may be a matter of perspective distortion. Vitruvius and
many Renaissance critics were much interested in that problem (see Figs. 91, 111–113).

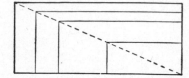
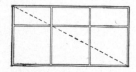

FIGURE 107 (LEFT). DIAGRAM OF SIMILAR RECTANGLES

All rectangles with a common diagonal have a similar ratio of length to width.

FIGURE 108 (RIGHT). A DIAGONAL USED TO DETERMINE MULLION AND TRANSOM DIVISIONS IN A WINDOW

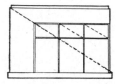
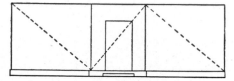

FIGURE 109. SIMPLE APPLICATIONS OF PARALLEL AND PERPENDICULAR DIAGONALS TO ARCHITECTURAL DESIGN

LEFT: The end of a wing of a building; RIGHT: The subdividing of a façade.

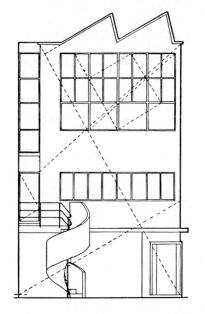
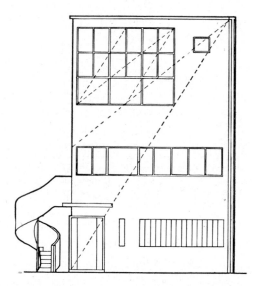

FIGURE 110. OZENFANT STUDIO, PARIS

Le Corbusier and P. Jeanneret, architects

Le Corbusier's use of directing lines—parallel and perpendicular diagonals and others—in determining the design of a façade.   Redrawn from Le Corbusier, *Vers une Architecture*

imposed one upon another with one corner constant, will have a common diagonal. Rectangles with common diagonals at right angles to the first diagonal

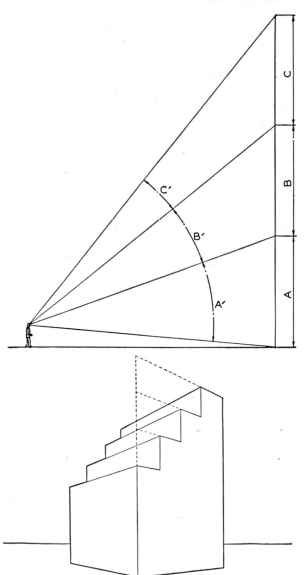

FIGURE III. PROPORTIONS
AS AFFECTED BY HEIGHT

A, B, and C are equal, but they
subtend unequal arcs for a spectator; hence visually A' (A as
seen) is much greater than B',
and that, in turn, than c'.

FIGURE II2. A STEPPED
MASS IN PERSPECTIVE

The upper steps seem progres-
sively smaller though all are of
equal height.

will also have identical ratios, though the longer dimensions of the second
group will be at right angles to the longer dimensions of the first (Fig. 109).
A simple method of developing harmonious door panels, window and door
proportions, and the like can be developed from these facts, and such graphic
aids to design have frequently been used, for on the basic angles made by the
diagonals and by perpendiculars to them a whole series of "directing lines" can
sometimes be developed. This system has been extensively used by Le Corbusier
(Fig. 110).

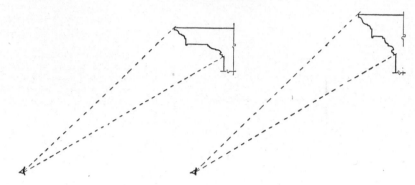

FIGURE 113. PROJECTING EAVES CORNICES AS AFFECTED BY HEIGHT

The thin, much projecting cornice at the left has the same visual impact as the deeper, less projecting cornice at the right. The designers of the early United States made great use of this fact.

More recently, Le Corbusier has advocated a system that uses elements derived by means of the Golden Section from three basic human dimensions—the height to the solar plexus, the height to the top of the head, and the height to the top of the extended fingers of the raised arms. The average height of a man is taken as six feet. It is found that the solar plexus divides in half the total height of the figure with upraised arms; that the distance between the ground and the solar plexus and the distance between the solar plexus and the top of the head are in Golden Section ratio; and that the distance from the head top to the fingers of the upraised arms and the distance from the solar plexus to the head top are similarly in extreme and mean ratio.

From these dimensions two series of related lengths are derived by successive Golden Section progressions; then the two are combined. On the basis of the lengths thus determined, networks are developed to form progressive rectangles of varying lengths and widths, all of which are related through the Golden Section; these rectangles, having been generated by a single system, can be related in all kinds of ways. The dimensions obtained can then be placed on a scale or rule and used for the rapid determination of lines on a drawing; this scale Le Corbusier calls the modulor.[3]

In contemporary architecture so much is fluid, and shapes are so entirely the results of the architect's choice, that the problem of proportion is of basic importance. Some such system of directing lines is often of considerable assistance in achieving harmonious proportion and pleasant spacings.

[3] See Matila Ghyka, "Le Corbusier's Modulor and the Concept of the Golden Mean," in *Architectural Review*, February, 1948. See also Le Corbusier, *New World of Space* (New York: Reynal & Hitchcock, 1948).

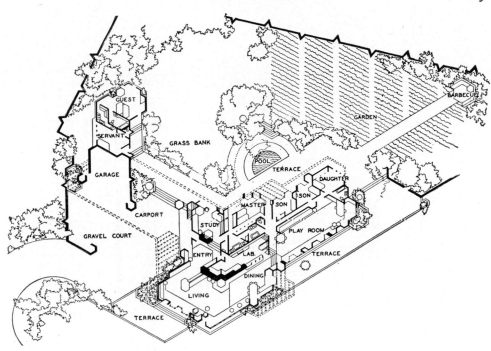

FIGURE 114. HANNA HOUSE, PALO ALTO, CALIFORNIA. PLAN

Frank Lloyd Wright, architect

A house designed on the basis of a hexagonal module in plan. This module controls the placing of all major elements and is expressed in the pavement patterns throughout.

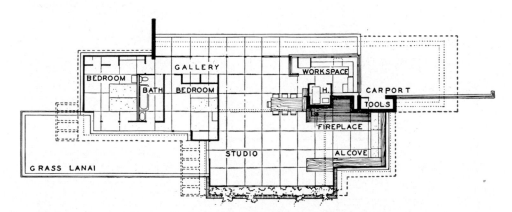

FIGURE 115. WINKLER-GOETSCH HOUSE, OKEMOS, MICHIGAN. PLAN

Frank Lloyd Wright, architect

A house planned on a square module; the module expressed in the pavement pattern.

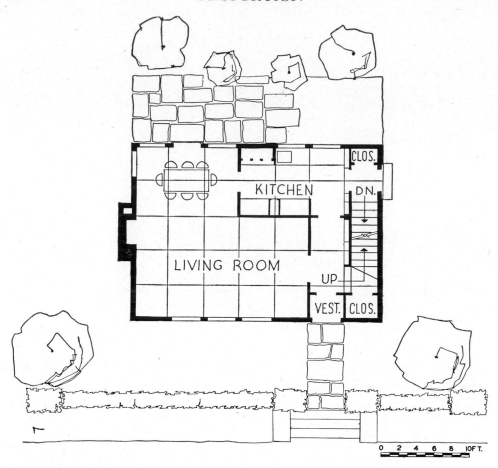

FIGURE 116. A MODULAR HOUSE DESIGN. FIRST-FLOOR PLAN

Harrie T. Lindeberg, architect

The module is 4'-0" square.   Redrawn from Lindeberg, *Domestic Architecture*

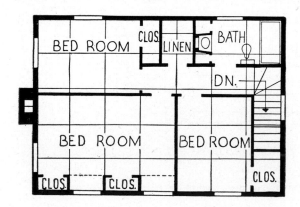

FIGURE 117. A MODULAR HOUSE DESIGN. SECOND-FLOOR PLAN

Harrie T. Lindeberg, architect

Redrawn from Lindeberg,
Domestic Architecture

FIGURE 118. A MODULAR HOUSE DESIGN. ELEVATION

Harrie T. Lindeberg, architect

Redrawn frcm Lindeberg, *Domestic Architecture*

The same may be true of the modular system; although there may be no inherent magic in the unitary ratios between the heights and widths of single elements, the use of the modular system, because it will produce many repetitions of the same dimension or of simple multiples of it, will often aid in establishing harmonious proportional relationships, just as the directing-line system does. Frank Lloyd Wright's use of an equilateral-triangle module in his so-called honeycomb houses is a characteristic example (Fig. 114), and Harrie T. Lindeberg's modular houses also show the frequently pleasant effects of this system (Figs. 116–118). It is possible that the growing use of prefabrication, sensitively handled by a true creative artist, will produce houses of harmonious proportion because of the application of such repeated dimensions.

These questions of simple geometrical ratios and proportions, of course, are only a part of the larger problem of architectural proportion. Structural elements inevitably create certain relationships, and it is the architect's task to see that they are beautifully combined. For instance, in the days of masonry and wood construction the width between supports was automatically regulated by the available length of beams strong enough to bear whatever they carried. That width was independent of the height of the supports. The architects of

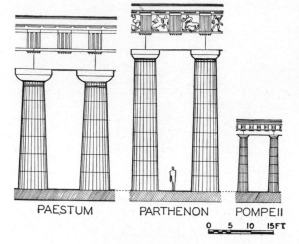

PAESTUM   PARTHENON   POMPEII

0   5   10   15FT

FIGURE 119. THREE DORIC OR-
DERS OF DIFFERENT SIZES

Proportion as affected by size. The lintel lengths control the spacing of columns; the larger the size of the order,
the more closely spaced are the columns in relation to their height.

Redrawn from Guadet,
Éléments et théorie . . .

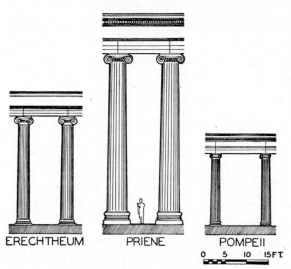

ERECHTHEUM   PRIENE   POMPEII

0   5   10   15FT

FIGURE 120. THREE DIFFERING
IONIC ORDERS

Proportion as affected by size. Lintel
lengths being limited, the intercolumniations of the smaller orders are, in
terms of column height, relatively
greater.

Redrawn from Guadet,
Éléments et théorie . . .

the classic styles realized this and, despite all the classic insistence on regular
proportions, tended to keep the distances between columns more or less the
same, whatever the height of the column might be. Thus, high colonnades have
the columns relatively close together; low colonnades or porches have them
relatively wide apart. Instinctively, on seeing such a porch or colonnade at a
distance, one is able to make quick conclusions as to its actual size (Figs. 119–
121). Even in the twentieth century the same is true in much simple building.

If one is using steel or reinforced concrete for beams, it becomes possible to
obtain spans visually much wider than those permitted by the older types of

FIGURE 121. PROPOR-
TION AND IMPLIED SIZES
One realizes instinctively
that the dimensions of the
columns in the foreground
are actually much smaller
than those in the background
because of their relatively
greater spacing.

FIGURE 122. MAISON CARRÉE, NÎMES, FRANCE
Masonry construction gives rise to high, narrow proportions.   Courtesy Ware Library

construction. At once an entirely new system of proportions is established. In
large buildings of the older, masonry type, the proportions tend to be high
and narrow (Fig. 123) because of the structural requirements, as, for example,
in the typical classic portico. The more modern steel-frame structures, on the

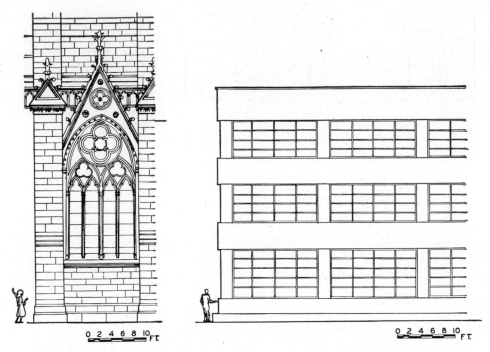

FIGURE 123 (LEFT). NOTRE DAME CATHEDRAL, PARIS. ONE BAY OF THE SIDE ELE-
VATION

Proportions based on materials (stone) and constructional system (Gothic vaulting). Bays are
naturally tall and relatively narrow.

FIGURE 124 (RIGHT). CORNER OF A TWENTIETH-CENTURY LOFT BUILDING

Proportions based on steel and concrete and on modern skeleton construction. Bays are naturally
low and relatively wide.

other hand, tend toward wide shapes (Figs. 124, 125), as in Sullivan's Carson-
Pirie-Scott department store in Chicago (Fig. 126).

Thus, there are tremendous differences in basic proportion which are due
to the use of different structural systems and different structural materials.
Such structural demands necessarily supersede any imposed mathematical systems of proportion. Yet the architect's duty to achieve what is called good proportion is as strong in the one case as in the other. Harmony of proportion,
at least, can be sought and obtained.

Many height-width-length relationships are dependent neither on arbitrary
choice nor on structural requirements but solely on the functional use of the
building or some portion of it. Room sizes vary according to use. Some uses
require long, narrow rooms; some uses require rooms nearly square; some uses

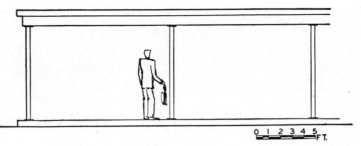

FIGURE 125. A COVERED WAY

The relatively low and wide proportions derive from the small size and from the materials and structure (Lally columns supporting a concrete roof).

FIGURE 126. CARSON-PIRIE-SCOTT DEPARTMENT STORE, CHICAGO, ILLINOIS. VIEW OF THE FLANK WALL

Louis H. Sullivan, architect

Low, broad proportions determined by the structural system and treated with delicate, sensitive imagination.

Photograph Sigfried Giedion

require height, others do not. The proportion of window openings will vary enormously, depending on the use to which a building is to be put as well as on the climate and the orientation. Here again, conditioning the sizes and shapes of building elements, there are a large number of forces which must of necessity supersede *a priori* aesthetic systems. Yet the proportions of interior spaces are architecturally and visually important. To be truly a work of architecture it is not enough for a building to achieve merely that which may be dictated by structure or function; it is also necessary that it have, in the whole and all its parts, that quality of design which we call beauty. Much of this aesthetic quality arises from proportion, and it is the architect's responsibility to achieve this under all circumstances. Again the problem of harmony in proportion becomes

FIGURE 127. PIETRO MASSIMI PALACE,
ROME. EXTERIOR

Baldassare Peruzzi, architect

Perfect proportional harmony, both in general
forms and in detail.

Courtesy Ware Library

FIGURE 128. PIETRO MASSIMI PALACE, ROME. COURT

Baldassare Peruzzi, architect

The same beauty of proportion seen on the façade characterizes the courtyard colonnades.

Courtesy Ware Library

FIGURE 129. PANDOLFINI PAL-
ACE, FLORENCE, ITALY

Raphael, architect

Precise relationship of piers and
windows establishes strong proportional harmony.

Courtesy Ware Library

FIGURE 130. CH'ING CHÊNG SHRINE, TEMPLE OF AGRICULTURE, PEIPING, CHINA
Chinese classic proportions based on subtle relations of equal and unequal dimensions.

From Imperial Museum, Tokyo, *Photographs of Palace Buildings of Peking*

FIGURE 131. PUBLIC LIBRARY, BOSTON, MASSACHUSETTS
McKim, Mead & White, architects
Long accepted as one of the most beautifully proportioned buildings in the United States.

Courtesy Avery Library

FIGURE 132. POST OF-
FICE, NAPLES, ITALY

Vaccaro & Franzi, archi-
tects

Harmonious and expres-
sive proportions in a
twentieth-century public
building.

Photograph
Leopold Arnaud

FIGURE 133. WINKLER-GOETSCH HOUSE, OKEMOS, MICHIGAN. EXTERIOR
Frank Lloyd Wright, architect
Modular proportion establishes visual harmony.   Photograph Leavenworth's

essential; in a good building all the rooms and spaces will be not only well
designed for their purpose and adequate in construction but also pleasing in
proportion and harmonious with one another.

Good proportion, therefore, is a matter of infinite complexity, but the need
for it is primary. The sources for proportion, as we have said, are shape, struc-

FIGURE 134. WINKLER–GOETSCH HOUSE, OKEMOS, MICHIGAN. INTERIOR
Frank Lloyd Wright, architect
Modular design helps harmony between exterior, interior, and plan.   Photograph Leavenworth's

ture, use, and harmony. To achieve good proportion from this complex basis requires not only the ability to discriminate between the more important and the less important considerations—not only a creative taste—but also a tremendous amount of study and a long series of experimental solutions, until, by means of constant adjustments here and there, a well-proportioned and harmonious solution finally emerges.

So far we have been discussing chiefly the proportions of the sizes and shapes of individual units. In architecture there is another great class of proportion relationships of major importance. This includes the size relationships of the various parts of a building to the entire composition. As has been suggested earlier, functional requirements will dictate in great measure the sizes and heights of individual rooms. One of the most important processes in architectural planning lies in making the correct choices in this field, and the efficiency and economy of a building will often depend largely on the correct adjustment of the relative sizes of the parts which compose it.

FIGURE 135. GERMAN BUILDING, BARCELONA EXPOSITION OF 1929. DETAIL
Ludwig Mies van der Rohe, architect
Simple and exquisite proportions distinguish this pavilion.   Courtesy Museum of Modern Art

Yet such an adjustment of size in accordance with functional requirements is by no means the entire story; there is, in addition, the problem of relative importance. Great buildings stress the most important elements so that they count from outside as well as within; these elements dominate the building, and their importance often is a matter of symbolic or expressive significance and not merely a question of the functionally necessary size. This is true of almost all large rotundas and vestibules and of many important circulation elements. It clearly may also be true of chapels and auditoriums and generally of the more public, as opposed to the more private, portions of a building. The good plan frequently develops a carefully composed hierarchy of sizes, varying from those of the most important and public elements—which are stressed in size, in position, and in design—down to those of the most humble and routine of service facilities. The good design will always indicate the relative position of any unit in the total scale of importance, and it will do this largely through the varying proportions of the unit sizes and their integrated relation to one another. It is that kind of proportion which Guadet had in mind when he said that one of the chief tasks of the architect was to discover the proportions which are naturally inherent in any architectural program.[4] He goes on to say: "There

[4] Julien Guadet, *Éléments et théorie de l'architecture* (Paris: Aulanier et cie., n.d.), Vol. I, Book II, Chap. 4.

is always some element which dominates, the dimensions of which must surpass the dimensions of all others, but in what approximate measure? Then there may be an element which seems to be of medium dimension, then another smaller than all the rest. Between these types there are nuances. If you have grasped firmly this scale of proportions, I do not say you will necessarily create a good composition—too many other things are necessary for that—but at least you will not make compositions which cannot be developed." In large and complicated buildings much of the final success must come from a careful study of proportions of this general type.

There is no royal road to good proportions; only intensive and careful study can achieve them. It is here that the cheapness and availability of tracing paper are of the greatest assistance; one must try everything over and over again. One must widen, narrow, lengthen, or shorten plan areas; one must test the effect of differences in height until the scale of the major relations of which Guadet speaks becomes finally crystal clear.

And one must study the shape and size of openings with the greatest care. Let us remember that aesthetically a building is primarily a visual object, depending for its effect on light and shade and on shape and color; only incidentally is it an expression of any doctrinaire theory. Thus, if we have glass areas in an exterior wall, the reflecting and transparent qualities of the glass will be so different from the visual qualities of the surrounding opaque materials that they will count as strong visual elements, even if the wall in which they are placed is a simple screen—carrying no weight—and not a bearing wall. It is true, of course, that such a screen may be of either opaque or transparent material, and great freedom in design will result from this fact. But, when the building is seen in the daytime and the sky is reflected in the glass or the darkness of the interiors shows through, the visual fact of the marked differences between the glass and the material around it becomes a dominant quality and will inevitably create problems in proportional design.

From the time of Serlio down to the early nineteenth century many architectural elevations showed all openings as completely black, and little or no attempt was made to indicate window-pane divisions or details of sash arrangement. In other words, the architects were making sure that the basic proportions of the openings were correct. No method brings out basic compositional values more clearly than this method of blacking in the openings; it is perhaps the surest method of studying elevation design for proportional value, and it is as useful today as it was four hundred years ago.

Another valuable and easy method of studying the heights of openings is to draw the head and the upper part of the jambs of an opening on a separate sheet of tracing paper and move it up and down until the most satisfactory position is achieved; the widths of the openings can be studied in much the same way. The sizes of chimney breasts and fireplace openings, the positions of mantel shelves, and the relations of built-in furniture and of openings in interiors must be studied with similar care before a completely integrated design can be achieved. Do not depend alone on small details to establish proportional relationships. The major elements must be considered first; generally the minor elements will then tend to take care of themselves.

In all this study we may well bear in mind the definition of good taste in architecture which Boffrand enunciated nearly two hundred years ago: Good taste is founded on convenience, appropriateness, structural strength, the requirements of health, and common sense. And we should also ponder the words of Viollet-le-Duc, who in his *Dictionnaire raisonné de l'architecture française* defines proportion as follows: "By proportion one means the relations existing between the whole and its parts—relations which are logical, necessary, and of such a character that at the same time they satisfy the reason and the eye."

SUGGESTED ADDITIONAL READING FOR CHAPTER 4

Blondel, François, *Cours d'architecture enseigné dans l'Académie royale d'Architecture*, 3 vols. (Paris: Vol. I, Lambert Roulland; Vols. II and III, Chez l'auteur et Nicolas Langlois, 1675–83).
Boffrand, Germain, *Livre d'architecture* . . . (Paris: Cavelier père, 1745).
Briseux, Charles Étienne, *Traité du beau essentiel dans les arts* . . . (Paris: Chez l'auteur et Chereau, 1752).
Butler, Arthur Stanley George, *The Substance of Architecture*, with a foreword by Sir Edwin Lutyens (New York: MacVeagh, 1927).
Cook, Sir Theodore Andrea, *The Curves of Life* . . . (New York: Henry Holt, 1914).
Frankl, Paul, "Secret of the Mediaeval Masons," *Art Bulletin*, Vol. XXVII (March, 1945), pp. 46–60.
Gardner, Robert Waterman, *The Parthenon, Its Science of Forms* (New York: New York University Press, 1925).
—— *A Primer of Proportion* . . . (New York: Helburn, 1945).
Ghyka, Matila, *The Geometry of Art and Life* (New York: Sheed & Ward, 1946).
Guadet, Julien, *Éléments et théorie de l'architecture*, 4 vols. (Paris: Aulanier, n.d.).
Hambidge, Jay, *Dynamic Symmetry: the Greek Vase* (New Haven: Yale University Press, 1920).

—— *The Elements of Dynamic Symmetry* (New York: Brentano's [c1926]).

—— *The Parthenon and Other Greek Temples; Their Dynamic Symmetry* (New Haven: Yale University Press, 1924).

Le Corbusier (Charles Édouard Jeanneret), *New World of Space* (New York: Reynal & Hitchcock, 1948).

—— *Vers une Architecture* (Paris: Crès, 1923); English ed., *Towards a New Architecture*, translated by Frederick Etchells (New York: Payson & Clarke [1927]).

Lund, Fredrik Macody, *Ad Quadratum; a Study of the Geometrical Bases of Classic & Medieval Religious Architecture* . . . (London: Batsford, 1921).

Perrault, Claude, *A Treatise of the Five Orders of Columns in Architecture* . . . made English by John James (London: printed by B. Motte, sold by J. Sturt, 1708); first published as *Ordonnance des cinq espèces de colonnes* (Paris: Chez Jean Baptiste Coignard, 1683).

Texier, Marcel André, *Géometrie de l'architecte* . . . (Paris: Vincent, Fréal, 1934).

Thiersch, August, "Proportionen in der Architektur," *Handbuch der Architektur*, Part IV, Vol. I (Leipzig: Gebhardt's, 1926).

Viollet-le-Duc, Eugène Emmanuel, *Dictionnaire raisonné de l'architecture française du XIᵉ au XVIᵉ siècle* . . . 10 vols. (Paris: Bance and Morel, 1854–68), article "Proportion."

Vitruvius Pollio, Marcus, *De Architectura*, the ten books on architecture translated by Morris Hicky Morgan . . . (Cambridge, Mass.: Harvard University Press, 1914).

5
Scale

THERE IS ANOTHER architectural quality closely related to proportion—the quality of scale. Scale in architecture is that quality which makes a building appear its correct, or any desired, size. This is a characteristic which seems instinctively to be demanded of buildings; all of us like to feel the great size or grandeur of large and important buildings or the intimate and personal quality of a small house. Delight in the size of things seems to be a widely felt quality of normal human thinking and to have been awakened at a fairly early stage in mankind's development; consequently we feel instinctively frustrated and distressed at buildings which appear markedly different in size from what they actually prove to be. The little house which, with spindly two-story posts over a four-foot-wide porch, aims to imitate the grandeur of a large southern mansion is an offense which hurts anyone with a sensitive taste. Similarly, the large building which belittles itself by using forms satisfactory only for a tiny structure produces an unpleasant sense of the puny, the toylike, even the unreal. False scale is always an offense against good manners in architecture, as well as a sign of a somewhat perverse exhibitionism. It is as unpleasant as the striving of an individual to seem richer, greater, or more important than he is, or of a "great man" to feed his own vanity by an artificial and play-acting modesty, and it is offensive for the same reason.

It follows, therefore, that a good building will have good scale. Good scale does not happen of itself. It is something to be consciously sought, and the consideration of scale must occupy the architect's mind almost continuously during the process of design. How, then, may scale be produced? We cannot produce it through the mere geometric form of the structure as a whole. Geometric forms in themselves have no scale. A pyramid can be anything from a paper weight to the Great Pyramid of Cheops (Fig. 136); it may be equally satisfactory in either case. A sphere may be a microscopic one-celled animal, a tennis ball, the perisphere of the New York World's Fair of 1939, or the sun itself. Obelisks have varied in common usage from the great stones the Egyptians

FIGURE 136. GREAT PYRAMIDS, GIZEH, EGYPT

Scale does not exist in the forms themselves; the sense of size is given only by their relationship to other elements. Courtesy Ware Library

loved, which were over one hundred feet high, or the 550-foot Washington Monument, on the one hand, to the little obelisks, three or four feet high, which decorate the balustrades of Colonial church towers or the steps of a Baroque garden, on the other. The parallelepiped, which is the ordinary major enclosing shape of buildings or of their larger elements, tells us nothing of its size; the same is true of the cylinder or the hemisphere.

Yet scale must be given to buildings. The first principle in achieving this important quality is that scale is produced by introducing into the design some unit which acts as a visual measuring rod and the size of which the human being appreciates easily, naturally, and instinctively. If such a unit is seen to be small in relation to the building as a whole, the building will appear large; if it is large in proportion to the rest of the building, the total will appear small. Moreover, if there are many such units in a building, the idea of the multiplicity of this easily judged unit will create a sense of great size; conversely, if there are but few, the natural tendency will be for one to consider the building small. Thus from that principle we may deduce a corollary: Generally speaking, a building with many motifs and subdivisions will tend to appear larger than one in which the subdivisions are few. This corollary, however, has many excep-

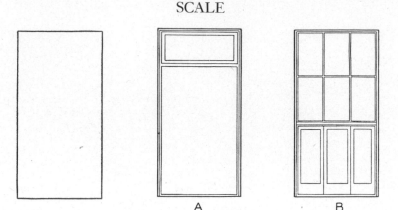

FIGURE 137 (LEFT). GEOMETRICAL SHAPES HAVE NO SCALE IN THEMSELVES
This rectangle might equally well represent a large doorway or a small one.

FIGURE 138 (RIGHT). SCALE BY THE ADDITION OF FUNCTIONAL ELEMENTS
A transom is added to the rectangle of Figure 137. In A, the transom being narrow and simple, the whole opening is presumed to be small. In B, where the transom is tall and subdivided, the opening is seen to be a large one.

tions, as we shall see; in any case, its validity depends on the fact that somewhere in the multiplicity or complexity of units there are elements which "the human being appreciates easily, naturally, and instinctively."

Such a well-understood unit, the size of which can be easily and naturally appreciated, leads us to the second great principle of scale: The elements in a building which have the closest and most direct touch with the activities and bodily functions of a human being are the most powerful elements in giving scale to that building. Among these are steps. No one can walk up stairs if the steps are wider or higher than a certain dimension or if, on the other hand, they are far below the size to which he is accustomed. Similarly, railings which are designed to keep one from falling must be of a certain height, or they will seem absurd. The child reaches for the moon, but before many years he will learn what is in reach of his arms. Such things as shelf heights of a natural dimension relate to our human potentialities, and the same is true of seats or benches or anything that seems to have the form of a seat or a bench. Long experience has taught us that anything lower, say, than 14 inches and anything higher than 18 or 19 inches is uncomfortable or actually impossible as a seat. Hence, when we see a form of bench type, we instinctively judge it to be of a suitable size in relation to our own bodies.

Thus we ourselves become the true measuring scales for buildings, and the sense of size can eventually be analyzed into some expression of human actions

FIGURE 139. SENSE OF SCALE ASSISTED BY ADDITIONAL SCALE-GIVING ELEMENTS

The railing, the steps, and the bench all help the observer to realize the small size and intimate character of the doorway.

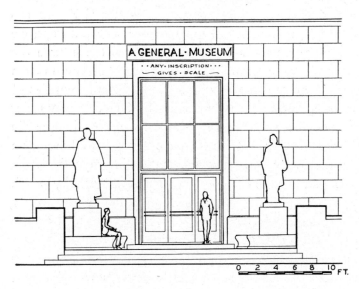

FIGURE 140. SENSE OF SCALE ASSISTED BY ADDITIONAL SCALE-GIVING ELEMENTS

In this case steps, benches, terrace wall, sculpture, stone courses, and inscriptions all help to make the opening appear large and important.

or of human body sizes. If there are steps in a building, we at once accept their size as relative to us. If there are railings or parapets, we instinctively attribute to them a height sufficient to prevent our falling but not so great as to prevent us looking over them. If there are benches, we assume that they are about the size of benches that we know and use. Then, by a sort of automatic comparison of the size of these units and that of the entire structure, the size of the whole in relation to human beings becomes at once apparent. The good architect will contrive to furnish ways in which this comparison can be readily made; he will build up from it, working from the small to the large, in such a way that the size of a building becomes evident almost at first glance. Let us take, for example, a simple problem. Imagine a rectangular opening which is to serve as a doorway in a building of a specific height relative to the opening (Fig. 137). In the figure shown there is absolutely nothing to indicate the size of the opening, except the very vague sense that the opening must be big enough for a person or persons to pass through. On the face of it, this diagram might equally well indicate either the great monumental entrance to a courthouse or the tiny back door of a cottage. It is a simple geometric form and accordingly has no scale. Suppose we add a transom. In Figure 138, A shows the transom high in the opening; B shows it at a lower level. At once we are beginning to have a sense of the actual size of the entrance. We realize that B is a much larger door than A because we know that human beings have to pass freely beneath that transom. Figure 139 illustrates this principle carried still further, showing developments to make apparent the smallness of the opening, and Figure 140 shows the door so designed as to increase the apparent size. We add steps; we add a porch or terrace railing; we add a bench or benches at the sides of the door; we add pedestals. In the larger example, we may add sculpture; in both we may add inscriptions. The extraordinary difference in the apparent size of the two examples thus treated becomes clear immediately. One doorway is developed into a monumental element, suitable perhaps for a courthouse or a civic hall; the other has become the intimate entrance to a private house or a private office. Yet both started out with rectangles identical in proportions.

These human-scale elements do not at all complete the list of means by which an architect can give scale to a building. There are, in addition, a great many dimensions of structural units to which we have become accustomed by the universality of their use. Almost anyone will realize instinctively the size of a brick and the general size of a brick course, and even simple brick buildings will thus have a truth of scale which is lacking in buildings covered with a plain unbroken surface like stucco. It is the same with shingles, clapboards, and sidings. In each case we have become used to certain limits of size, and much of the beautiful scale we associate with old country houses of the Colonial and Classic Revival periods derives from this source. In addition, if the observer has frequented cities or noted many buildings faced with cut stone, he will develop a similar sense of size with respect to stone courses and, feeling the number of stone courses in the height of an opening or the height of a wall, he will at once gain a sense of the building's scale.

FIGURE 141. CATHEDRAL, FLORENCE, ITALY. SECTION

The extraordinary width of the nave bays—62 feet—makes it almost impossible for the observer to grasp the colossal size of this interior; similarly, the simplicity of the vertical composition tends to belittle the actual height.

In a similar way, we have become accustomed to the usual size of the larger structural elements. In modern American cities the normal spacing of steel columns in stores and office buildings—at intervals usually of 16 to 20 feet—has built up in most of us a sense of scale quite different from that possessed by people a hundred years ago (see Fig. 528). We instinctively grasp the size of an office building from the repetition of this bay spacing, whereas individuals of an older culture would find it merely confusing.

The same is true of the general bay spacing of Gothic cathedrals, which averages somewhere in the neighborhood of 20 feet from center to center (Fig. 508). So strongly engraved upon our minds has this sense of Gothic scale become that marked deviations from the usual bay spacing at once produce the most puzzling effects of scale. Many Gothic Revival churches in all countries give a puny and toylike impression because the bay spacing is sometimes not over half the normal spacing. On the other hand, a vast increase in distances from pier to pier in a Gothic church, instead of making the interior look larger, has quite the reverse effect. It is almost impossible, for example, to appreciate the enormous size of the Cathedral at Florence; even after one has walked its entire length, it still appears as a structure of only moderate dimensions because of the excessive width of its bays (Figs. 141, 142).

FIGURE 142. CATHEDRAL, FLORENCE, ITALY. INTERIOR
The wide spacing of the piers prevents any conception of the great scale.

Courtesy Ware Library

FIGURE 143. ST. PETER'S, ROME. INTERIOR OF THE NAVE
Bramante and Michelangelo, architects
The oversized detail hinders realization of the true size.   Courtesy Ware Library

One other element in architectural scale deserves to be mentioned—the use of contrast. When two objects of similar shape or type, one large and one small, are close together, the contrast between them enhances the apparent size of the larger. Thus in buildings, if a succession of small similar motifs is suddenly interrupted by a similar motif of larger size, the effect of great scale in the whole will be increased. In the interior of St. Peter's, for instance (Fig. 143), the scale of the great arches at the crossing is vastly increased by the succession of small arches in the side aisles and the niches. One secret of the satisfactory scale of many classic buildings lies in the fact that similar motifs of different sizes have been used in the same composition. In somewhat the same way, the existence of the transept in Gothic churches adds greatly to the sense of the size of the interior because of the contrast between the succession of the smaller nave bays, with their pier arches, and the much higher and wider arch of the transept vault. In order to use successfully this method of obtaining scale, it is necessary that the smaller units have in themselves a scale that is readily grasped; this may be accomplished by any of the means suggested earlier. The great difficulty in appreciating the scale of St. Peter's is caused by the fact that the pier arches and the other smaller arched units are themselves so large that it is only after repeated visits that one comes to realize their architectural grandeur.

As we have stated above, another fact that contributes to the apparent size of buildings is concerned with the number of units composing them. In general, a building with many units will appear larger than one in which there are but few. Thus, in the Colosseum, the sense of immense size comes largely from the parade of arches repeated indefinitely, it would seem, around its vast circuit, as well as from the repetition of the tiers of arches, one over the other. A simple and unbroken cylindrical wall of the same size would have conveyed no such sense of magnitude. This relationship of the number of units to the scale of buildings, however, is subject to many qualifications and numerous exceptions. An unbroken wall pierced by one large entrance of great scale may have a power which the wall with too many members lacks. But, in order to achieve such an impression, the careful scale treatment of the single penetration is of the utmost importance. Buildings of many units may fall into mere confusion, and confusion has no scale. Looking at such structures, one sees only the individual units and cannot grasp their relation to the whole; such a building will appear ineffective. It is only when the multiplicity of units is bound together by the strongest possible integral relationship to the totality of the design, therefore, that the sense of size is created through the use of many units. As we have seen, a building to be a work of art must be a unified experience; similarly, it must be a unified structure to have adequate scale.

Since architecture is concerned alike with the inside and outside of a building, interior scale is quite as important as that of the façade. The building must have scale in plan as well as in its other aspects. Scale in plan means that the supports, the walls, the doors, and all the other internal elements—the position of which is determined by the plan—must be so related and so designed that the observer will gain from them an intuitive sense of the size of each part, their distances, one from the other, and the size of the whole. Just as in exterior design, this sense of size will be produced largely by the use of elements which have close relationships to the human body and its activities—such as chairs, benches, doors, tables, and the like—and also by the use of "measuring rod" details or elements close to the eye or familiar to the general user of the building.

The sense of size imparted by identical objects when seen outdoors and indoors is quite different, and the scale problem varies accordingly. Objects outside always look relatively smaller than they do inside; a doorway 4 feet wide and 8 feet high, for instance, might seem almost monumental in many interiors, but the same door as the chief entrance to a monumental building would look absurdly small. This principle holds true for almost every conceivable element. Exterior steps which provide the same rise and tread as those which seem comfortable and pleasant in interior stairs appear cramped and tight and uncomfortable. Moldings and projections which are delicate and refined on exteriors look coarse and even gigantic inside. Similarly, in classic buildings a 15-foot interior column might be dignified and impressive, whereas a column of the same height used on the exterior would be puny and weak.

This is especially true of sculpture, which, as we have noted, is one of the great means by which buildings of the past have achieved scale. A life-size figure outdoors always looks dwarfed and smaller than it is in reality; for that reason exterior figures are almost always made somewhat larger than life size. One of the difficulties with museum presentations of sculpture lies precisely in this fact, for figures designed with exterior scale are usually shown inside buildings and little attempt is made to separate outdoor from indoor sculpture. This is one of the problems which arise in modern buildings where sculpture is used; it also discloses one of the reasons for the need of the closest co-operation between sculptor and architect, for both must understand the scale desired and the sculptor must work intelligently with this end in view.

The problem of scale in architecture involves more than the mere achievement of some impression of size; it involves also a choice as to what size impression the designer wishes to produce. The question of actual dimensions as measurable with a tape is without importance; within limits, a designer can make his structure appear either larger or smaller by the way in which it is designed. What, then, is the desirable sense of size he should seek to convey?

FIGURE 144. ARC DE L'ÉTOILE, PARIS. ELEVATION

François Chalgrin, architect

Heroic scale achieved through simplicity of form and large dimensions but more especially through careful adjustments of the parts to the whole. Each detail makes the whole seem larger; each smaller part furnishes a measuring rod for the greater elements and the whole. A bench around the base and the base molds immediately above it give a natural sense of size because easily seen and grasped by the mind. The relation of these to the sculpture pedestals follows—then to the colossal sculpture—then to the arch pier—then to the arch—and so on. The ornament in the attic is made large in order to count from a long distance; when one is close to the arch the attic is invisible or forgotten.

The answer is inherent in the program of each individual building and is to be approached only by an imaginative consideration of the building's function.

Generally speaking, three types of scale impressions can be differentiated—natural, heroic, and intimate scale. The first of these, natural scale, is the attempt to make a building express its actual dimensions, to make the observer measure his own normal being and personality against it. Natural scale is obviously to be sought in the ordinary workaday structures of the world—that is, in the usual houses, commercial buildings, factories, shops, and so on. The second, what is known as heroic scale, is the attempt to make a building appear as large as possible and to do it in such a way that, instead of making the individual feel small by contrast, it will make him feel enlarged, liberated, somehow part of a unit bigger, stronger, and more powerful than himself.

Heroic scale is not a falsification of scale, because the longing of people for some sort of superpersonal enlargement is a common and a valid emotion (Fig. 145). The great buildings of heroic scale are the expressions of man's longing to transcend himself, to rise above the limitations of time itself. As an expression of this essentially religious and contemplative point of view, heroic scale is appropriate in great churches, in monuments, and in much official and governmental architecture; here the effort is not to build for the individual or merely for a fleeting moment of time but to build for a social group united in a com-

FIGURE 145. ARC DE L'ÉTOILE, PARIS. GENERAL VIEW
François Chalgrin, architect
Heroic scale achieved by careful handling of detail.   Courtesy Avery Library

mon end and in a way that expresses the continuity of humanity. When people build a city hall, they are building not just a place where people work; they are also building an expression of their united purpose. They are seeking to make clear to the passer-by not only individual pride in accomplishment but, still more, a true civic pride. Any valid expression of that purpose necessarily as-

FIGURE 146. ARC DE L'ÉTOILE, PARIS. DE-TAIL SHOWING THE SCULPTURE BY RUDE

The bench, moldings, and treatment of the sculpture all assist in building up a sense of colossal scale.

Courtesy School
of Architecture,
Columbia University

sumes an appropriate scale, and this is what we call heroic scale. (See Figs. 144–146, 148, 149.)

Frequently heroic scale is based on a certain large size in units, a size larger than that to which people are generally accustomed; but large-sized units will not, alone, create heroic scale. One cannot, for instance, take a design of satisfactory scale for a given set of dimensions, enlarge it fifty per cent in every detail, and expect to have the result a building of good heroic scale. The result in that case is likely to be quite the reverse. The building will look smaller than it actually is; furthermore, whatever sense of size it has will be achieved only by making the observer feel small. (See Fig. 151.)

Thus Baroque designers frequently attempted to get heroic scale by an unnatural enlargement of many motifs. The front of the Basilica of St. John Lateran in Rome, designed by Alessandro Galilei in 1734, is an example in which a type of design in many ways fitted for a small building is enlarged to colossal scale (Fig. 150). The effect is almost terrifying; not only is it impossible to gain a true sense of the great size of the whole, but in addition one has the unpleasant feeling that somehow individuals are contemptible and dwarflike. This kind of Brobdingnagian detail in architecture has the same quality of

FIGURE 147. CAVE TEMPLE, ABU-SIMBEL, EGYPT

A sense of great size created by the use of sculpture varying in size and closely related, with the smallest elements closest to the eye.   Courtesy Ware Library

nightmare repulsion which Gulliver felt at what seemed to him the horrible size of the natural imperfections of the human skin in that land of giants. The balustrades at the summit of St. John Lateran, instead of being the normal maximum 4 feet or 4 feet 6 inches high, are 7 or 8 feet; the colossal figures silhouetted against the sky are over 25 feet tall. It is possible that the architect did this consciously with the idea of producing some kind of dramatic surprise when one finally discovered the true size. Similarly, in the front of St. Peter's, by Carlo Maderna, there is the same fault—niches, panels, moldings, and statues all gigantic. The discrepancy in scale becomes obvious when one sees a bell, apparently about the size of a locomotive bell, hanging high up on the front, start to swing and hears its tone as deep-pitched and sonorous as that of Big Ben in London. In Aix the colossal garland of leaves and fruit decorating the entire width of the front of the Mint has somewhat the same effect.

Baroque designers, we know, were sometimes fond of playing practical jokes, as in the garden fountains which sprayed unsuspecting visitors when they stepped on certain stones in the pavement. Perhaps their enormously overscaled church façades are merely different expressions of a similar intent to

FIGURE 148. PALAIS DE JUSTICE, BRUSSELS

J. Poelaert, architect

Great scale achieved by multiplicity of closely related parts.

From Poelaert, *Le nouveau Palais de Justice de Bruxelles*

FIGURE 149. PALAIS DE JUSTICE, BRUS-
SELS. DETAIL OF ENTRANCE

J. Poelaert, architect

Note how small elements are placed against
larger ones to increase the sense of size.

From Poelaert, *Le nouveau Palais de
Justice de Bruxelles*

FIGURE 150. ST. JOHN LATERAN, ROME. FAÇADE

Alessandro Galilei, architect

False scale, perhaps consciously sought for its shock value, is the inevitable result of oversizing almost every element in this composition. Especially misleading are the sculpture and the upper balustrade.

surprise and astound; yet to us such humor seems essentially out of place, and the total effect is depressing and unpleasant. The south front of the Grand Central Station in New York has almost the same faults (Fig. 152). Its composition is one that might be suitable for a medium-sized structure. Its detail is dainty and almost frivolous; enlarged to colossal size, it seems absurd and the whole front but a fraction of its actual dimensions.

It is equally fatal to reduce the scale of architectural elements and hope to retain any of the grandeur of the original scale; here the only result is confusion and frustration. This is well illustrated in St. James's Cathedral in Montreal, which has an interior that is a half-scale model of St. Peter's at Rome. Its dimensions are large, even monumental, but the effect upon the observer is anything but a feeling of great size. The total result is an interior which, despite its large dimensions, appears puny, ineffective, even funny.

FIGURE 151. VÖLKERSCHLACHTDENKMAL, LEIPZIG, GERMANY

Bruno Schmitz, architect

Complete absence of scale resulting from the deceptive oversizing of all elements; the whole appears but a fraction of its colossal size. From Schliepmann, *Bruno Schmitz*

FIGURE 152. GRAND CENTRAL STATION, NEW YORK. VIEW FROM THE SOUTH

Reed & Stem and Warren & Wetmore, associated architects

The small number of motifs and the oversized sculpture combine to minimize the apparent size of this large structure.

Courtesy Fellheimer & Wagner, architects

FIGURE 153 (LEFT). FONTHILL ABBEY, ENGLAND. EXTERIOR

James Wyatt, architect

Intimate and heroic scale dramatically combined.

From Nichols, *Historical Notices of Fonthill Abbey*

FIGURE 154 (RIGHT). FONTHILL ABBEY, ENGLAND. INTERIOR

Great size emphasized by the stairs and total height.

From Nichols, *Historical Notices of Fonthill Abbey*

The problem of natural scale is simpler, but it still requires a careful handling of size relationships in the details and in their relation to the whole structure. Good natural scale will usually follow from the unforced solution of the functional problems involved in the design; for, if the observer feels himself carrying on his activities, whatever they may be, in the midst of elements that

FIGURE 155. ELM HAVEN HOUSING, NEW HAVEN, CONNECTICUT. TWO VIEWS

Orr & Foote, architects; Albert Mayer, consultant

Excellent domestic scale achieved by careful detail, normal size for the usual elements, and
occasional variations in height.   Photograph Richard Garrison

are of the proper size for those activities, a pleasant sense of adequacy in scale
will almost necessarily arise (Fig. 155). Thus, in a house, the doors, windows,
porches, and steps must be designed as directly in relation to their use as possible; any ostentatious attempt to make any element excessively large will
merely result in producing, at best, a bizarre effect of play-acting—an effect
which may be amusing at first sight but one which after a longer acquaintance
becomes oppressive and unreal.

Intimate scale—the desire to make buildings or rooms appear smaller than
their actual size—is seldom desirable and is difficult to achieve. There are places,
however, where it is permissible, as, for example, in a large restaurant, where

FIGURE 156. CENTER THEATRE, ROCKEFELLER CENTER, NEW YORK

Reinhard & Hofmeister; Corbett, Harrison & MacMurray; and Hood & Fouilhoux, associated architects

A search for intimate scale in a large theater by means of oversized ornament, simplicity of wall surfaces, and the use of horizontal emphasis.   Photograph Gottscho-Schleisner

the management wishes to produce a feeling of informal and personal intimacy, or in theaters, in which the desire for a large seating capacity conflicts with the wish to make the relationship of every spectator to the stage as close and personal as possible. To produce intimate scale successfully one can never simply reduce the size of elements to dimensions smaller than the usual; this will often produce directly the reverse effect. Occasionally, indeed, intimacy of scale can be gained by the use of oversize ornament combined with great simplicity of scheme, as in the Center Theatre in New York (Fig. 156). In other cases, the subdivision of large areas and large elements into smaller sections will achieve the desired result, provided that each of these units is of a size easily appreciable. In many large restaurants this scheme has been adopted successfully through the mere disposition of the furniture. And in many library reading rooms of recent date, such as that of the Brooklyn Public Library (Fig. 157), a similar division by means of bookcases or furniture has served to produce pleasant reading areas of intimate scale.

FIGURE 157. PUBLIC LIBRARY, BROOKLYN, NEW YORK. READING ROOM

Githens & Keally, architects

The scale of the large reading room is humanized by the arrangement and type of furniture and by subdivision by bookcases.   Photograph Gottscho-Schleisner

One of the designer's chief tasks is the choice of the correct scale for any individual problem. Here the natural solution of the dimension problem will usually determine the choice. A conscious and *a priori* effort to impose on any building a type of scale treatment which does not follow from the demands of the building usually achieves only ostentatious confusion. There is a necessity for good manners in architecture as there is in life, and the basis of architectural good manners lies largely in the question of whether or not a building is trying to be more important, more strident, or more impressive than its use or size justifies. The day of the ostentatious private palace, we hope, is over. Those enormous palaces, unpleasant to live in and existing only as examples of what Veblen called conspicuous expenditure, seem to us today merely vulgar. Similarly, the little bank that insults a village street with a parade of undue magnificence, the office building that pretends to the dignity of a capitol or a temple—these are essentially ill-mannered, and their bad manners are expressed in false scale. The greatest offenders of all, at least in the United States, are the meretricious movie houses which, on the streets of almost every town, scream at the observer with their monumental schemes, oversize façades, and vulgar ornaments. False heroic scale shackled to commercialism is one of the major American architectural vices.

One other principle in architectural scale must be stressed—the necessity for harmony of scale in any single structure. Once the essential scale feeling of a building has been determined, the designer must see to it that the same type of scale is carried through the entire structure. Of course numerous gradations are possible within this harmony; large and complicated buildings which require space for many different purposes will demand a similar variation in the type of size relationships. In a small bedroom or in an office we do not wish to see the large size and the bold forms appropriate to large public rooms or important and much used halls or lobbies. Each space will have its own scale, depending on its use and the emotional effect desired within it. Yet the great designer succeeds in giving even to the most complicated of buildings a scale harmony which will run through every part. Here again the resemblance between scale and proportion is extremely close. As we have seen, there is a sort of hierarchy of proportions inherent in every complicated building program. So, too, in the matter of scale there is a somewhat similar hierarchy of values. It is one of the marks of the sensitive designer to be able to achieve, within this variety, a true and unforced harmony.

Scale, we have said, is essentially a quality which relates buildings to human beings. As such, it is of the first importance; for buildings exist for people to use and to love, and the closer and simpler the relationships set up between buildings and the physical and emotional potentialities of human beings the more beautiful and the more useful the buildings will be.

SUGGESTED ADDITIONAL READING FOR CHAPTER 5

Butler, Arthur Stanley George, *The Substance of Architecture*, with a foreword by Sir Edwin Lutyens (New York: MacVeagh, 1927), p. 84.

Edwards, A. Trystan, *Style and Composition in Architecture* . . . (London: Tiranti, 1944), Chap. 5.

Greeley, William Roger, *The Essence of Architecture* (New York: Van Nostrand [c1927]), pp. 43–44.

Guadet, Julien, *Éléments et théorie de l'architecture*, 4 vols. (Paris: Aulanier, n.d.).

Nobbs, Percy Erskine, *Design; a Treatise on the Discovery of Form* (London, New York, etc.: Oxford University Press, 1937), Chap. 8.

Scammon Lectures for 1915; Six Lectures on Architecture, by Ralph Adams Cram, Thomas Hastings, and Claude Bragdon . . . (Chicago: University of Chicago Press [c1917]), the two lectures by Thomas Hastings.

6

Rhythm

RHYTHM in visual art is an attribute of any object that is marked by a systematic recurrence of elements having recognizable relationships between them. In architecture such recurrences must naturally be recurrences of visual elements produced by the building design, such as lines of light and shade, color differences, supports, openings, interior volumes, and so on. Much of the effect of a building will depend on the harmony, the simplicity, and the power of these rhythmical relationships.

Rhythm is one of the inescapable facts of life. The heartbeat, breathing, and many other physiological functions (including those of the greatest emotional power) are strongly rhythmical in nature. Sense perception in sight and hearing is based on rhythmical waves. And rhythms of many kinds run through the entire cosmos, from the whirling of the electrons in the atom, through the great orbits of the planets, to what seem to be rhythmical expansions and contractions in the entire universe. Rhythm is therefore one of the most pervasive facts in all life; *The Dance of Life*, by Havelock Ellis,[1] describes the importance of rhythm in human psychology and human experience. In art, a strong rhythmical pattern will increase the intensity of the experience, because each recurrence of a recognizable factor brings with it increasing awareness of its form and of its richness. Recognition aids understanding, and emotional understanding creates intensity.

Rhythm is one of the surest ways of giving pattern to any set of more or less incoherent experiences. A random series of spots, for example, is purely incoherent; it is difficult, if not impossible, to remember, and its only effect is one of confusion or monotony. If, however, the same number of spots is grouped in such a way that the effect of the whole is one of repetition of a recognized kind, the series at once becomes coherent; we say that it has pattern. Often the eye will group experiences instinctively into a rhythmical system; thus, in looking at the stars one will frequently tend to pick out those which

[1] Boston and New York: Houghton Mifflin Co., 1923.

FIGURE 158. RHYTHM AND REPETITION

ABOVE: Repetition of the same shape gives rhythm despite differences in spacings. BELOW: Repetition of the same spacing gives rhythm despite differences in shape.

are more or less equidistant or more or less equally brilliant. In this way a pattern will be established, and a sense of aesthetic satisfaction will arise, even though one is unconscious of the grouping that has gone on. Much of our sense of rhythmical experience never reaches consciousness as rhythm; yet the pleasantness of the experience as a whole is definitely based on this unconsciously apprehended pattern.

That is the reason for the continued persistence of such classic musical forms as the sonata and the symphony, where the repetition and expansion of musical phrases or ideas create a certain massiveness in the total effect of the work which no amorphous succession could produce. But in music there are other types of rhythm besides strict repetitions. There are the freer rhythms of tone poems or études, in which the recurrences creating the rhythm may be general patterns of stress or cadence.

Both of these musical types have their architectural analogies. In the strict repetition of arch after arch circling the Colosseum, in the beauty of the colonnades of Greek temples, and in the repetition of the pointed arches and vertical lines of Gothic cathedrals there is a type of formal repetition similar to that found in these classic musical forms. But architecture would be weak indeed if it depended entirely on such strictness of rhythmical pattern. The beautiful country house, the informal village, and the town square frequently have a rhythmical beauty quite different—a beauty which comes from a flowing variety of recurrent crescendos swelling to climaxes and of diminuendos sinking to rests. But it has been remarked that the musical analogy of much good architecture is to be found in the rhythm of well-written prose rather than in the more fixed forms of poetry or music.

There are many types of rhythm which are of special importance in building. First, there is the repetition of shapes—windows, doors, columns, wall areas,

FIGURE 160. GREEK APPLICATIONS OF REPEATED RHYTHMS (ALL FROM GREEK
VASES)

ABOVE: Three types of Greek fret and two types of vine border; BELOW: Three examples of
anthemion band.

In all these there is regular rhythm in spacing, but the units repeated are individually rich in
progressive rhythms of detail. This combination is one cause of the strong grace of Greek
decorative forms.

and so on. Second, there is the repetition of dimensions, such as the dimensions
between supports or those of bay spacing. In the first case—the repetition of
shapes—the spacing can vary without destroying the rhythmical character
(Fig. 158, above). Conversely, where dimensions are equal, the units may vary

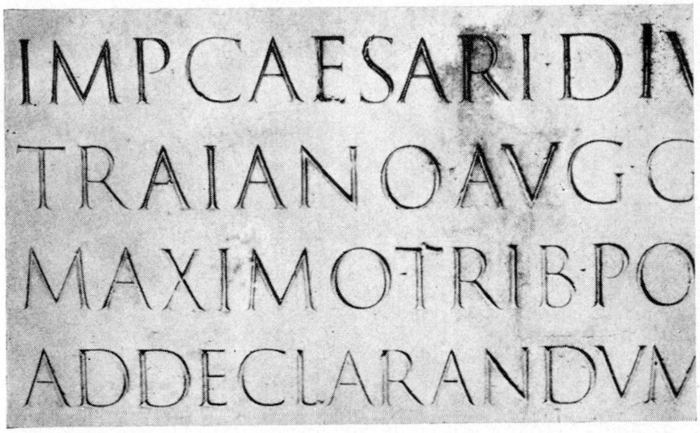

FIGURE 161. LETTER-
ING AS RHYTHM

The beauty of good let-
tering is the result of the
subtle rhythms between
the letters and the spaces
between them.

Courtesy Ars Typo-
graphica

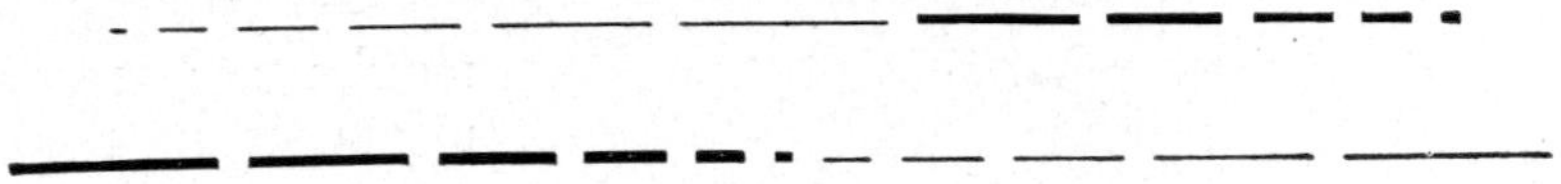

FIGURE 162. PROGRESSIVE HORIZONTAL RHYTHMS
ABOVE: Small—large—small; BELOW: Large—small—large.

in size or shape and rhythm will still remain (Fig. 158, below). It is this rhythmical quality of dimension repetition which accounts for much of the beauty
of well-designed lettering—a quality that is especially marked in carved inscriptions (Fig. 161).

A third and more complex type of rhythm is based on the repetition of differences. Thus, if we have a series of lines, parallel to each other, in which the
distance between the second pair is greater than that between the first pair and
the distance between the third pair greater than that between the second pair,
we inevitably establish an irregular, progressive rhythm. And so with lines of
varying length, placed continuously: we may start from a dot, have a dash,
then a longer dash, then one longer still; the effect will be definitely rhythmical
and will, moreover, imply a strong sense of motion, either from the small to
the large or from the large to the small (Fig. 162). We can even combine as-
cending and descending progressions in the same rhythmical series, building
up from small to large and then gradually returning to small again, or, conversely, working from large to small to large. In the latter case, however, the
relationship may be felt as constricted. More useful is the combination in which
the large is in the center, with a sense of swelling to an important element and
diminishing to a small one—progressing from a quiet beginning to a climax and
then relaxing again (Fig. 163).

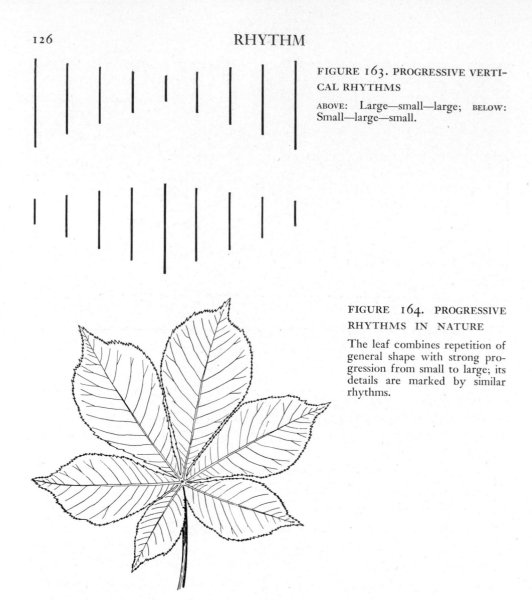

FIGURE 163. PROGRESSIVE VERTI-CAL RHYTHMS

ABOVE: Large—small—large; BELOW: Small—large—small.

FIGURE 164. PROGRESSIVE RHYTHMS IN NATURE

The leaf combines repetition of general shape with strong progression from small to large; its details are marked by similar rhythms.

The architectural implications of these rhythmical principles should be self-evident. The ranges of windows in a Renaissance palace (Figs. 166, 167), the repeated brackets of a cornice (Fig. 168)—these do much to create rhythmical beauty, and perhaps one of the reasons why modern kitchens are often visually so satisfactory lies in the quiet regular rhythms of repeated cabinet doors and drawers punctuated by the staccato notes of latch and handle. It is also undoubtedly the rhythmical richness of classic molding decoration and of classic design generally which makes the layman so loath to give it up.

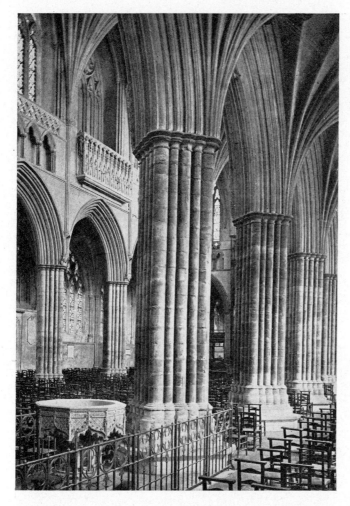

FIGURE 165. CATHE-
DRAL, EXETER, ENGLAND.
INTERIOR DETAIL
Rhythmical development of
decorative and structural detail in pier treatments and
arch moldings.

Courtesy Ware Library

But in architecture the rhythmical pattern is not merely, or perhaps even chiefly, a matter of exterior arrangement. As one walks through an interior he is faced by a series of changing views; he sees ahead of him doors, piers, windows, wall surfaces; perhaps he passes through opening after opening—these all form a rhythmical series, and the quality of this rhythmical experience will determine much of his final judgment of the building. And, because visual impressions in interiors are so complicated and are composed of so many different elements, it is all the more necessary to design carefully to make the experienced rhythm coherent and satisfactory.

Rhythms may be indefinite and open or definite and closed. A mere repetition of similar units, equally spaced and without a defined beginning or a

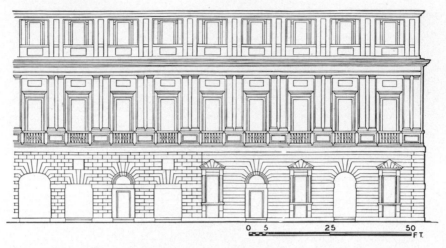

FIGURE 166. STOPPANI-VIDONI PALACE, ROME. ELEVATION

Powerful architectural rhythms, both vertical and horizontal, achieved by repetitions of windows, pilasters, band courses, panels, and horizontal moldings. This rhythm, horizontally, is repeated but complex; vertically, it is a subtle progression: small—large—small.

Redrawn from Sturgis, *European Architecture*

FIGURE 167. VENDRAMINI PALACE, VENICE, ITALY

Pietro Lombardo, architect

Complex vertical and horizontal rhythms exquisitely integrated.

Courtesy Ware Library

defined end, is called an open rhythm. Its effect in architecture is usually disturbing; it has about it something indeterminate and confusing. In the case of circular or oval buildings, like the Colosseum or the Temple of Vesta at Tivoli, continuous regular rhythms are satisfactory because the actual regular rhythm

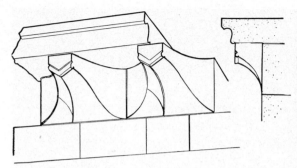

FIGURE 168 (LEFT). CORNICE FROM A CHAPEL IN NOTRE DAME, DIJON, FRANCE, THIRTEENTH CENTURY

The brackets form strong rhythmical elements of light and shade that accent the cornice line.

Redrawn from Viollet-le-Duc,
Dictionnaire raisonné . . .

FIGURE 169 (RIGHT). SO-CALLED TEMPLE OF VESTA, TIVOLI, ITALY

In a circular building, the regularly spaced columns, seen from any point of view, count as a closed, progressive rhythm.

FIGURE 170. BASILICA, VICENZA, ITALY

Andrea Palladio, architect

Rich rhythmical composition, both vertical and horizontal.

Courtesy Ware Library

of spacing is apparently closed at either end by the effect of perspective (Fig. 169). If an open rhythm is closed by a definite marking of each end, this sense of confusion disappears. Rhythms can be closed by changing the shape of the units at the ends, by changing the size of the units at the ends, or by combinations of both types of change; it can also be closed by adding to each end a strongly marked opposing rhythm. In architecture, an example of the first

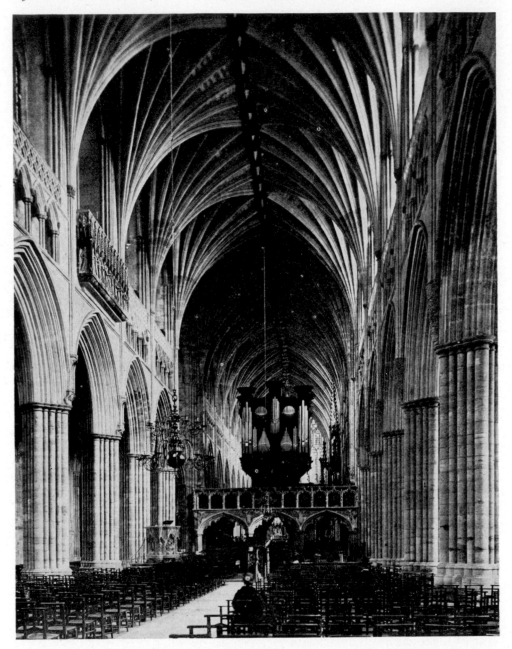

FIGURE 171. CATHEDRAL, EXETER, ENGLAND. NAVE

The repetition of richly developed structural elements gives a compelling rhythm to many Gothic buildings.   Courtesy Ware Library

FIGURE 172. SCHOCKEN STORE, CHEMNITZ, GERMANY
Eric Mendelsohn, architect
Strong rhythmical balance between the central horizontals and the end verticals.

Courtesy Museum of Modern Art

scheme can be seen in Palladio's Basilica at Vicenza (Fig. 170), where the bay spacing remains constant but the end bays have smaller openings. A somewhat similar variation occurs in the coupled columns which distinguish the end bays of the Vendramini Palace, and in many office buildings and apartment houses the open rhythm of the bay spacings is varied in the end bays by diminishing the glass area or by omitting glass entirely. Many contemporary architects have used the system of opposing rhythms to close a series—often with powerful effect. Thus, Holabird & Root's Forest Products Laboratory in Madison has a central vertical rhythm closed by strong horizontals at the sides; in Mendelsohn's Schocken department store in Chemnitz, the powerful horizontals which curve around the front are stopped at each end by the tall glazed openings in front of the exit stairs (Fig. 172). A still more subtle modification of the same system can be seen in the Philadelphia Saving Fund Building, in Philadelphia, by Howe and Lescaze (Fig. 173), where the horizontal rhythms of

FIGURE 173. PHILADELPHIA SAVING FUND BUILDING, PHILADELPHIA, PENNSYL-
VANIA

Howe & Lescaze, architects

Interesting and powerful balance between the horizontals on the façade and the verticals on the
flank　　　　　　　　　　　　　　　　　　　　　　　　　　　Photograph Ben Schnall

FIGURE 174. A PAINTING BY PIET MONDRIAN (1)

Strongly marked progressive rhythms from the center out.

Collection, Museum of Modern Art, New York

the cantilevered floors are stopped by, and, as it were, engaged in, the vertical rhythms of the columns on the flank.

There is another type of rhythm of great importance in architecture—the rhythm of lines. Such rhythms may be merely systematic variations of linear lengths or curvatures. The abstract painters of the Styl group in the Netherlands, especially Mondrian, have made an intensive study of linear rhythm, and many of Mondrian's paintings show his preoccupation with it. This group exercised a strong influence on certain important modern architects, especially Oud and Mies van der Rohe; the resemblance between many plans by the latter and the paintings of Mondrian has frequently been noted (see Figs. 174, 175). These Mies van der Rohe plans, by their brilliant use of isolated stretches of walls, freely placed under a single horizontal slab, create in the buildings an actual visual rhythm of the greatest interest; at the same time the plan pattern

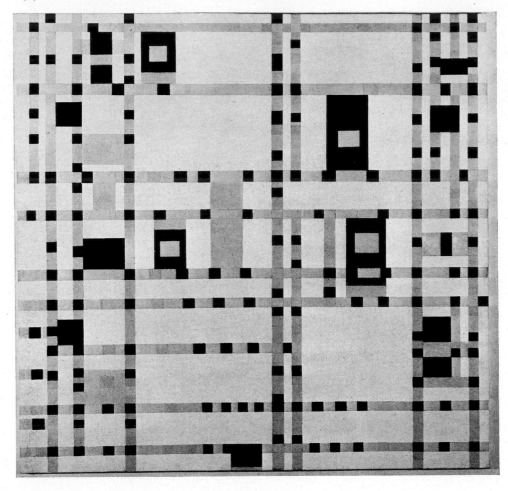

FIGURE 175. A PAINTING BY PIET MONDRIAN (2)

A rhythmical arrangement of vertical and horizontal lines.

Collection, Museum of Modern Art, New York

has the abstract quality of pure line (Fig. 176). For architectural composition, some of the earlier Mondrian experiments are perhaps even more stimulating, as, for example, the picture illustrated, which is based entirely on the progressive rhythms of linear lengths (Fig. 174). Somewhat similar rhythms distinguish the exteriors of many of the most successful freely designed buildings erected between the First and Second World Wars. They are also marked in the work of most Dutch and Italian architects and are found superbly developed in the best work of Eric Mendelsohn. Chinese architecture makes con-

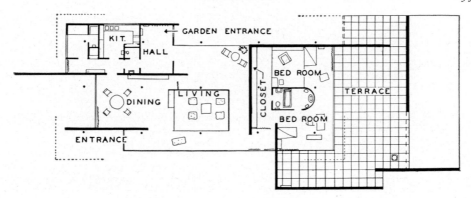

FIGURE 176. HOUSE IN THE BERLIN BUILDING EXPOSITION OF 1930. PLAN

Ludwig Mies van der Rohe, architect

A plan of marked rhythmical character, based on repetitions of wall planes and of supports, and on alternations of closed and of open views.

FIGURE 177. GERMAN BUILDING, BARCELONA EXPOSITION OF 1929. PLAN

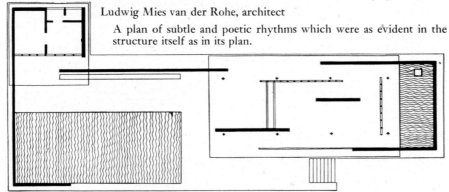

Ludwig Mies van der Rohe, architect

A plan of subtle and poetic rhythms which were as evident in the structure itself as in its plan.

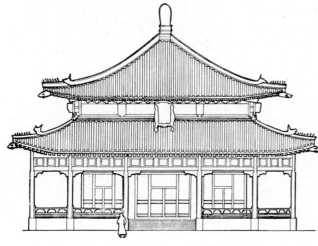

FIGURE 178. HALL OF CLASSICS, TEMPLE OF CONFUCIUS, PEIPING. DIAGRAM ELEVATION

Vivid progressive rhythms, both vertical and horizontal, distinguish this exquisitely designed, small, square pavilion. Every important architectural line bears definite rhythmical relations to all other lines parallel to it. The progressive horizontal rhythm is accented by the square panels in the frieze.

FIGURE 179. TAI-HO HALL IN THE FORBIDDEN CITY, PEIPING

As in all Chinese architecture, the rhythmical content is rich, subtle, and progressive.

From Imperial Museum, Tokyo, *Photographs of Palace Buildings of Peking*

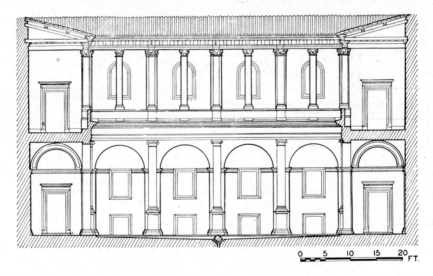

FIGURE 180. CLOISTER OF SANTA MARIA DELLA PACE, ROME

Donato Bramante, architect

A beautiful example of architectural counterpoint, with the smaller, more graceful elements grouped two and two above the single openings below. The whole is organized with horizontal lines which create subtle, progressive, vertical rhythm.

stant and effective use of progressive rhythms. The Hall of Classics of the Temple of Confucius in Peiping is typical (Fig. 178).

Just as we can have rhythms of linear length, so we can have repetitions of line motions in curves. Thus the progression from a circle to an ellipse is based on a related change in the radius of curvature (Fig. 182). Spirals similarly have

FIGURE 181. SO-CALLED PRISON, BRE-SCIA, ITALY

An interesting example of architectural counterpoint: seven units above integrated with two below.   Courtesy Avery Library

FIGURE 182. RHYTHMS OF CURVES

ABOVE: The progressive rhythms of the change from ellipse to circle; BELOW: Applications of curved rhythms in French ironwork: left, balcony from the rue Royale, Versailles; right, part of the choir grille of St. Germain-l'Auxerrois, Paris. Both make use of circles, ellipses, and spirals.

interesting progressions in the radius of curvature from small to large. The spiral is one of the most rhythmical of forms because of its combination of repeated curves around a focus and the continual progressive change in the radius

FIGURE 183. SPIRALS

Spirals are one of the most universally popular of rhythmic curves, susceptible of an infinite variety of expressive form. The branching scroll, shown at the top, consists of a wave curve with spirals swinging from it on alternate sides; it is the basis of the classic rinceau.

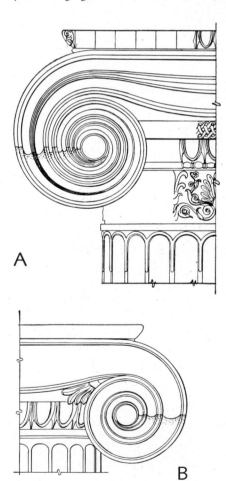

FIGURE 186. COLLEGIO DI SAPIENZA, ROME. VIEW IN THE COURT

The richly rhythmical curves of Borromini's Chapel of Sant' Ivo form a powerful climax to the quieter rhythms of the court.

Courtesy Ware Library

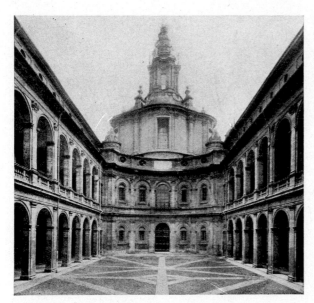

of curvature (Figs. 183, 184). The fact that the spiral finally winds around to a point of minimum curvature gives it a powerful close; this accounts for its popularity during the Baroque period as a decoration for shields and even for pediments. In fact, rhythmical curves are at the basis of much Baroque design alike in plans, interiors, and exteriors, and it is the frequent use of changing rhythmical curves which creates much of the vitality in Baroque design (Figs. 185, 186, 200).

Rhythm in architecture is not limited to matters of mere façade composition and interior detail; even more important are the larger rhythms of interior spaces. One enters through a small vestibule into a sizable lobby; from this he proceeds into a space of a different character, smaller perhaps than the lobby but larger than the entrance vestibule; from here, in turn, he may pass into the chief and most important element of the building. In buildings of some complexity, this changing and progressive rhythm of alternations—of large and

FIGURE 184 (OPPOSITE PAGE). TWO GREEK IONIC CAPITALS

A: From the Erechtheum, Athens; B: From the Propylaea, Athens.

The Ionic capital shows the beauty of the progressive rhythm of the spiral.

FIGURE 185 (OPPOSITE PAGE). ZWINGER PALACE, DRESDEN, GERMANY. GATEWAY

M. D. Pöppelmann, architect

The swinging rhythms of strongly contrasted curves create dynamic character.

Courtesy Ware Library

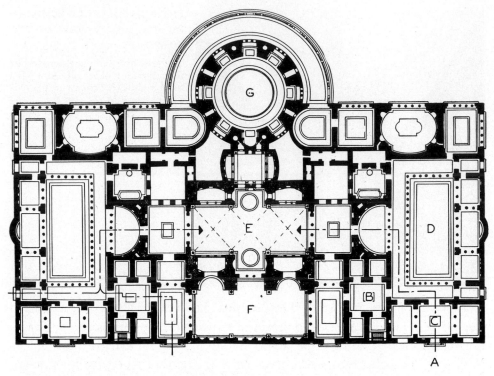

FIGURE 187. CENTRAL BUILDING, BATHS OF CARACALLA, ROME. PLAN

A: Entrance; B: Dressing rooms and clothes storage; C: Vestibule; D: Exercising court; E: Tepidarium and lounge; F: Swimming pool; G: Calidarium and steam baths.

The dotted lines show various methods of approaching the central lounge. Examination will show that in every case this passage will be through interiors producing a rich progressive rhythm of shapes, with alternations of open and closed, big and little, wide and narrow—all climaxing in the superb great space of the central lounge.

small, of wide and narrow, of rooms running transversely and corridors running longitudinally—creates an ordered variety of effect which has much to do with the power of great and monumental structures. The main entrance to the Pennsylvania Station in New York and those to the Roman thermae offer many examples of such changes (Figs. 187–189).

Moreover, as we have seen, all open rhythms, to be satisfactory, must be closed at the ends. In any interior, a series of supports on either side invites passage through between them. Forms which in plan are rhythmically related necessarily create a sense of motion and a sense of direction. One passes through a building as these shapes suggest, and, as he passes, the rhythmical character not only builds up in him a pleasant and continuing interest but also prepares

FIGURE 188. BATHS OF DIOCLETIAN, ROME. THE GREAT HALL AS RESTORED BY MICHELANGELO

The strong climax of a rhythmical approach.

Courtesy Avery Library

FIGURE 189. PENNSYLVANIA STATION, NEW YORK. ARCADE

McKim, Mead & White, architects

Repeated rhythms in a circulation which emphasize its transitional nature.

From *A Monograph of the Work of McKim, Mead & White*

him for something important, something tremendous, something exciting at the end. An open rhythm needs closing, and the closing must be a climax of sufficient importance to justify the preparation that has been made for it.

Exterior rhythms, too, are more complex and more important than matters of detail or the simple arrangement of openings; here there is the whole prob-

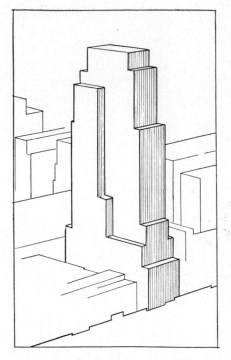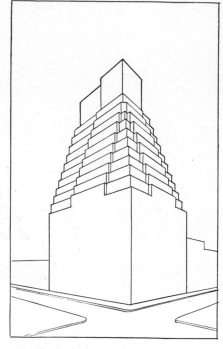

FIGURE 190. VERTICAL RHYTHMS IN ARCHITECTURE

LEFT: Daily News Building, New York, Howells & Hood, architects; RIGHT: A loft building in New York.

In the Daily News Building, progressive, subtle rhythms combine to produce a mass of the greatest interest. In the building at the right, the regular rhythms of the setbacks, unprepared for and leading to nothing, achieve only monotony in themselves and incoherence in the whole.

lem of the rhythm of the masses themselves. There is rhythm in the relation of the end wings to the point of central interest; there is rhythm in the outline of a good tower as it narrows from the bottom upwards.

This problem of the rhythm of masses is perhaps better illustrated in tower design or in the handling of high buildings than anywhere else. We say that a tower is too soft, or that its silhouette is awkward, or that it lacks unity; chiefly we mean that there is no recognizable rhythmical basis for the changing heights and widths and the setbacks, all of which determine its major design. The secret of the effect of many a simple Colonial church steeple lies in the architect's intuitive sense of rhythm in the relation between the solid square base and the various stages of square or octagonal plan which rise above and between these and the pyramid of the spire itself (Fig. 192).

The same, of course, is true of much of the design of tall office buildings.

FIGURE 191. DAILY NEWS BUILDING, NEW YORK

Howells & Hood, architects

Satisfactory and strongly marked vertical rhythms.   Courtesy *Daily News*

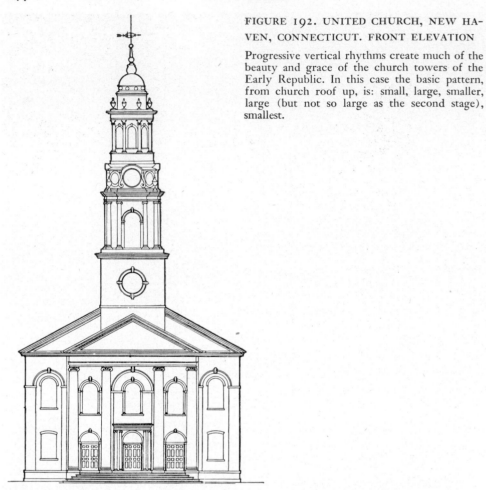

FIGURE 192. UNITED CHURCH, NEW HA-
VEN, CONNECTICUT. FRONT ELEVATION

Progressive vertical rhythms create much of the
beauty and grace of the church towers of the
Early Republic. In this case the basic pattern,
from church roof up, is: small, large, smaller,
large (but not so large as the second stage),
smallest.

Most cities require setbacks as a tall building rises from the street; these offer
the architect amazing opportunities for successful rhythmical treatment. Thus
the suave beauty of the 250 Sutter Street Building in San Francisco derives
largely from the delicacy of its rhythmical treatment. The repeated masses of
Rockefeller Center (Fig. 193) are similar to each other yet different, and all,
with their subtly designed breaks, form a rhythmical composition of the greatest interest. Perhaps the climax of rhythmical volume design in buildings of
this type can be seen in the New York Daily News Building, where the setbacks required by law have been modulated into a composition of sure and
poetic beauty (Figs. 190, 191). It is interesting to notice the comparison between this and some of the loft buildings not far from it; there a literal ad-

FIGURE 193. ROCKEFELLER CENTER, NEW YORK. GENERAL VIEW FROM THE NORTH

Reinhard & Hofmeister; Corbett, Harrison & MacMurray; and Hood & Fouilhoux,
associated architects

Varied but coherent vertical and horizontal rhythms.   Courtesy Rockefeller Center, Inc.

FIGURE 194 (LEFT). FRIEZE AND CAP MOLD FROM THE ERECHTHEUM, ATHENS
Definiteness, grace, and regularity distinguish Greek ornament.   Courtesy Ware Library

FIGURE 195 (RIGHT). A TYPICAL ROMAN RINCEAU, FROM THE ARA PACIS AUGUSTAE
Roman rhythms are freer and more varied than the Greek.   Courtesy Ware Library

herence to the zoning act, and not the architect, has controlled the volume and produced dull and incoherent structures.

Rhythm has an undeniable attractive power over the human mind. Thus, if from one spot two views are possible, the first rhythmical and the second not, an observer will turn naturally and instinctively to the former. Rhythmical design, therefore, constitutes one method by which the eye and the mind can be guided in one direction rather than in another, and attention can thus be directed toward an important element in a building. This is true of both exterior and interior, of both plan and elevation. The rhythmical piers of a basilican church, for example, serve to direct the attention forward to the climax, the altar.

Preferences in rhythm type have varied greatly in different architectural periods. Greek ornament, for example, indicates an intense love of small, regular, and perfectly studied rhythms; the egg-and-dart molding, the water-leaf

FIGURE 196 (LEFT, ABOVE). ROMAN RINCEAU, POSSIBLY FROM THE FORUM OF
TRAJAN   Courtesy Ware Library

FIGURE 197 (LEFT, BELOW). DETAIL OF THE RINCEAU SHOWN IN FIGURE 196
This shows the variations in light and shade, as well as in line, which generate the rhythms of the
typical Roman rinceau.   Courtesy Ware Library

FIGURE 198. (RIGHT). NOTRE DAME CATHEDRAL, PARIS. DETAIL OF THE FLANK
Repeated crockets, gables, and arches develop the characteristic Gothic rhythmical power.
                                                          Courtesy Ware Library

decoration, and the patterns of repeated anthemions all show this quality of
definiteness, and they also indicate a love for alternations of curved and straight
lines. Nothing could demonstrate this better than the famous ornament from
the Erechtheum (Fig. 194), which illustrates the intricacy and the definiteness
which the Greeks loved. This Greek rhythm is essentially a linear rhythm: the
relief is regular throughout; shadows count almost as purely linear elements.
Some of the same feeling for shape and well-defined linear rhythms characterizes the deeply cut ornament of Byzantine architecture, although here the
motifs are quite different.

FIGURE 199. NOTRE DAME CATHEDRAL, PARIS. DETAIL OF TOWER CORNICES

Note the exaggeration of the crockets to emphasize the rhythmical richness of the towers as seen from the ground.

Courtesy Ware Library

The Romans, on the other hand, loved rhythms of a much freer and more plastic type. Relief is often remarkably varied in Roman ornament, some elements projecting boldly and some dying away into the background; the shadows thus are no longer linear, as in the Greek examples, but instead form varied areas of changing value. The basic composition of much Roman ornament is further distinguished by great rhythmical freedom; strong progressions from big to little, from high relief to low relief, and from free swinging curves to tight spirals mark the gorgeous rhythmical patterns of the typical acanthus rinceaux, which the Romans so loved (Figs. 195–197).

Gothic is extraordinarily varied in its rhythmical content. In the earlier examples the rhythm is generally more definite, and in the later ones freer and more progressive; but throughout the Gothic period architects liked to establish many clearly defined and persistent rhythms in their ornament, such as the repeated vertical lines of Gothic wall panels and the sharp staccato notes of crockets on the edges of spires and gables (Figs. 198, 199).

The earlier Renaissance architects, in turn, tended toward simple and definite rhythms—handled sometimes, however, especially in Venice, with the freer type of relief which the Renaissance designers developed from Roman sources. Later, in the so-called Manneristic period, there was a tremendous freeing of rhythmical content both in general design and in decoration, so

FIGURE 200 (LEFT). THE SHELL FOUN-
TAIN, ROME

Lorenzo Bernini, architect and sculptor

Vivid progressive rhythms establish the dynamic, typically Baroque character.

Courtesy Ware Library

FIGURE 201 (RIGHT). HÔTEL SOUBISE,
PARIS. SALON OVALE

Germain Boffrand, architect

Orchestrated rhythms of shapes, lines, relief, and color all integrate the lavish complexity into a
compelling unity.   Courtesy Metropolitan Museum of Art

much so that at times rhythmical definiteness was almost lost. In developed
Baroque architecture, rhythm again asserted its sway over all architectural design; here, both in the larger rhythms of building design and in the minor
rhythms of ornament, the designers achieved a kind of ordered and dramatic
rhythmical complexity of line, of mass, and of shape which has never been sur-
passed.

The rhythmical feeling of the twentieth century is confused and tentative.
Modern architecture, like modern music, varies in its rhythmical ideals from
the most clean-cut and regular rhythms, like those in an office building, to
those in which there is a search for such free and so-called natural rhythms
that the rhythmical basis is almost entirely lost and the result appears to many
people amorphous and without meaning. Just as in music, where on the one
hand we have jazz with its extreme dependence on definite but complex rhythmical patterns and, on the other hand, such music as that of Satie, who refused
to mark any measures in his music at all, so, in architecture, rhythmical taste

FIGURE 202. "LES TERRASSES," GARCHES, FRANCE

Le Corbusier, architect

Strong rhythms of window and wall, of closed and open areas, and of curved and straight surfaces. Courtesy Museum of Modern Art

varies from the definiteness shown in the work of Frank Lloyd Wright to the completely indefinite rhythms of some of the work of Le Corbusier.

In the complex process of modern design, with its insistence on economy, efficiency, functional expression, and the avoidance of useless parts, the problem of rhythm may sometimes seem an unimportant and even unnecessary complication. Nevertheless, the modern architect should bear it in mind that great architecture has always been distinguished by strong and definite rhythmical content and that one of the greatest needs, in order to make the architecture of today an architecture that will in the best sense of the word be appealing, is the need for clarification of rhythmical pattern.

From what has preceded, it should be obvious how important rhythm is in architectural design. Rhythm in mass and in line is one of the surest ways of achieving coherence and interest; rhythms in the spacing and type of openings, when correctly handled, inevitably produce exteriors and interiors which have organized beauty (Figs. 200–202); rhythm in the arrangement of supports and in the handling of interior volumes creates system and pattern through the interior spaces of a structure. Moreover, interior rhythms do much to direct a visitor through the complexities of a building plan; they help to create climax and to accentuate the effect of the climax itself. Rhythm is thus one of the most important means at the architect's command for developing a systematic organization in any building he may be designing. Rhythmical relationships arise simply and naturally from constructive and functional necessities; controlled and, as it were, orchestrated by the creative imagination, they become one of the chief elements in architectural beauty.

SUGGESTED ADDITIONAL READING FOR CHAPTER 6

Belcher, John, *Essentials in Architecture* . . . (London: Batsford, 1907), pp. 71 ff.

Birkhoff, George David, *Aesthetic Measure* (Cambridge, Mass.: Harvard University Press, 1933).

Ellis, Havelock, *The Dance of Life* (Boston: Houghton Mifflin, 1923).

Greene, Theodore Meyer, *The Arts and the Art of Criticism* (Princeton: Princeton University Press, 1940), pp. 219 ff.

Hamlin, Talbot [Faulkner], *Architecture, an Art for All Men* (New York: Columbia University Press, 1947), pp. 81–87.

Hitchcock, Henry Russell, *J.-J. P. Oud* (Paris: Éditions Cahiers d'art [c1931]).

Johnson, Philip C., *Mies van der Rohe* (New York: Museum of Modern Art [c1947]).

Nobbs, Percy Erskine, *Design; a Treatise on the Discovery of Form* (London, New York, etc.: Oxford University Press, 1937), p. 146.

Raymond, George Lansing, *The Essentials of Aesthetics in Music, Poetry, Painting, Sculpture, and Architecture*, 3rd ed. rev. (New York: Putnam's [c1921]).

Whittick, Arnold, *Eric Mendelsohn* (London: Faber [1940]), Mendelsohn sketches.

7

Sequences in Planning

ANY BUILDING, in order to justify its inclusion in the ranks of good architecture, is necessarily a single continuing aesthetic experience, outside and in, as long as the interested spectator remains in aesthetically sensitive contact with it. Architecture, therefore, is quite as much an art of time as of space, and the building as an aesthetic entity exists in time as well as in space. Frequently, no purely momentary perception of a building will enable the observer to get more than a faint hint of the entire richness of its composition or the significant message which it has to offer. One must visit a great building again and again. One must approach it from all sides, walk around it; one must enter it and pass through its ordered interiors. Only then will its real greatness begin to appear; only by such study, over a considerable period of time, can its true richness, its real message, be appreciated.

This is the great reason why any two-dimensional representation of a building is of necessity inadequate. Elevations and plans are by their nature diagrams only. Perspectives which aim to present a "real" aspect of a structure can each give only one of many possible views of a building. Even photographs have the same limitations; however factual, however carefully chosen, interior and exterior photographs are only fragmentary representations. Perhaps carefully directed motion pictures might be the closest representation of a building possible in another art, but even there basic difficulties would arise between the reaction of the spectator to the movie and his reaction to the building itself. For there are definite contrasts between the more fixed and static eye (which the lens of even a motion-picture camera is) and the actual wandering of the human eye over the changing field of view presented by a building. Architecture, like music, cannot be adequately represented by anything other than itself. And all so-called representations of buildings are, at best, mere approximations.

There is another and most important difference between any static representation of a building in two dimensions, such as a drawing or a still photograph, and the actual structure. In a good building every view has a definite relation-

FIGURE 203. NOTRE DAME CATHEDRAL, PARIS. VIEW IN AMBULATORY

Motion, sequence, and accordingly the factor of time are inevitable in large structures and visually expressed in many.

ship to all the views of it which may come to a spectator in definite sequence; there are many possible aspects of even the greatest buildings which are meaningless in themselves and achieve meaning only through their relation to this before-and-after experience. As pictures such aspects might be simply incoherent and confusing, yet as parts of a continuing experience in time they are inevitable and right.

Moreover, when looking at a drawing or a photograph, one cannot help judging it as a work of two-dimensional art in its own right. It is well balanced or ill balanced, it is beautiful or ugly, because of qualities which may be purely accidental when applied to the actual building. One thinks, for instance, of the dark skies with which the smart architectural photographer frequently overdramatizes his prints, or of the clouds and trees by which the architectural delineator gives composition to his rendering. Yet the essential difference between the drawing or the photograph and the building itself is one of *time;* it must be recognized that an appreciative understanding of a work of architecture is built up of a series of different experiences, one after the other, organically related. The aesthetic experience of a building is as much a stream of successive and changing factors as is the experience of a symphony (Fig. 203).

The architect must definitely consider this fact in the design of anything but the simplest of elements. He is both the composer and the conductor of a visual symphony—the building. By his planning he directs the steps of the observer through the whole. It is he who determines what the spectator will see first, what second, what third, and the success of the building often depends just as much on the correct order of the impressions as on the excellence of each one in itself.

What does one actually see within a building as he passes from point to point? He *sees* masses and shapes of light and shade or of different colors; he *sees* vertical and horizontal accents of value or hue. But what he *perceives* is quite different; for every visual experience necessarily, and fortunately, associates itself with the whole background of his total remembered experience—his apperception mass, as the psychologists call it. Out of this confusion of shape and line and color, therefore, he builds up a meaning; he infers, from his sense experience, a structural, or aesthetic, or functional fact. The vertical accents of line and shade are perceived as columns or posts or edges of openings. The planes of light and color are realized as walls or openings in those walls. Bifocal vision has already developed in the raw sense experience some appreciation of distance and size; from these, in turn, one infers the ideas of space and height. Thus, from his changing impressions in the building and from the meaning of these experiences to him, he is enabled to infer the formal structure of the building, the shape and size of its rooms, the position of its openings, the relationships of one part with another. Moreover, those formal relationships will suggest to him ideas of function and feelings of beauty or grandeur, and the whole succession of these experiences of form will, if the building is well designed, have coherence, unity, and beauty.

But the ordinary spectator's inferences do not stop with the perception of mere shape; he will also infer qualities of construction and qualities of use. He will realize that columns and walls, or both, hold up something; he will realize that the ceiling above him is supported. He will imagine the strength in post or

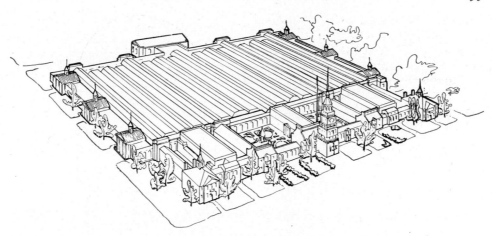

FIGURE 204. FORD MUSEUM, DEARBORN, MICHIGAN. BIRD'S-EYE VIEW

A glance at this drawing reveals at once a basic disparity between the Colonial exterior pavilions and walls and the central core of standardized industrial bays with monitors. Any sequences between the two portions reveal basic contradictions in structure and in appearance.

beam or arch or vault, and he will also realize the purposes for which these shapes exist. He will note that this space is a hall or corridor, that this is a lecture hall or that a chapel. From what he sees, he will understand that one space is for relaxation or recreation, another for eating, that this area has been designed for sleeping and that one for work. In this way, from experiences acquired earlier in life, even the person uneducated in architecture will gain at least an elementary conception of the building as a structure and as a shelter for human activities. It is the architect's responsibility to make these successive impressions of structure and of use just as harmonious and meaningful, just as coherent, as is the purely formal succession of shape experience. In other words, we say that in the good building the *structural sequence*, the *functional sequence*, and the *aesthetic sequence* must all be thoroughly coherent and organized. One of the chief tasks of the architect, therefore, is to design in such a way that this will be true. It is impossible to black out that process in the observer's mind, for the mind cannot help making these automatic inferences, seizing upon these inferred relationships, without a definite and difficult exercise of the will. The experience will go on for every person in any building, whether he wants it to or not. It will be either a pleasing experience or an exasperation, and it is the architect's responsibility to see that it is pleasing. Unfortunately today the world is so full of ill-designed buildings, many of them with definite architectural pretensions, that the average person has become deadened to the quality

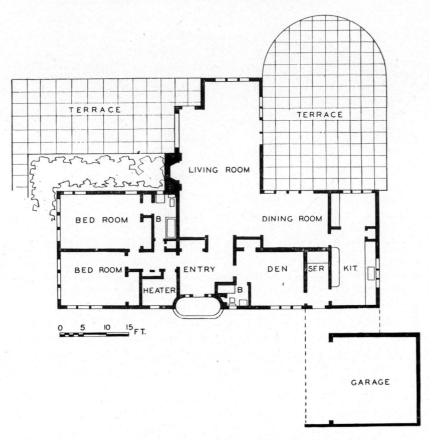

FIGURE 205. HOUSE IN MARIN COUNTY, CALIFORNIA. PLAN

W. W. Wurster, architect

This plan illustrates the essence of logical as well as beautiful sequence design. From service entrance to kitchen to dining room, or to front door, there is direct and simple communication. From main entrance to living room, or to bedroom wing, the approach is equally simple, with a careful regard for the relative importance of each separate sequence. The den is so placed as to be flexibly usable as guest room or maid's room as necessity arises.

of the experience he receives from buildings, just as the person who lives close to a railroad may, sooner or later, become completely unconscious of the noise of passing trains.

Let us take examples of both good and bad structures and functional sequences. In the Ford museum at Dearborn (Fig. 204), already cited, the structural sequence—from the Georgian ceilings, walls, and isolated openings of the front part of the building to the steel beams and glass areas of the exhibition halls behind them—is shocking. Each portion of the experience contradicts every other, even to the untutored eye. By contrast, one of the reasons why a

FIGURE 206. TYPICAL TWO-FAMILY HOUSE PLAN

Illogical sequences in domestic planning; the dining room becomes a passageway between living room and sleeping areas.

Redrawn from Wright, *Rehousing Urban America*

Gothic cathedral is effective lies in the absolute coherence of its structural system, which is obvious from every point of view, both outside and in. Any well-designed house shows the pleasant quality of logical and organized functional sequence: thus the passage from front door, through vestibule, through hall, to living room suggests a pleasant organization of living activities; similarly, a sequence from back door through kitchen and pantry to dining room has an organized and meaningful unity (see Fig. 205). If, on the other hand, one had to pass through a pantry to get from a hall to a living room, or through a kitchen to get from a bedroom to a bath, the patent absurdity of the arrangement and its denial of all functional logic would go far to destroy any beauty of detail or furnishing; yet in the United States there are many double houses where a bedroom has to be entered through a dining room and one finds numerous altered apartments where the only way of reaching the bath is by traversing the kitchen. Not only do these systems make for bad and disorganized and difficult living; they also inevitably produce bad architecture (see Fig. 206).

FIGURE 207. DIAGRAM OF APPROACH TO A CLIMAX

Minor elements balanced on each side assist progress toward an axial climax; this climax must be strong enough to justify its position.

There is one principle which holds true of sequences in all the arts—every sequence must have a beginning and a recognizable end. In this respect architectural design resembles the principles of rhetoric in writing. The sequences within a building begin naturally at the entrance, and they should lead just as naturally to some definite end. This end should be both the artistic and the

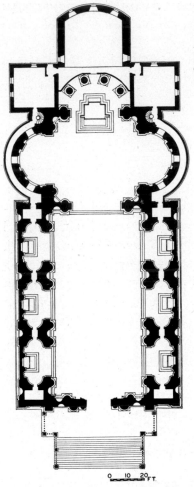

FIGURE 208. IL REDENTORE, VENICE, ITALY. PLAN

Andrea Palladio, architect

A plan with the major sequence carried through and beyond the major climax—the high altar. The sacristy vault
can be seen between the columns of the apse and suggests
spaces beyond; the sequence is visual rather than actual.

functional climax of the sequence (Fig. 207). If it is not sufficiently important
or sufficiently beautiful to make the passage to it seem worth while, a sense of
frustration will inevitably develop and the building will appear inconclusive
and disappointing. Herein lies much of the secret of great architectural planning—to provide the end of each natural sequence with a sufficient climax.

But this is not the whole story. The entire sequence through a building may
entail passage through or beyond the climax, perhaps to a natural exit or else
to necessary portions of less importance; this sequence, too, can be as much a
subject of careful and imaginative design as the original sequence from entrance
to climax (Figs. 208–210). Just as the passage from entrance to climax is designed to produce a gradual crescendo of interest, so the sequence through or

FIGURE 209. IL REDEN-
TORE, VENICE, ITALY.
INTERIOR

Andrea Palladio, architect

Views beyond the apse columns express a sequence
that passes beyond the altar
climax.

Courtesy Metropolitan
Museum of Art

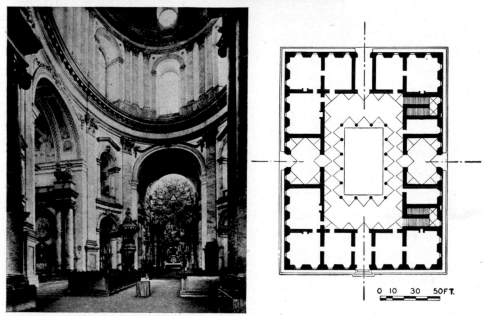

0 10   30   50 FT.

FIGURE 210 (LEFT). KARLSKIRCHE, VIENNA. INTERIOR

Johann B. Fischer von Erlach, architect

A sequence beyond the climax is suggested by the open nature of the altar piece.

Courtesy School of Architecture, Columbia University

FIGURE 211 (RIGHT). STROZZI PALACE, FLORENCE, ITALY. PLAN

A plan distinguished by four simple axial sequences from door to court; the court is the climax.
The placing of the stairs at the ends of the wider court arcades gives them importance; they
become links in a further sequence to the upper floors. These sequences all work equally well
in both directions, forming a crescendo from door to court and a diminuendo from court to door.

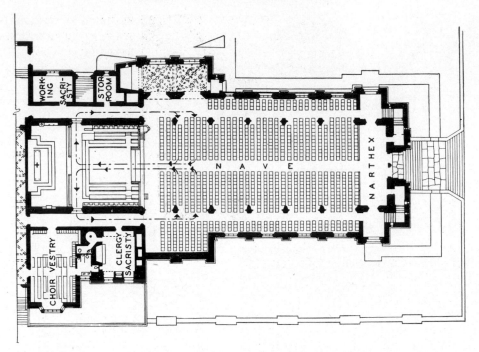

FIGURE 212. INTERCESSION CHAPEL, NEW YORK. PART PLAN

Cram, Goodhue & Ferguson, architects

The dot-and-dash lines indicate the path taken by communicants during the Communion rite. This sequence, important because of the emotional impact of the service, is carefully designed to build up a crescendo in the approach to the Communion rail before the altar and then to produce a restrained but gracious diminuendo to the side aisles and back to the pews.

past the climax to less important elements, or to an exit, can be planned to have coherence and meaning; it can form a balanced diminuendo from the excitement of the climax to a general level of pleasant relaxation (Figs. 211, 212).

Thus it will be seen that the essence of much successful sequence planning lies in adequate preparation for what is to come later. We have seen, too, how important is the climactic psychological reaction which may be produced by any visual experience (Fig. 212). The problem then arises of how aesthetic preparation is produced. To begin with, we may say at once that everything that happens to us in the aesthetic appreciation of a building modifies any succeeding experiences in the building. Just as in music we attain a feeling of the coherent design only by carrying over from one moment to the next a memory, conscious or unconscious, of what has preceded, so in architecture, by a similar carry-over, successive visual experiences are related. And we may go further. A new stimulus added to the memory of a related, immediately pre-existent

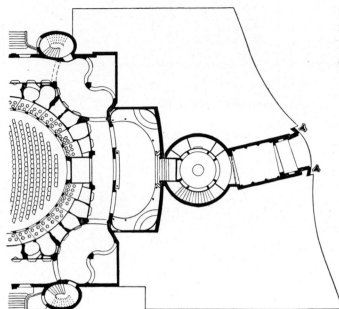

FIGURE 213. KOMOE-
DIE THEATER, BERLIN.
PLAN OF ENTRANCE

Oscar Kaufmann, architect

This illustrates the way in which the rococo spirit of the exterior and interior is preserved in the plan, as well as the harmony of form and the natural flow of the sequences. Ticket offices and control are in the rotunda; the foyer has little bars in the corners, and coatrooms are placed in the corners of the theater proper.

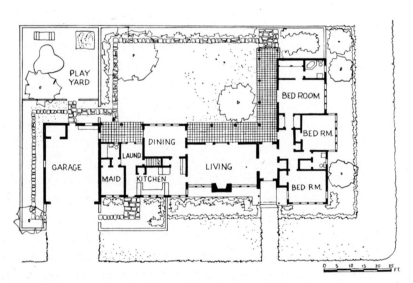

FIGURE 214. HOUSE AT LELAND MANOR, CALIFORNIA. PLAN

B. M. & D. B. Clark, architects

A plan distinguished by rich and varied sequences well handled. The entrance hall acts as a transition to, and a preparation for, the living room and the patio colonnade. Yet all sequences finally lead through to the garden climax—at least visually. Thus the importance of outdoor living and the oneness of outdoors and indoors are expressed. There is also an efficient and logical service sequence.

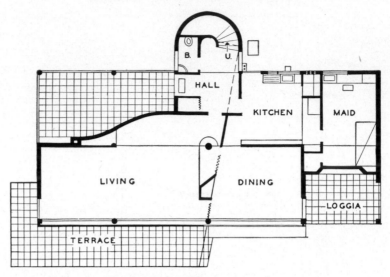

FIGURE 215. HOUSE IN ENGLAND. FIRST-FLOOR PLAN

Oliver Hill, architect

A plan of rich and effective sequences: entrance porch to hall, hall to living room, living room to terrace. Note that the curved living-room wall tends to direct attention toward the opposite side. The angle of the living-room end wall is prepared for by the hall ceiling treatment, and the importance of the living-room entrance is accented by the curved-end cabinet and column.

stimulus creates an expectation of what is to follow, and the quality of this expectation and its relation to the climax are most important elements in architectural design.

Preparation for a climax, therefore, is essentially a question of building up an expectation for it, and this can be done in many ways. In the first place, if we have a succession of elements of generally similar types, each one larger than the one before it, an observer passing through this series will experience a progressive rhythm, from small to large, which will make him eager for still larger elements to come (Figs. 214, 215). Thus, as one passes through a door of relatively small size into a vestibule, also small but higher than the door, and from that into a larger hall, an expectation is built up of a still larger space beyond. This type of sequence is common in many well-designed houses, where the climax furnished naturally by the large living room seems a logical finale to what has preceded. Here the effect is one of satisfaction and aesthetic pleasure. In many small houses where the living room is entered directly from an entrance door, so little preparation exists that the living room frequently appears even smaller than it is and less important; accordingly, it gives less aesthetic satisfaction (Fig. 216). Where such a plan type is necessary, the architect must

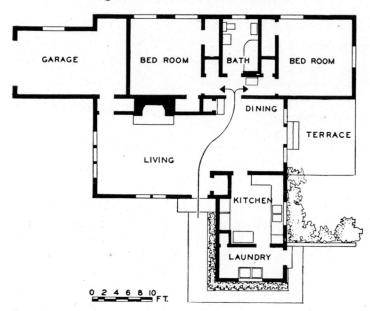

FIGURE 216. TYPICAL ONE-STORY HOUSE WITH THE LIVING ROOM ENTERED DI-
RECTLY FROM OUTDOORS. PLAN

A glance at this plan shows confused sequences and a lack of preparation for any climax. The living room becomes largely a passageway; the dining area is the only approach to the bedrooms and the kitchen; the garage is approached from the living room; the living room is entirely open to view from the front door. Such a house would be both inconvenient and banal.

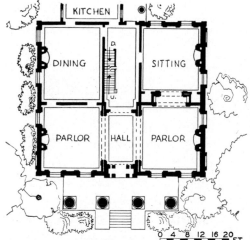

FIGURE 217. GENERAL LEAVENWORTH HOUSE, SYRACUSE, NEW YORK. FIRST-FLOOR PLAN

Formal, classic preparation and climax in a Greek Revival house. The hall forms a directional intersection and in its treatment a superb transition to the parlors on either side; also, the recess in the right-hand parlor forms a subtle transitional element between parlor and sitting room. The whole is firmly composed; every detail form has a meaning in the total sequence composition.

be extremely careful in the relation of the living-room door to the rest of the room and must attempt to build up, through its detail, some kind of gradual transition—essentially a preparation between the outside and the actual climax

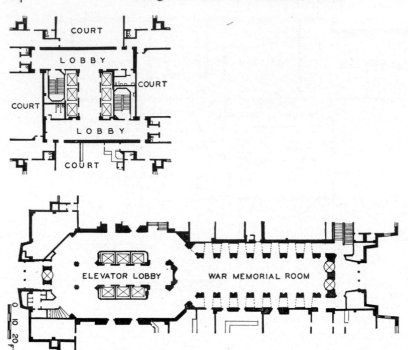

FIGURE 218. COURTHOUSE, MILWAUKEE, WISCONSIN. PLAN OF GROUND FLOOR
AND TYPICAL COURTROOM FLOOR

Holabird & Root, architects

ABOVE: On the typical courtroom floors the courtrooms have ample lobbies opening off the elevator lobby, which is large enough to accommodate those waiting for elevators and those having business in the courts, with ample space for both. The actual entrances to the courtrooms may be criticized as being badly placed and unimportant both in size and position, with nothing in the plan to distinguish them from less important doors to corridors and service areas. BELOW: A complex sequence pattern working from either entrance to or through the War Memorial and to the elevator lobby. Repeated rhythms of supports create a strong preparation for climax, and the diagonal openings at the inner end of the War Memorial suggest passing beyond the climax niche wall to the elevator lobby beyond.

of the living room, which may be the fireplace or some interesting furniture group. A somewhat similar preparation is found in many churches, where there may be a vestibule and an ample narthex to prepare one for the greater height and space sense of the body of the church. In the Cathedral of Notre Dame in Paris, the heavy piers which support the internal angles of the towers act in a somewhat similar manner. This first general type of preparation depends on a simple progress from the smaller to the larger. (See also Fig. 217.)

A second type of preparation results from the experiencing of a regular open rhythm of a series of strongly marked elements, such as a row of columns or piers (Fig. 218). As we have seen, open rhythms, whether regular or progres-

FIGURE 219. UNION STATION, WASHINGTON. VIEW IN ARCADE

D. H. Burnham, architect

Strong sequence expression leading to the climax furnished by the greater dimensions and larger arches of the main entrance.

From *The Architectural Work of Graham, Anderson, Probst & White*

sive, demand a close; when in a building, for instance, one passes through an open rhythm of apparently indefinite length, an expectation of something beyond is inevitably produced. Furthermore, the longer the rhythm, the more intense becomes the feeling of expectation and the more important and dramatic must be the climax to which it leads. Thus, as one walks through the colonnades of the piazza of St. Peter's in Rome, the flashing by, one by one, of those apparently innumerable columns builds up an expectation so strong that only the tremendous size and magnificence of St. Peter's itself is a sufficient climax. It is a definite fault in many contemporary plans, otherwise systematic and efficient, that no adequate climax exists. For example, in the main lobby and the side corridors of the RCA Building at Rockefeller Center (Figs. 223, 224), the strongly marked open rhythm of the supporting columns of the building, by which one inevitably passes, creates an expectation of climax which is frustrated; not even the turgid Sert murals can serve as a sufficient satisfaction. This example is instructive in another way; it reveals that sequences through a building may work better in one direction than in another. Here, if one enters on the Sixth Avenue side, the sequence is more satisfactory than it is from the other

FIGURE 220. CATHEDRAL, GLOUCESTER, ENGLAND. VIEW IN THE CLOISTER

Strong, rhythmical sequence emphasis, with the turn at the corner clearly expressed.

Courtesy Avery Library

FIGURE 221. PIAZZA OF ST. PETER'S, ROME. GENERAL VIEW

Lorenzo Bernini, architect

The colonnades furnish a powerful sequence element leading to the church façade.

Courtesy Ware Library

FIGURE 222. PIAZZA OF ST. PETER'S, ROME. DETAIL OF THE COLONNADE

Lorenzo Bernini, architect

The rhythmical march of the ranged columns both suggests and enriches progress through the composition.   Courtesy Ware Library

direction, for the progress is generally from smaller to larger elements and Rockefeller Plaza itself acts as a sort of climax. Yet the main entrance of this building is on Rockefeller Plaza, and the sequence through the building from this direction is inconclusive and frustrating; in a sense, therefore, the building contradicts itself.[1]

[1] Actually, of course, the sequence most apparent to those who have business in the building is not from one entrance to another but from either of the entrances to the elevators. This sequence seems undistinguished, for the elevator lobbies are almost concealed and the approaches to them require turning from the main corridor at points that are not architecturally marked in any way.

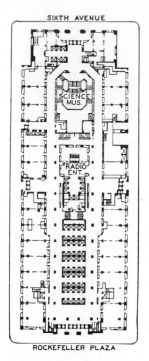

SIXTH AVENUE

SCIENCE MUS.

RADIO ENT.

ROCKEFELLER PLAZA

FIGURE 223. RCA BUILDING, ROCKEFELLER CENTER, NEW YORK. FIRST-FLOOR PLAN

Reinhard & Hofmeister; Corbett, Harrison & MacMurray; and Hood & Fouilhoux, associated architects

Note how the corridors pass on either side of the rows of columns; note also the concealed character and small size of the elevator lobbies. No particular reason is apparent to the visitor for their placing; no architectural emphasis is given them; no architectural indication of their presence is made.

FIGURE 224. RCA BUILDING, ROCKEFELLER CENTER, NEW YORK. VIEW IN LOBBY

Reinhard & Hofmeister; Corbett, Harrison & MacMurray; and Hood & Fouilhoux, associated architects

The columns give rhythmical interest to the sequence.

Courtesy Rockefeller Center, Inc.

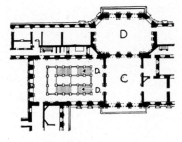

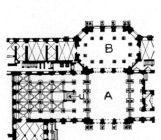

FIGURE 225. RESIDENZ, WÜRZBURG, GERMANY. PART PLAN OF GROUND FLOOR AND OF MAIN FLOOR SHOWING CHIEF ENTRANCE AND STAIRS

De Neumann, Boffrand, and others, architects

One enters a nearly square vestibule, A. Directly ahead is a garden room, B, but the flood of light coming down from the stair hall at the left turns one naturally towards it. Proceeding up the stairs, beneath the famous ceiling by Tiepolo, one arrives at an anteroom, C; from this is entered the throne room, D, almost unbelievably lavish and the climax of the entire sequence.

Changes of level can also produce definite expectations. Here the purely aesthetic consideration is reinforced by the common-sense feeling that the effort required to go up steps must have some definite purpose in view; the greater the rise, the more important must be the climax to make the rise worth while. This idea of a change in level as a preparation for climax has frequently been used, particularly in the Baroque period and in many eclectic buildings of the nineteenth century. As a notable example one may cite the Residenz at Würzburg (Figs. 225–228), where, from a square vestibule, one proceeds up one of the most magnificent flights of stairs in the world to arrive eventually in the great oval throne room or audience hall, the amazing richness of which, together with the interest of its curved lines, makes it an adequate climax, all the more exciting because of the stairway approach. Garnier's Opéra in Paris offers a similar example of a magnificent stair leading to the climax, the great auditorium itself (Fig. 229).

In rare instances, the preparation for the climax may also be achieved by a gradual progress from the large to the small; in such a case, however, there must be a functional reason for the smallness of the climax and, furthermore, a generally increased richness as one progresses through the sequence. This is notably the case in many Egyptian temples (Figs. 231–233), where the climax may be a tiny shrine, to which the entire series of spacious halls and courts is merely an introduction.

FIGURE 226 (LEFT). RESIDENZ, WÜRZ-
BURG, GERMANY. ENTRANCE HALL

De Neumann, Boffrand, and others, architects
See caption of Figure 225.

From Sedlmaier and Pfister, *Die
fürstbischöfliche Residenz zu Würzburg*

FIGURE 227 (RIGHT). RESIDENZ, WÜRZBURG, GERMANY. VIEW IN STAIR HALL

De Neumann, Boffrand, and others, architects

From Sedlmaier and Pfister, *Die fürstbischöfliche Residenz zu Würzburg*

FIGURE 228. RESIDENZ, WÜRZBURG, GERMANY. THRONE ROOM

De Neumann, Boffrand, and others, architects

From Sedlmaier and Pfister. *Die fürstbischöfliche Residenz zu Würzburg*

FIGURE 229. OPÉRA, PARIS. GRAND STAIRS

Charles Garnier, architect

A sequence of level changes grandiloquently expressed.

Courtesy Avery Library

FIGURE 230. FARNESE VILLA, CAPRAROLA, ITALY. STAIRS AND CASCADE

G. B. Vignola, architect

A strong axial sequence embodying a change of level and emphasized by the flanking walls and the central cascade.   Courtesy Ware Library

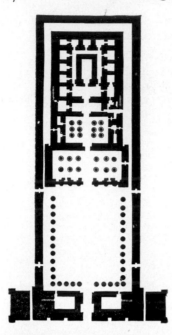

FIGURE 231. TEMPLE, EDFU, EGYPT. PLAN

Here the sequence is from large to small, thus emphasizing the hieratic quality and otherworldliness of the shrine. Only the priests had access to this, yet the whole plan suggested even to the casual visitor the existence of the withdrawn and mysterious Holy of Holies within.

FIGURE 232. TEMPLE, EDFU, EGYPT. FRONT OF HYPOSTYLE HALL AND HOLY OF HOLIES

These two views illustrate the sequence from large to small that characterizes Egyptian temple design.   Courtesy Ware Library

Another dramatic method of preparation may result from the quality of lighting found in each interior space; this quality of light may be one either of intensity or of color. Generally speaking, a brilliantly lighted climax can be prepared for by gradually increasing the amount of light as the climax is ap-

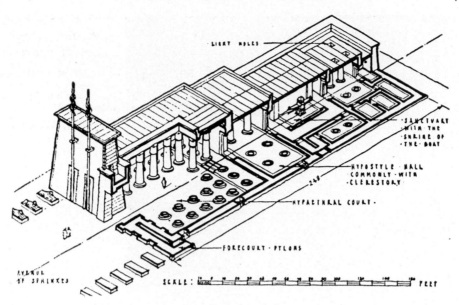

FIGURE 233. TEMPLE OF KHONS, KARNAK, EGYPT. ISOMETRIC SECTIONAL VIEW

Another example of sequence from large to small; in this case, as in most Egyptian temples, also a sequence from high to low.

From Richardson and Corfiato, *The Art of Architecture*

proached. Thus, in the greater number of Gothic cathedrals the design of the chancel is such that one is more conscious of light there than anywhere else; since the windows in the nave are seen only in steep perspective, their apparent width is much reduced, but the choir windows appear with their full breadth in the chancel. Where transepts are important, the flood of light which comes in at the crossing from the hidden transept windows acts as a preparation for the brilliance of the light or color of the chancel itself. The Dome of the Invalides in Paris offers a dramatic effect of climax through the change in the color of the light; here the sudden introduction of glass of a golden-yellow tone at either side of the chancel bathes the altar with a glow that is unforgettable. (See also Figs. 235, 239.)

Certain general principles may be deduced from these considerations. One is that the large prepares for the large, the small for the small. This, however, is subject to many exceptions, for in many superb buildings the importance of the climax of a large room is increased by contrast and by the use of small elements in the preparation for it. Nevertheless there are many cases where the general rule will hold true.

Another related idea was much developed in the eclectic architecture of the

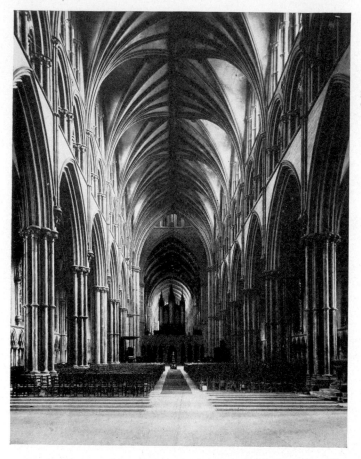

FIGURE 234. CATHE-
DRAL, LINCOLN, ENG-
LAND. INTERIOR

A sequence magnificently
developed   to   suggest
great length and powerful
climax.

Courtesy Ware Library

nineteenth century. This was the rule that large rooms should have thick walls
so that any approach to them would be by doors or openings piercing those
walls with deep reveals. Without a doubt, in many masonry buildings of the
past, the effectiveness of the composition is enhanced by the depth of the
reveals. Without a doubt, also, in masonry construction, the great weights involved in roofing over large halls made thick walls, heavy piers, or deep buttresses inevitable. But today the problems are different, and these old so-called
principles are largely without meaning. Modern methods of construction in
steel and reinforced concrete now enable us to carry weights of almost any desired size on supports relatively tiny, and the walls dividing the spaces in a
skeleton construction are merely screens and can be made as thin as desired; any
application of the old rule thus becomes a patent absurdity.

This is one of the things which make the design of modern structures diffi-

FIGURE 235. CHURCH OF ST. BONIFACE, FRANKFURT AM MAIN, GERMANY. INTERIOR

Martin Weber, architect

Climax to a simple sequence as achieved by the greater height and the brilliant illumination of the chancel.

Courtesy School of Architecture, Columbia University

cult aesthetically. The architect is still confronted with the necessity of producing adequate preparation for a climax. He is still confronted with the fact that, from the visual point of view, the preparation for large elements must somehow involve the impression of largeness. It is therefore a challenge to the architect to see that, despite slim supports, thin screens, and openings without appreciable reveals, this preparation is made. And it is here too, fortunately, that modern materials offer hints of possible solutions. Thus the use of glass screens, with the possibilities they offer of views through and beyond the immediate enclosure, creates an opportunity for completely new types of visual preparation. We cannot accept the conclusion that modern methods of building have necessarily destroyed the opportunities for organized architectural effect, or that architects can tamely and thoughtlessly in their design forget types of aesthetic pleasure which people have demanded for centuries. What we must realize is that modern construction has changed the bases of our solutions but has not destroyed the possibility of new solutions, that it has made new types of visual effect possible, and that a great architect will use these new types in as imaginative, as creative, and as organized a way as the architects of preceding ages used the old.

A caution is desirable here—the fact that there are various types of purely practical building in which the existence of climax would be illogical, as, for instance, in a warehouse made up of a great number of small storage rooms of equal importance. There are other types in which the existence of a climax might prove an actual disadvantage, because people would be inclined to stop for at least a moment where a climax occurred, whereas the whole purpose of the building might be to assist the public to rapid progress through it. In such a building, for example, as a subway station, where the aim of the design should be the most continuous, the most direct, and the most rapid circulation, the existence of any striking climax or any element which would tend to retard circulation would be both unnatural and inefficient. In that case it is clearly the architect's duty to seek for complete continuity and to avoid anything which could build up a demand for a climax. Similarly, a market hall divided into a great many little booths might require no climax but simply some kind of convenient and regular arrangement. Yet, in actual fact, there is in all people a tendency to develop or to impose the climax sensation on almost any experience of life, even in the experience of marketing; such a purely accidental climax might be, for instance, the bright color of fruit and flower stands against the quieter colors of the vegetables. Generally speaking, one may say that in the greater number of buildings some kind of climax, either muted or stressed, is desirable. Even in such a purely utilitarian structure as a factory, climax is imaginable; there could be a careful and organized sequence from the entrance through locker rooms and service areas into the machine room itself, where the greater volume, the brighter light, and the interest in the form—and perhaps in the color—of the machines would produce a satisfactory and enjoyable climax.

Sequence planning naturally has developed along two different lines, which have given rise to two great classes or methods of organization. These are generally termed the formal and the informal types of planning and are closely related to the problems of formal and informal balance mentioned in Chapter 3.

The first of these, formal sequence planning, depends in general on a progress through spaces which are themselves in formal balance. But formal sequence planning entails other considerations also. It entails the most careful and conscious preparation for the climax. Frequently it is based on straight-line progress through a plan, so that all the important elements will lie on the main axis and the relationships of all new experiences along that axis are consciously organized with a definite end in view. Generally speaking, too, formal plans will minimize curves in major plan elements, unless these curves are symmetrically balanced or are of dominantly large size, as, for instance, in the Roman Pantheon and in some domed churches (see Figs. 187, 208, 231, 236, 248).

The second great class of sequence planning is the informal or romantic type (Figs. 267–279). Plans of this kind are often based on curved progressions and involve experiences balanced freely instead of symmetrically. Equally important is the fact that in informal planning the preparation for the climax is more subtle, less conscious. The informal planner seeks for the quality of dramatic surprise—the sudden emergence from dark into light, or from small into large. He knows that the element of surprise adds frequently to the emotional intensity of any experience. He may feel, also, that a too conscious preparation for climax in his building is stilted and impersonal. But what he often forgets is the fact that surprise can be shocking, disturbing, and unpleasant instead of exciting and delightful. In many romantic public buildings erected in the last quarter of the nineteenth century, the lack of conscious preparation for important functions or climax elements produces such incoherence that the feeling of pleasure in any surprise one may have is deflated at the outset. The minute the observer questions the position or the rationality of some building element, pleasure in surprise becomes impossible. For this reason, preparation of some kind, however subtle, is necessary even in the most informal plans, and the great architects of informal buildings have always realized this and known how to obtain it. It is this quality of subtle preparation which has characterized much of the best house design of recent years.

8

Formal and Informal Sequence Design

FORMAL AND INFORMAL sequences produce completely different effects and are therefore appropriate to different types of edifice. The impression produced by the formal sequence is one of dignity, of directness, and of definite and stressed climax. It arouses necessarily a sense of the impressive. The element of conscious design is always obvious; there is little opportunity in the formal sequence for accidental and unexpected charm. Thus formal sequences are emotionally appropriate only in those instances where the emotional effects they produce are appropriate. Generally speaking, they seem best suited for large, imposing buildings constructed for use by associations, clubs, religious bodies, governments, or large crowds of people; in such buildings the directness of approach which formal planning produces is an aid to the functioning of the structure. It seems, therefore, in many cases, the logical choice for theaters, auditoriums, and churches, as well as for large railroad stations and many government buildings.

Informal sequences, on the other hand, are full of the sense of dynamic and varied motion; they may have units which yield an element of surprise and lead to effects of apparently unpremeditated charm; thus they are naturally more personal in effect than are formal sequences. There is in them, usually, nothing of the awe-inspiring feeling that sometimes accompanies formal planning; they seem natural and, as it were, human. They are therefore more fitting for houses, clubs, informal community buildings, and the like.

But there are other considerations besides the type of effect which each kind of sequence produces. There is the problem of mere size, for instance. In many important structures the architect must give an organized pattern to a large composition of great complexity. It is much easier to preserve a sense of coherence and of definiteness in an arrangement basically formal. Too many items of the accidentally charming type become cloying, and too many changes of

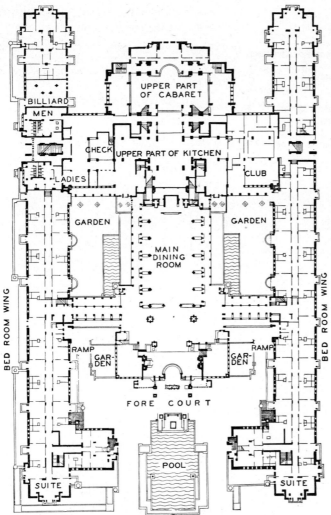

FIGURE 236. IMPERIAL HOTEL, TOKYO. MAIN-FLOOR PLAN

Frank Lloyd Wright, architect

A building embodying formal sequences of the greatest interest: pool, forecourt, hall, main dining room on the main axis; the sequence from hall through the side porticos to the bedroom wings is likewise beautifully handled. There are also many superb visual sequences in and around the building, where views over water, garden, ramp, and railing, or through open porches, or under covered ways all reveal careful composition, with sequences, rather than individual items, stressed.

direction only confuse; accordingly, it is much more difficult to keep informality under control and to avoid confusion in a large informal group than in one of the same size which is handled with formal or carefully organized sequences. It is noteworthy, for instance, that Frank Lloyd Wright in the Imperial Hotel in Tokyo (Fig. 236) developed an essentially formal plan with formally organized sequences of great richness; on this strong framework all the detailed complexities of the large building take definite and easily understandable positions.

The Romans well understood this difference. In designs such as the great

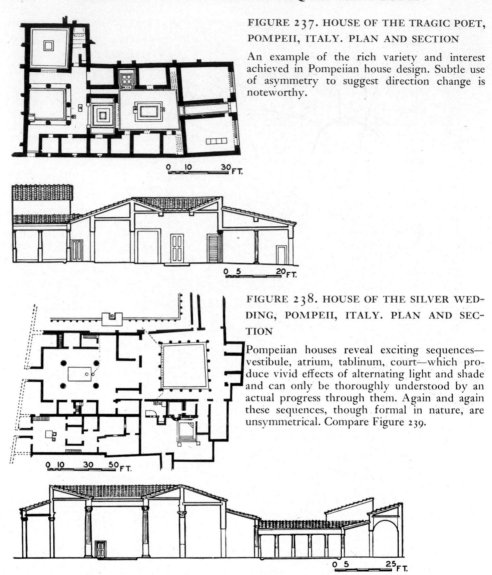

FIGURE 237. HOUSE OF THE TRAGIC POET, POMPEII, ITALY. PLAN AND SECTION

An example of the rich variety and interest achieved in Pompeiian house design. Subtle use of asymmetry to suggest direction change is noteworthy.

FIGURE 238. HOUSE OF THE SILVER WEDDING, POMPEII, ITALY. PLAN AND SECTION

Pompeiian houses reveal exciting sequences—vestibule, atrium, tablinum, court—which produce vivid effects of alternating light and shade and can only be thoroughly understood by an actual progress through them. Again and again these sequences, though formal in nature, are unsymmetrical. Compare Figure 239.

public baths they sought for monumental balance and formal sequences of powerful visual effect based on strongly marked axes, but when they came to small or middle-sized houses, either in the city or the country, they seem to have preferred sequences of a much more informal and indirect type. Practically all the Roman villas and practically all the houses of Herculaneum, Ostia, and Pompeii are laid out with carefully designed sequences of the changing and informal type. They often approach symmetry—evidently the Roman architects felt strongly the need for general balance—but in the details, in the general

FIGURE 239. HOUSE OF THE SILVER WEDDING, POMPEII, ITALY. VIEW FROM ATRIUM

An excellent example of light-dark sequence distinguished by subtle axial development combined with a delicate freedom.

Photograph Ernest Nash

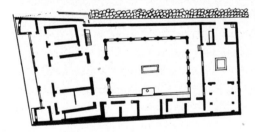

FIGURE 240. HOUSE OF THE MOSAIC ATRIUM, HERCULANEUM, ITALY. PLAN

A Roman house with a sequence even more subtle and rich than in most Pompeiian houses. From street entrance to atrium, with a superb and monumental tablinum as climax; from atrium, at right angles, into the large gardened court, with its splendid recessed exedra at one side; from court through a large triclinium with wide doors and a dramatic window, and finally to the portico and terrace, once overlooking the Bay of Naples —this all forms a whole of extraordinary visual richness.

views through a plan, and in the sequence pattern subtly changing axes and studied informalities frequently occur. Le Corbusier's analysis of Pompeiian houses in *Towards a New Architecture* is most enlightening in this respect. Thus the Romans appear to have been sensitive to the difference between the balanced formality they felt appropriate in many of their larger structures and

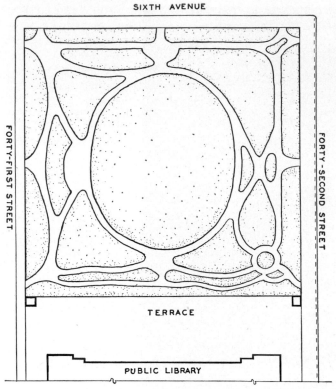

SIXTH AVENUE

FORTY-FIRST STREET

FORTY-SECOND STREET

TERRACE

PUBLIC LIBRARY

FIGURE 241. BRYANT PARK, NEW YORK. EARLY PLAN

This plan shows the informal combination of winding walk and lawn that characterized the park in its earlier decades. With growing congestion, it became impossible to maintain.

the intimate scale and informal sequences they desired in the private portions of their houses and in house design generally (Figs. 237–240).

There are also functional reasons which underlie the choice of formality or informality in sequence design. If, for instance, one is designing a building with one large element, and if a central entrance to that element is the most efficient scheme, a formal approach seems almost inevitable. The same would be true in a composition of three elements of almost equal importance which are to be entered from the same general area. Unless other extraneous conditions enter in, formality becomes the natural answer to many problems of this general nature.

Another functional control lies in the number of people who may be expected to use an area or a structure. The greater the number, the more important it is that the circulation shall be direct and untrammeled. This will naturally mean an axis as straight and direct as possible (for the axis is merely an abstraction of the natural line of progress), and this axis itself will often develop sequences of an essentially formal nature. We have already noted that people tend to walk toward a center of balance; if we wish them to walk in a straight line, naturally we develop a balanced formality.

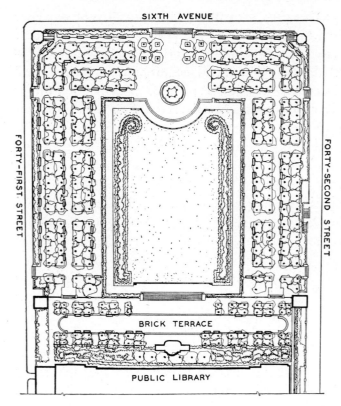

SIXTH AVENUE

FORTY-FIRST STREET

FORTY-SECOND STREET

BRICK TERRACE

PUBLIC LIBRARY

FIGURE 242. BRYANT PARK, NEW YORK. PLAN IN 1948

The new, formal plan, by sinking the lawn and bordering it with balustrades, discourages use of the park as a mere passageway; the massed benches along the formal walks, well shaded by the close-spaced plane trees, furnish ample seating accommodation. Paths are planned to serve the park alone. Because of this careful, formal arrangement, the whole is not only visually most effective but also easy to maintain.

Courtesy of the New York City Parks Department

The problem of human congestion has other effects on this question of formality versus informality in planning. An instructive example is furnished by Bryant Park in New York City. This is not only one of the most used and congested of city parks, because of its location in the middle of a shopping and office district, but it is also one of the best maintained and one of the easiest to maintain because of its strictly formal nature. Bryant Park had originally been designed with the informality usual in the park design of the period when it was first laid out, with winding walks, lawns with curved edges, and scattered trees and bushes (Fig. 241). As the district grew more crowded, this informality made the park impossible to maintain. People walked straight lines from gate to gate and cut across curves, until the lawns became bare, beaten earth and the shrubbery merely pathetic groups of broken trunks and branches. It was only by carefully canalizing the crowds of people along straight walks and by concentrating seating areas under ranked trees, as the new design has done, that it became possible to control the crowds and produce a park that will retain its beauty (Figs. 242, 626). As a general rule, therefore, the more congestion there is, the more necessary a formal arrangement becomes.

In order, then, to decide between formality and informality of sequence planning in any given problem, we must, as far as possible, clear our mind of any *a priori* decision and attempt to find indications for the answer in the conditions of the program itself. In the mid-twentieth century general architectural taste prefers the informal to the formal, just as architects a generation earlier strove for formality wherever they could achieve it. Accordingly, we must bear in mind with particular care the fact that forced and unnatural informality is just as great an architectural error, just as much an offense against logic and common sense, as was the forced and unnatural formality which we so severely criticize in nineteenth-century buildings. If we follow the program logically, sympathetically, and naturally, bearing in mind use and appropriateness, we can never go far wrong in our decisions.

Formal Sequences. It has already been said that the basis of formal sequence planning lies in formal balance and in the conscious and often elaborate preparation for the climax of the composition. It is necessary here to go more deeply into the implications of these ideas. First of all, one must remember that the architect, by his planning, controls the rate of progress which the ordinary observer will make through a building. Look at a person visiting a structure for the first time. You will see that in some parts he will hurry, in other places he will check his speed and look around, and in still others he may stop entirely for a longer or shorter time in order to appreciate and enjoy what he sees. Longer observation will show that, in this respect, most people will act in a similar fashion. They will hurry at the same places, they will slow down at the same places, they will stop at the same places. The hurry and the stop, therefore, are not mere accidents; they occur because of the visual experiences the building offers. If this is so, it follows that there are not only some types of sequence arrangement which suggest, and even seem to compel, motion but also others which just as strongly suggest or compel a cessation of motion. The architect, by the correct arrangement of building elements in the plan, can therefore plan buildings or portions of buildings which literally hurry the observer through them, and he can also arrange places in which the motion sense is definitely checked.

In general, an open architectural rhythm, either progressive or regular, suggests motion; a visitor seeks unconsciously to arrive at its finish. Similarly, wherever the summation of visual interest increases suddenly by the interruption of the rhythm or by the introduction of richer, larger, or contrasting elements, an equilibrium of attention, as it were, is established, and the visitor's speed is instinctively reduced. If this equilibrium of interest is produced by

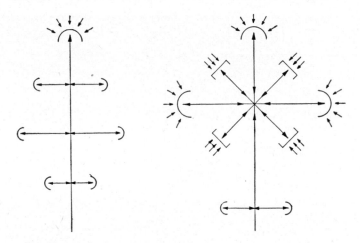

FIGURE 243. CLIMAX TYPES IN DIAGRAM

LEFT: Minor sequences balanced on either side of a major sequence, which leads to a climax at the end. This is the type of sequence characteristic of basilican churches. RIGHT: A sequence with the most powerful formal climax possible. There is a small secondary sequence balanced across the main sequence at the front. This is the type of composition characteristic of many domed churches and of public buildings with a central distribution rotunda.

some strong element directly on the line of progress and closing the progression—stopping the axis—then the person will inevitably come to rest, as does a piece of iron placed between four equally spaced magnets at right angles to each other (Fig. 243, right). In the diagram shown, the various elements of interest may be of any type—large and important doorways or openings, altars in a domical church, mural paintings—but whatever their nature, if they arouse sufficient interest because of their shape and color, the observer's attention will tend to be held equally on all sides, and he will stop to observe in more detail.

If these interest elements, however, exist only at the sides (Fig. 243, left), the effect will be a reduction in the speed of the progress but not a total stop. The observer will first be checked in his rate of progress, his attention called first to one side and then the other; he will then, seeing the repetition of the progression beyond, continue on. These side elements, like those in Figure 243, left, may be of any type; frequently they are themselves minor sequences, and the check in the visitor's speed serves not only to break the monotony of the building but also to give him the moment which he requires to decide whether he shall turn to left or right, into one of the minor elements, or proceed straight ahead. Thus they are minor distribution points in the plan and have a functional as well as an aesthetic significance.

From all this we may conclude that a climax of some type will be developed

FIGURE 244. SAN APOLLINARE NUOVO, RAVENNA, ITALY. INTERIOR
The simple formal sequence of the typical basilican church.   Courtesy Ware Library

wherever interests are balanced across a main axis or a line of progression and
that a major climax is produced where the balancing of interests achieves a
complete equilibrium. Such climaxes, both major and minor, must always be
sufficiently rich, interesting, or even visually exciting so that the observer will
not feel that the time lost has been wasted. For the moment the feeling of waste
arises in his mind it will be accompanied by a sense of frustration, and this frustration will defeat any attempt on the part of the architect to arouse a sense
of beauty. It follows, therefore, that the good plan will not only establish definitely the position of climaxes but also provide climaxes of the correct relative
importance.

Any number of examples may be cited, varying from the simplest to the
most complex arrangements. Such an Early Christian basilica as San Apollinare
in Classe at Ravenna (Figs. 82, 83, also 244) illustrates perfectly the simplest
form. The pier arches on either side of the nave, together with the columns

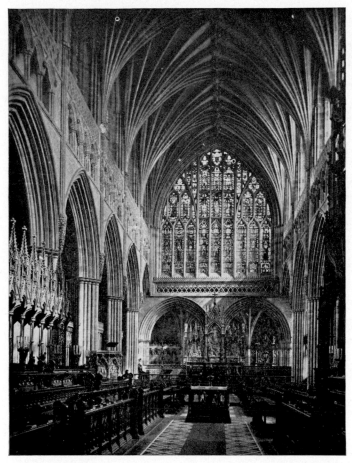

FIGURE 245. CATHE-
DRAL, EXETER, ENG-
LAND. INTERIOR

Gothic development of
formal sequence with rich
climax.

Courtesy Ware Library

supporting them, form an open rhythm of simple power which leads inevitably
onward; the climax, of course, is the altar, and the triumphal arch and half dome
of the apse not only frame the altar perfectly but also serve to form a tie between the arcades and the climax. In any Romanesque or Gothic church that
has groined or ribbed vaults, the repeated lines or changes in the light and shade
of the vault form a strong open rhythm above, which parallels the rhythm of
the pier arches below and, as in the case of the Early Christian basilica, leads
one inevitably toward the climax formed by the chancel. Undoubtedly one of
the reasons for the development of the richness of the Gothic church interior,
with its pier arches, triforium, and clerestory, its vaulting shafts and vault ribs,
was the desire to enrich as much as possible the nave sequence in order to make
the preparation for the climax the stronger. In a somewhat similar way the

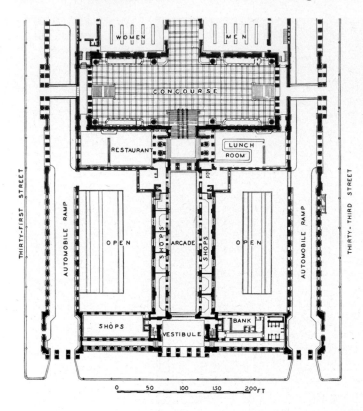

FIGURE 246. PENN-
SYLVANIA STATION,
NEW YORK. PART
PLAN OF MAIN FLOOR

McKim, Mead & White,
architects

The sequence from Sev-
enth Avenue to the con-
course illustrates alternation of shape and direc-
tion, continuous rhythms
as a directional element in
the arcade, a minor stop
and climax between res-
taurant and lunch room,
and a powerful major cli-
max at the concourse.
There is also a strong sequence through this cli-
max to the train con-
course and the trains.

Redrawn from *A Mono-
graph of the Work of
McKim, Mead & White*

simple arcades of the court of the Collegio di Sapienza in Rome act as a strong
preparation for the complex curves and the exciting outline of Borromini's
chapel, which forms the climax (Fig. 186).

Much more elaborate systems of formal sequence are also commonly used;
in general, they are formed by a series of minor sequences balanced across the
main axis and leading to a major climax. These minor sequences, which create
minor climax points, increase the feeling of anticipation or suspense on the part
of the observer; accordingly, the preparation for the final climax must itself
be strong enough to satisfy this increased expectation. One may therefore say
that the greater the number of minor climaxes, in an architectural sequence, the
more powerful is the sense of preparation and the stronger must the final climax
appear. This is well illustrated in the Seventh Avenue approach of the Pennsylvania Station in New York (Fig. 246), where the climax—the main concourse
—is approached through a portico, a vestibule, an arcade, another vestibule,
and finally a broad flight of steps. The great size and increased height of the
concourse form a sufficient climax to this rich sequence. In fact, one of the

FIGURE 247. PENNSYLVANIA STATION, NEW YORK. MAIN CONCOURSE

McKim, Mead & White, architects

The formal climax of a strongly axial formal sequence.

From *A Monograph of the Work of McKim, Mead & White*

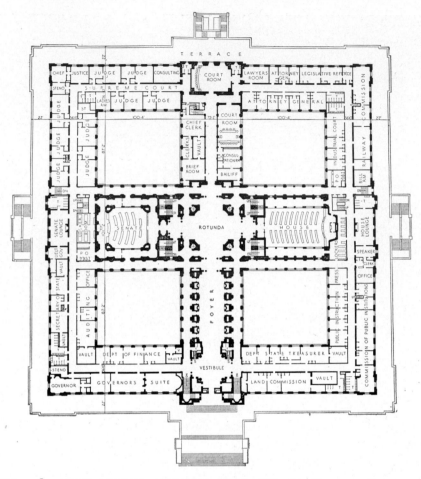

FIGURE 248. STATE CAPITOL, LINCOLN, NEBRASKA. PLAN

B. G. Goodhue, architect

A plan distinguished by the most carefully composed formal sequences. Relations of major and minor sequences are skillfully adjusted, and the sizes and shapes of all elements, the widths and heights of openings, and the richness of form are all designed in close accordance with their circulation function.   From the *American Architect*

reasons for its impressiveness lies in that strong preparation. The same is true of the main floor of the Nebraska State Capitol (Fig. 248). Here, since the first domical vestibule leads on either side to important offices, this element is given considerable size and richness and creates a minor climax of some power. From there one proceeds into the vaulted entrance hall, with its strong, open rhythms, and from this, in turn, through a series of arches and cross passages into the great rotunda. Many large theaters and opera houses have sequences

FIGURE 249 (ABOVE, LEFT). STATE CAP-
ITOL, LINCOLN, NEBRASKA. VESTIBULE

B. G. Goodhue, architect

See caption of Figure 248.

Photograph Gottscho-Schleisner

FIGURE 250 (ABOVE, RIGHT). STATE
CAPITOL, LINCOLN, NEBRASKA. EN-
TRANCE CORRIDOR

B. G. Goodhue, architect

Photograph Gottscho-Schleisner

FIGURE 251 (BELOW, LEFT). STATE
CAPITOL, LINCOLN, NEBRASKA. RO-
TUNDA

B. G. Goodhue, architect

Photograph J. B. Franco

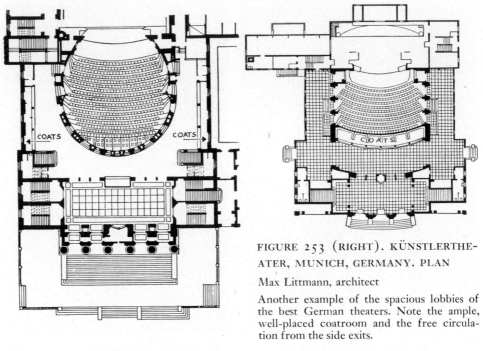

FIGURE 253 (RIGHT). KÜNSTLERTHE-
ATER, MUNICH, GERMANY. PLAN

Max Littmann, architect

Another example of the spacious lobbies of
the best German theaters. Note the ample,
well-placed coatroom and the free circulation from the side exits.

FIGURE 252 (LEFT). STADTTHEATER, POSEN, POLAND. PLAN

The ample lobbies, characteristic of Euorpean theaters, create interesting and meaningful sequences from the entrances through the lobbies to the auditorium.

of a similar type (Figs. 252, 253). It is an almost universal fault of theater planning in the United States that the circulation sequences are unplanned and ineffective; the result is as functionally disastrous as it is architecturally stupid,
for confusion and delay are the almost inevitable results.

There are many formal sequences which are based on one or more right-angle
turns in direction. These bring up the problem of ways in which the direction
of motion through a plan can be altered. This has already been referred to in
Chapter 3 on balance. The most important method is to block the axis of the
original direction by some minor climax and to indicate the directional change
by using a different treatment for the two sides of the sequence at the point of
change (Fig. 254). It is well to remember that wherever the direction is changed
an enlargement of a sequence is logical, as is the existence of a minor climax at
this point, for people generally walk more slowly when they are turning a
corner.

But there are many other ways of indicating a directional change. One is
by the frank use of a curved wall (Figs. 87, 88, 254); this allows no doubt in

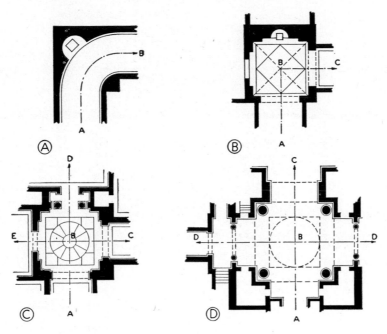

FIGURE 254. CHANGE OF DIRECTION, FORMAL

ABOVE, LEFT: The simplest possible scheme. The niche, with its statue or other accent, closes the view from either A or B and, combined with the curved walls, gives positive notice of the change of direction from A to B. ABOVE, RIGHT: A more complex problem, with corridor direction changed, ABC, and with an unimportant room opening from the intersection.
BELOW, LEFT: An expression of a still more complicated condition. Its design informs anyone approaching from A that at B he must choose whether to follow the side corridor, C, or to enter either of the rooms, D or E. The elaboration of the opening into D states that this is the most important of the elements C, D, and E and is the direction to follow in normal cases. BELOW, RIGHT: Plan based on the entrance to the Nebraska State Capitol. The entrance is at A. The domed rotunda, B, creates a natural stopping, or choice, point. The corridors, D, lead to important public offices and are given an important expression, but the width of the arch leading to C, as well as its position directly opposite the entrance, establishes C—the public entrance to the two legislative chambers—as the dominant direction.

the observer's mind that a change is coming. It is the swiftest kind of warning and, as such, is suitable where crowds have to be handled in the shortest possible time, as, for instance, in the exit stairs of theaters. In many cases, direction change in larger elements can be controlled by a judicious placing of the openings in the enclosing wall. Thus in a hall or court, if the wall opposite a visitor, as he enters, has no opening—or only minor openings at such unimportant points as the corners—and if the wall at one side has an important axial opening, the ordinary person will invariably use the important axial opening at the side.

Such a plan as that of the Baths of Diocletian in Rome is full of suggestions

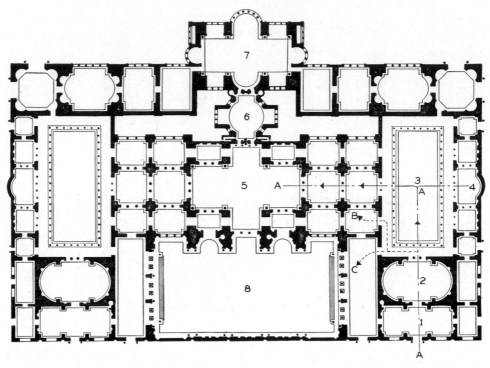

FIGURE 255. CENTRAL PORTION, BATHS OF DIOCLETIAN, ROME. PLAN

(1) Entrance; (2) Dressing room; (3) Exercising court; (4) Court exedra; (5) Tepidarium or central lounge; (6) and (7) Hot and steam baths; (8) Swimming pool.

The chief entrance A-A, shown in dash-and-dot lines, follows the stresses set up in the plan and achieves magnificent sequence effects. The dotted lines, A-B and A-C, show other less important and less used routes, which permit free circulation but are less emphasized architecturally.

in this respect. Study reveals that in every case the doorways on the axes are important and indicate the normal progress from the dressing area to the central hall, whereas doors off the axis are unimportant; in that way the freest possible circulation is furnished. One can hurry from part to part by the shortest lines if necessary, but the chief and most important circulation (which is not the shortest) is subtly stressed throughout (Fig. 255). Many Baroque plans have a similar type of circulation pattern, although in most cases a change of level is also part of the major sequence. In the Residenz at Würzburg already mentioned (Figs. 225–228), for instance, one enters a square vestibule and on the left finds openings to the great stair. The vestibule is fairly dark; the stairway is flooded with light, and there is consequently no doubt of the direction intended. One proceeds up the main stair and arrives in a great, square antechamber. Here the large size of the door indicates the correct turn into the

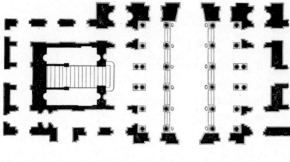

FIGURE 256. VESTIBULE, MINT, PARIS. PLAN AND TWO SECTIONS

J. D. Antoine, architect

The forms themselves are such as to suggest and to accent the approach to the important rooms of the upper floor, as well as the passage through to the court. The recessing of the stairs gives them strong emphasis. The position of the entrances from the arcade to the ground floor indicates that the ground floor is secondary to the floor above.

Redrawn from Guadet, *Éléments et théorie . . .*

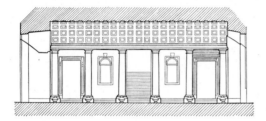

gorgeous finale, the throne-room climax, which is given even greater importance by its curved plan. The porte cochère entrance to the Mint at Paris (Fig. 256) also illustrates how directional changes can be indicated. Naturally the directional quality of the entrance vault is strong, yet the main entrance to the building is at right angles to this, and to create a correct sequence pattern required meticulous care. It is brilliantly achieved here by the careful arrangement of the supports. Because of the recess at the foot of the stairs and the size of the openings, no one could fail to receive the suggestion that he is supposed to turn to the left and proceed up the monumental stairway to the important rooms above. One of the most interesting of complex sequence patterns which incorporates a level change is that of the Hôtel de Ville in Paris (Figs. 257, 258). Here the approach to the Salle des Fêtes is by means of a great vaulted porte cochère. The broad supports of the vault give a natural transverse feeling and thus assist one's entrance into the long cloakroom or checkroom (the Salle St. Jean). From one side of this space, axial elements lead into a square hall with

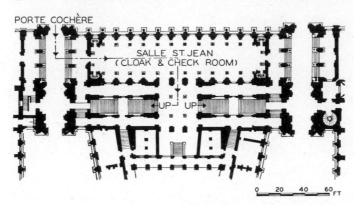

FIGURE 257. HÔTEL
DE VILLE, PARIS. PART
GROUND-FLOOR PLAN

Ballu and Deperthes,
architects

The dot-and-dash line in-
dicates the normal ap-
proach from the portes
cochères to the Salle
des Fêtes above, passing
through the check room
(Salle St. Jean). The
shape of the piers in the
portes cochères suggests a
turning into the Salle St. Jean; here the wider central openings invite the visitor to pass on to
the stair.   Redrawn from Guadet, *Éléments et théorie* . .

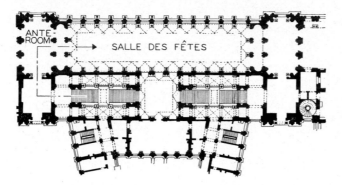

FIGURE 258. HÔTEL DE
VILLE, PARIS. PART PLAN
OF MAIN FLOOR

Ballu and Deperthes,
architects

The visitor, climbing the
great stair, arrives in a series
of vestibules and anterooms
which by their shape and design invite progress through
them and lead at last into the
vast and lavish Salle des
Fêtes. This long preparation,
this progress through space after space of growing richness—made easy by ample size and careful
planning—is one reason for the extraordinary power of the climax of the Salle des Fêtes itself.
To have approached it directly, without preparation, or to have arrived at it only after passage
through meaningless and ill-designed vestibules would have deprived it of much of its effect.
Note, too, the balconies overlooking the stairs, from which early comers may observe those
arriving later. The whole is an elaborate and marvelously successful "machine" for accomplishing
its purpose—the holding of great state receptions or other social functions of an official character.

Redrawn from Guadet, *Éléments et théorie* . . .

majestic flights of steps sweeping up on either side, which, in turn, lead to a
double anteroom at either end of the great Salle des Fêtes. These chambers build
up a most interesting crescendo effect with their continually growing richness,
until the main hall, with its lavish architecture and brilliant murals, is reached.
Off this is another square hall, similar in feeling, where groups may collect and
talk, gaze down at the guests arriving, and yet be out of the major crush. It is
an ingenious arrangement, and for its particular purpose—the handling of the
multitudes at official functions—it works well. Aesthetically it has a compelling
power; the sequence is one of great variety—of alternations of wide and nar-

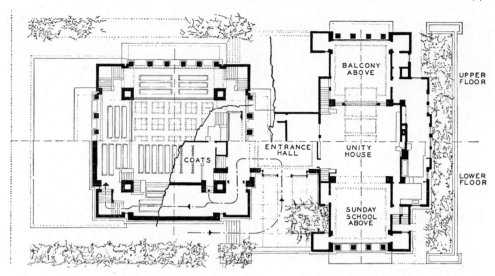

FIGURE 259. UNITY TEMPLE, OAK PARK, ILLINOIS. PLAN

Frank Lloyd Wright, architect

Another example of Wright's power as a designer of rich and meaningful sequences. Approach to the church is through the entrance hall, where the pastor greets the congregation, then through passages and stair halls that prepare one for the climax of the auditorium. The entrance hall also serves as the connecting link between the church proper and its social annex, the parish house.

row, of big and little, and of high and low—but with a basic crescendo which acts as a superb preparation for the final climax, the great reception hall.

A simpler, though brilliant, and more recent example of effective sequence based on direction change as well as on a change of levels can be seen in Unity Temple at Oak Park, Illinois, designed by Frank Lloyd Wright (Figs. 259, 260). Here the main entrance to the church is through an interesting and generally square reception room, which also serves as an entrance to the parish house behind and furnishes a most usable gathering place before and after church services. From this, one proceeds down a few steps to cloakrooms under the gallery, then up to the church gallery or to the church floor. Here again the preparation for the climax is excellently handled and there is a beautiful alternation of the dim and the brilliant, the large and the small.

At certain periods in the history of architecture, and in certain countries, architects have not been satisfied with sequences of the pure crescendo type or with climaxes which seem to be too definitely enclosing. They have preferred a progress through and beyond the climax—a progress of the generally diminuendo type—and, even when actual physical progress was cut off by the

FIGURE 260. UNITY TEMPLE, OAK PARK, ILLINOIS. EXTERIOR AND INTERIOR
Frank Lloyd Wright, architect
A brilliant sequence connects exterior and interior. Compare Figure 259.

Courtesy Museum of Modern Art

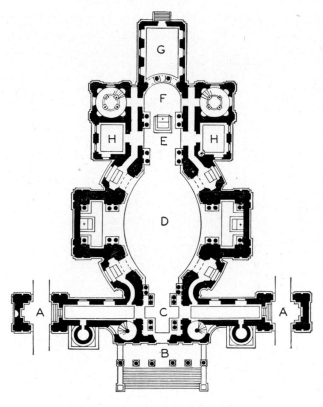

FIGURE 261. KARLSKIRCHE,
VIENNA. PLAN

Johann B. Fischer von Erlach,
architect

A plan distinctive through its
use of implied sequence beyond
the climax altar, E, because of
the views possible into the apse,
F, and the sacristy, G. Like many
Austrian Baroque plans, it has
superb entrance sequences, both
from the portico, B, and the
portes cochères, A. Note too the
minor passages creating other
sequences from the chapels to
the service rooms, H. C is the
narthex and D the oval domed
nave, the climax of the whole.

climax, they have frequently liked to suggest the existence of spaces beyond.
This is true of such a church as Il Redentore in Venice, by Palladio (Figs. 208,
209), where behind the altar is an open choir screen of columns, through which
the simpler and lower vault of the sacristy beyond can be seen. The Karlskirche in Vienna, by Fischer von Erlach (Figs. 210, 261), shows a somewhat
similar treatment, for behind and beyond the explosive brilliance of the reredos
one is conscious of rich, lavish spaces.

Many Chinese plans carry this idea even further. Again and again the Chinese will develop minor climaxes which block a main axis and then will furnish
passage around the climax on either side and back to the main axis again, where
a new and more important climax is seen. In the typical Chinese temple, the
major climax is often approached in this manner through two or even three
courts, and beyond it will be other courts similarly arranged but less important.
The visual experience created by an arrangement of this kind is extremely rich
and varied, though formal and orderly to the last degree. From a distance one
is conscious of the great roofs rising, one behind the other, along the main axis.

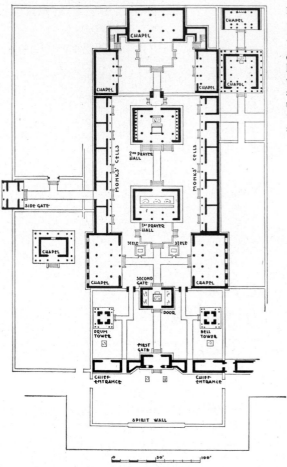

FIGURE 262. BO LIN SSÜ TEMPLE, WESTERN HILLS, PEIPING. PLAN

This plan illustrates the Chinese system of placing gates and halls with their long dimensions across a main axis, as well as the usual Chinese avoidance of any long-continued progress along that axis; periodically the observer or worshiper has to leave it to pass around axial altars or axial buildings.

Drawn by E. P. McMullin, Jr., from T. Hamlin, *Architecture through the Ages*

On approaching he finds the way barred by a rich "spirit wall," around the ends of which he has to pass. The main gate to the building also is often blocked on the main axis; one enters in the middle but passes out on one side or the other. Each of the great halls has a wide central altar, rich with sculpture, votive offerings, and ritual furniture; the observer or the worshiper, after enjoying this climax, can pass by and around the side and into another court behind, where the experience may again be repeated, although on a different scale of size and importance (Figs. 262, 263).

It will thus be seen that formal sequence planning is a matter requiring the most brilliant imagination, yet the greatest discipline, and an ability to discriminate between the more important and the less important, both functionally and aesthetically. Always one must bear in mind that in true formal sequence

FIGURE 263. SUMMER PALACE, NEAR PEIPING. VIEW OVER THE AXIS

The powerful formality of monumental Chinese planning.

From Imperial Museum, Tokyo, *Photographs of Palace Buildings of Peking*

planning the axis is not a line on paper; it is the way in which people naturally walk and an indication of the direction in which they naturally look.

It may be well here to list a few of the general types of sequence which have proved of architectural importance:

Sequences of open spaces, as in Roman forums and Chinese temple courts.

Sequences of structural elements, such as the columns of an Early Christian basilica, the piers of a Gothic cathedral, or the ribs and groins of a vault.

Sequences of enclosures, such as a simple series of rooms.

Sequences of level change, such as important ramps or stairs, and in addition, outdoors, the use of banks, terrace walls, etc., as in typical Italian gardens.

Sequences of light and dark, as, for instance, in the Residenz in Würzburg.

Sequences with alternations of direction or of size.

Sequences in which minor sequences leading to minor climaxes are balanced on the chief and most important sequence.

Sequences of growing degrees of complexity or richness.

FIGURE 264. ROMANESQUE CHURCH, CORNETO TARQUINIA, ITALY. NAVE

A simple example of the rhythmical sequence of structural elements.

Courtesy Ware Library

In a study of sequence planning one must always keep in mind the double purpose of organized sequence design—the desire to produce a building which will take the visitor where he wishes to go, and the necessity of building up preparation for the climax.

Informal Sequences. Informal sequence planning is based on two concepts. The first is the idea of surprise; the second is the use of curved or bent axes and of informal visual balance. We have seen above how, in formal sequences, the preparation for the climax is made in the most definite and conscious way. In informal sequences, the architect frequently seeks to make his climax a sudden and dramatic surprise. This does not mean that he avoids preparation entirely or that he consciously attempts to give no hint, in what comes before, of the shapes and the type of climax. In fact, a surprise entirely without preparation of any kind may be for the observer a distinct shock; if, moreover, the visual quality of the climax is totally different from that of the rest of the building, the result will be not only a shock but an unpleasant one and will give rise only to a feeling of incoherence and confusion.

What informal sequence planning does aim for is to keep visual preparation to a minimum and to make it subtle rather than obvious. We may take for an example the church of Santa Sophia in Istanbul. This, although based on a fundamentally symmetrical plan, has a climax effect that is a dramatic surprise and

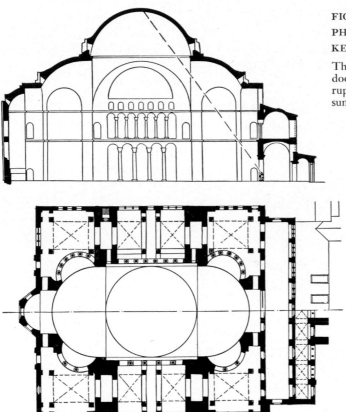

FIGURE 265. SANTA SO-
PHIA, ISTANBUL, TUR-
KEY. PLAN AND SECTION

The moment one enters the
door, he obtains an uninterrupted view direct to the
summit of the dome.

hence illustrates one of the main qualities of successful informal sequence planning. When one approaches the church from the front, the dome, though
large, is accepted merely as a simple device for completing the exterior composition and roofing over the interior. The entrance narthex is relatively modest
in size; consequently, when a visitor passes through the door between it and
the body of the church, the extraordinary height and width of the interior
breaks upon him as a most dramatic experience. From the door, his eye can
take in the entire spread of the area and can follow the arches and vaults straight
up to the summit of the dome (Fig. 265). The effect is totally different from
that produced by the long vaults and the ranges of piers of most Western
churches, as well as from the gradual building up of the sense of size which
characterizes the great plans of ancient Rome and of the Baroque period. It is
this drama of sudden revelation which the informal planner is seeking.

Yet it is to be noticed that preparation does exist in this case. The interior

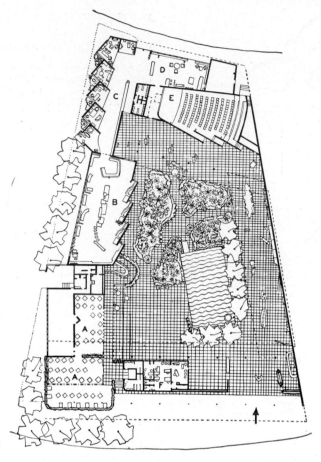

FIGURE 266. SWEDISH BUILDING, NEW YORK WORLD'S FAIR OF 1939. PLAN

Sven Markelius, architect

An informal plan of the greatest beauty. The sequences from the public entrances, beneath the shelter, and by the pool and garden to the auditorium, E, the exhibition halls, B, C, D, and the restaurant, A, are natural and produce successive views of great interest. Informality is here combined with a sure sense of coherence and order. F indicates the administration offices.

dome is expressed on the outside. All the arched forms of the exterior are paralleled by similar forms within, and the marble and mosaic of the narthex are harmonious in material with the similar but much richer treatment of the walls and vaults of the main church. In other words, the surprise exists within a harmonious context; it is a surprise basically rewarding and not an unpleasant shock.

The greater number of recent houses can only artificially be forced into formal sequences; the principles of informal sequence planning, therefore, are of especial importance to the modern architect. In every case the climax which is usually furnished by the living room, after an approach through the simplest of halls or vestibules, must be a climax within a harmony of exterior and interior forms. The treatment of the door and the shapes and furnishings and colors of the hall or vestibule must form a suitable preparation for a climax of

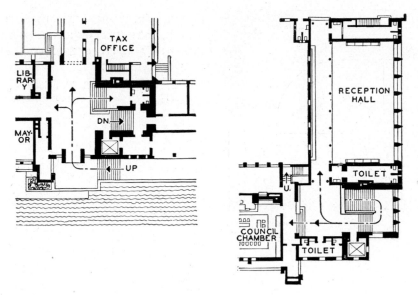

FIGURE 267 (LEFT). TOWN HALL, HILVERSUM, THE NETHERLANDS. PART PLAN
GROUND FLOOR

W. M. Dudok, architect

An informal entrance sequence of great richness. The projection of the building directs one
approaching to the door. Within the vestibule, four paths may be taken—into either of two important corridors, down stairs, or up stairs. Of these four, the lavish materials and projection of
the main stairs, leading up, and the view of the landing to which they lead make it the most
important although it is off axis.

FIGURE 268 (RIGHT). TOWN HALL, HILVERSUM, THE NETHERLANDS. PART PLAN
MAIN FLOOR

W. M. Dudok, architect

The upper vestibule continues the lavish material of the stairs and leads to the two most important
elements of the building—the council chamber and the reception hall. Entrances to both are
stressed, though differently, one by steps and a railing, the other by columns set within it, a
preparation for the gold mosaic columns of the reception hall.

some kind. Because of the relatively small importance of the average entrance
front of a modern house and the generally small dimensions of halls, this preparation will necessarily be a subtle one, and the surprise of the large openness of
the living room will form a dramatic climax; to be successful, this climax must
be harmonious with what has gone before.

The same kind of subtle preparation is found in many public buildings (Figs.
266–268). The universal necessity for economy and the reluctance of architects and clients alike to build elements merely for aesthetic reasons both tend
to reduce the relative size of corridors, lobbies, rotundas, and similar elements

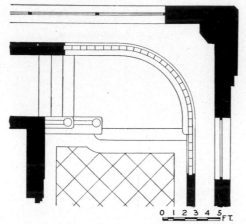

FIGURE 269. INFORMAL DIRECTIONAL CHANGE, BEAUTIFULLY STRESSED BY THE CURVING WALL, THE STEPPED STAIR RAIL, AND THE LIGHTING

Alfred S. Alschuler and R. N. Friedman, architects

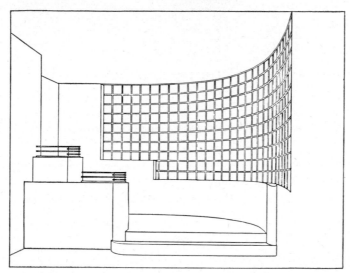

below that common in many earlier periods. It therefore becomes all the more important that designers use these reduced elements as efficiently from the aesthetic point of view as they do from the practical standpoint. In a public building, a corridor is more than a means of getting from one place to another; by its very design, whether meager or adequate, good or bad, it will inevitably build up in the minds of those who use it some kind of expectation; and the important or climax elements to which it may lead will themselves be more effective if this preparation, however subtle, involves no contradiction and no incoherence. Thus a mean and ill-designed lobby outside a fine courtroom will diminish the effect of the courtroom as well as be an eyesore in itself. Nowhere

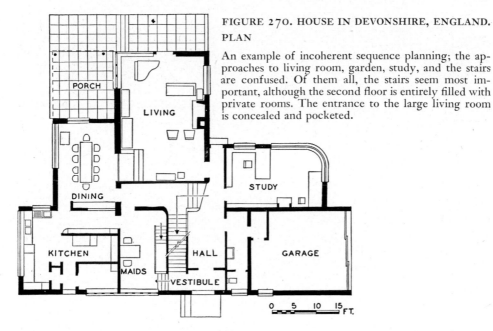

FIGURE 270. HOUSE IN DEVONSHIRE, ENGLAND. PLAN

An example of incoherent sequence planning; the approaches to living room, garden, study, and the stairs are confused. Of them all, the stairs seem most important, although the second floor is entirely filled with private rooms. The entrance to the large living room is concealed and pocketed.

can this be more readily appreciated than in the average American theater, where the ill-planned stairways and the crowded and inadequate lobbies do much to destroy whatever effect the auditorium itself may possess.

The second great element which distinguishes informal sequences from those of a formal nature lies in the informal balance which predominates and in the use of curved and bent axes. (See Figs. 87, 90, 275.) Here good sequence planning will have much to do with the functional success of a building, for, as we have seen, the architect's plan will itself serve to direct the visitor. In Chapter 3 the importance of balance as a directing quality has already been discussed; good informal sequence planning will take advantage of the various methods of obtaining the effects desired.

Much of the ineffectiveness of certain types of modern houses, particularly those built in the early years of the so-called International Style, arises from the fact that in them the sequence pattern is confused and incoherent. In an effort to produce plans which aid the maximum economy and efficiency, their architects often produced buildings which, however excellent they were as theoretical diagrams of usable space, seemed completely neglectful of the actual visual experience which they provided. In the living room shown in Figure 216, for instance, there is neither beginning nor end; there is no focus or climax, and the sequences of approach are visually confused. Similarly, in the sequence

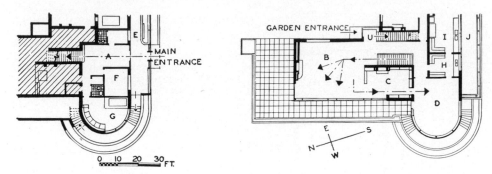

FIGURE 271. MANDEL HOUSE, MOUNT KISCO, NEW YORK. PART PLAN OF ENTRANCE FLOOR AND FIRST FLOOR

Edward Stone, architect

A: Hall; B: Living room; C: Library; D: Dining room; E: Flower room; F: Office; G: Bar; H: Pantry; I: Kitchen; J: Terrace.

Here the sequence from entrance to living room, B, is direct and impressive, with no possibility of error. The climax of views in the living room establishes its importance. The subsidiary sequence from living room through the library, C, to the dining room, D, is also beautifully handled, and the interesting shape and glass walls of the dining room furnish a sufficient climax.

illustrated in Figure 270, the passage from the exterior door to the living room is full of suggested false turns and is crowded and indirect; consequently, the climax furnished by the large living room itself seems so unexpected as to belong almost to another building. This is a surprise which defeats the first principle of design unity.

The greatest architects of twentieth-century houses have not made these errors. They have always remembered that architecture is a visual, as well as an intellectual, art. They have always, therefore, borne in mind the importance of the axis—the true visual axis, which is simply the line of the easiest and the most direct vision. When a turn has been desired in the natural progress, they have indicated it, made it definite, and built up subtle preparations in all sorts of imaginative ways—especially through the use of built-in furniture, correctly placed. For instance, in the Mandel house, by Edward Stone, the approach from the main entrance through the hall, up the entrance stairs, and into the living room is a sequence experience as visually exciting as the plan is natural and efficient; similarly, the sequence from the living room to the dining room through the library is well designed (Figs. 271, 272). In the Tugendhat house at Brno, by Mies van der Rohe (Figs. 273, 274), there is a much more elaborate informal sequence from the door to the reception area of the living room. Here the design is extremely subtle and extremely conscious, but the visual experience throughout is organized and exquisite. A simpler, but equally successful,

FIGURE 272. MANDEL HOUSE, MOUNT KISCO, NEW YORK. ENTRANCE STAIRS AND LIVING ROOM

Edward Stone, architect; Donald Deskey, decorator

See caption of Figure 271.

Photographs John Gass, courtesy Edward Stone and Donald Deskey

sequence can be seen in the little house by Wurster shown in Figure 205. Here the off-center door from the small vestibule furnishes a beautiful view into the living room so that the climax of the room itself is both powerful and harmonious. In the house at Westwood Hills, by Gardner Dailey (Fig. 275), the preparation is more conscious; from the front hall one looks over a built-in cabinet

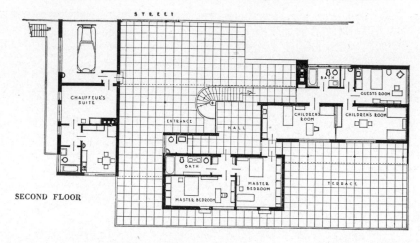

SECOND FLOOR

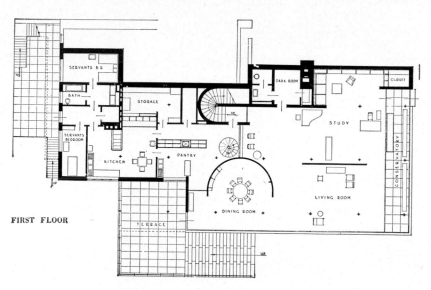

FIRST FLOOR

FIGURE 273. TUGENDHAT HOUSE, BRNO, CZECHOSLOVAKIA. PLANS

Ludwig Mies van der Rohe, architect

The house is entered from the street on the upper floor. In the hall the curved glass screen around the stair is the most salient element; one therefore progresses naturally down the stair and into the living room. This sequence is subtly handled, but nonetheless controlling; there is no doubt about directions or of the satisfaction of the final climax.

From Hitchcock and Johnson, *The International Style*

and receives a preparatory impression of the size of the living room, although the cabinet furnishes complete privacy and shelter. This entire plan is full of subtleties of a similar type.

FIGURE 274. TUGENDHAT HOUSE, BRNO, CZECHOSLOVAKIA. VIEW IN LIVING ROOM

Ludwig Mies van der Rohe, architect

The sequence leads inevitably from the front door on the upper level to this rich and inviting interior.   Courtesy Museum of Modern Art

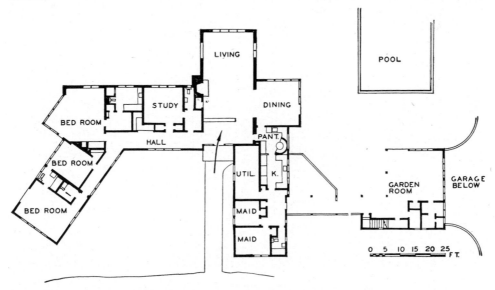

FIGURE 275. HOUSE AT WESTWOOD HILLS, CALIFORNIA. PLAN

Gardner Dailey, architect

The sequences are direct, simple, interesting, and with the appropriate visual importance. Note that the less important passages from the entrance to pantry and to bedrooms are near the front corners where they are least conspicuous to one entering.

FIGURE 276. GOODYEAR HOUSE, LONG ISLAND, NEW YORK. CORRIDOR TO DINING ROOM

Edward Stone, architect

Sensitive treatment of an important sequence emphasized by the sculpture and the lighting.

Photograph Ezra Stoller

FIGURE 277. KERSHNER HOUSE, LOS ANGELES, CALIFORNIA. LIVING ROOM

Harwell Harris, architect

The suggestion of the continuation of the hall sequence into the living room gives richness and variety without destroying repose.   Photograph Maynard L. Parker

FIGURE 278. TALIESIN, SPRING GREEN, WISCONSIN. VIEW IN LIVING ROOM

Frank Lloyd Wright, architect

A composition of surpassing richness, the climax of the entrance sequence; this suggests in addition other sequences to other portions of the house.   Courtesy Museum of Modern Art

But the necessity for careful sequence planning is not limited to the approach to the living room from the front door. The same sense of meaningful change in visual pattern, the feeling that there is a beginning and an end, should apply in all buildings wherever progress from part to part occurs. One of the commonest of such minor sequences, for instance, may be that furnished by progress from a bedroom to a dressing room and bath or through the various related spaces of a public office.

As an excellent example of many types of carefully designed sequences, we show the plans of a house designed by Peter Behrens in the Taunus Mountains (Fig. 279). In this, notice particularly the richness of composition running through the ground floor and the relation of sequences, more or less formal, as more or less generally used. On the second floor the planning of the master's suite, with its private living room or study and its bedroom, boudoir, and bath, is also imaginative and carefully studied; it shows an ordered variety of an extremely high quality. This is true architecture.

The problem of achieving ordered sequences within buildings is thus as

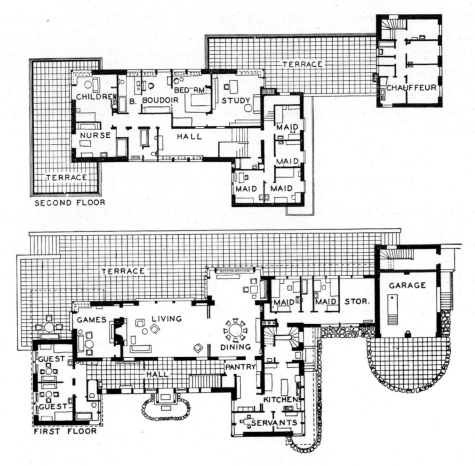

FIGURE 279. HOUSE IN THE TAUNUS MOUNTAINS, GERMANY. PLANS

Peter Behrens, architect

A plan of carefully studied formal informality, distinguished by rich and efficient sequences both upstairs and down. Symmetry is here used to emphasize the mountain view and to create a strong tie between living and dining rooms. On the upper floor the informal sequences in the master's bedroom, study, and boudoir are carefully designed, both for functional convenience and visual interest.

broad as the entire process of planning itself. To arrange a complex plan, designed for complex uses, in such a way that its sequences may be not only logical and efficient but also visually effective, that is, to provide the necessary major and minor climaxes where they assist the building's functions as much as they enrich its effect—this is a difficult task, but architecture is a difficult as well as a noble art.

And, on examination, many of these difficulties will yield, provided the architect always bears in mind that a plan is not a diagram and a building is not a theorem, that the plan establishes visual qualities in the building it represents, and that the building can be a visual experience of exciting and enriching beauty. No one who uses a building can avoid receiving visual impressions from it. It is the task of the architect to see that these visual impressions are themselves beautiful and are received in a designed, ordered, and meaningful sequence.

SUGGESTED ADDITIONAL READING FOR CHAPTERS 7 AND 8

Curtis, Nathaniel Cortlandt, *Architectural Composition*, 3rd ed. rev. (Cleveland: Jansen, 1935).

Giedion, Sigfried, *Space, Time and Architecture* (Cambridge, Mass.: Harvard University Press, 1941), especially pp. 39–67.

Greene, Theodore Meyer, *The Arts and the Art of Criticism* (Princeton: Princeton University Press, 1940), p. 225.

Gromort, Georges, *Essai sur la théorie de l'architecture* . . . (Paris: Vincent, Fréal, 1942).

Guadet, Julien, *Éléments et théorie de l'architecture*, 4 vols. (Paris: Aulanier, n.d.), especially Vol. I, Liv. II, and Vol. IV, Liv. III.

Hamlin, Talbot [Faulkner], *Architecture, an Art for All Men* (New York: Columbia University Press, 1947), pp. 36–65.

Harbeson, John Frederick, *The Study of Architectural Design* . . . with a foreword by Lloyd Warren (New York: Pencil Points Press, 1927).

Le Corbusier (Charles Édouard Jeanneret), *Vers une Architecture* (Paris: Crès, 1923); English ed., *Towards a New Architecture*, translated by Frederick Etchells (New York: Payson & Clarke [1927]), especially Sec. II, "The Illusion of Plans."

Stratton, Arthur, *Elements of Form & Design in Classic Architecture* . . . (New York: Scribner's [1925]).

Woelfflin, Heinrich, *Principles of Art History* . . . translated by M. D. Hottinger (London: Bell, 1932).

—— *Renaissance und Barock* . . . (Munich: Bruckmann, 1926).

Wright, Frank Lloyd, *Modern Architecture; being the Kahn Lectures for 1930*, Princeton Monographs in Art and Archeology (Princeton: Princeton University Press, 1931), pp. 71–72.

9

Character

CHARACTER in buildings is a quality dependent on the close relationship of the general aspect of a building and its purpose. As Louis Sullivan expressed it, "Outward appearances are the mirror of inner purpose." It is also a quality which has something to do with a building's homogeneous expression, its consistency throughout. Just as the character of a person indicates the sum total of the qualities which make him what he is, so the character of a building is the result of all of those qualities which are apparent in it.

In one sense any building has character, for there are things in it which set it apart from other buildings; but the word "character," in the sense in which it is used in architecture, usually means distinctive character, coherent character, and, especially, that kind of character which results from the clear and consistent expression of the building's basic human purpose. It is thus a quality arising out of the close relationship between architecture and human beings. It is determined for the average person by the emotional reaction aroused in him by the building.

It should be obvious that no such reaction can exist in a mental vacuum. Expression depends on some kind of intelligibility, and intelligibility depends on the existence of some kind of symbols which arouse recognizable association. What makes a person recognize character in a building, therefore, involves a certain memory; the person recognizes in a new building some qualities that recall to him other buildings the purpose of which he knows, and therefore he infers a similar purpose in the new one. It seems to him to have character because its forms are similar to the forms of many other buildings with like purposes which he has seen in the past.

But there is another kind of emotional reaction which buildings arouse, a reaction based on the direct psychological effect of certain types of lines and volumes that have definite shape and quality. This reaction, at the simplest, is one of mere pleasure or displeasure; but beneath, and forming a large part of, the general sense of pleasure lies another concept, the concept of *appropriate-*

FIGURE 280. COTTAGE AT SIASCONSET, NANTUCKET, MASSACHUSETTS

Domestic character at its simplest.   Photograph Talbot Hamlin

ness, the concept of the *easy performance of a function*. We may say, then, that part of the character of a building arises from the use of basic forms that are obviously appropriate to their purpose. From this point of view it is sometimes difficult to judge whether or not a building has character unless we know its purpose, for obviously window sizes, ceiling heights, and many kinds of general shape that would be appropriate to one purpose would be inappropriate to another. If we find such architectural forms used in buildings to which they are manifestly inappropriate, we realize at once that the building has an unsatisfactory character; a sense of shock is developed, and the possible effectiveness of the building is seriously compromised. Yet, if precisely the same forms are used where they are appropriate, a strong sense of character is produced and a consequent pleasantness. It thus follows that the actual aesthetic effect of a building may be definitely bound up with the clarity of its composition and the perfection with which it has developed the most appropriate forms for its functional purpose.

But the question of character in the functional forms of a building goes even deeper than this. Not only does the building with character use forms that are basically appropriate to its purpose, but in many cases it actually tells us what that purpose is. In this way the observer is enabled to judge it directly, without depending on *a priori* knowledge to identify its purpose. The building itself is its own label.

FIGURE 281. RIBERSHUS APARTMENTS, MALMÖ, SWEDEN. GENERAL VIEW

E. S. Persson, architect

Domestic character preserved in a sizable group of large apartment houses.

Courtesy American Swedish News Exchange

It is here, of course, that memory most strongly enters in. This is one reason why new or revolutionary forms have difficulty in winning acceptance in those types of building where people hold the existence of character as most important. Through the past century, and in some cases for periods much longer than that, people have become so accustomed to the use of specific kinds of forms for specific kinds of buildings that their first reaction to the use of forms of a different type is one of shock, and they feel that the building has a misleading character.

The existence of this popular mythology of building forms may be illogical and superficial enough, but its existence is a fact which architects must somehow face and with which they must cope. The clergyman and the congregation usually desire a Gothic church, because Gothic has come to them to mean "church"; only the Gothic, they feel, has the correct religious character. The committees in charge of public buildings like classic; memories of Washington or of classic capitols and courthouses have created in them a feeling that only in the classic styles can the right public character be given. How often, too, does the house builder demand a little Cape Cod cottage or a larger Colonial house because his memory is stored with Colonial images, all of which to him are eloquent of the idea "home." A "modern" house is to him, he says, like a hospital—hard and impersonal—because to him memories of clear, simple, and

FIGURE 282. RIBERSHUS APARTMENTS, MALMÖ, SWEDEN. BALCONY DETAIL

E. S. Persson, architect

Residential quality achieved by careful detailing and arrangement of the dwelling details.

Courtesy American Swedish News Exchange

logical forms are more often associated with hospitals (an unpleasant connotation) than with the cheerful confusion which he associates with home.

Howard Greeley, in *The Essence of Architecture* [1] (page 27), has well expressed the resulting difficulty:

It has been suggested by one recent writer on architectural composition that the expression of function often leads architects into the use of stereotyped designs. If a bank is to be designed, it is made to look like other banks that have already been designed. In this way it soon becomes possible to recognize a bank from its resemblance to a type established by usage in a given locality. The tendency is strong to follow this propensity until the type of design is in fact stereotyped and perhaps dry and uninteresting with over repetition.

Such a process is not in any true sense the expression of function. It is merely the development and preservation of specific conventionalities. It is a form of advertising, and is reduced to simple terms in the chain store architecture of America. A certain corporation painted all its drug stores, whether in Maine or New Mexico, in canary yellow. Another company finished all its lunch room interiors in the Tudor style. Every ten cent store in America is vermilion. This is a mode of publicity. It enables the public to recognize the proprietorship with ease. It is not, however, an expression of function in terms of architecture. It is a trade-mark.

[1] New York: D. Van Nostrand Co. [c1927].

FIGURE 283. CROW ISLAND SCHOOL, WINNETKA, ILLINOIS. ENTRANCE
Saarinen & Swanson and Perkins & Will, associated architects
Invitation, quiet detail, and human scale combine to produce excellent school character.

Photograph Hedrich-Blessing

To express the function of a ten cent store in architectural terms is to embody in the building the features that are adapted to the needs and uses of merchandizing small articles of negligible value. It means usually a street façade one story high, in materials indicating economical management and moderate overhead costs. It means display windows and ample ingress and egress. It means a large undivided floor area with maximum facilities for counter display and circulation. Counter display requires abundant light. Circulation requires ample lanes or aisles, with floors that are not only of durable material, but easily kept clean.

There is thus an inevitable difficulty in the creation of character in recent architecture, as there probably was in the architecture of many transitional periods in the past. One might conceive, for instance, of some good conservative monk, brought up in a Romanesque monastery, looking appalled at the new cathedral going up in the town and wondering how people could possibly worship in such a bird cage with such enormous windows. Yet the cathedrals continued to be built, and today, six hundred years later, we accept them as criteria of precisely those qualities in which the conservatives of their day must have found them lacking.

FIGURE 284. EXETER UNION HIGH SCHOOL, CALIFORNIA. VIEW IN THE COVERED WAY
Franklin & Kump, architects
Quiet, direct treatment establishes an excellent expressive quality.   Courtesy Ernest J. Kump

Yet, however difficult the problem of giving character to modern buildings may be, because they are unable to appeal to a large body of remembered buildings as background, we must not weakly retire to the defeatist idea that character does not matter or that it is impossible to achieve. Character in buildings is of great social and practical value; the emotional reaction which the character of buildings produces in general on people is one of the great contributions which architecture can make to the richness of living. Character is therefore one of the most necessary of qualities, and it is an interesting fact that sensitive architects in times of transition have always been able to bridge this gap in background and to force an acceptance of character in appropriate new forms. Little by little, as a greater and greater amount of work of the new type is built and as more and more schools, houses, factories, and public buildings appear in which the ideals of twentieth-century design are dominant, the public will amass a new collection of memory images which will make the realization of good architectural character increasingly easy.

It is obvious, then, that we cannot yet depend on memory images alone as a determining factor in achieving character in modern buildings. The Gothic church, the Collegiate Gothic university building, the Colonial house, the classic-temple bank are now concepts impossible for a thinking person to en-

FIGURE 285. CHICKAMAUGA POWERHOUSE, TVA

Roland Wank, chief architect

A magnificent expression of the tremendous power generated here, the character of this building
expresses both its industrial and its public purposes.   Courtesy TVA

tertain; to depend on the use of any given historic style, ancient or modern, to
establish character in any building whatsoever is today impossible. The whole
nineteenth-century theory of the relation of architectural styles to character
is merely silly, for we know that at all times of great architecture in the past
the styles then current have controlled buildings of *all* types, and that the
supposed relationship between any of these styles and building types was nothing but the thoughtless expression of an uncreative and grab-bag eclecticism,
which fortunately has in a great measure passed away.

Accordingly, to find ways in which to produce character in modern buildings, we must appeal to deeper and more universal conceptions than those concerned with any superficial style. Just as through serious study we have
achieved a truer command of functional requirements in planning, so we must
find the way to achieving effective character by the same kind of functional
examination. Where, in public buildings, the demands require large amounts
of daylight, we must see that daylight is provided and that large windows or

FIGURE 286. BORDEN COMPANY BUILDING, OKLAHOMA CITY, OKLAHOMA
Designed and constructed by the Austin Co.
Industrial character of a different sort designed to harmonize with a rural setting.

Courtesy the Austin Co.

glass areas are made a major feature in design. Similarly, where large exits are required to handle crowds of people, these should be frankly expressed. The same will be true of general factors of dimension; the design will be such as to make the necessarily large elements appear large, the necessarily small ones small. All sorts of functional connections between various elements in a design can be expressed so that the basic functional relationships of the whole building will become evident to the observer. The scale will be that which the purpose of the building suggests, and so on.

Thus a building will in a way form a kind of intellectual picture of what goes on in it. It will, if the design is clear and definite, tell the observer the story of the particular functions it shelters and in that way, perhaps, enrich his whole concept of life. The basis of this type of character is the simple one of functional clarity; it accounts, for instance, for much of the satisfactory effect of large industrial groups and of some modern schools.

But character arises also from reactions that are not entirely intellectual. The pleasure one gets from perceiving character in a building is not merely a cold realization of the mechanical fitness of its forms to the purpose they serve; it is

FIGURE 287. THOMAS HOUSE, SOMES SOUND, MOUNT DESERT, MAINE

George Howe, architect

Character developed from construction and material: walls of wood and stone, with cantilevers of reinforced concrete. Photograph Ben Schnall

FIGURE 288. AUTOMATIC POST OFFICE, STUTTGART, GERMANY

Simple design, good proportions, and the ample recessed shelter all suggest public use.

Courtesy Museum of Modern Art

a definitely emotional reaction as well. The good building puts one in the right emotional state; it prepares one for the activities that go on in it. Thus the good school should make the child happy in learning; it should have forms and colors that will combine to produce in him a quiet and happy attention. The good church will assist worship in its every form; it will arouse those emotions which not only are appropriate to religious services but also serve as definite aids to them. The good house will not only make housekeeping easy but also tend to arouse those emotions which make family living restfully pleasant—general

FIGURE 289. CITY HALL, FRESNO, CALIFORNIA

Franklin & Kump and associates, architects

Dignity, openness, permanent materials, and unforced symmetry combine to produce its excellent twentieth-century public-building character.   Photograph Roger Sturtevant

emotions of relaxed ease yet marked individual ones as well, such as the feeling of protection from the outside world, where that is important, or a sense of the close relationship of the inside of the house to a garden, where that is possible. Seen in this way, even a factory can be much more than an efficient and well-lighted enclosure around a productive process; it can be a place which, in its careful visual design, has the quality of freedom from distraction as well as that underlying humanity in color and shape which will make the workers feel not merely wage slaves but individuals co-operating in a productive enterprise. The same kind of emotional rightness must be the foundation of character in buildings of all types. Public buildings, of course, must suggest that they are for public use; they must seem to be the creations of the community and not of an individual. Yet they must also emphasize, in the individual's reaction, the qualities of dignity, self-respect, and control, and they must be buildings in which all the individuals of the community feel a common interest and a collective pride.

The first necessity in designing a building of character, then, is that the designer be fully cognizant of the place of the building in the life of society and in the life of individuals. He must know what emotions are appropriate to each kind of building, for functional arrangements alone will frequently give ambiguous results. Almost any educational building, for instance, will require big windows and ample exits, but factories also will demand big windows and ample exits. Yet obviously the character must be different in the two cases, and the proper character can come solely through an expression of the appropriate human emotion; it is only then that the difference between school and factory will become at once obvious. The school that is for children must avoid anything that is terrifyingly large. It must seem intimate and have perhaps a touch of the domestic in its character; it is the child's second home and must be so designed. The factory, on the other hand, is for adults, working with a known purpose, sure of themselves, and interested in efficiency; its design is conditioned on the fact that here relatively large numbers of people will be doing similar things at the same time. The good factory will reflect these qualities.

Similarly, the character of houses and apartment houses must be based essentially on the emotions ordinarily evoked by homes. Here, and particularly in the design of individual houses, there will be great differences, for families themselves are infinitely different in their ways of living and feeling. Ideally, each house should express primarily the attitudes of those who live in it. Some will desire the maximum of privacy, the feeling of the world shut out; others will desire a more public life, a sense of welcome to the outside world. Good architecture will develop appropriate characteristics in either case; yet both will seem essentially homes, for in both certain basic emotions will be expressed —the emotions which are common to all families of considerate people. The architect's responsibility here is very great, for by the character he gives to his buildings he not only expresses the qualities of the people who live in them but actually creates in those same people some of the attitudes which the building possesses. The architect, by his designs, can make people actually more relaxed, more co-operative; or he can make them aggressive, arrogant, even exhibitionistic. He both expresses and, to some degree at least, determines the emotional life of the world.

In various types of building, it is difficult to decide on the appropriate emotions to be expressed. In theater design, for example, it has been traditional to consider that a character of gaiety and even of lavishness was correct, because people usually went to theaters or motion-picture performances seeking recre-

FIGURE 290. VOLKS-THEATER, VIENNA. INTERIOR

A typical nineteenth-century Rococo theater auditorium designed to emphasize its festal character.
Courtesy Ware Library

ation, seeking a divorce from the hampering restrictions of daily life, eager for merriment, for fun; in order to express this common emotion, theater designers have sought to give appropriate character through extravagance or even frivolity of design. But now there is a new and contrary idea abroad: since the performance itself is the end in view, everything else should be subordinated to it, and theater lobbies and auditoriums should be as simple as possible; nothing should disturb the emotional tone set by the drama, for which the structure was built.

How is the architect to choose between these two concepts? Is there not a certain validity in both? People need and want parties, they want relaxation, and gaiety of style will express this very common feeling. Moreover, there are always people who use such buildings more purposefully and are seeking not merely random escape from daily existence but some definite emotional experience to be gained from screen or stage, and for such persons the quieter character will be appropriate.

FIGURE 291. THEATER AND ART CENTER, UNIVERSITY OF WISCONSIN, MADISON
Michael Hare and Corbett & MacMurray, associated architects
The simplicity of the walls and the curve of the ceiling focus attention on the stage.

Photograph Hedrich-Blessing

There has been a somewhat similar discussion with regard to the appropriate character for churches. Is the church building a frame for the service, or is it rather, in its way, a part of the service itself, as definitely an assistance as is church music? Again different answers to this question will give different interpretations of the character appropriate for the building. In governmental buildings, too, there has been a somewhat similar split between those on the one hand who say the expression of the individual reaction should be the aim rather than that of the community reaction and those on the other who believe that a certain impersonality, to express the more than personal quality in government or community activities, is necessary. Every architect, of course, has his own individual feeling about these problems, his own personal answer to these questions. Yet, by and large, it might almost be said that it is not his duty to answer them for others or to force his own answers upon a program to which they may not be appropriate. He is designing a structure for a definite client, who has undoubtedly some answer of his own; provided he can do so with intellectual honesty, the architect's first job is to carry out his client's wishes

FIGURE 292. SANTA MARIA IN
TRASTEVERE, ROME. CHANCEL

Gold mosaics, lavish materials, and dynamic lines create the strong emotional
climax associated with religious rites.

Courtesy Avery Library

in the best possible way. Naturally he will explain something about these basic
problems and make sure that the client's reaction is founded on knowledge and
thought and not merely on ignorance and habit. But, once the client's mind is
made up, it becomes the architect's duty to follow his wishes. For the theater
client who wants a *Festhalle* he will design a gay and carefree building. For
the one who wishes a serious framework for serious drama he will provide an
atmosphere appropriate to such an approach.

It is obviously the architect's first duty, then, to determine in any program
what emotions are appropriate for it; only then can he create buildings designed
to produce those emotions. Architecture, of course, can arouse only certain
emotions. Its effect is limited to feelings of the less personal and the more generalized types. Thus buildings can express, and by expressing help to produce,
feelings of ease, repose, homelikeness, stress, aspiration, welcome, gaiety, solemnity, or awe.

For these particular emotions may be aroused directly by form. Some persons are more sensitive to forms than others, yet for practically everyone form
itself carries some emotional message. The whole subject of this emotional

FIGURE 293. ST. THOMAS MORE CHAPEL, PORTLAND, OREGON

Pietro Belluschi and A. E. Doyle Associates, architects

Religious character gained by the greatest simplicity and the elimination of all extraneous or disturbing features.   Courtesy Pietro Belluschi

effect still needs much research and greater clarification. It seems to a large degree founded on empathy, or *Einfühlung*—the fact that people feel themselves into the objects which they contemplate; they feel themselves enlarged in big spaces and constricted in small ones, they sense the actual supporting nature of columns, they feel almost physically the crushing load of heavy weights. In actuality, a person's emotional response to a building is probably produced by a combination of this direct feeling with a mass of memories and

FIGURE 294. GREAT PYRAMIDS, GIZEH, EGYPT

Their gigantic size and pyramidal shape denote weight, permanence, and awe.

Courtesy Ware Library

conventions. But, since the architect today can no longer appeal to memory in his effort to achieve character, he must become all the more sensitive to the emotional effects of pure form and line.

Some generalized indications of these effects can be definitely listed. There are effects of mass and volume, effects of weight and support, effects of complexity or simplicity, effects of line, and effects of color.

Effects of Mass and Volume. Great size and unity combined almost always produce some feeling of grandeur, and, if developed to a sufficient degree, the combination may arouse effects even of *awe.* This is the secret of the power of the pyramids, for example. Small masses generally arouse feelings of *personality* and *individuality* and, if rightly related to their surroundings, produce a sense of *intimacy.* Small volumes always suggest the idea that a single individual can somehow encompass them, surround them, become part of them. Large volumes suggest, similarly, the feeling of the enlargement of personality; they may suggest the idea that mankind is somehow greater than it appears on the surface. If the enlargement is on the horizontal plane this feeling of personal enhancement, of added life value, will be felt in the more physical and obvious sense. If, however, the enlargement is essentially vertical, the enhancement may seem one of intellectual and spiritual quality, a sort of transcendence of human limitations; hence the religious inspiration inherent in tall spires and high interiors. The same qualities to a lesser degree may be produced by vertical masses seen from outside themselves. It is no accident that the religious buildings of so many different civilizations have sought again and again for effects of great height, both exterior and interior. Greek and Roman temples, to be sure, were horizontal rather than vertical in design, and the same is generally true of the temples of China and Japan; perhaps this expresses the definitely

FIGURE 295. RED ROCKS AMPHITHEATER, DENVER, COLORADO

Burnham Hoyt, architect

Superb monumental character achieved by combining the imaginative use of natural cliffs with a minimum of visible construction.   Photograph Hedrich-Blessing

humanistic and anthropocentric quality of the cults of these countries. Indian temples, with their tall towers, on the other hand, and Christian edifices express a basic mysticism through their search for height. The aspiration expressed in the Gothic has been so often commented on as to seem a truism.

Effects of Weight and Support. Shapes of apparent weight, such as pyramids, truncated or pyramidal buildings with heavily battered walls, and the like, nearly always create the impression of permanence and power. The expressed sense of gravity seems to relate them to the whole cosmos itself. Such buildings appear to be part of the earth. They seem to have a oneness with elemental things—a power and permanence like that of the force of gravity itself. The great temple terraces of Mesopotamia, the pyramids of Aztec and Mayan America, the battered walls of Inca fortresses—these owe much of their impressiveness to this sense of enduring weight. Thus such forms are appropriate only for those structures in which the emotional effects of power, permanence, and solemnity are the first aim—structures like monuments, memorials, tombs, and so on.

Related to the sense of gravity is the sense of support—of great weights efficiently and pleasantly supported. It is this feeling which Schopenhauer considered the foundation of architectural aesthetics. It is certain that in this effect of perfect support there lies a great source of pleasure for the sensitive observer. Today we feel this not only in the column—wood, steel, stone, or concrete—but also in the thin lines of rod and cable which support so easily and so gracefully the arcs of great suspension bridges. In this sense of support, easily and gracefully achieved, men feel instantly an emotion of quiet satisfaction—a deep kind of repose which comes from the knowledge that here, at least, man has been adequate to the problems which faced him.

Effects of Complexity and Simplicity. In general, buildings of simple shape with simple lines and masses tend to produce the feeling of ease. If the building is large in size, the result may be a sense of power; if small, it will produce a feeling that here is an object that one can love and cherish without strain. A designed and organized complexity, on the other hand, produces the effect of victory over great odds—the triumph of man's organizing ability over a multitude of varying and even conflicting demands. It expresses a great sense of human co-operation toward a single and definite end, both through the exquisite ordered character of the details and the unity of the smaller parts and through the oneness and the power of the whole. This combination is one of the most powerful emotions that architecture can give; it lies at the base of the appeal which many great buildings have had for the human imagination. Yet in complexity there is almost always some sense of struggle or of stress. It is the triumphant integration of this sense of struggle or stress into final and purposeful achievement which constitutes the so-called inspiration that great architecture produces.

Effects of Line and Rhythm. The emotional effects of line have been studied more carefully and for a longer time than have the emotional effects of mass or volume. The importance of line in painting and the graphic arts has forced this problem into the consciousness of artists and critics. It is of almost equal importance in architecture, because here lines are created by the intersections of the planes surrounding masses and by many types of necessary building elements, such as supporting piers, the bottom of beams, the projection of eaves, and so on.

The sense of repose and of relaxation inherent in horizontal lines has long

FIGURE 296. THE CREMATORIUM, STOCKHOLM

E. G. Asplund, architect

Geometric simplicity, brilliant handling of scale, and imaginative use of the site create a strong character of dignity, solemnity, and repose.   Courtesy American Swedish News Exchange

been recognized. This sense of repose is perhaps due to the relationship of the horizontal line to the principle of equilibrium, as, for instance, in the beam of a pair of scales equally weighted on either side. It also owes a great deal of its effect to its recall of the long horizon of the sea, of the levelness of water at rest, of the flatness of broad, stretching plains. Horizontals also have a connotation of oneness and of unity, and, as Frank Lloyd Wright has pointed out, in a building they accent the close relationship between the building and the earth itself; the long horizontals which characterize many of Wright's designs produce an extraordinary sense of quiet and contentment. And one of the strong notes which recent architecture has made more and more common is the repose that arises from the horizontal feeling of long bands of windows. The same accent on horizontal lines accounts for much of the effectiveness of some of the work of Eric Mendelsohn, such as the Schocken store in Chemnitz, and of the best work of many of the Dutch architects, like Dudok or Brinkman & Van der Vlugt.

Horizontals can be reduplicated almost indefinitely, and the effect will even be increased by rhythmical repetitions of horizontal lines; much of the serene grandeur that distinguishes great buildings in the classic styles arises from the dominant horizontal lines of base course, string course, entablature, and cornice.

Strongly marked vertical lines, on the other hand, seem to produce effects

FIGURE 297. TEMPLE OF NEPTUNE, PAESTUM, ITALY. INTERIOR

Character achieved by simple structural forms and admirably executed architectural detail expressive of the material.

Courtesy Ware Library

of effort or stress; if these lines are carried high, they suggest aspiration and transcendence. This effect is undoubtedly related to the idea of pushing upward, of resisting the power of gravity, of forcing one's attention somehow away from the limitations of earth. The power inherent in much developed Gothic architecture illustrates these effects, as does the dynamic lift which many people feel at the silhouette of a modern skyscraper or the view of New York from the harbor. Whether or not this emotional expression is the correct one for buildings devoted merely to business is a moot question; to give such an extraordinary and dynamic expression to buildings for mere money-making purposes perhaps indicates a basic unbalance in our character. Bruno Taut, in his inspiring early book *Die Stadtkrone* [2] develops the concept that the crown, or the most important and the most highly stressed element, of a modern community should be the group of structures in which the town's governmental, educational, and recreational life is centered. This center he would place on the highest rise so that from afar men could see the town dominated and, as it were, brooded over by the buildings which it has created for social welfare, just as in earlier days towns were dominated by the tall mass of a cathedral or the vertical note of a church spire.

The use of many verticals repeated rhythmically seems sometimes to have a less dynamic effect than the use of a few. It is as though one felt each line helping the next so that in the combined efforts of all a certain sense of ease is

[2] Jena: Dieterichs, 1919.

FIGURE 298. QUINCY
MARKET, BOSTON,
MASSACHUSETTS

Alexander Parris,
architect

Simple dignity and a sense
of permanence arising
from the sympathetic use
of granite.

Photograph
Talbot Hamlin

produced. Furthermore, since the vertical line is closely related to the question of support—the effort to resist gravity—whereas the horizontal line is related directly to the earth, combinations of vertical and horizontal lines, wherever the sense of equilibrium is achieved by careful integration, almost necessarily produce a sense of power efficiently used; in other words, they represent the resolution of a struggle. It was for this reason that Schopenhauer found in the perfect relation of support (externalized in the column) and of burden (externalized in the long horizontals of the entablature) the most perfectly satisfying of architectural experiences; it was this which dictated his preference for Greek architecture over Gothic.

In the twentieth century, with our new feeling for the strength of metallic supports, much of the same quality of an inherent struggle satisfactorily resolved can be found in such exquisite relationships of slim column and horizontal slab as appear in the best work of Mies van der Rohe or in the spreading concrete columns of Wright's Johnson Wax Company Building in Racine.

The effects of curved lines have also received much study. Gentle undulations of basically horizontal development seem to produce the same feeling of relaxed effortlessness as do horizontal lines. In fact, lines of the type of the sine curve, which undulate and change direction without any break, always produce a feeling of rhythmic serenity. Silhouettes of hills and of long ocean swells have this character; in plan, the same quality is responsible for the beauty of many roads and paths. Circles are always enclosed, definite, and unified, either in plan or in elevation elements; the related curves of ellipses and ovals add to this strong sense of quiet enclosure a certain dynamic stress. Curves that are broken produce a feeling that is nervous and tense; they build up an expectation of some purpose behind this tension, and they demand resolution in order that the final effect shall be one of equilibrium. Spirals are among the most

FIGURE 299. BAKER HOUSE, WILMETTE, ILLINOIS
Frank Lloyd Wright, architect
The repose resulting from stressed horizontal lines.   Courtesy Museum of Modern Art

dynamic and interesting of curves and have been favorite ornamental elements through many cultures for thousands of years.

The structural requirements of architecture have definitely restricted the use of curves in building. Except in the cases of domes and curved plans, curves have been more frequently used in decorative details than in major building forms. Certain cultures, however, have developed this use of curves to an extraordinarily high degree. The richness and the power of much of the best Baroque architecture are due to the resolved tensions and the subtle equilibriums of the developing dynamic stresses resulting from the disciplined use of exuberant curves of all kinds. Thus in the work of Bernini, Borromini, Fischer von Erlach, and Prandtauer an inspiring sense of purposeful power is built up by the balanced, but not necessarily symmetrical, use of carefully related dynamic curves, both in plan and in elevation. The main gate of Pöppelmann's Zwinger Palace in Dresden, also an example of the best of this work, has the elaborate contrapuntal emotional richness of a Bach fugue.

Many types of emotion—conflict, gaiety, even humor—can be expressed in buildings by the use of curves and broken lines. Yet it requires a creative imagination of great brilliance to command the infinite variety that is possible. In the hands of unskillful, dishonest designers the result becomes mere incoherence and a feeling of meaninglessness and vulgar splurge; all too many movie houses bear eloquent witness to this fact.

FIGURE 300. HOFBIBLIOTHEK, VIENNA. INTERIOR

Johann B. Fischer von Erlach, architect

Here lavish detail under perfect control creates regal and dignified grandeur.

Courtesy School of Architecture, Columbia University

Effects of Color. The problem of color in architecture will be considered in Chapter 11. Here we need only suggest some of the basic problems of character which color induces. The simple fact that most of the ordinarily accepted adjectives used for color are words with strong emotional connotations should indicate the emotional power which color has. We speak of drab colors as we speak of drab lives. There are cold colors and hot colors, colors cool and colors warm; there are gay colors and sober colors; in fact, our entire color vocabulary, except for the actual names of the colors themselves, is based on the human emotions that colors produce.

With the extraordinary color freedom which modern types of building material make possible for the architect, both in exterior and interior design, there is in color an opportunity for gaining character which architects as yet have little developed. Generally speaking, modern designers of buildings too often

FIGURE 301. GERMAN BUILDING, BARCELONA EXPOSITION OF 1929. INTERIOR VIEW
Ludwig Mies van der Rohe, architect
A perfect expression of the refined elegance appropriate for a public building.

Courtesy Museum of Modern Art

think in terms of gray and cream, with occasional touches of black; they are still under the traditional dominance of stone. The use of clear, bright colors to assist in giving architectural character might be much more frequent than it is. The contemporary architects of the Netherlands seem to have achieved this ideal to a greater extent than have others, and bright colors on doors, window frames, and steel elements go far in producing the human and lived-in character that is so strongly a feature of the best Dutch houses. Bold interior color is also an excellent means of achieving the correct expression of character. The interiors of most, if not all, the great Gothic cathedrals were richly polychromed. The brilliant mosaics of Constantinople and Venice help immeasurably to give the particular character of dignified richness which marks the interiors of Santa Sophia and St. Mark's, and the gold ground of these mosaics seems to have a touch of glory almost heavenly. Let us hope that eventually our architects will learn to evolve similar bold color compositions which will help a building communicate its character to those who enter it.

In addition, there are three other sources of character in buildings; these are of a more general nature, and each of them is more important than any of those listed above. First of all, there is the matter of correct subordination. A good building to have an appropriate character must keep its main purpose always in evidence and must somehow, both from far away and from near at hand, set the proper note. This means, of course, that the designer must subordinate all the minor complexities entailed in any building design to the major architectural elements which enclose, and naturally express, its major purpose. In the search for interest in detail this must never be forgotten, and the entire structure must be so designed that all its lesser elements fall into the less important positions. In that way the major forms, which will be more likely to express the correct character, will dominate the whole and assist in helping the building tell the story it should.

The second of these general sources of character lies in correct scale. This should be obvious; the public building, to seem public, will need a different scale treatment from that of the individual house. The governmental building will have a scale which suggests some purpose greater than a personal one. Heroic scale will set apart buildings which seek permanence or suggest ideas and ideals that are permanent. Thus the architect, merely by the careful handling of the scale of each individual building he designs, can do much to give it the right character, the right emotional overtones.

The third general character-giving quality lies in the directness and clarity of functional expression. This is perhaps the most important of all, for nothing is more destructive of the entire sense of true character in buildings than an attempt to make a building express uses or emotions that are foreign to its true nature. Such deception, which is as disastrous in architecture as it is in many of the other arts, can never arise if the functions of any building are thoroughly understood and clearly and logically expressed. The office building that poses as a cathedral and the bank that imitates a temple are offenses alike against the ideals of good architecture and good citizenship. Human lives are full of variety. The whole complex of individual and social relationships in a modern community is endlessly fascinating. If all the buildings in a community have true character, the community itself will have an equal fascination, because it will be a mirror of the life which that community engenders.

SUGGESTED ADDITIONAL READING FOR CHAPTER 9

Belcher, John, *Essentials in Architecture* . . . (London: Batsford, 1907), especially Chap. 3, "The Factor of Significance," and Chap. 5, "The Adjustment."

Greeley, William Roger, *The Essence of Architecture* (New York: Van Nostrand [c1927]), Chap. 6.

Greene, Theodore Meyer, *The Arts and the Art of Criticism* (Princeton: Princeton University Press, 1940), pp. 321 ff., especially p. 329.

Hamlin, Talbot [Faulkner], *Architecture, an Art for All Men* (New York: Columbia University Press, 1947), pp. 15 ff.

Ledoux, Claude Nicolas, *Architecture de C. N. Ledoux . . . l'architecture considerée sous le rapport de l'art, des moeurs, et de la législation*, ed. by D. Ramée (Paris: Lenoir, 1847). Ledoux demanded an "architecture parlante."

Lethaby, William Richard, *Form in Civilization; Collected Papers on Art & Labour* (London: Oxford University Press, 1922).

Lurçat, André, *Architecture*, in the series "Les Manifestations de l'esprit contemporain" (Paris: Au Sans Pareil, 1929).

Mendelsohn, Eric, *Three Lectures on Architecture* (Berkeley: University of California Press, 1944).

Ruskin, John, *The Seven Lamps of Architecture*, 1st American ed. (New York: Wiley, 1849).

Taut, Bruno, *Modern Architecture* (London: Studio [1929]).

IO

Style

THE WORD "style" is one of the most puzzling and misused words in the entire field of architecture. This arises from the fact that the term has many different and even contradictory meanings and is loosely used by writers who have not sufficiently discriminated with regard to the exact meaning they are seeking to convey. Broadly speaking, style in architecture simply indicates a manner of building or of design which is in some recognizable way different from other manners. As such, it differs entirely from fashion. Style and fashion have little to do with each other, and many things that might be considered fashionable are destitute of true style.

If style, then, indicates any easily distinguishable type or effect of design, it naturally follows that there may be different definitions of style, depending on the particular *kind* of differences in buildings under consideration. We may say that each designer has his own style. Equally well we may say that, generally speaking, different periods or cultures have different styles, and equally correctly we may say that there are styles that arise from the use of specific materials.

The most common use of the term in architecture is undoubtedly the historical one. We speak of the Gothic, the Romanesque, the Renaissance styles, and so on; used in this sense, the word carries a recognizable meaning in each case. It is an attempt to summate into one concept all the elements of planning, of construction, and of aesthetic effect which characterize the major structures of certain periods. As a simplification of an extremely complicated body of data, this concept of style in the historical sense is a valuable one.

Nevertheless, the thorough student of architectural history soon begins to find out that the gradual development of architecture from one period to another produces again and again buildings which fall with great difficulty into any of the so-called styles; he also discovers that even in the more highly developed periods of civilization, when any one of the so-called styles was at its

FIGURE 302. BROAD-CASTING STATION IN CALIFORNIA

An arbitrary use of a historical "style" results in a total absence of true style.

Photograph
Talbot Hamlin

height, many exceptional structures were erected in which the accepted qualities of the then current style can scarcely be recognized. In other words, if we wish to keep this historical use of the word accurate, we must define it thus only in the broadest sense possible—either as a matter of simple date or as a matter of general spirit—and only in the most general way construe it as a matter of the use of any set category of forms.

It is this indefiniteness of meaning which causes Le Corbusier to state that styles are an illusion. "Style," in the historical sense, he writes, "is a unity of principles animating all the work of an epoch, the result of a state of mind which has its own special character." [1] Such a definition is broad enough to be difficult to refute, but it is also so broad as to be generally useless as a description. "Style," therefore, should be used even in history and historical writing with the greatest discretion, for the question of whether or not a certain building of the past is in a given style is critically almost without meaning.

If this is so in historical writing, how much more is it true in the case of buildings of the recent past or of our own time. It is only after generations that we can begin to pick out from the complexity of structures produced by a civilization those common elements which are the hallmarks of its style. In the historical sense, therefore, our concept of what the modern style is, or may be, or may become, is necessarily of the vaguest kind, and critically it becomes almost meaningless to ask whether or not a building is in the modern style. As Le Corbusier says, "Our own epoch is determining day by day its own style." [2] The historical style of the twentieth century is being inexorably developed, even pressed upon us, willy-nilly, by many forces—economic, sociological, in-

[1] *Towards a New Architecture*, translated by Frederick Etchells (New York: Payson & Clarke [c1927]), p. 3.
[2] *Ibid.*, p. 3.

FIGURE 303. HOUSING AT THE HOOK OF HOLLAND, THE NETHERLANDS
J. J. P. Oud, architect
Distinguished style resulting from an exquisite sense of appropriate detail.

Courtesy Museum of Modern Art

dustrial, political—which combine to create the life we live. We are expressing our own culture, whether we will or no; just because we are architects living at a certain time and in a certain place, what we do, good or bad, imitative or creative, is largely the result of the net of cultural influences in the center of which we sit. It should thus be apparent that any use of the word "style" or "styles" in this modern sense is worse than useless in true criticism of contemporary work; it is also a hampering influence rather than a help to the designer. (See Fig. 302.)

But, as we have said, there are other possible style concepts according to which a building may be classified besides that concerned with their date or general spirit. Just as there are brilliant authors and stupid authors—and we say of the work of the first that it has style and of the work of the second that it lacks style or its style is bad—so in architecture the sensitive critic or the sensitive designer soon comes to recognize the fact that there are buildings of which he says instinctively, "This is beautiful, it has style," or "This is stupid and lacks style entirely." In that sense, then, the word has true critical meaning and it behooves us to understand what is inherent in the concept.

Style in architecture implies two things: the imposition of some idea or ideal

FIGURE 304. "FALLING WATER," BEAR RUN, PENNSYLVANIA
Frank Lloyd Wright, architect
Style resulting from materials: stone and concrete.

Photograph John McAndrew, courtesy Museum of Modern Art

upon design and the creation of that design in such a way that in every least
detail the idea or the ideal is made clear. Such an expression can never come
from the mere factual functionalism of an efficient building. As expressed, for
instance, by Le Corbusier, who is perhaps above all others the prophet of functionalism, "The naked fact is a medium for an idea only by reason of order that
is applied to it." In that conscious ordering of facts in accordance with a basic
idea lies much of the secret of true style in architecture. Coherence, both inner
and outer, both of factual arrangement and of artistic expression, is thus at the
basis of good architectural style. In a building there must be the same quality
or expression throughout—in plan, in composition, in detail. Nothing in the
building must contradict this feeling or expression.

The unifying ideal which runs through the building that has style may be

FIGURE 305. GAM-BREL-ROOFED HOUSE, WICKFORD, RHODE IS-LAND

Style resulting from materials: wood in shingles and clapboards as a surfacing material.

Photograph
Talbot Hamlin

FIGURE 306. "JIG-SAW" PORCH ON A HOUSE IN VINEYARD HAVEN, MASSACHU-SETTS

Style resulting from materials: wood detailed to express its strength and workability.

Photograph
Talbot Hamlin

any one among many different kinds. It may be the ideal of delicacy, of eloquence, of power, of strength, even of economy or of efficiency. It must, however, be an ideal that has some relation to the major function of the building; for, if there is a contradiction here, inner coherence will be destroyed and the design, however excellent it may be in other ways, will seem purposeless and superficial. Style, therefore, is not unrelated to character.

This concept of style as some kind of basic coherence should enter into the process of architectural design at every stage; every choice should be made with it in mind. In basic conception, for instance, style implies a perfect clarity of unified design, a design so clear and so unified that there are no loose ends, no raveled edges. The best work of Oud illustrates this perfectly. How clear and simple and unified, for instance, are the houses he built in the Hook of Holland (Fig. 303). The best recent factories (Figs. 286, 370) have style for the same reason; the perfect clarity of the conception in each case is obvious.

FIGURE 307. WATZEK HOUSE, PORTLAND, OREGON. VIEW IN COURT

John Yeon, architect; A. E. Doyle & Associated Architects, associated

Style resulting from materials: wood imaginatively treated in a fresh way.

Photograph Photo-Art Commercial Studios

FIGURE 308. SANTA MARIA DEI MIRACOLI, VENICE, ITALY. INTERIOR

Pietro Lombardo, architect

Style resulting from materials: marble and wood exquisitely combined.

Courtesy Avery Library

FIGURE 309. RAILROAD STATION AT MONTECATINI-TERME, ITALY
Style resulting from materials: marble used as a veneer on a modern functional building.

Courtesy Avery Library

The same kind of considerations will arise in the choice and treatment of building materials. Style in the handling of materials comes from a combination of the strictest honesty and the most sensitive imagination. Truth to material has become an architectural cliché which is not sufficiently understood. It is not enough merely to avoid untruths, or the pretense that a material is something other than it is—that is a problem not of achieving style but of plain architectural decency. What style in the use of materials implies is a search for the most expressive treatment possible; it should be based on a sensitive knowledge of the qualities of the material, as well as on an imagination which will suggest treatments that will bring out those qualities in the clearest and most beautiful way. One thinks at once of the work of Frank Lloyd Wright as being outstanding in this respect, in its use both of masonry (Fig. 304) and of wood (see also Figs. 305–307). Many modern Italian buildings, like the railroad station at Siena or Montecatini and the post office at Naples (Fig. 309), owe at least part of their indubitable style to treatments as imaginative as they are expressive of marble and of metal. Many of our own West Coast architects, such

FIGURE 310. CUSTOM HOUSE, NEW BED-
FORD, MASSACHUSETTS. PORTICO

Robert Mills, architect

Style resulting from materials: granite detailed to
express its hardness, strength, and natural origin.

Photograph Talbot Hamlin

FIGURE 311. MILL HOUSING, MANCHESTER, NEW HAMPSHIRE

Style resulting from material: brick.   Courtesy John Coolidge

FIGURE 312. PUBLIC MARKET FOR MEAT AND FISH, PORT-LOUIS, GUADELOUPE
Ali Tur, architect
Style resulting from climate and material: tropical heat and a sympathetic treatment of reinforced
concrete.   From *Architecte*

as Harwell Harris, Dinwiddie, and Belluschi, have attained great style in their
work through a similar and exquisite use of wood (see Figs. 318, 319).

Even climate can give rise to certain types of style coherence based on the
complete harmony of the building with the air and light, the rain and sunshine,
and the winds in which it lives. Thus the extraordinary work of Ali Tur in the
French Antilles has a poetry of openness which is the true result of the climate;
he has made this the basis for that striking coherence which gives his buildings
style (Fig. 312). In the matter of climate, a comparison between two houses
by the same architect may be instructive—Eric Mendelsohn's own house near
Berlin and the house which he built for Chaim Weizmann in Palestine (Figs.
313, 314). In each case the climate has served as the controlling feature in setting
the style, and the requirements it has dictated have become, not limitations to
design, but rather sources of expressive style.

Style in detail involves, first of all, an extraordinary coherence in spirit between the concept of the entire building and the design of all its smallest parts.
Good architectural detail not only accomplishes the practical work for which
it exists but also aids immeasurably in creating or in destroying the artistic coherence of the whole (see Figs. 315–317). A building powerful in conception
and finicky in detail can have no style; similarly, a delicate and intimate structure with details that are careless or coarse appears brutal and unlovely. Herein

FIGURE 313. THE ARCHITECT'S OWN HOUSE, CHARLOTTENBURG, GERMANY. GARDEN FRONT

Eric Mendelsohn, architect

Restrained composition and reticent detail create a style of quiet, appealing elegance, expressive of purpose and climate. Courtesy Eric Mendelsohn

FIGURE 314. CHAIM WEIZMANN HOUSE, REHOBOTH, PALESTINE. COURT

Eric Mendelsohn, architect

Here the dry warm climate has inspired architectural forms of great distinction.

Courtesy Eric Mendelsohn

FIGURE 315. COLUMBUSHAUS OFFICE BUILDING, BERLIN. DETAIL

Eric Mendelsohn, architect

Distinguished style gained through a successful expression of purpose, construction, and materials.   Courtesy Eric Mendelsohn

lies one of the great dangers of an unthinking acceptance of standardized details. The good designer uses standard details frequently, of course, but he uses
them intelligently and keeps them in tune with the building design as a whole.
The great beauty of Mies van der Rohe's German Building at the Barcelona
Exposition (Figs. 135, 301) is inherent to a large extent in the exquisiteness of
its sensitive detail. The Conger Goodyear house on Long Island, by Edward
Stone (Figs. 276, 322–324) is another excellent example of a building with real

FIGURE 316. DE LA WARR PAVILION, BEXHILL-ON-SEA, ENGLAND

Mendelsohn & Chermayeff, architects

Style expressive of the public and recreational purpose of the building, as well as of its site, which commands a broad sea-and-shore view.   Courtesy Museum of Modern Art

FIGURE 317. ELM HAVEN HOUSING, NEW HAVEN, CONNECTICUT

Orr & Foote, architects; Albert Mayer, consultant

Quiet composition and carefully detailed porches and cornice combine to produce a winning and livable domestic style.   Photograph Talbot Hamlin

FIGURE 318. THOMAS HOUSE, SOMES SOUND, MOUNT DESERT, MAINE. VIEW FROM
BEDROOM WING

George Howe, architect

Style as the result of materials, purpose, and site.   Photograph Ben Schnall

FIGURE 319. HOUSE AT WESTWOOD HILLS, CALIFORNIA

Gardner Dailey, architect

Purity of detail and formality combine with livability to create a style of distinguished elegance.
                                                                Photograph Talbot Hamlin

FIGURE 320. APARTMENT HOUSE, 40 CENTRAL PARK SOUTH, NEW YORK. EN-
TRANCE

Mayer & Whittlesey, architects

Distinctive style achieved by the combination of urban dignity and human scale.

Courtesy Mayer & Whittlesey

FIGURE 321. GREAT
LAKES NAVAL TRAIN-
ING SCHOOL, CHICAGO,
ILLINOIS. RECREATION
HALL

Skidmore, Owings &
Merrill, architects

Style resulting from the
unforced expression of
construction designed for
the economic shelter of
social recreation.

Photograph Hedrich-
Blessing

style, for the same kind of elegant delicacy which underlies the concept of the
building as a whole is to be found everywhere in each smallest detail.

Essentially, style in buildings comes largely from the quality of the designer's
personality. It is founded on a series of choices between different methods and
different solutions; if the building is to have style, every single one of these
myriad choices must be made in accordance with a single and coherent basic

FIGURE 322. GOODYEAR HOUSE, WESTBURY, LONG ISLAND, NEW YORK. EXTERIOR

Edward Stone, architect

Style resulting from the exquisite treatment of glass, metal, and concrete.

Photograph Ezra Stoller

FIGURE 323. GOODYEAR HOUSE, WEST-
BURY, LONG ISLAND, NEW YORK. DIN-
ING ROOM

Edward Stone, architect

Shape, the details of windows, and the furniture combine to create a style of refined gaiety.   Photograph Ezra Stoller

FIGURE 324. GOODYEAR HOUSE, WESTBURY, LONG ISLAND, NEW YORK. LIVING ROOM

Edward Stone, architect

The breadth of the glass, the delicacy of the metal work, and the suave beauty of line and proportion distinguish the style here.   Photograph Ezra Stoller

ideal. To achieve this requires a mind and a personality clear-cut enough to realize what the implications of a single ideal are and sensitive and imaginative enough to make each choice inevitably right. At its best this ability is a matter not merely of talent but almost of genius itself.

SUGGESTED ADDITIONAL READING FOR CHAPTER 10

Giedion, Sigfried, *Space, Time and Architecture* (Cambridge, Mass.: Harvard University Press, 1941).

Greene, Theodore Meyer, *The Arts and the Art of Criticism* (Princeton: Princeton University Press, 1940).

Gropius, Walter, *The New Architecture and the Bauhaus*, translated by P. Morton Shand, with a preface by Joseph Hudnut (New York: Museum of Modern Art [1937]).

Hamlin, Talbot [Faulkner], *Architecture, an Art for All Men* (New York: Columbia University Press, 1947), Chap. 9.

Johnson, Philip C., *Mies van der Rohe* (New York: Museum of Modern Art [c1947]).

Le Corbusier (Charles Édouard Jeanneret), *New World of Space* (New York: Reynal & Hitchcock, 1948).

—— *Vers une Architecture* (Paris: Crès, 1923); English ed., *Towards a New Architecture*, translated by Frederick Etchells (New York: Payson & Clarke [1927]).

Mendelsohn, Eric, *Three Lectures on Architecture* (Berkeley: University of California Press, 1944).

Sullivan, Louis H., *The Autobiography of an Idea*, with a foreword by Claude Bragdon (New York: Norton [c1926]).

Wright, Frank Lloyd, *Frank Lloyd Wright on Architecture; Selected Writings 1894–1940*, edited with an introduction by Frederick Gutheim (New York: Duell, Sloan & Pearce, 1941).

—— *Modern Architecture; being the Kahn Lectures for 1930*, Princeton Monographs in Art and Archeology (Princeton: Princeton University Press, 1931).

II

Color in Architecture

BY JULIAN E. GARNSEY
COLOR CONSULTANT

PROBLEMS of color relations cannot be ignored in architectural design, since every building material has color and will relate agreeably to adjacent materials in proportion to the care and wisdom exercised in its color choice. A mediocre design may be improved by distinguished effects of color, but careless or unintelligent color treatment is likely to defeat the purpose of the most thorough study in form. Refuge cannot be taken by the designer in "safe grays," for all gray materials are tinged with one hue or another; visually perfect neutral grays can be found only in laboratories. Nevertheless, most color decisions during the progress of design and construction are made at haphazard, usually from small samples, frequently by different persons not in liaison with each other, working under differing conditions of light, and always under pressure of time schedules. Yet experience proves that the relatively few buildings whose color schemes have grown in step with their form have been generally successful.

It is curious, however, that architects engaged in planning American world's fairs, from the Chicago Exposition of 1893 to the New York and Chicago fairs forty-odd years later, have consistently taken color into account as an integral element of design. One wonders whether the inference is justified that, to the architectural mind, planned color has value for ephemeral but not for permanent structures. Or can it be that architectural invention, freed of the responsibility of permanence, expresses itself joyously and naturally in color? An argument might be found here for designing no structure for a longer life than five years. The net gain in pleasant surroundings and psychic health might overbalance the financial cost of such frequent rebuilding. In this chapter the term "color" will be understood to include not only the gay polychromy suitable to an exposition but also, and especially, the inevitable psychological effects and interactions which result, for better or worse, from the juxtaposition of colored materials.

Part of the blame for the architect's neglect of color in permanent buildings may be laid at the door of architectural education in the nineteenth and early twentieth centuries. At the École des Beaux Arts, during that period, some archaeological renderings in color were required, but the presentation of any serious problem in design was limited to the warm blacks and grays of Chinese ink washes, in the belief that monochrome put students upon an equal footing or canceled the advantage which a skillful colorist might have over one not so endowed. The fact escaped notice that a view of a proposed building that is shown in monochrome with conventional shades and shadows gives an entirely erroneous forecast of its appearance when built, but this false procedure accompanied Beaux Arts graduates to their homes throughout the world. It still prevails in many American architectural competitions, with the effect that not a few building committees have been astonished with the result upon viewing the finished structure which they had approved as drawn on paper.

In American schools of design, mental images of architectural precedents were then, and for the most part still are, derived from black-and-white photographs or slides. Thus students can hardly fail to assume that worthy architecture is a colorless affair. Even graduate students so fortunate as to visit Europe bring back measured drawings in monochrome or freehand sketches in ink or pencil. Their records in color are confined to a few water colors of picturesque views. By the time they have become practicing architects, they are thoroughly conditioned to the neglect of color. Those who have taken the trouble to observe and to match for future reference the honey-colored Pentelic marble of the Parthenon, the porphyry or verd antique of Roman columns, or the color notes, based upon a lovely greenish gray, which compose the interior harmonies of Garnier's Opéra, are rare indeed.

Yet architecture of the past, prior to the nineteenth century, is rich in precedents showing the use of color as one element necessary for complete expression. Shocking though the thought may be to persons who regard themselves as purists, the Greeks used color to reinforce the visual effect of their marble temples. In the Ionic capitals of the Erechtheum, for instance, the volutes were defined with red, edged with gold, against a blue drum. At Olympia, the rows of acanthus leaves upon terra-cotta Corinthian capitals were picked out alternately in blue and gold, and the inner faces of the leaves, rolling forward into view, were painted red. Even the Doric order, purest of the three, was visually strengthened by a logical, constructive disposition of red upon horizontal members, of blue upon verticals, and of yellow (as a substitute for gold) upon dividing strips. Ornamented moldings were rendered in alternations of red and blue, with yellow between those colors, to give greater definition to the modeling. In fact, the Greeks relied upon color to emphasize form. Fortunately, being themselves the classics, they were uninhibited by false ideas as to the necessity of "classical" monochromy.

The point need not be labored further. Merely to mention the intricate, colored patterns on red, black, or yellow grounds in Pompeii (where an act of God has preserved the sophisticated decorations of Graeco-Roman times); the glowing mosaics and marbles of Santa Sophia or St. Mark's; the richly decorated ornamentation of Gothic moldings and vaults throughout Europe; the splendor of Arabic, Persian, and Spanish tiled facings; and those supreme examples of color allied to architecture, French and English stained-glass windows, is to illustrate by contrast the colorless character of building in the last hundred and fifty years. But, since the examples cited were products of civilizations and philosophies different from those of the nineteenth and twentieth centuries, any unintelligent latter-day use of them as precedents must be disparaged. Principles may be deduced, but imitation of color treatments results in sterile eclecticism. Although the twentieth-century architect may well adopt the Greek *principle* of using the most ornament, and hence the most color, on the least structural elements, nevertheless he will not find the brilliant, primitive Greek *hues* satisfactory in a northern environment.

In modern times much progress has been made in the investigation of color physics and psychology. Five centuries ago Leonardo da Vinci, applying his incredible genius to color theory, set down observations and recipes, some of which remain valid today; but truly scientific research did not begin until the very period when architects were avoiding color. Robert Boyle in the late seventeenth century and Sir Isaac Newton at the dawn of the eighteenth pioneered in studying the behavior of light when passed through a transparent prism and developed the first hue circle. After them Goethe, Schopenhauer, Young, Field, Maxwell, Helmholtz, Brewster, and others made their contributions to the growing sum of knowledge but, by conflicts in theory and point of view, brought about confusions not yet entirely resolved.

Michel Chevreul, however, who lived for 103 years, from 1786 to 1889, greatly clarified the situation, especially in regard to the use of color in architecture and the crafts. Neither a physicist nor a psychologist by training, but observant and inquiring, he realized the necessity of approaching color prob-

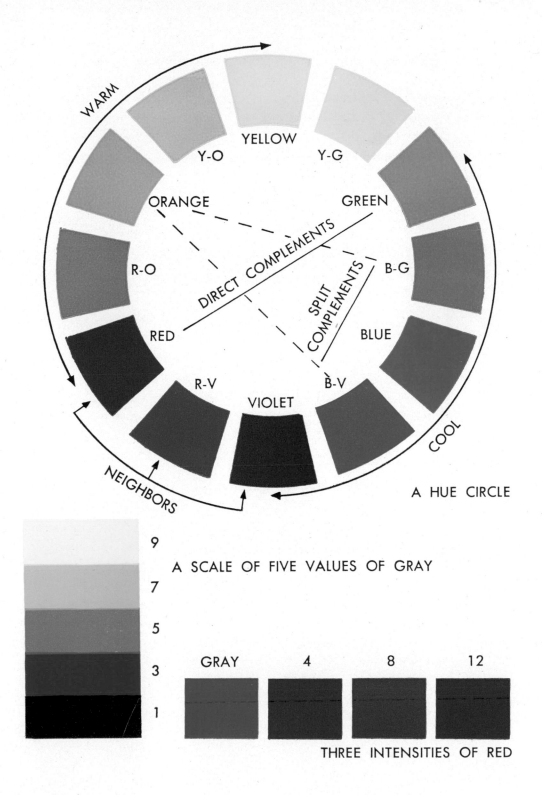

A HUE CIRCLE

A SCALE OF FIVE VALUES OF GRAY

9
7
5
3
1

GRAY   4   8   12

THREE INTENSITIES OF RED

FIGURE 325

lems primarily as visual phenomena rather than as ratiocinations in physics or philosophy. From his empirical attack on difficulties encountered in the supervision of the Gobelin tapestry factory, and by discovery and experiment, he arrived at practical conclusions which were published in 1835 under the title, *The Principles of Harmony and Contrast of Colors*. Here he stated eleven propositions which, together with his other remarks on the peculiarities of human vision, have greatly influenced present-day understanding of what color is and does. They constituted the principal foundations of the Impressionist School of painting (especially of *pointillisme*), furnished new inspiration to designers of textiles and interior decoration, and are much used today. After Chevreul, Ogden Rood (1831–1902), Wilhelm Ostwald (1853–1932), and Albert Munsell (1859–1916) carried further the study of color as visual sensation and also organized systems for color identification.

Of these various systems, the one properly in widest use, despite certain technical shortcomings, is that of Munsell. Borrowing the three dimensions of space (length, breadth, and height) to represent the three characteristics of color—hue, value, and intensity [1]—it permits the exact designation of any color by indicating its hue along with two numbered coefficients, one for value and one for intensity. Pending invention of a better system, and in view of the fact that failure to identify exactly a desired color is a frequent source of error, the Munsell system may well be studied and used by anyone who has to make color decisions.

The remainder of the present chapter will be devoted to a description of the phenomena of color vision and the ways in which they may be used to advantage in planning color for architecture.

Color occurs only where light exists. It is perceived through the response of eyes and brain to the impact of light, that narrow series of waves of radiant energy which, alone of the vast sequence extending from miles-long vibrations of radio to infinitely short cosmic rays, is recorded by the eye. The vibrations of light, when dispersed by passing through a transparent prism, are seen to vary in color according to their wave lengths, which range from 700 to 400 billionths of a meter. Every light source sends out a characteristic sheaf of

---

[1] *Hue:* first impression of a color, disregarding value or intensity. We say a "red" apple, a "green" leaf, with no further definition. All hues except purple are found in the solar spectrum.

Value: relative lightness or darkness, disregarding hue or intensity. It is usually measured by reference to a scale of equal steps between black and white. Adding white "raises" the value of a color, adding black "lowers" it. An eggplant is lower in value than a lemon.

Intensity (also called chroma): strength or weakness, disregarding hue or value. It is usually measured by reference to a scale of equal steps of visual perception from a neutral gray pole outward, increasing in strength, to the most vivid pigment available.

colored rays, and these when separated comprise the "spectrum" of its light. Diverse coloring of the rays results from the combustion of the elements composing their source; iron, cadmium, or sodium, for example, emits its typical combination of colored rays and so announces its presence in stars or other heavenly bodies. The color of any earthly object depends upon its inherent ability to absorb certain light rays and to reflect others into the eye of an observer.

As a convenient basis for color identification, the spectrum of sunlight coming from the zenith on a clear day is generally used because of its even balance in colored rays. It progresses in color from one limit of visibility at red, through orange, yellow, green, and blue, to violet at the other limit. Each hue melts smoothly into its neighbors, but about one hundred and fifty separate differences in hue are discernible by the normal human eye. The number and proportion of these hues reflected by an object determine its color: a tomato reflects many red, some orange, and some yellow rays but absorbs most of the blue and green.

The six principal hues of the solar spectrum—those mentioned above, which are located at points of greatest purity—together with the six hues located at halfway points between them and as many further subdivisions as are desired, may be arranged upon the circumference of a circle, equidistant from each other, to form a "color circle," better named a hue circle. (It should be noted that the Munsell system is constructed on the basis of five principal hues instead of six, for reasons too technical to be related here. The difference in point of departure is unimportant.) By this device, thought in terms of color may be organized, as follows: First, at the ends of diameters are found "complementaries," the hues most opposed in character to each other—Red is the complement of Green, Orange of Blue, and so on. When mixed together in pigments, these pairs neutralize each other toward gray, since each hue absorbs those light rays which its complement reflects. When placed in proximity, but not mixed, each enhances the other. Second, the hues on one side of the circle—the Red-Orange-Yellow sequence—are "warm" and visually advance; the hues opposite, the Green-Blue-Violet sequence, are "cool" and seem to retreat. Between those two sequences, Red-Violet and Yellow-Green are neither warm nor cool but conform visually to their actual position in space. Third, "neighbors" may be located and defined as colors which have one hue in common—such as Red, Red-Violet, and Violet—all of which contain some red.

Emphasis should be placed on the point that the interrelations of color just mentioned occur only within the seeing mechanism of the eye and brain. So far as is now known, they correspond to no mathematical relationships of wave lengths nor to any other natural law, such as that controlling the vibrations of music, except the phenomena of human vision. Therefore, the primary consideration in planning any color scheme must be, not what colors have previously been used in other situations nor what colors are momentarily fashionable, but what reactions will be transmitted by a color scheme through the eye to the mind of an observer. It is the job of the colorist to manipulate color relations toward desirable results in function, fitness, and pleasure. In order to predict color reactions accurately, he must know how the human eye behaves when it receives the colored rays reflected by one or more objects.

Avoiding an unnecessary discussion of conflicting theories regarding the mechanics of seeing, the principal visual phenomena are as follows:

1. Simultaneous Contrast. Chevreul observed that no color within the field of vision exists as a fixed quantity by itself. Every color influences and is influenced by every other color in view with respect simultaneously to hue, value, and intensity, and this mutual reaction increases as the colors are brought closer together. In other words, the hue of each will induce a tinge of its complement upon an adjacent color; a light value will make a dark value near by appear darker, and vice versa; and intense color will weaken the apparent intensity of its neighbor. All three reactions occur in concert. For instance, a light, intensely red book lying on a billiard table will make the green cloth appear darker, greener, and less intense than it is without the book. In architecture, a blue-gray stone exterior wall may be forced farther toward blue by a complementary burnt-orange doorway or by a planting of zinnias, or it may be forced toward gray by an intensely blue doorway or a blue roof. The color of shutters on houses and of window shades in skyscrapers may be chosen to serve the same purpose.

2. After-Image. The eye quickly tires of any color on which it is focused, and the rate of fatigue is proportional to the intensity of that color. Moreover, immediately after viewing the fatiguing color the eye tends to record its complement. Thus, after one has looked fixedly at a bright orange spot for fifteen seconds and then turns his eyes to a white card, he will see a spot of pale blue on the card. This peculiarity of the eye was utilized at the New York World's Fair of 1939; here the golden effect of a group of buildings at the Long Island

Railroad entrance was enhanced and made doubly powerful by the blue-violet glaze employed for tinting the windows of the long station through which visitors approached the Golden Circle. Another more dramatic illustration of the use of similar complementary hues is found in the windows surrounding Napoleon's tomb at the Invalides. Yet the phenomenon occurs less theatrically in every movement of the eyes from one color to another.

One of three effects may result from the phenomenon of after-image: a color may be enhanced by the complementary tinge remaining in the eye from the color previously seen, as in Red seen after Green; it may be vitiated, as in Pink seen after Red; or it may be modified toward an unanticipated, but not necessarily unpleasant, hue, as in Chartreuse seen after Blue. To use this peculiarity of the eye, or any of the others mentioned, for obtaining desired effects in color is not to play childish tricks but to take advantage of physiological and psychological constants which exist, whether admitted or not.

3. *Fusion of Colors.* When the eye perceives a field of many small areas of one hue closely interspersed with equal areas of another hue, as in a checker-board pattern, at a certain distance it will invent a third hue sensation, allied to but different from both of the parent hues. For instance, a mosaic field composed of alternating red and blue tesserae, seen from forty or fifty feet away, will appear to be violet or purple in hue and unlike either red or blue. Inspection through a magnifying glass will show that half-tone color printing is based on this habit of the eye, and many interesting textures in woven materials depend upon it for their effect. In architecture care should be taken to insure that the total visual effect of a random stone wall, made up of blocks contrasting in hue and value, shall present no unpleasant surprises when built. Per contra, handsome textures may be achieved by a courageous use of contrasting materials in close juxtaposition. Eighteenth-century stonework in Pennsylvania and New Jersey presents many successful combinations which may serve as precedents. In paint, surfaces at a distance from the observer may be given greater interest by using "broken color," that is, by alternating in small areas two different hues which, in combination, produce the vibrant color desired.

4. *Effects of Illumination.* It is common knowledge that colors change in visual appearance according to the hue and intensity of light falling upon them. Rugs bought under fluorescent lights in a shop often prove disappointing when laid in a home lit by incandescent bulbs or daylight. The reason is plain: since the color of an object results from the absorption of some colored rays of light and the reflection of others, it is evident that unless the object receives from a

SIMULTANEOUS
CONTRAST

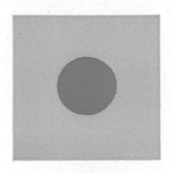

THE CENTER DISCS ARE
THE SAME GRAY

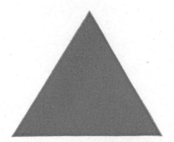
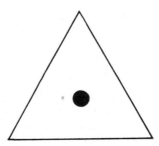

FUSION OF COLORS   IN THE EYE

AFTER-IMAGE

IRRADIATION

THE STARS ARE THE SAME SIZE

FIGURE 326

light source the rays appropriate to its own color nature it cannot reflect them. Hence a blue rug under light from a "daylight" fluorescent tube, which is rich in blue rays but poor in rays from the warm side of the spectrum, may appear to be just the color desired; in a living room, however, under the plentiful red, yellow, and orange but relatively few blue rays of the incandescent bulb, it may seem dull or faded. Human skin is similarly affected but in the reverse direction; under cold fluorescent light the rosiest girl looks sickly.

It follows that the choice of colors for architecture should be made under the same light conditions as those under which the surfaces for which they are intended will be seen. To select under the cold north light of a drafting room exterior colors later to be lit by sunlight may result in disappointment in the finished building. Direct sunlight (not that reflected from the zenith) abounds in yellow and orange rays and its shadows are relatively violet or bluish—forced in that direction by the simultaneous contrast of the surrounding warm surfaces in light—hence in this light warm colors will be intensified and cool colors will be somewhat neutralized. A hint may be found here for planning exterior color according to orientation; a red door, which is too brilliant on the south façade, may be correct on the north. The same considerations will dictate the choice of interior colors to compensate for the colors in the light itself which fall upon them.

Not only the color of the illuminant but also its intensity must be adjusted to the effect desired. The stronger the light, the higher in value and the weaker in intensity will a color appear; yet lessening the illumination will both darken a color and weaken its intensity. Under either very strong or very weak light, visual acuity decreases so much that adjacent colors tend to approach each other in hue, value, and intensity. This means that contrasts intended for dimly lit interiors must be magnified if their differences are to be perceived and also that extreme contrasts may be endured under strong lighting which would be unpleasant in normal light. The agreeable effect of intense colors under tropic sunlight is an example.

5. *Irradiation.* This term refers to the apparent increase in dimensions of a light object when seen against a dark background and the apparent decrease of a dark object when seen against light. Designers of printers' type faces and of advertising layouts are aware of this visual reaction, but architects often ignore it. Elements that are light in value may seem to expand and become stubby when placed before a dark wall or opening, whereas others of dark material when placed against a light background may appear thinner than the designer had

intended. Success in laying out inscriptions or applied lettering depends upon taking this matter into account. Fortunately, since irradiation occurs at any scale, its effect may be determined in advance by colored sketches.

6. Color Harmony and Disharmony. Much nonsense and not a little misleading information have been published on this topic, ranging from the defeatist belief that ability to compose harmonious relationships is a gift from God or the result of a felicitous arrangement of chromosomes, on through attempts to prove that Mother Nature lays down infallible rules in her foliage and skies, to elaborate mathematical calculations based on arbitrary measurements of hues, values, and intensities. Since the final judge of any color combination is the human eye, a more logical procedure would seem to be a study of the eye's preferences and dislikes as the safest guide for planning appropriate color schemes.

The following preferences have been substantiated by examples in past history and by survey and investigation in recent times:

(a) The eye prefers combinations of few rather than of many hues. More than three basic hues are seldom successful, and an assortment of hues becomes less satisfying as their number increases beyond three. In fact, countless successful schemes have been attained by variations in the value and the intensity of only one hue; these are termed monochromatic schemes. A partial list of colors to be derived from one hue, Red, suggests the richness possible in such a scheme: Shrimp, Strawberry, Flesh, and Coral pinks; Scarlet, Dragon's Blood, Etruscan, Brazil, Brick, and Morocco reds; Claret and Hessian browns. From a monochromatic scheme one may gain an impression of dignity, cohesion, and strength, but he may also soon lose interest. In that case, the introduction of a small area of a near complement to the original hue may enliven the scheme.

(b) Schemes based on two or three basic hues satisfy the eye's desire for simplicity and give variety as well, but the eye has preferences as to the optimum intervals between hues. It prefers the hues to be either close neighbors (analogous) or definitely far apart (contrasting). Neighboring hues, as mentioned earlier, are those which have one constituent in common; twelve sets of three hues each may be identified on the hue circle. Contrasting hues, of which the most obvious are the complementaries, are located at the ends of the long chords of the hue circle. In spite of advice sometimes given in writings about color, the eye is not much interested in direct complements, perhaps because each exactly balances the other. It much prefers split complements, that is, a three-hue combination in which two of the hues are neighbors to the complement of the third. Such combinations might be: Red, Yellow-Green, Blue-Green; Yellow, Blue, Red-Violet. Here it is not to be understood, however, that the three hues in full intensity will be pleasing; adjustments in value, intensity, and area, as shown below, will be necessary.

(c) The eye likes variety in both the area and the intensity of hues. It prefers that colors shall vary in area inversely as their intensity; that is, the grayer the color, the larger its area may be. Designers who believe that graying all colors will insure harmony fail to observe that this preference of the eye works both ways; not only should large areas be reduced in intensity but smaller areas should be relatively intensified to satisfy the normal color sense. Also, those modern colorists who spread strong color over entire walls of interiors, ignoring this preference, condemn the occupants of those interiors to a mild feeling of malaise which is likely to be attributed to any other cause than to color intensity.

Perhaps the easiest way of thinking out a design in color is to assign the term "dominant" to the hue of greatest area and least intensity, "relief" to the next smaller in area and more intense, and "accent" to the least in area and most intense. The richest color schemes result from modulations in the value and intensity of a few hues. Within the framework of dominant, relief, and accent colors, therefore, as many variations of light or dark and of strength or weakness may be introduced as the designer wishes. Even minor divergences in hue will be found acceptable if not overworked.

(d) Colors have particular psychological associations of an obscure origin, and these hold great importance for the designer in color. Everyone knows that green is the hue of spring, orange of autumn, and blue of the sky, but more subtle distinctions are necessary for the colorist. Colors to him may be warm, cold, "edible," repellent, hospitable, formal, soothing, depressing, exciting. For instance, the general wall color of a bank interior may be chosen to influence clients toward feeling either that the bank welcomes small accounts or that it prefers the patronage of the exceptionally well-to-do. In a factory, employees working in high temperatures can be made more comfortable if their surroundings are painted in light, cool colors. In hospitals, the therapeutic value of colors accurately related to the function of the various rooms has been proved beyond a doubt; a pure-white hospital interior implies an institution behind the times.

A trial balance may now be struck to summarize the color tools previously mentioned, before proceeding further to a consideration of planning color schemes. These tools are:

1. A working palette of colors such as is supplied by any good color system like Munsell's.
2. An understanding of the hue circle and of the relationships to be discovered through its use.
3. An appreciation of the visual phenomena of simultaneous contrast, after-image, fusion of colors, effects of illumination, and irradiation.
4. A knowledge of the preferences of the eye as to the number, area, and hue relationship of the colors used.

With these tools any architectural color problem may be attacked with confidence. Planning in color, like planning in form, must fulfill primarily the requirements of function and fitness. Difficulty in choosing appropriate hues lies not in the complexity of color itself but in defining beforehand exactly what results are sought. The program of functional requirements which guides the architect toward appropriate form will also direct him in color. For instance, a maternity room in a hospital may be skillfully designed to answer every need of the patient, but only color will persuade her, first, to be content in her temporary surroundings and, second, to go home as soon as safety permits in order to free the room for another occupant. Quick turnover is one of the functional requirements of such a room.

The most important color choice in any architectural problem will be that of the dominant hue. For exteriors, this will be determined by the prominence desired for the new building in its environment. Shall it melt into its surroundings, shall it be projected into public notice, or shall it take its place on a modest equality with adjacent structures? The client's wishes, the character of the neighborhood, the purpose of the building, and the architect's own taste are to be taken into consideration. Here a completely untrammeled, courageous point of view will pay dividends. One surmises that the generally drab look of all American cities is due to failure on the part of architects to search with an open mind for the most appropriate basic hue for his building, wherever that search may lead. Yet here is an opportunity for the exercise of the architect's creative imagination. Everybody loves a good try, even if it is not completely successful. Confidence in the use of color may be developed by the architect not only by practice of the suggestions here set forth but also through exposure to colorful objects, such as fabrics, enamels, mosaic, pottery, and

ADVANCING AND RETREATING COLORS

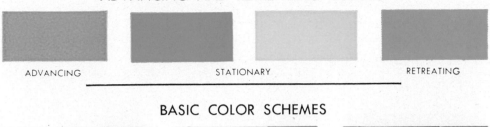

ADVANCING   STATIONARY   RETREATING

BASIC COLOR SCHEMES

MONOCHROMATIC   ANALOGOUS   CONTRASTING
(VARIATIONS OF 1 HUE)   (NEIGHBORS)   (SPLIT-COMPLEMENTS)

NUMBER OF HUES IN A COLOR SCHEME

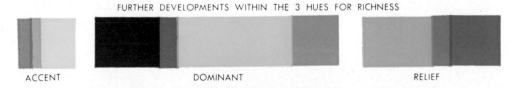

3 HUES: SAFE   4 HUES: POSSIBLE   5 HUES: DOUBTFUL

ADJUSTMENTS OF 3 HUES IN AREAS · VALUES · INTENSITIES

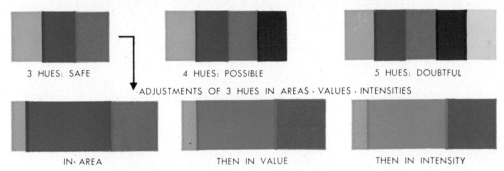

IN·AREA   THEN IN VALUE   THEN IN INTENSITY

ANY 3 HUES MAY BE HARMONIZED BY ABOVE ADJUSTMENTS

FURTHER DEVELOPMENTS WITHIN THE 3 HUES FOR RICHNESS

ACCENT   DOMINANT   RELIEF

EXAMPLES OF PSYCHOLOGICAL ASSOCIATIONS OF COLORS

EDIBLE   REPELLENT   HOSPITABLE

SOOTHING   EXCITING   DEPRESSING

FIGURE 327

other visual treats to be found in museums or books. One brave and splendid scheme exists for all to see on Raymond Hood's American Radiator Building, in New York, which stands as a monument to his unfettered imagination in color.

To accompany the dominant hue, two subsidiary hues, in either analogous or contrasting relationship with it, will then be chosen for relief and accent. Where a recessive effect is desired, the purpose would obviously be defeated by the choice of contrasts, and analogy would be ineffective where prominence is appropriate. After all three hues have been chosen, their values and intensities must be decided. From the most closely related values to the most extreme oppositions, an almost infinite series of combinations is at the disposal of the designer for expressing his intentions exactly. Here again courage and a thorough exploration of the possibilities will bring rich rewards. Every American city furnishes examples of opportunities missed, especially in tall buildings. One might imagine the slender soaring towers, made possible by steel, not only emphasized by vertical lines but also growing vertically in color interest and exploding in magnificence at the apex. So far such crowning glories for proud cities exist only in the imagination.

Beyond this point every color problem becomes a special case, and counsel gives way to the architect's own point of view, his experiments, and intelligent study. The logical procedures here advocated are no hindrance to his freedom of expression. Though great artists in color, as in all arts, have no need for rules, the general practitioner of architecture will find that regularized thinking opens unexpected resources for suitable, fresh, and stimulating color schemes solidly based on human reactions.

SUGGESTED ADDITIONAL READING FOR CHAPTER 11

Birren, Faber, *Functional Color* (New York: Crimson Press, 1937).

—— *Monument to Color* (New York: McFarlane, Warde, McFarlane, 1938).

Burris-Meyer, Elizabeth, *Historical Color Guide* (New York: Helburn [c1938]).

Chevreul, M. E., *The Principles of Harmony and Contrast of Colours* (London: Bell & Daldy, 1870).

Guptill, Arthur L., *Color in Sketching and Rendering* (New York: Reinhold, 1935).

International Printing Ink Corporation, *Three Monographs on Color* (New York: the Corporation, 1935).

Katz, David, *The World of Colour* (London: Kegan Paul, Trench, Trubner, 1935).

Luckiesh, M., *Color and Colors* (New York: Van Nostrand, 1938).

—— *Light, Vision and Seeing* (New York: Van Nostrand, 1945).

—— and F. Moss, *The Science of Seeing* (New York: Van Nostrand, 1937).

Munsell, A. H., *Book of Color* (Baltimore: Munsell Color, 1929).

—— *A Color Notation* (Baltimore: Munsell Color, 1929).

Ostwald, Wilhelm, *Colour Science*, Parts I and II (London: Winsor & Newton, 1931–33).

Sargent, Walter, *The Enjoyment and Use of Color* (New York: Scribner's [c1923]).

12

Architectural Design and Structural Methods I: Types of Construction

I F, AS WE HAVE INSISTED throughout the course of this book, architecture is a complete integration of structure, use, and beauty, it follows that the connection between structural systems and architectural design is extremely close. During the course of human history, man has learned to build his shelters in many ways and to use many different kinds of materials, depending on the climate and the natural resources of the particular part of the world in which he lived. With our wide archaeological and historical knowledge, the development of these various construction systems and the use of these various materials have become more and more clear, and we are now enabled to discuss architecture with some definiteness and accuracy according to the structural principles involved and the materials used.

In order to make this discussion fruitful and to reduce confusion, it has become customary to clarify construction according to certain basic classifications. The first and most common of these is the classification according to the way in which voids are spanned—post and lintel or wall and lintel, arch and vault, and truss. The first classification, post and lintel or wall and lintel, covers all constructions in which the voids are spanned by simple horizontal beams, girders, or lintels, whatever their material may be (Figs. 328, 329). The second classification includes all arched and vaulted structures (Figs. 337–340). The third is based on the use of trusses (Figs. 348–351). It will be noticed that the last two of these are both concerned with roofing over an interior or spanning an opening with lengths of material which, taken singly, are too short to bridge the space. To this degree they are more advanced types of construction than the first, and they actually appeared in the history of building at a somewhat later date. Nevertheless, arched construction goes back at least to the third

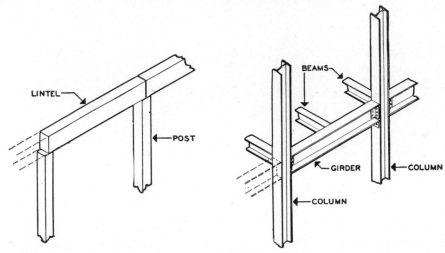

FIGURE 328. POST-AND-LINTEL CONSTRUCTION

LEFT: The elements of the system; RIGHT: Modern post-and-lintel construction in steel.

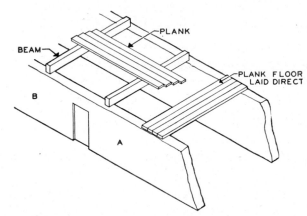

FIGURE 329. DIAGRAM OF TYP-ICAL WALL-AND-LINTEL CON-STRUCTION

The covering can be laid direct on the walls as at right, A, or by means of beams or girders as at left, B. The weights at A are uniformly distributed; at B they are concentrated beneath the beams, therefore the door is placed between the beams.

millennium B.C., and trussed construction is at least as early as the Roman Empire and may represent a timber-building tradition of a much earlier date, although this problem—the birth of trusses—is still obscure.

Post-and-lintel construction indicates, of course, that all openings are rectangular and that the sections of rooms and the interiors are also, in general, rectangular. This type of construction limited the widths of openings and rooms to spans which beams of the known materials could bridge (Figs. 335, 336). In monumental buildings of stone, it resulted in comparatively small spans and openings that tended to be relatively high in proportion to their width (Figs. 331–333), a point which has been referred to in Chapter 5 on scale. The use of

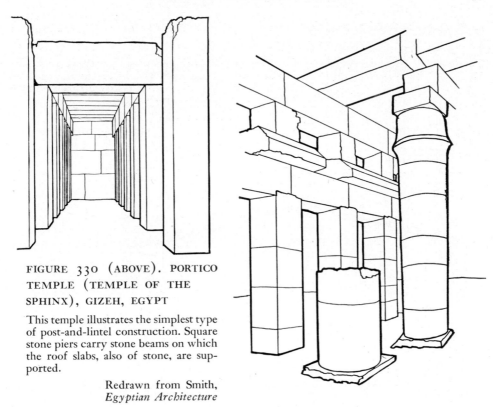

FIGURE 330 (ABOVE). PORTICO TEMPLE (TEMPLE OF THE SPHINX), GIZEH, EGYPT

This temple illustrates the simplest type of post-and-lintel construction. Square stone piers carry stone beams on which the roof slabs, also of stone, are supported.

Redrawn from Smith,
Egyptian Architecture

FIGURE 331 (RIGHT). TEMPLE OF AMON-RE, KARNAK, EGYPT. A VIEW IN FESTIVAL HALL OF THUTMOSE III

This drawing illustrates a slightly more developed example of Egyptian post-and-lintel construction, with columns used for the central post rows. Note how all the major architectural forms result from the simple use of lintel beams or slabs resting on piers or beams. This hall was lighted by clerestory windows.   Redrawn from Smith, *Egyptian Architecture*

wood, because of its greater bending strength in relation to its weight, made larger spans possible; therefore large halls came to be roofed in wood. Lintel construction is the type most commonly used today, and the development of steel and reinforced concrete has made it possible to roof spans of great width by means of simple beams and girders. The basic rectangularity of the typical modern city is derived naturally from the almost universal use of the lintel type.

Arched and vaulted construction is the natural building method where good timber is rare and where strong building stones of large dimensions are likewise difficult to obtain. It therefore seems to have come into use first in the Mesopotamian Valley; it was also used to a certain extent in Egypt. Arches and

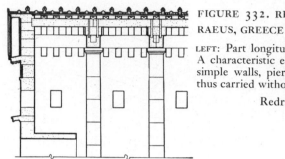

FIGURE 332. RESTORATION OF THE ARSENAL, PI-
RAEUS, GREECE

LEFT: Part longitudinal section; BELOW: Cross section.
A characteristic example of Greek construction based on
simple walls, piers, and lintels; even the sloping roof is
thus carried without ties or trussing.

Redrawn from Choisy, "L'Arsenal du Pirée"
in *Études épigraphiques* . . .

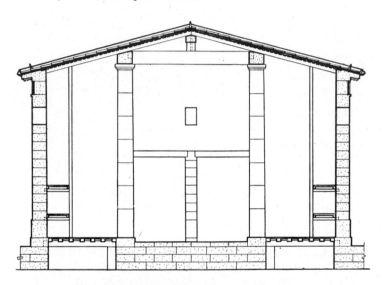

FIGURE 333. TEMPLE
OF NIKE APTEROS,
ATHENS

Characteristic rectangular
simplicity of typical post-
and-lintel and wall-and-
lintel construction.

Courtesy Ware Library

FIGURE 334. CARSON-PIRIE-SCOTT DEPARTMENT STORE, CHICAGO, ILLINOIS
Louis H. Sullivan, architect
The wider rectangles of post-and-lintel construction in steel.
Photograph Chicago Architectural Photograph Co., courtesy Museum of Modern Art

vaults have since remained an important factor in the architecture of the Near East and the Middle East. The peoples of Italy—first the Etruscans and later the Romans—were noted for their brilliant use of arches and vaults.

Structures vaulted in masonry possessed the enormous virtue of being fire-proof, and this is one of the facts underlying the tremendous importance given to vaulting throughout the history of architecture. It was losses from fires in wooden-roofed basilicas which induced Romanesque architects to attempt the construction of completely vaulted churches and thus gave birth to a

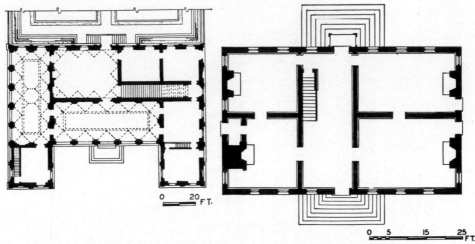

0   20 FT.

0   5   15   25 FT.

FIGURE 335 (LEFT). VILLA FARNESINA, ROME. PLAN

Baldassare Peruzzi, architect

A characteristic bearing-wall, generally post-and-lintel, plan of the Renaissance, characterized by regularity of rhythm, parallelism of walls, and rectangularity of basic room shapes.

FIGURE 336 (RIGHT). WESTOVER, VIRGINIA (FIRST HALF EIGHTEENTH CENTURY). PLAN

A typical wall-and-lintel construction plan; bearing walls subdivide the area into smaller, easily spanned units, and walls are relatively thick with relatively small openings. General rectangularity is a natural result of the structural system. Floor joists cross the hall parallel to the length of the house; the joists over the rooms are at right angles, with their inner ends supported on the central walls.

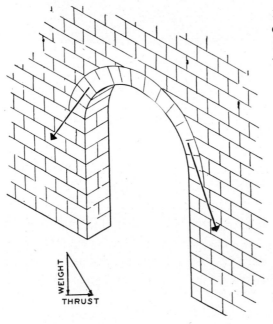

FIGURE 337. DIAGRAM ISOMETRIC OF A STONE ARCH, SHOWING STRESS LINES AND RESOLUTION INTO THRUST AND WEIGHT

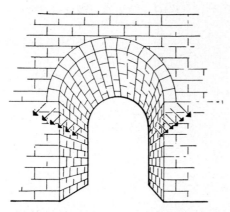

FIGURE 338. TYPICAL BARREL OR TUNNEL VAULT

Note that the thrusts are continuous for the entire length of the vault on both sides and require thick walls or heavy continuous abutments to withstand them.

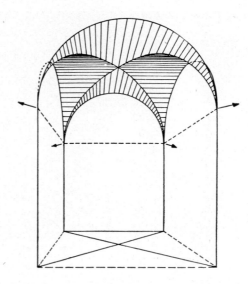

FIGURE 339 (RIGHT). DIAGRAM OF A SIMPLE INTERSECTING OR GROINED VAULT OVER A SQUARE BAY

The groins are in the plane of the diagonals of the square and form ellipses. The thrust is diagonally outward at the corners.

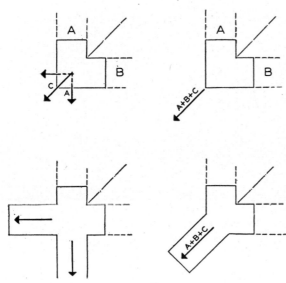

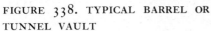

FIGURE 340. SUPPORTS AND ABUTMENTS FOR SQUARE GROINED VAULTS

ABOVE: The simplest support of an actual square groined vault is L-shaped, supporting two arches, A and B. The thrust of arch A is shown at A. Arch B thrusts at right angles to it, and the groin exerts a diagonal thrust C. BELOW: These forces can be combined and abutted by a diagonal buttress (lower right) or analyzed into rectangular components and resisted by buttresses at right angles (lower left). Gothic towers show both usages.

FIGURE 341. OSPE-
DALE DEGLI INNO-
CENTI, FLORENCE,
ITALY. LOGGIA

Filippo Brunelleschi,
architect

Arched and vaulted con-
struction with exposed tie
rods.

Courtesy Ware Library

FIGURE 342. OSPEDALE DEL CEPPO, PISTOIA, ITALY. ARCADE

Another example of the typical Italian use of tie rods.   Courtesy Avery Library

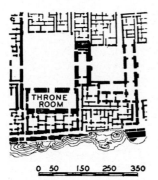

FIGURE 343. ROYAL PALACE, BABYLON. PART PLAN

The influence of vaults on plan can be seen in the throne room and the gateway hall, or guard room, between the two courts; both of these have the thick walls necessary to resist the vault thrust.

THRONE ROOM

0 50 150 250 350

movement that eventually resulted in Gothic architecture. Similarly, in the early years of the American Republic masonry-vaulted structures were popular for important buildings because of their fire-resistant qualities.

It is not necessary here to discuss the qualities of arches and vaults, since these have already been covered in Volume I, Chapter 14; but the precise way in which these qualities are reflected in plan and in aspect does require a brief note. The major effect of this type of construction depends on two things: first, the relatively great width of the opening or span which can be covered; and, second, the fact that all arches and vaults—even when apparently monolithic, like those of concrete—exert a side thrust which requires a heavy weight or a counterthrust to resist it. Thus it follows that arches adjacent to each other in the same line, because their thrusts meet and counteract each other, can be supported on isolated piers to form an arcade but the end arches of any arcade must have suitable abutments or buttresses. In the case of many Italian arcades and in much Italian medieval and Renaissance vaulted construction, the thrust is taken care of by exposed tie rods rather than by means of abutments. Whether or not this is an adequate artistic expression is debatable. From the standpoint of pure logic, there seems to be no more reason here to condemn tie rods than to condemn the tie beams or tie rods of a triangular truss. Nevertheless, if the problem of expression in architecture involves more than pure logic, if it entails the development of the construction qualities in such a way that they may be obvious to anyone, then it may be said that tie rods in this case are less expressive than heavy abutments or buttresses because they are less evident (Figs. 341, 342).

Other results of this type of construction are apparent in the heavy walls necessary for continuous vaults (domes or barrel vaults), such as are found in some Mesopotamian work (Fig. 343), in the Pantheon at Rome, and in many

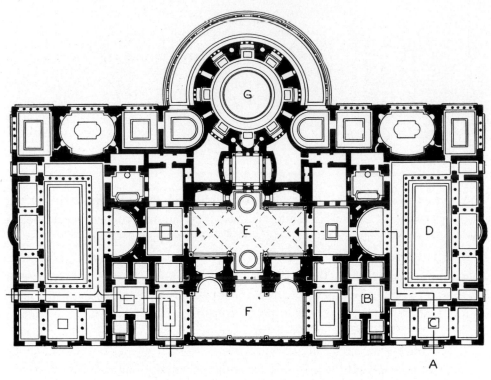

FIGURE 344. BATHS OF CARACALLA, ROME. PLAN OF CENTRAL BLOCK

This plan is a characteristic result of the logical application of the Roman vaulting system. The concentrated thrusts of the great groined vaults over the central hall, E, are abutted by heavy cross walls which also act as major plan divisions. Longitudinal thrusts are abutted by the walls on either side of the passages leading from E to the open court, D, and enormously thick walls around the calidarium, G, buttress the thrust of its huge dome.

Romanesque churches. The same qualities can be found in the broadly projecting buttresses at the points of support where groined vaults are used, as, for instance, in the great halls of the Roman thermae (Fig. 344), in the Basilica of Constantine, and in most Gothic churches (Figs. 345, 506, 507).

The nineteenth-century industrialization of building processes contributed strongly toward the substitution of lintel construction for arched construction. The necessity for speed in building, the fact that beams and girders could be easily machine-produced, and the comparatively heavy weights of the usual masonry vaults all combined to eliminate, generally speaking, vaulted construction. It had too many aesthetic advantages, however, to allow it to disappear completely, and further study produced at least two types of light masonry vaulting of minimum thrust—a system of light tile vault building named after its developer, Guastavino, and vaults of reinforced concrete. Guastavino

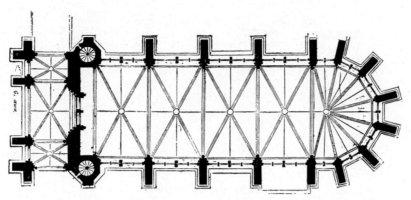

FIGURE 345. STE CHAPELLE, PARIS. PLAN OF UPPER CHAPEL

A plan typical of the developed French Gothic of the thirteenth century. Ribbed groined vaults concentrate weights at points rhythmically spaced, and thrusts are counterbalanced by buttresses projecting boldly at right angles to the wall. The wall as a supporting member is entirely eliminated, and great stained-glass windows occupy the entire space from pier to pier.

From Viollet-le-Duc, *Dictionnaire raisonné* . . .

vaults have continued in use for various types of religious and public structures; they seem to fit easily and naturally into buildings of solid masonry construction. Reinforced concrete vaults have the advantage that in their design the use of correctly spaced reinforcing rods in tension eliminates much of the thrust and therefore allows comparatively thin supports; the result is a construction that is light and airy.

Various types of thin concrete vault have played an increasingly important part in much industrial construction, especially in hangars for dirigibles and airplanes. And the growing popularity of this flexible building method is projecting a new note of variety and interest into mid-twentieth-century architecture.

A somewhat similar development of arched construction in wood has taken place; this is based either on the uniting of small framing members into a cylindrical network (lamella construction) or on the use of laminated arches. Such laminated arches have been utilized in many types of building; although not entirely fireproof, they permit graceful interiors of great height and width.

In general it may be said that arched and vaulted construction gives rise to plans of almost unlimited variety; the necessary buttressing elements as essential parts of the plan, as well as the rhythms of the supports, are dependent on the size and membering of the vaults. In exterior and interior aspect the curved lines of arches and vaults are dominant expressions, and in some cases the buttresses also are of major importance. The expression problems inherent

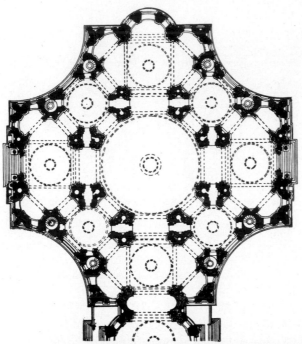

A plan entirely based on the brilliant combination of domes on
pendentives, cross vaults, and
niche vaults. The supporting
piers are concentrated and arranged so that the thrusts of the
central dome are adequately buttressed.

FIGURE 347. WREN'S FIRST DESIGN FOR ST. PAUL'S CATHEDRAL, LONDON. INTERIOR
PERSPECTIVE

This interior view shows the richness of visual effect created by a succession of arches and domes.

From the *Wren Society*

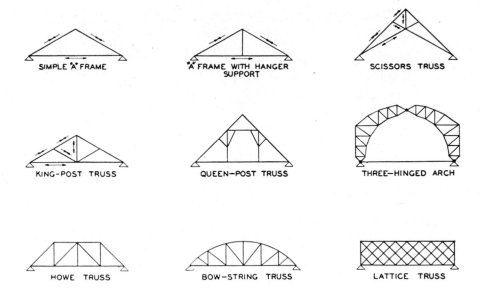

FIGURE 348. VARIOUS TYPES OF COMMONLY USED TRUSSES

Note the triangular basis of all except the queen-post truss. Here the central rectangle is statically unstable; hence the diagonal braces introduced at the top of the queen posts. The lattice truss, though apparently formed of diagonal squares, can be analyzed into a series of overlapping triangles. It is used where small pieces of material are more easy to obtain than larger and stronger elements. Thus the Town truss, invented by Ithiel Town, was a lattice truss which used timbers of uniform size connected by the simplest stock bolts.

in modern types of vault, where thrusts are minimized, are difficult and as yet not entirely mastered. If the architect follows carefully and simply the nature of the construction, as he feels it, his design is likely to have the correct expression.

Trussed construction depends on the fact that a triangle is a rigid form; so long as the sides of a triangle are unbroken and constant in length, its shape cannot be changed. Consequently, any systematic combination of triangles will remain rigid provided its members are strong enough to resist the strains imposed on them. All true trusses are merely combinations of such triangular forms. The simplest truss is formed by a pair of roof rafters and a tie beam connecting them at the bottom. Fortunately it is possible to work out mathematically the force at work in any member of a truss and to design it accordingly; trusses therefore can be used to span widths of great size, and many different types have been developed for spans of different widths and for halls of different sizes. Because of their rigidity true trusses exert no thrust, and, because trusses are most often used on comparatively wide spans, the vertical weights

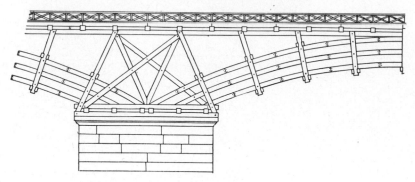

FIGURE 349. A ROMAN MILITARY WOODEN BRIDGE, BASED ON ONE SHOWN ON THE
COLUMN OF TRAJAN

The Romans were well acquainted with the truss principle, though apparently ignorant of its
scientific refinements. Here they have combined truss and arch principles in a design of brilliant
ingenuity. The Column of Trajan shows many other examples of wooden trussed construction.

Redrawn from Choisy, *L'Art de bâtir chez les Romains*

which they transfer to their supports are frequently enormous. Trusses and
trussed construction therefore will generally suggest plans with widely spaced
isolated supports and with aspects, both exterior and interior, of great openness
and lightness. Trusses are of all shapes—horizontal panels, triangles, trusses
with sloped sides and bottoms, and trusses with under sides which take curved
or arched outlines (Fig. 348). This gives the architect abundant freedom in the
design of trussed interiors. It also gives additional force to the fact, as noted
before, that it is one of the characteristics of modern construction to break
down former hard-and-fast categories.

Many great arched trusses are hinged to allow expansion and contraction
with changes in temperature. The moment this is done the rigidity of the whole
is lost, and we find that these hinged-arch trusses exert enormous thrusts which
have to be taken care of by heavy abutments in the foundations (as in many
arched-truss bridges) or by tie rods, sometimes placed under the floor of a
great trussed hall (as in the case of certain armories and similar structures).
One of the finest of such great trussed halls was the Galerie des Machines of
the Paris Exposition of 1889 (Fig. 353), where the design of the trusses showed
a great refinement, both structurally and aesthetically.

Another type of construction which it is difficult to classify consists of various kinds of portal-arch and rigid-frame structures in steel or concrete—constructions which are not susceptible of theoretical mathematical analysis (Figs.
355–362). Many of these partake somewhat of the nature of the arch and some-

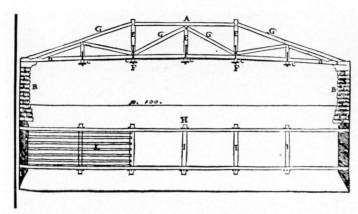

FIGURE 350. TRUSSED
BRIDGES DESIGNED BY
ANDREA PALLADIO

Palladio's bridges show an
almost perfect applica-
tion of truss principles—
the most scientific pro-
duced up to their time.

From Palladio, *I Quattro
Libri dell' Architettura*

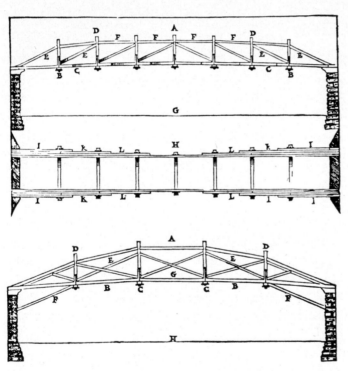

what of the nature of post-and-lintel construction. They are increasingly used
because of economies in material and labor and because of the generally clean,
untroubled effect which they produce. Thus, in some of the powerhouses of
the TVA, rigid-frame construction in steel was used because its simple form
not only allowed an inexpensive and efficient roof construction but also produced an interior easy to illuminate, without the disturbing shadows which

FIGURE 351. GRAND CENTRAL STATION, NEW YORK. TRAIN SHED
A characteristic example of iron-arched construction over a large span.   From *Harper's Weekly*

the usual construction would have produced and yet without the necessity of a hung ceiling. (See Fig. 359.)

Rigid-frame construction in reinforced concrete has many applications. By means of balanced rigid frames it is possible to produce cantilevers of great length, as in various race tracks and stadiums, where the grandstand seating and the cantilevered roof above it are both held on a series of rigid frames; here the seating itself serves as a counterweight for the cantilever. Good examples are the Stadium Giovanni Berta at Florence, by Nervi (Fig. 362), and the Buenos Aires race track, by Acevedo, Becu & Moreno. Simpler and more normal rigid frames offer enormous possibilities for creating large interiors and have frequently been used in industrial buildings—hangars, assembly halls, and so on. An excellent example of their use for a more monumental purpose is the superb church in Dortmund by Pinno and Grund (Figs. 360, 361), the beauty of which arises almost entirely from the frank yet subtle expression of its construction.

Expression of this kind of structure is a particularly fascinating problem. The depth of the frame members allows them to be expressed strongly either

FIGURE 352. BIBLIOTHÈQUE STE GENEVIÈVE, PARIS. UPPER READING ROOM

Henri Labrouste, architect

An early but highly architectonic use of iron arches and iron supports combined with masonry walls.   Courtesy Ware Library

FIGURE 353. GALERIE DES MACHINES, PARIS EXPOSITION OF 1889. INTERIOR

Dutert, architect; Contamin, engineer

Arched steel trusses, elegant and efficient in form, span more than 450 feet.

Courtesy Ware Library

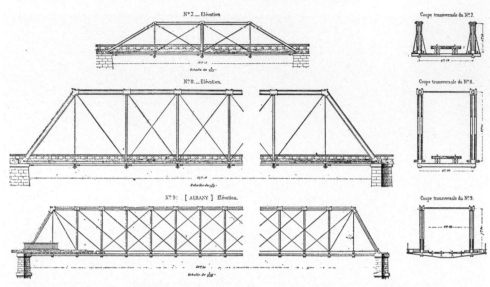

FIGURE 354. THREE BRIDGES OF WROUGHT AND CAST IRON AS DEVELOPED IN THE
UNITED STATES CIRCA 1870

Note that the compression members are in cast iron and the tension rods in wrought iron.

From Malézieux, *Travaux publics des États-Unis d'Amérique en 1870*

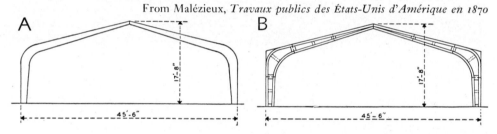

FIGURE 355. RIGID FRAMES IN LAMINATED WOOD

A: Solid rigid frames of rectangular section, made of strips parallel to the general curvature;
B: Laminated rigid frame formed of thin webs, with heavy flanges and stiffeners.

Redrawn from Huntington, *Building Construction*

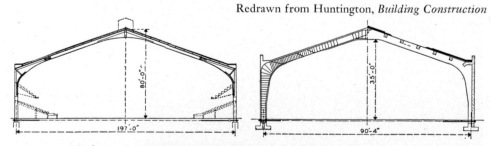

FIGURE 356 (LEFT). RIGID FRAME IN STRUCTURAL STEEL

This frame is from the Chicago Amphitheater in the Stock Yards and shows the elegance of form
and the lightness possible with this system, even over large spans.

FIGURE 357 (RIGHT). RIGID FRAME IN REINFORCED CONCRETE

This example is from an armory. The left-hand side shows the general pattern of the reinforcement.   Figures 356 and 357 redrawn from Huntington, *Building Construction*

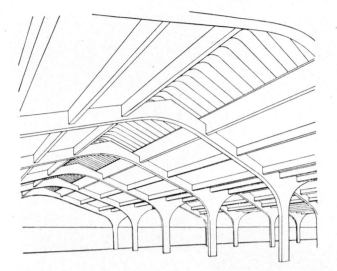

FIGURE 358. AN INDUS-
TRIAL INTERIOR WITH
CONCRETE SKYLIGHTED
ROOF SUPPORTED ON
CONCRETE RIGID FRAMES

This drawing illustrates the
interesting visual character
possible through an imaginative use of reinforced concrete rigid frames.

Redrawn from Huntington,
Building Construction

FIGURE 359. CHICKA-
MAUGA POWERHOUSE,
TVA. INTERIOR

Roland Wank, chief archi-
tect

The direct simplicity of
rigid frames in steel.

Courtesy TVA

FIGURE 360. CHURCH OF ST. NICHOLAS, DORTMUND, GERMANY. EXTERIOR AND INTERIOR

Pinno & Grund, architects

Rigid concrete frames, simply treated, allow floods of light and develop expressive forms.

From *Deutsche Bauzeitung*

on the exterior or on the interior (or both) of ceilings or roofs. Roof surfaces can be kept well below the tops of the frames, and the sturdy haunches that are often necessary will make a forceful and handsome pattern. A rich and original example of such a treatment may be seen in the concrete church of Ste Thérèse at Elisabethville, by P. Tournon (Fig. 363); another excellent instance is in the Le Corbusier design for the Palace of the Soviets (mentioned later), where the ends of the rigid frames are hung from a great parabolic arch. Yet a warning is necessary here—one must realize the difficulty of making watertight connections between the frames and the roof surfaces between them; an especially careful handling of flashing is necessary.

Two other important types of construction remain to be treated: cantilevered, or corbeled, construction and suspended construction. Both are old types of building which have received fresh, intensive study in recent years and a growing application in new ways. Both exert a tremendous influence on the aspect of structures utilizing them.

Corbeled, or cantilevered, construction has been in use since brackets were first introduced (Fig. 364). Essentially, it entails merely the carrying of weights which project beyond the face of the supports below. Classic cornices in stone

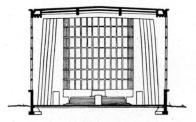

FIGURE 361. CHURCH OF ST. NICHO-
LAS, DORTMUND, GERMANY. PLAN
AND SECTION

Pinno & Grund, architects

This church owes its form and character
almost entirely to the type of construction
used. A succession of rigid frames in concrete supports the roof, and almost the
entire vertical area between these frames
is glazed with stained glass set in simple
rectangular concrete mullions and tran-
soms. The construction is left entirely exposed, and the effect is monumental and
dignified.

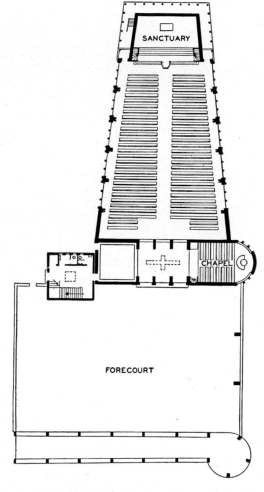

are excellent examples. Many log cabins or plank-built chalet types of building
employ quite elaborate corbels made simply by projecting each course of logs
or planks beyond the one below in order to support galleries, balconies, or projecting roof eaves. (See Figs. 388, 393.) But it is only in recent decades that
cantilevered construction has been developed to such a degree as to control
large elements in the basic design of structures.

The essential difference between the corbel and the cantilever lies in the fact
that generally the corbel is relatively small in size and is built into another construction in such a way that the weights above the embedded portion are sufficient to prevent the whole from overturning. The cantilever is usually a beam
or girder of comparatively large size and relatively great length; it is supported

FIGURE 362. STADIUM GIOVANNI BERTA, FLORENCE, ITALY. GRANDSTAND

P. L. Nervi, architect

Each rigid frame supports both the seat ranges and the overhanging roof; only concrete permits such freedom in design.   From *Encyclopédie de l'architecture*

at some distance from its outer end by a post or wall, and at its inner end it is attached to a support so arranged that it cannot rise vertically. Then, if the beam is of sufficient strength, its outer, unsupported end will be held rigidly in position and enabled to bear the desired weight. The first major use of such cantilever beams probably occurred in the construction of the projecting upper stories so familiar in late medieval houses. Its most common modern use is in commercial or industrial buildings, where a maximum amount of outside light, unbroken by columns, is desired; for only by this method is it possible to have buildings with absolutely continuous openings on every floor (Figs. 367, 371).

It is the continuity of opening which must form the basis for any true architectural expression of cantilevered construction, for that very continuity is the unique contribution to building shape which this type of construction has

FIGURE 363 (OPPOSITE). STE THÉRÈSE, ELISABETHVILLE, FRANCE. PLAN, PERSPECTIVE, AND TWO SECTIONS

Paul Tournon, architect

This ingenious concrete church is supported by a series of braced rigid concrete frames, with a light shell vault between them, all so arranged as to form a sort of modern Gothic. The side aisles are low and roofed with flat slabs.

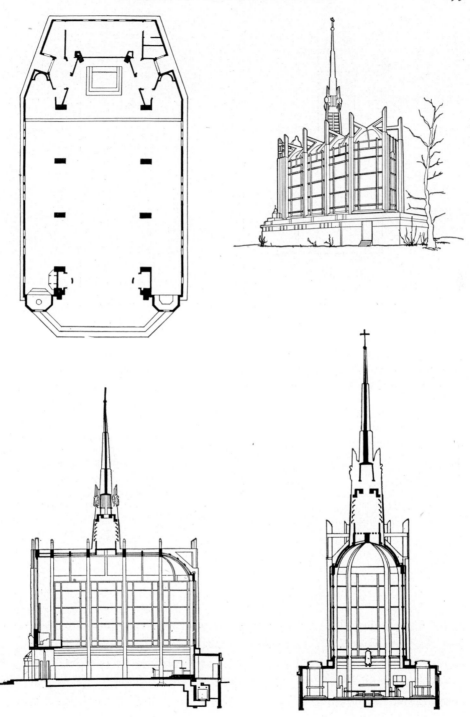

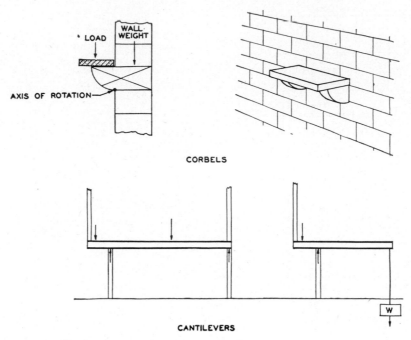

CORBELS

CANTILEVERS

FIGURE 364. CORBELS AND CANTILEVERS

Corbels are usually built into a wall; cantilevers are formed by the ends of girders or beams which project beyond one of the two necessary supports.

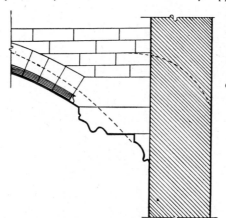

FIGURE 365. SEGMENTAL ARCH ON CORBEL

This is based on a system much used in the halls of twelfth-century châteaux, as in Hoch Koenigsburg. Note the way the general thrust line of the arch (shown dotted) works with the profile of the corbel.

Redrawn from Viollet-le-Duc,
Dictionnaire raisonné . . .

made. Cantilevered buildings or cantilevered portions of buildings will therefore tend to place emphasis on horizontal bands of windows through the use of horizontal spandrels or horizontal balcony railings or parapets. Any considerable amount of strong vertical separations between individual sash becomes undesirable, and nothing should exist which might be mistaken for a column.

FIGURE 366. PALAZZO VECCHIO, FLOR-
ENCE, ITALY. EXTERIOR

Daring corbeling in stone; the face of the
tower overhangs the front wall and itself
bears a boldly corbeled crown.

Courtesy Ware Library

FIGURE 367 (BELOW). HUNGER-
FORD FISH MARKET, LONDON, 1835

Charles Fowler, architect

Ingenious cantilevered construction in
cast iron. The hollow cast-iron columns
also act as down spouts for water from
the roof.

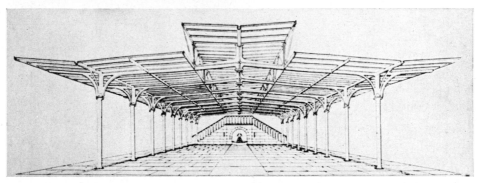

Such horizontal compositions can be seen in the Schocken store at Chemnitz,
by Eric Mendelsohn (Fig. 172), and in the Embassy Court Apartments in
Brighton, by Wells Coates.

Cantilevers of unprecedented length, weighted at their inner ends by entire
buildings, carry the great shelter slab over the embarking and debarking area
of the Tempelhof Airfield in Berlin (Fig. 371). Here the protected area is wide

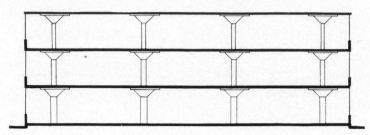

FIGURE 368. CANTILEVERED CONSTRUCTION IN REINFORCED CONCRETE

This section shows the typical system used in many industrial plants.

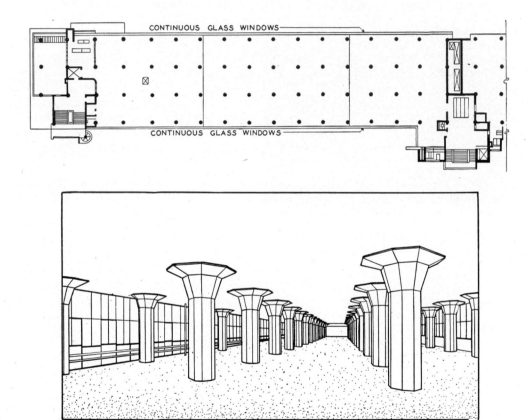

FIGURE 369. VAN NELLE TOBACCO FACTORY AND WAREHOUSE, ROTTERDAM, THE NETHERLANDS. PART PLAN AND INTERIOR

Brinkman & Van der Vlugt, architects

A plan characteristic of reinforced concrete cantilevered structures; the columns are inside the external wall, which can thus be made to consist of long unbroken bands of windows on each floor. The view of the interior shows the refined type of column used and the great amount of light this system allows.

FIGURE 370. VAN NELLE TOBACCO FACTORY AND WAREHOUSE, ROTTERDAM, THE NETHERLANDS

Brinkman & Van der Vlugt, architects

Bold and logical use of cantilevered construction handled with discriminating skill.

Courtesy Museum of Modern Art

and high enough to permit the largest transport planes to enter and load under cover.

One other factor may frequently furnish a clue to the successful design of cantilevered structures—the fact that, as normally developed, cantilevered construction is simpler when the projection beyond the columns occurs only on one side, or at most on two sides, of a building than when an attempt is made to cantilever all four walls. Thus, the normal cantilevered industrial building will be cantilevered on the two long sides but not on the two short ends (Fig. 369). If, then, a striking difference in expression exists between the portions that are cantilevered and the portions that are not, interesting and dramatic effects of great power can often be developed. A telling contrast can be produced between the vertical expression of columns in the walls where there is no cantilever and the unbroken horizontal lines of those parts which are cantilevered beyond the columns. This rhythmical pattern not only is aesthetically forceful in its own right but is also a true expression of the actual construction of the building. It is one of the reasons for the brilliancy of the tower portion

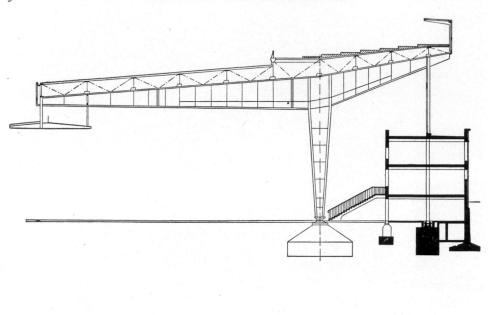

FIGURE 371. TEMPELHOF AIRPORT TERMINAL STRUCTURE, BERLIN. SECTION AND VIEW OF THE EMBARKING AREA

Ernst Sagebiel, architect

Alone among airports, the Berlin Tempelhof air terminal furnished an area covered over by a permanent structure large enough for transport planes to enter. The shelter here is provided by some of the largest cantilevers ever used in a building. Made of steel, they project a total of 132 feet beyond the supports and are counterweighted by the office structures as well as by huge underground counterweights. Large windows above the office buildings protect the area on that side. Part of the roof is used as an observation platform.

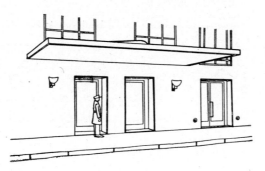

FIGURE 372. MARQUEE OF ROCKEFELLER APARTMENTS, NEW YORK

Harrison & Fouilhoux, architects

The chief cantilever beam which supports the marquee slab is concealed as far as possible by its position in the center of the marquee and by its detailing.

of the Philadelphia Saving Fund Building by Howe and Lescaze (Fig. 173).

The expression of smaller-scale brackets, or corbels, is a similar problem. It simply requires that the architect bear in mind the actual structure and that he somehow suggest in the appearance of the final composition the integral nature of the brackets, despite their portions built into the wall or otherwise concealed. When these corbeled or cantilevered details are of larger size, as, for example, in the case of broadly projecting shelters—a slab over an entrance or perhaps even over an entire terrace area—the problem becomes one of greater difficulty and brings up the puzzling question of whether the truest expression is best produced by the naked display of structural facts or by a more subtle, and perhaps more deeply felt, suggestion.

Many modern architects, for instance, have gone to great lengths to conceal the actual brackets or cantilevers which support a marquee or a terrace shelter slab (Fig. 372). They have apparently tried to produce the effect of a thin, almost over-thin, broadly protecting slab hung in the air by some hidden magic. Without question the effect is one of brilliant lightness; it astonishes, yet it is doubtful whether this appearance expresses or suggests the true type of construction which makes the element possible. It may well be that here the search for the simplest unbroken forms of pure geometric quality has led to an undue oversight of the potential beauty—the possible sense of satisfying strength— which a franker display, or at least a franker suggestion, of the cantilever beams would give. Thus, in the case of the marquee of the Rockefeller Apartments on West 54th and 55th Streets, by Harrison & Fouilhoux, the cantilever beams are placed above the slab in such a way that they can only be seen from over-

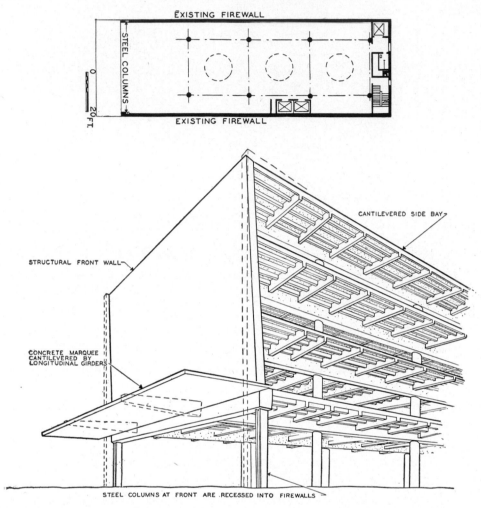

FIGURE 373. RENBERG'S CLOTHING STORE, TULSA, OKLAHOMA. PLAN AND CONSTRUCTION DIAGRAM

Joseph Boaz and Parr & Aderhold, associated architects

This store, built between party walls, shows an interesting and economical use of cantilevered construction.   Redrawn from the *Architectural Forum*

head. And in Frank Lloyd Wright's "Falling Water" the entire projecting terrace is formed with a great two-directional cantilever, which to some persons seems unduly fragile and light in appearance. Here, however, the two main cantilevers are expressed as powerful brackets beneath the terrace floor, so that at least from below one can gain the feeling of the nature of the support although not of its details.

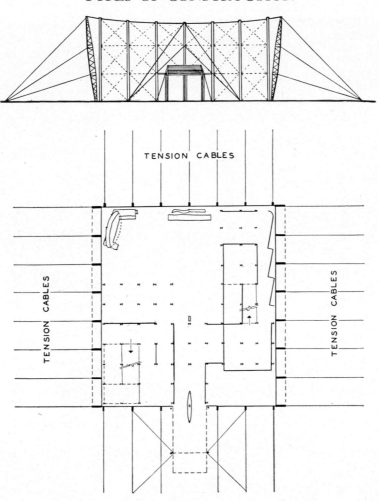

FIGURE 374. EXPOSITION PAVILION FOR "ESPRIT NOUVEAU," PARIS EXPOSITION OF 1937

Le Corbusier, architect

This pavilion is an excellent example of simple suspended construction. In essence it is a large tent, with walls and roof of textiles, supported on steel open-webbed struts held in place by tension cables. Redrawn from Le Corbusier, *Oeuvre complète*

The problem of the smaller projecting slabs that are common in contemporary buildings—slabs in which the reinforcement incorporated in the slab itself gives it sufficient strength—is perhaps a simpler one, for common sense tells the observer that the slab thickness is sufficient to prevent collapse, provided the slabs are well anchored in the building. This question of the expression of cantilevered construction, like the expression of all new architectural forms

FIGURE 375. BRONX-WHITESTONE BRIDGE, NEW YORK
The delicate strength of steel in tension admirably expressed.

Courtesy Triborough Bridge and Tunnel Authority, New York

and structural systems, is thus a challenge to the sensitivity and the imagination of all architects of the twentieth century.

Another type of construction which is of growing importance is the one we have called suspended construction; here the large elements of a structure, instead of being built up from a foundation, are hung from an overhead support. This, like many of the types of construction already mentioned, is in essence a primitive form. Tents, for instance, are excellent examples of a simple

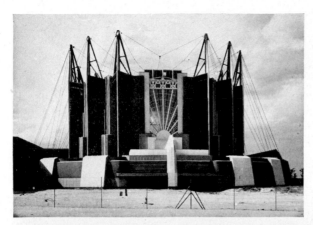

FIGURE 376. TRAVEL AND TRANSPORT BUILDING, CHICAGO EXPOSITION OF 1933

Bennett, Burnham, and Holabird, associated architects

A pioneer example of suspended construction in a large building.

Photograph Hedrich-Blessing

FIGURE 377. EXPOSITION HALL PROPOSED FOR PARIS
Baudouin & Lods, architects
A French suggestion for the use of suspended construction to roof a hall 1,300 feet in diameter.
From *American Architect*

type of suspended construction. Suspension bridges of various kinds have been used from a very early period in some parts of the world—notably in the mountainous parts of western China and the near-by portions of central Asia. Both tents and suspension bridges have continued in use to the present day. In the Paris Exposition of 1937, for instance, the pavilion of the group "Esprit Nouveau," designed by Le Corbusier, was a highly developed tent structure of textiles hung on delicate, braced, steel posts (Fig. 374). The Bronx-Whitestone Bridge (Fig. 375) illustrates the extraordinary delicacy possible in a modern suspension bridge.

What has given a fresh importance to suspended architecture has been a growing realization of the remarkable strength of steel and certain other ma-

FIGURE 378. COMPETITION DESIGN FOR NEW YORK CRYSTAL PALACE (1852). SECTION

Bogardus & Hoppin, architects

This design contemplated a circular structure with cast-iron walls and in the center a cast-iron tower, from which the roof was to be suspended. The circular form of the wall prevented it from yielding inward because of the pull of the suspended roof.

From Silliman, *World of Science, Art, and Industry* . . .

terials and alloys when in tension. Buildings naturally have to be supported from the ground in some way; but, if steel is relatively stronger in tension than in compression, it would appear logical that in some types of building great economies would result if the supports could be concentrated into the fewest possible areas and if the building could be hung from these supports by tension members. This type of construction was used on a large scale in the Travel and Transport Building, by Edward H. Bennett, Hubert Burnham, and John Holabird, at the Chicago Century of Progress Exposition in 1933 (Fig. 376). It was also the essence of a brilliant proposal for an exposition building at the 1937 Paris Exposition (Fig. 377). This design, by Baudouin & Lods, contemplated a colossal circular building with a trussed-arch exterior framework. The roof was to hang from the framework by means of tightly stretched catenary cables. Theoretical spans of an almost indefinite width could thus be roofed, and buildings a thousand or more feet in diameter, with no interior supports, would be possible.

In a way, this solution of a large-span roof had been anticipated nearly nineteen centuries earlier in the great awning over the Colosseum in Rome. Here the awning was supported by masts around the circuit of the building; these

FIGURE 379. COMPETITION DESIGN FOR THE NEW YORK CRYSTAL PALACE (1852)
Leopold Eidlitz, architect
An early suggestion for the use of suspended construction.   Courtesy Avery Library

masts, closely spaced, were themselves supported and held in place by brackets and sockets projecting from the exterior face of the top-story wall. The inward pull at the mast tops was resisted by the strength of the masts themselves, by the weight of the stone wall, and, still more important, by the fact that the curving of the wall, acting as a horizontal vault or arch, gave it great strength against any inward-directed forces.

In the Paris project, the inward tension of the roof catenaries is resisted in a somewhat similar way. The plan is circular and the great surrounding upper

FIGURE 380. FIRST DYMAXION HOUSE. MODEL
Buckminster Fuller, designer
A closely reasoned application of suspended construction to house design.

Courtesy Museum of Modern Art

beam or roof-plate element is non-compressible inward because of its shape. Just as in a bicycle wheel thin tension spokes not only furnish ample support for the hub but also give great strength to the fragile rim, so in this Baudouin & Lods design the thin tension catenaries support the roof and are in turn supported by—and even strengthen—the circular rim to which they are attached.

This idea had been anticipated nearly a century earlier by two designs submitted in the competition for the New York Crystal Palace in 1852 (Figs. 378, 379). One, for example, by the architect Leopold Eidlitz, consisted of a long, high nave flanked by lower side aisles; the roofs of both were supported by catenaries hung from masts at the edge of the nave and at the outside of the aisles. The tension members and anchorages took the form of triangular buttress-like forms projecting at the sides. The whole was treated in a sort of modified neo-Gothic. Although impractical for its time, it was an interesting and prophetic suggestion.

The other design was by Bogardus & Hoppin. Bogardus was a great designer of cast-iron commercial buildings and one of the originators of this type. His Crystal Palace design contemplated a circular building nearly 400 feet in diameter, with cast-iron walls 60 feet high (which, he pointed out, consisted of sections that were demountable and could be re-used) and a high central tower. This tower was to serve two purposes—as an observatory, to be reached by an elevator, and as a support from which the roof was hung. The circular roof was to be of thin iron sheets suspended on iron catenaries. On a smaller scale, suspended construction was the essence of Buckminster Fuller's first Dymaxion house (Fig. 380)—a hexagonal house suspended from a central steel mast designed to contain all the necessary mechanical facilities. Thus the house would require only one small foundation, that for the mast, and the erection as well as the demounting of the house itself would become almost as easy as setting or furling the sails of a racing yacht.

One difficulty was inherent in almost all these early schemes for the use of metal in tension. If the system is based on catenaries—long suspension cables running from support to support—tremendous inward pressures are generated at the top of their supports and require resistance—by means of cables and anchorages, as in the case of suspension bridges; by shrouds or stays, as in the case of smaller buildings; and by shrouds to brace a central mast, as in the Dymaxion house. Such shrouds or cables would necessarily vary in length according to the temperature. Long catenary-supported roofs would sink and rise as the weather turned warm or cold, and this variation in the case of large buildings brings up extremely difficult problems, for various portions of the building must be adjusted so that they can move according to the temperature and yet remain tight to wind and water.

Aesthetically, such constructions raise troublesome problems of expression. This was apparent, for instance, in the Chicago Exposition building referred to above, which earned the name "Grasshopper Building" because of the ungainly shapes of the supporting stanchions and their braces. It is entirely possible, however, that further study in this promising field of large-scale construction will indicate approaches more fruitful and will develop designs both more frank and more beautiful, until the vast structures which such a method makes possible will achieve the compelling grace of the world's best suspension bridges.

There is another type of suspended construction in which various elements of a structure are hung from permanent and rigid supports designed specifically for them. These may take the form of cantilevered beams or even of great steel or concrete arches. Le Corbusier's unaccepted competition design for the Palace of the Soviets in Moscow made brilliant use of a great hyperbolic arch of reinforced concrete, from which the roof of the mammoth auditorium was supported by vertical cables. Because of the size and power of the forms which construction like this produces and because of the perfect expression of the forces at work, designs of this character might brilliantly achieve a sense of striking power. On a smaller scale, the suspension of minor building elements, like balconies, from beams, girders, or trusses overhead is common, although little has been made of them architecturally and architects as far as possible seem to have sought to conceal or neglect the suspension bars or rods that form the essence of the construction. There is, however, at least one building in which the entire side walls, together with the floor panels adjacent to them, are hung from cantilevered girders at the roof level. This building, designed by Thompson & Churchill, is on the northwest corner of 57th Street and Lexington Avenue in New York. The combination of suspension and cantilevered construction was adopted here because, by means of this scheme, the entire weight could be supported on six interior columns and because extremely difficult foundation problems could thereby be avoided along the lot lines. The architects have expressed the hangers by using vertical metal bands which stop on the lowest spandrel in a series of intersecting horizontal planes. This bottom detail of the hangers is a most interesting attempt to express in decorative form the forces at work in an architectural member, and it reveals unusual care in the search for expressive shape.

Lightness, delicacy, the avoidance of the least suggestion of support in the enclosing walls, and the powerful development of supporting struts or masts or towers—these seem the essential qualities in buildings of suspended construction, and it is through the further study of those qualities in the suspended buildings of the future that successful architectural expression is to be achieved.

SUGGESTED ADDITIONAL READING FOR CHAPTER 12

Choisy, Auguste, *L'Art de bâtir chez les Romains* (Paris: Ducher, 1873); English translation in *Brickbuilder*, Vols. III–VI (1894–97).
—— *Histoire de l'architecture*, 2 vols. (Paris: Gauthier-Villars, 1899).
Crane, Theodore, *Architectural Construction; the Choice of Structural Design* (New York: Wiley; London: Chapman & Hall, 1947).

Fitch, James Marston, *American Building; the Forces That Shape It* (Boston: Houghton Mifflin, 1948).

Hamlin, Talbot [Faulkner], *Architecture, an Art for All Men* (New York: Columbia University Press, 1947), Chap. 2.

Huntington, Whitney Clark, *Building Construction* . . . 2nd ed. (New York: Wiley; London: Chapman & Hall [1944]).

Michaels, Leonard, *Contemporary Structure in Architecture* (New York: Reinhold [c1950]).

Scammon Lectures for 1915; Six Lectures on Architecture, by Ralph Adams Cram, Thomas Hastings, and Claude Bragdon . . . (Chicago: University of Chicago Press [c1917]), the two lectures by Thomas Hastings.

Viollet-le-Duc, Eugène Emmanuel, *Dictionnaire raisonné de l'architecture française du XIe au XVIe siècle* . . . 10 vols. (Paris: Bance and Morel, 1854–68).

—— *Entretiens sur l'architecture*, 2 vols. (Paris: Morel, 1863–72); translated as *Discourses on Architecture* . . . with an introductory essay by Henry Van Brunt, 2 vols. (Boston: Osgood, 1875–81).

—— *Rational Building; being a Translation of the Article "Construction" in the Dictionnaire* . . . by George Martin Huss (New York and London: Macmillan, 1895).

13

Architectural Design and Structural Methods II: Block or Gravity Construction

ANOTHER METHOD of classifying structures—which is more fundamental than that discussed in the preceding chapter because it considers fundamental differences in the way in which basic materials are
used and put together—is to class them as follows: (1) block or gravity construction, (2) mass or cohesive construction, and (3) framed construction.
Block or gravity construction is that type in which blocks of building material
of relatively large size are piled one on top of another and held in place chiefly
by their own weight and the friction between adjacent units. Mass or cohesive
construction is that type in which material units of relatively small size, or of
a fluid or semi-fluid nature, are held together by the strong adhesiveness of the
basic materials so that the mass, when hardened or set, is almost monolithic.
Framed construction is that type in which the materials and members used for
supporting or giving rigidity to a structure are completely separate and usually
different from the materials which create shelter. The present chapter will be
devoted to the first of these three methods, block or gravity construction.

Block construction has been used from an early period. In stone it is typical
of all of those primitive culture centers which built stone beehive shelters or
huts or piled great stones on each other to form tombs or religious monuments.
In wood the system appears in the type of log cabin found in forested northern
Europe as early as the Middle Ages and perhaps earlier. It is used in more developed forms in many Russian churches, in the elaborately detailed log constructions of Scandinavia, and in the chalet construction of the Alps.

The typical log cabin shows remarkably well how both the plan types and
the appearance follow inevitably from the type of construction. Log cabins
are made by placing on the ground, or on a foundation, two logs parallel to

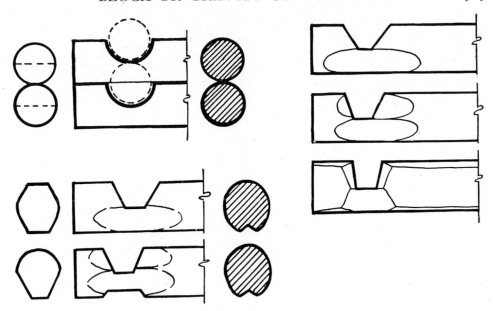

FIGURE 381. TYPICAL LOG-CABIN LOG NOTCHING

ABOVE, LEFT: The simplest form of notching, used in both Scandinavia and America; ABOVE, RIGHT: Various types of log shaping and notching from Sweden; BELOW: Top notching; top and bottom notching; two types of log grooving to give a tighter joint between the logs.

Redrawn from Erixon, "The North-European Technique . . ." in *Folkliv*

FIGURE 382. A TYPICAL LOG CABIN, NEAR DARBY, PENN-SYLVANIA

Photograph Rau Studios, reproduced from Talbot Hamlin, *The American Spirit in Architecture*, Vol. 13 of "The Pageant of America" (copyright, Yale University Press)

each other and separated by a distance equal to the desired width of the building. Across their ends other logs are place at right angles to the first pair, and notches are cut in either the lower logs (Fig. 381), or in both lower and upper logs, to hold them rigidly in position. On the rectangular basis so created more logs are piled in pairs, first longitudinally, then transversely, the ends being

FIGURE 383. HOUSE DOOR FROM MORA PARISH, DALE-CARLIA, SWEDEN (CIRCA 1000–1100). NOW IN THE ZORN MUSEUM

One way of finishing openings in log structures was by the use of vertical jamb planks, into which the log ends were rebated. In ancient Scandinavian work these jambs were sometimes richly carved.

From Erixon, "The North-European Technique . . ." in *Folkliv*

FIGURE 384. CORNER OF A BARN, SAND-SELE VILLAGE, SORSELE PARISH, SWEDISH LAPLAND

A simple form of notching, with logs roughly hewn to shape.

Redrawn from Erixon, "The North-European Technique . . ." in *Folkliv*

notched as in the first set of logs. Thus the four walls of the house rise, the log ends usually projecting beyond the notched corners. Whatever cracks occur in the horizontal joints between the logs are caulked or chinked with moss, clay, or cement. (See Figs. 382–386.)

Openings are made in various ways. Sometimes the logs are merely sawed through in the proper places and perhaps the ends pegged to give strength. If the opening is large, as in the case of doorways, vertical posts of planks or logs are placed on either side of it and the wall-log ends are notched or mortised into the posts. Roofs also are made in many different simple ways, either by using log rafters or by carrying up the gable ends in logs and supporting log purlins upon them.

The result produces an extraordinary similarity in the basic appearance of

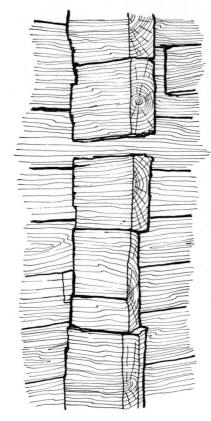

FIGURE 385 (LEFT). CLOSE-TIMBERED CORNER OF A WINDMILL FROM HABLINGBO PARISH, GOT-LAND (1794). NOW IN THE BUNGE MUSEUM, GOTLAND, SWEDEN

A typical block-construction corner in squared timber showing the intersections of plank ends coming through from a wall at right angles.

Redrawn from Erixon, "The North-European Technique . . ." in *Folkliv*

FIGURE 386 (RIGHT). LOG CABIN WITH SQUARED TIMBERS, DOWNINGTOWN, PENNSYLVANIA

Photograph L. A. Sampson, reproduced from Talbot Hamlin, *The American Spirit in Architecture*, Vol. 13 of "The Pageant of America" (copyright, Yale University Press)

these log buildings wherever they may be found. They are strictly rectangular in plan, and the size in each case is limited by the available lengths of straight logs and by the primitive types of roof construction used. Openings are small and always rectangular since they are spanned by the continuous log that runs through above them. Doors will often be framed by doorposts or doorjambs. In early Scandinavian examples these frequently consist of wide planks, care-fully smoothed and sometimes elaborately carved (Fig. 387). The corners of the buildings will be emphasized by the projecting log ends.

As building skills increased, many different kinds of corner notching were developed, and often the log ends which projected beyond the notches were roughly axed to form definite shapes, either squarish or hexagonal (Figs. 381, 383). In some cases the entire logs were squared into heavy planks without causing a change in the basic concept of the construction.

Log cabins probably first came into use in the United States in the second

FIGURE 387. A "HARBOR" (STOREHOUSE) FROM LÄLANDA, UPPLAND, SWEDEN. NOW AT DISA-GÅRDEN, GAMLA UPP-SALA, SWEDEN

A block construction of logs hewn to hexagonal section. The view illustrates the ease with which corbeling can be formed in this type of wood building.

Redrawn from Erixon, "The North-European Technique . . ." in *Folkliv*

half of the seventeenth century—in all probability introduced in the early Swedish settlements along the Delaware. Since this type of construction was eminently fitted for heavily forested areas and required little skilled labor, it was rapidly taken over by other colonists and became almost the standard building method used by the pioneers who little by little filled the country, spreading ever westward. The American log cabin probably was most highly developed during the first half of the nineteenth century in the country between the Alleghenies and the Mississippi. It is still in occasional use for summer camps and summer cottages, although many such buildings, apparently of logs, are actually ordinary wood-frame buildings with an applied covering of half logs or log slabs. Naturally such imitative construction is without architectural

FIGURE 388. LOFT-
BOWER AT ORNÄS,
TORSÅNG PARISH,
DALECARLIA, SWEDEN

A characteristic example
of highly developed
Swedish timber construc-
tion.

From Erixon, "The
North-European
Technique . . ."
in *Folkliv*

importance and is significant only as it indicates a widespread habit of imitative
design.

It should be obvious that corbels may be most easily made in log buildings by
merely extending the ends of the logs over those below, each projecting farther
than the one beneath. This method of corbeling with logs is frequently used in
the more highly developed Scandinavian examples to carry widely projecting
eaves or upper-floor balconies. (See Fig. 388.)

In the complex development of this basically simple log construction, some
of the seventeenth-century Russian churches of the Archangel area are pre-
eminent. Here the towering spires, which frequently cover the church body

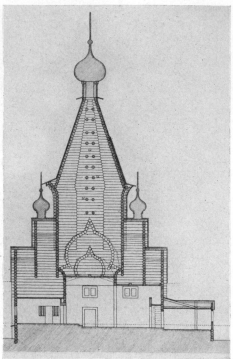

FIGURE 389. LOG-BUILT CHURCH AT OUNA, ARCHANGEL, RUSSIA. ELEVATION AND SECTION

A typical example of the northern Russian wood church; note especially the construction of the great central tower.

From Souslow, *Monuments de l'ancienne architecture Russe* . . .

proper, are formed in the typical manner, the logs of each course being slightly shorter than, and set slightly in from, those of the course beneath (Fig. 389). Thus a sort of corbeled vault in wood is produced. These churches also show a romantic complexity in plan, with details ingeniously worked out for the kind of timber used. Many village houses in Russia are also highly developed examples of ingenious log building.

Squared-log or plank construction was carried to its peak of development in the Alpine region of central Europe. Swiss and Tyrolese carpenters are especially skillful in developing houses of great size, with both exterior walls and bearing partitions made of squared timbers (Figs. 390–393). These are notched and intersect at the corners as in the case of ordinary log construction. Much corbeling is used to carry the wide, spreading eaves and the ever present open balcony across the front. Generally through the center of the building there is a heavy longitudinal bearing partition which carries the ridge.

FIGURE 390. CHARACTERISTIC CHALET OF THE UPPER RHINELAND

Built of squared planks, intersecting and halved at the corners, such a building expresses perfectly the qualities of block construction in wood. Its plan is the natural result of the type of construction used; the ridge of the roof is directly supported on a plank wall running through the center of the plan.   Redrawn from Viollet-le-Duc, *Dictionnaire raisonné* . .

Numerous attempts have been made at various times to develop other types of wooden construction based on the block or gravity system. Its advantages lie in its simplicity and in the high insulating quality inherent in the heavy, solid wood walls; yet the average log cabin is difficult to keep tight or insect-free. It was natural, therefore, for men to search for some system which would retain the advantages and correct the disadvantages of this type of construction. The most interesting of such types is the horizontal plank wall, seemingly invented by Orson Fowler (Fig. 394).

Block construction of a special type in concrete is common. Concrete can be easily cast in blocks of almost any desired shape; the most frequent kind uses a light aggregate, like cinders or pumice, and is formed into hollow blocks so that walls of it not only are easily built but also have a certain insulating value. But such blocks are usually neither sightly nor waterproof; consequently a covering of stucco or paint becomes necessary in any finished building. In general appearance, therefore, these concrete-block structures resemble any other stuccoed buildings, and any attempt to give them a special and expressive nature can only be based on using simple walls and piers that can be built easily from the stock block units available. Moreover, since such light concrete blocks have only a moderate compressive strength, their use is generally restricted to one-story houses, small shops, garages, and the like or to the erection of screen walls in framed constructions.

But there is another type of concrete-block construction which has produced important and beautiful architectural results. This type, developed by Frank Lloyd Wright and used in a series of remarkable houses in the Los Angeles

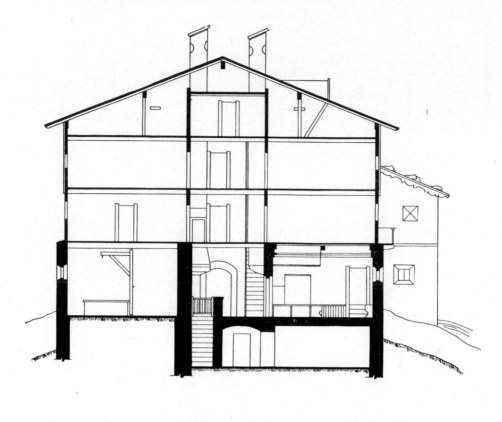

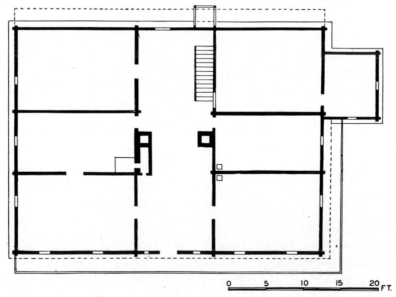

FIGURE 392. CHALET-CONSTRUCTED HOUSE AT GUT MAYRLEITHEN, SALZBURG, AUSTRIA. FRONT VIEW

A characteristic chalet exterior, showing the effect produced by the projecting corner inter-sections and the easily cantilevered roof and balcony.

Redrawn from Eigl, *Das Salzburger Gebirgshaus*

neighborhood, is based on the building of a two-shell wall, each shell being composed of thin, square concrete blocks set in a web of reinforcing rods (Figs. 395–397). These blocks are made of a rich mixture of specially selected materials and are formed with a semi-cylindrical sinkage running the full length of all four edges. The rods are spaced the width of one block apart and fit into the sinkages; the blocks are bedded in cement mortar. Thus a strong, rigid wall is built, amply reinforced, and its appearance is dominated by the continuous vertical and horizontal joints to which the system itself gives rise —joints which express the continuity of the rods embedded in them.

FIGURE 391 (OPPOSITE). CHALET-CONSTRUCTED HOUSE AT GUT MAYRLEITHEN, SALZBURG, AUSTRIA. PLAN AND SECTION

A characteristic plan and section of a chalet-type house. Note that the plank walls carry through all intersections; also note the general simplicity of rectangular planning. The roof is carried on purlins resting directly on the plank walls.   Redrawn from Eigl, *Das Salzburger Gebirgshaus*

FIGURE 393. CHALET IN LEYSIN, SWITZERLAND

Swiss skill in squared-timber construction.   Courtesy Avery Library

The square unit blocks are cast in metal forms; decorated blocks can thus be produced as needed, the only added expense being the cost of one special form from which casts can be taken indefinitely. Walls built in this fashion have a most definite and characteristic appearance. The over-all pattern of the

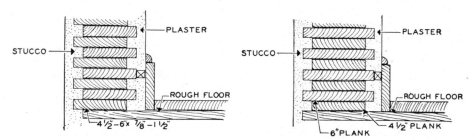

FIGURE 394. WOOD WALL CONSTRUCTION OF PLANKS SUPERPOSED AS PROPOSED BY ORSON FOWLER

The wall thus produced is a solid wooden structure of block type. The alternation of plank edges provides a key for the exterior stucco and the interior plaster. The cross-grain shrinkage of the timber would undoubtedly prove severe.

joints (usually emphasized by beveling the exposed edges) and the incorporation of patterned blocks in bands or spots, to give heightened interest, make a whole that is brilliantly effective under the play of the sun. Here effective expression not only is due to the pattern of the surface but also depends on the careful composition of the walls, the dimensions of which agree with the

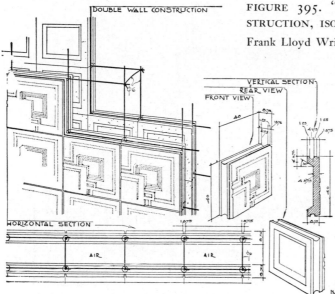

FIGURE 395. "TEXTILE BLOCK" CON-
STRUCTION, ISOMETRIC DIAGRAM

Frank Lloyd Wright, architect

This system of construc-
tion is based on the use
of precast square concrete
blocks, with rebates in the
edges. Continuous vertical
and horizontal reinforc-
ing rods are enclosed in
all the joints and weave
the whole together. Dou-
ble walls are thus built to
give an insulating air space
between them. Since the
blocks are precast, it is
simple to give them a pattern if desired. Contrasts
between plain and pat-
terned blocks create much
of the interest.

From the *Architectural
Record*

module of the unit block; in addition, the shapes of the whole may themselves
partake organically of the basic blocky, rectangular nature of the units. The
Freeman house in Los Angeles (Figs. 396, 397) is an especially happy and
daring composition; in Pasadena the Millard house, called "La Miniatura," is
a dwelling of great beauty which recalls in its simple cubical shape the basic
geometry of its structural system.

But it is block construction in stone which has had the greatest effect on
architecture (Figs. 398–403). In fact, because of the permanence and inherent
dignity of stone and the almost limitless variety with which it can be used,
block construction in stone has characterized the greater part of the important monumental architecture of the Western world. The early beehive-hut
builders along the western Mediterranean and Atlantic coasts of Europe were
merely using a natural material, amply available, in a natural and primitive way.
Later, as the stones came to be squared or shaped for their positions, buildings
of such imposing appearance as the nuraghi of Sardinia or the beehive tombs of
pre-Hellenic Greece came into being. Farther east and south, the Egyptians
were beginning more and more to use the hard granites and sandstones lining
the Nile Valley and were developing with them an architecture of austere
power and compelling beauty, the basic forms of which, however, are often
derived from earlier traditions developed in mud brick rather than from the

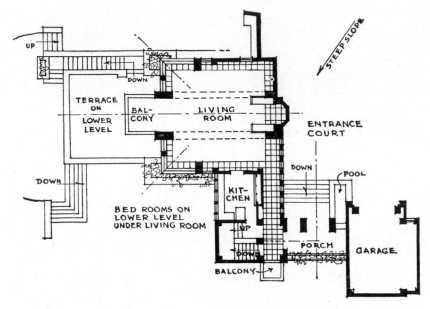

FIGURE 396. FREEMAN HOUSE, LOS ANGELES, CALIFORNIA. PLAN

Frank Lloyd Wright, architect

Every feature of this house is influenced by its constructional materials and techniques—the use of so-called Textile Block construction. The block size determines the sizes and rhythms of openings and the thickness and design of walls; it is recalled in the floor tile pattern which surrounds the living room and fills the corridor.

shapes suggested by the stone itself. In the meantime, too, stone was being increasingly used for fortification walls, at first made merely of piled rough stones and then of stones crudely shaped to fit together more closely; finally there developed the wall of finished square-cut ashlar. A tangential early development, which produced many interesting monuments but exerted little other influence on the main stream of Western architecture, was the use, by certain peoples, of stones of huge size—megalithic construction—which reached its climax in the temples of Malta and in certain of the fortifications of ancient Peru (Fig. 401).

Stone architecture in block construction is naturally controlled by the qualities of the material. Thus a certain thickness in walls is necessary in order to give a base sufficient to avoid their overturning and a bearing ample enough to carry the inevitably great weight. Since stone is brittle for use as a beam, openings in stone walls will tend to be relatively narrow, although their height is almost unlimited. If arches are used to permit wider openings, there must be enough weight on either side to resist the arch thrust. Where large areas of

FIGURE 397. LA MINIATURA, MILLARD HOUSE, PASADENA, CALIFORNIA

Frank Lloyd Wright, architect

Textile tile blocks used organically in a building that partakes of their nature both in form and detail.   Courtesy Museum of Modern Art

opening are desired, the natural answer is the use of colonnades or rows of piers, regularly spaced and relatively close together, or of arcades closed at each end by heavy piers, walls, or buttresses. The plans for this type of building will

FIGURE 398. A COTTAGE AT SENNEN, CORNWALL, ENGLAND

This shows the power of simple stone walls simply treated. The stones are roughly squared and laid with basically horizontal beds, but there is not careful continuous horizontal coursing. Strength, weight, and the influence of gravity are at once apparent in such walls.

Redrawn from Batsford and Fry, The English Cottage

tend toward basic simplicity, for stone is difficult to work and to place, and the amount of stonecutting will be minimized by concentrating the walls and supports and by eliminating as far as possible any complexities in the plan (Figs. 233, 399).

The appearance will result largely from the character of the material. Stone is heavy and hard. It is the most natural of building materials in the sense that it requires no fundamental change in physical or chemical make-up and no sur-facing with a foreign material to make it strong and durable. Furthermore, stone seems something essentially of the earth itself. It is the foundation of mountains, and it edges many coast lines with mighty cliffs or jagged teeth. It seems to short-lived mankind as something well-nigh permanent—the everlasting rock —and as such it has entered deeply into the folk mind. Because of all these quali-ties Western man has always chosen stone for those buildings for which he cared the most, feeling that his material conveyed upon them something of its own dignity.

Good stone construction has always emphasized this character. It has been the medium for the most dignified and the most emotionally significant of architectural forms. And, wherever it is rightly used, it still exerts this com-pelling influence today. It is therefore not a material for frivolous or merely smart and fashionable effects, and the architect who plans to use it must come to its use with a due sense of both its permanence and its power; he must ap-proach it with a certain basic humility. How strong may be the influence of this

FIGURE 399. PORTICO TEMPLE (TEMPLE OF THE SPHINX), GIZEH, EGYPT
Stone block construction of the simplest, most direct type.   Courtesy Ware Library

material can be seen in many stone structures of all periods. In the Scotch town of Aberdeen, for instance, which is built almost entirely from a very hard, silver-gray granite, locally plentiful, the various fashionable styles of the nineteenth century have swept by leaving scarcely a trace, for the material was too hard to cut into the tortured shapes of mid-Victorian whimsey. The town therefore has an extraordinary and effective unity, the direct result of its building stone.

Another quality in good stonework comes from the fact that it uses individual stones, laid most frequently in horizontal courses (Fig. 403); out of these elements can be produced walls as quiet or as "busy" as one wishes. Interest is given most easily by varying the texture of the wall, through emphasizing either

FIGURE 400. EARLY GREEK WALLS AT OLYMPIA AND OLUS

The Olympia example, left, shows stones only roughly shaped; in Olus, right, squared stones are used in alternating courses of headers and stretchers.   Courtesy Ware Library

FIGURE 401. TAMBO-MACHAY, PERU. INCA STONEWORK

The exquisite workmanship evident in ancient Peruvian stonework is shown in the careful cutting of stones of different sizes and shapes to fit together with close joints.

Courtesy Professor William D. Strong

the courses or the individual blocks (Figs. 407–413). Stone is usually split from quarry rock, although occasionally blocks are axed or hammered from rough or rounded boulders. In either case the result is likely to be stone faces which, being somewhat uneven, will catch the light in various ways; stonework laid with this kind of surface is called *quarry-faced*. If, in addition, a line is drawn around the faces of each stone to indicate the theoretical plane of the wall and if the edges of the stone are then cut roughly back to this line with a broad chisel, the result is called *drafted* masonry. This method will serve to outline

FIGURE 402. CASTLE, MATSUYAMA, JAPAN. FOUNDATION WALLS

Carefully constructed battered walls of polygonal masonry characterize many Japanese palace and castle buildings.

Courtesy Avery Library

the individual stones with shadows of various widths, depending on the roughness of the surface. Drafted masonry was occasionally used by the Romans with extraordinary effect (Fig. 410), as in many of their aqueducts and in the great

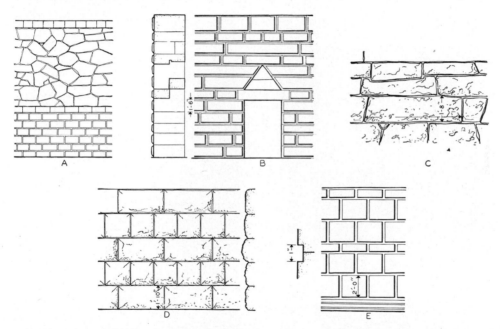

FIGURE 403. TYPICAL GREEK, ETRUSCAN, AND ROMAN STONE TREATMENTS

A: From Cnidus, a wall in ashlar and polygonal masonry; B: Wall from the theater at Iasus, showing rustication, with a door, above which is a lintel and corbeled opening; C: Rock-faced masonry from an Etruscan building at Fiesole; D: Drafted masonry from an Etruscan building at Falerii; E: Roman rusticated masonry from the Round Temple by the Tiber, Rome.

Redrawn from Atkinson and Bagenal, *Theory and Elements of Architecture*

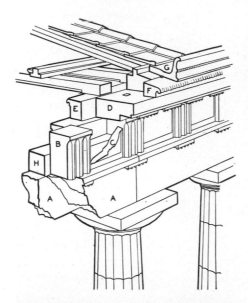

FIGURE 404. GREEK BLOCK CONSTRUC-
TION. DIAGRAM OF A TYPICAL DORIC EN-
TABLATURE

Here all the forms, though probably developed
from wooden prototypes, are instinct with the
feeling of stone or marble. The main beams, A,
form the architrave; on them the triglyphs, B,
carry the cornice—the metopes, C, being non-
structural slabs between them. The inner face,
H, E, is designed to carry gracefully the portico
crossbeams. The corona, D, is essentially a corbel
course, strong enough to support the projecting
cymatium, F, and the gutter, G, above it. Thus
the three elements of the classic entablature—
architrave, frieze, cornice—follow naturally
from the constructional necessities.

Redrawn from Sturgis, *European Architecture*

FIGURE 405. THESEUM,
ATHENS. FLANK COLON-
NADE

The qualities of block construction determine the column spacing, the wall design,
and the ceiling beams and
panels.

Courtesy Ware Library

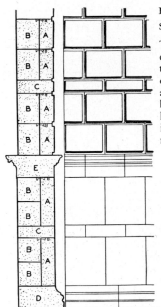

FIGURE 406. ROUND TEMPLE BY THE TIBER, ROME. SECTION OF LOWER PART OF WALL

Typical classic solid block wall construction. In general two layers of stones, outer, A, and inner, B, are used. These layers are tied together by metal cramps; still more important there are periodic through, or header, courses, C. The molded courses, D and E, are also formed of through stones. This is frankly expressed and beautifully designed block construction. Such construction is, however, suitable for moderate climates only, for it has little insulating value except what comes from the mere mass of the material.

Redrawn from Viollet-le-Duc, *Entretiens sur l'architecture*

FIGURE 407. GATE HOUSE, NORTH EASTON, MASSACHUSETTS

H. H. Richardson, architect

Field stones brilliantly used to produce an effective wall.   Courtesy Ware Library

FIGURE 408. TEMPLE AT KHAJURAHO, IN-DIA

Indian expression of block construction emphasizing the sense of gravity and stratification.

Courtesy Metropolitan Museum of Art

FIGURE 409. PITTI PALACE, FLORENCE, ITALY

Filippo Brunelleschi, architect

The boldest Italian use of drafted and rusticated stone masonry at colossal scale.

Courtesy Ware Library

Roman gate known as the Porta Maggiora. In this gate the contrast of the drafted masonry below and the carefully smoothed stones above is exceedingly effective. Many medieval fortifications are of drafted masonry and consequently have just the right expression of disciplined power. Drafted and rock-faced masonry is still used frequently for retaining walls, bridge abutments, and the like. Some of the structures of the Riverside Park extension in the city of New York and some of the older bridges in the Bronx River Parkway are excellent examples of its expressive use.

FIGURE 410. FORUM OF AUGUSTUS, ROME. ENCLOSING WALL

Ancient Roman drafted masonry of superb power, with alternating courses of headers and stretchers.

Courtesy Avery Library

Much of the work of Henry Hobson Richardson (Figs. 407, 411) reveals a remarkably sure genius in using stonework of this generally rough type, characterized by an expert handling of scale based on the careful combination of large and small stones; by subtle variations in roughness and by the restrained use of smoothed or tooled areas, he produced walls that are unmatched in their expression of the material. More recently, Frank Lloyd Wright has displayed an almost similar genius in the use of stone; in Taliesin (Fig. 412), as in the stonework of "Falling Water," he has built walls of the greatest interest which seem somehow to partake of the nature of ledge stone itself.

But stone faces can be more carefully finished. The roughnesses can be hammered off with different kinds of hammers, which leave a plane pockmarked in various ways, depending on the type of hammer used and the direction of the stroke. Stone can also be chiseled or tooled to a plane surface with toothed chisels which give a surface of parallel ridges. It can be sawn to a plane by either diamond or wire-and-shot saws, and the saw marks will give

FIGURE 411. LIBRARY, NORTH EASTON, MASSACHUSETTS. DETAIL OF WING
H. H. Richardson, architect
Drafted, rock-faced masonry handled with an exquisite sense of scale and texture.

From *Monographs of American Architecture*

a characteristic surface. In addition, stones may be cut to a plane or else grooved or molded on a mechanical planer. Some stones can also be rubbed to a perfectly smooth surface, either by rubbing two blocks of the material against each other or by the use of whirling wheels or pads and some foreign abrasive; certain other stones, especially granites and marbles, can be polished to a high gloss. In the twentieth century the chief stones used are granites, limestones, and marbles, as well as a few selected sandstones. The almost complete mechanization of quarries and stonecutting plants has led to the general substitution of sawn, planed, or rubbed finishes for the tooled finishes more usual at an early period. Polished stone is frequently employed as a veneer, more often for very limited areas than for larger surfaces.

This alphabet—of extraordinary variety in both color and texture—which stonework offers is one with which the architect must become familiar if he

FIGURE 412. TALIESIN, SPRING GREEN, WISCONSIN. VIEW IN GARDEN COURT
Frank Lloyd Wright, architect

Photograph Ezra Stoller—Pictorial Services

is to achieve the best results in block construction in stone. A study of the wide range of effects achieved in the past will help him enormously in gaining this command. Especially interesting is the great variety of rustications and toolings to be found in the buildings of the Italian Renaissance (Figs. 415–417). An observant study, too, of more modern examples will be well worth while— from the beautiful dry stone walls that border the fields of New England, through the split-stone masonry of many Philadelphia suburbs and the dignified granite of many Greek Revival public buildings, to the rubbed limestone of Rockefeller Center and the "cobweb" walls of Le Corbusier (Fig. 418). These will show that it is fundamentally by designing simple wall spaces in such a way as to bring out the character of the material—its weight, its natural quality, and its dignity—and by giving to the stonework the surfaces and textures appropriate to it that the most expressive stone walls can be achieved.

FIGURE 413. CHÂ-
TEAU, MAISONS LA-
FITTE, FRANCE

François Mansart,
architect

Block construction in
smooth ashlar expressed
in the basic geometry of
the architecture.

Courtesy Avery Library

FIGURE 414. BRAZER'S BUILDING, BOSTON, MASSACHUSETTS

Isaiah Rogers, architect

The power and hardness of granite expressed with monumental simplicity.

Courtesy J. M. Howells and Metropolitan Museum of Art

FIGURE 415. CHARACTERISTIC ITALIAN ROCK-FACED AND HAMMERED STONE FINISHES

LEFT: Rock-faced, Palazzo Vecchio, Florence; RIGHT: Hammered, Palazzo Grifoni, Florence.

Photographs Myron Bement Smith

FIGURE 416. CHARACTERISTIC ITALIAN TOOLED STONE FINISHES

LEFT: Palazzo Nonfinito, Florence; RIGHT: Borghese Palace, Rome.

Photographs Myron Bement Smith

All the details in stone walls are similarly dependent on the physical qualities of the material (Figs. 419–422). Most stones are porous and will absorb a certain amount of water. When the water freezes, it is likely to crack or spall the stone. Thus it becomes essential to keep water out of stone walls and, wherever possible, to avoid conditions under which water will run down the wall faces for long distances.

This will mean, first of all, copings for all parapets or otherwise unprotected

FIGURE 417. CHARACTERISTIC ITALIAN SMOOTH OR RUBBED STONE FINISHES, CHIEFLY IN TRAVERTINE

LEFT: Pietro Massimi Palace, Rome; RIGHT: Cornice of the Strozzi Palace, Florence.

Photographs courtesy Myron Bement Smith

stone walls. It will mean also that projecting horizontal surfaces, such as sills, band courses, projecting cornices, and the like, must be made with an inclined upper surface, or wash, so that water will run off. In addition, it will mean that these projecting members must be finished with drips on the under side in order that water may drop off their outer edges and not run back on the soffit and thus percolate into the joints or run down the wall (Fig. 421). Since the proper detailing of all such elements has already been discussed in Volume I, it is not necessary here to go into the matter at great length.

The careful detailing of projecting elements in block-constructed walls has important aesthetic implications. Rain in any urban locality will contain large amounts of impurities—soot, dust, and various smoke acids. Where the rain runs down walls, it not only deposits its burden of dirt but also tends to disintegrate the surface of the stone. The result will be unsightly stains or the gradual flaking off of the surface. It is one of the great advantages of certain historical forms of detail and ornament that they direct and limit this inevitable staining in such a way that the discolorations will seem to be a coherent part of the intended design of the building. W. M. Dudok, the architect of the Hil-

FIGURE 418 (OPPOSITE). A STONE HOUSE. PLANS AND ELEVATIONS

Le Corbusier, architect

This house shows Le Corbusier's characteristic type of stone wall, formed of rough stones in a sort of coursed rubble bond. Note in both plan and elevation that walls are as continuous as possible, with but few small openings; where he desires larger windows he changes to a framed type of structure in wood and glass. This design illustrates the total difference in effect given by the two types of construction as well as the fact that they may be successfully combined in one building.   From Le Corbusier, *Oeuvre complète*

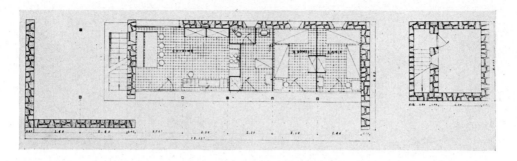

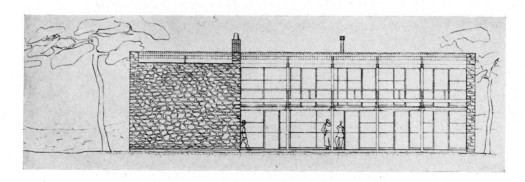

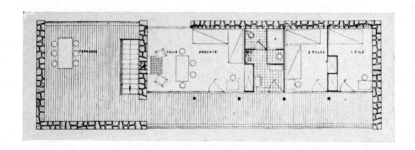

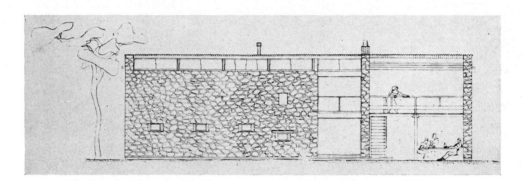

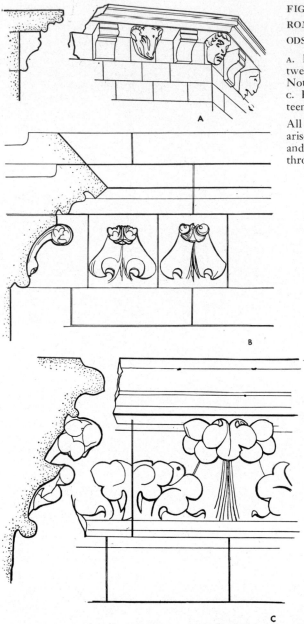

FIGURE 419. CORNICES OF THE ROMANESQUE AND GOTHIC PERIODS

A. From the Cathedral of Langres, twelfth century; B. From choir of Notre Dame, Paris, thirteenth century; C. From Cathedral of Troyes, thirteenth century.

All three show cornice forms which arise naturally from the use of stone, and all are furnished with drips to throw water away from the wall face.

Redrawn from Viollet-le-Duc, *Dictionnaire raisonné* . . .

versum Town Hall, in the Netherlands, once said that the real architectural value of any structure could not be judged until ten years after its completion; the good building will look better after ten years of use and exposure to the elements, whereas bad buildings grow more ugly with age. He added that God

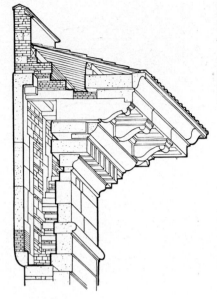

FIGURE 420. STROZZI PALACE, FLORENCE, ITALY. DIAGRAM OF THE CORNICE CONSTRUCTION

The modillions are actual corbel brackets supporting the corona and cymatium above and are held in place partly by the treatment of the base of the parapet wall. Again the forms express the actual construction.

Redrawn from Guadet, *Éléments et théorie* . . .

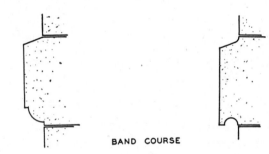

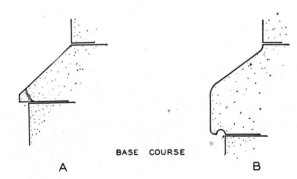

BAND COURSE

BASE COURSE

A

B

FIGURE 421. BAND COURSE AND BASE SECTIONS FOR MASONRY WALLS

The examples at A illustrate bad detailing; those at B, good detailing from the practical point of view. Thus the left-hand band course has the top of its splay on the line of a horizontal joint and has no drip. Water running down the wall would tend to run into the joint above, and the remainder would continue down the wall below. These errors are avoided in the right-hand example. The base sections show a similar comparison; in addition, the lip of the left-hand example is too thin and might crack as shown.

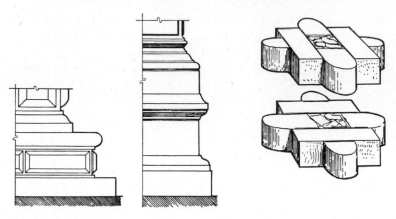

FIGURE 422 (LEFT). TWO RENAISSANCE BASE COURSES

LEFT: From the Strozzi Palace, Florence; RIGHT: From the Giraud Palace, Rome.

Both bases are composed of moldings which look strong and are strong; all are detailed so that there is no possibility of fracture, and the depths of the members are therefore proportioned in relation to their projection.

FIGURE 423 (RIGHT). STONE COURSING OF A ROMANESQUE PIER

The alternate courses shown illustrate not only the fact that the center of the pier is built of rough material, but also the fact that courses in good stonework should vary in plan above each other and that the fewest possible vertical joints should carry vertically through more than one course. In this way a good *bond* is produced and the whole is unified.

Redrawn from Viollet-le-Duc, *Dictionnaire raisonné* . . .

seemed good to the Baroque because Baroque buildings aged and stained so beautifully. Twentieth-century design ideals, with their insistence on plain surfaces and their emphasis on pure, unbroken geometric forms, have made this problem a pressing one, for even the most beautiful surface of the most beautiful material can become squalid and unsightly when blotched and streaked with water stains. Furthermore, the amount of stain to be expected will vary greatly on the different sides of a building; in the general northeastern region of the United States it will be the east, northeast, and southeast faces which stain the most, because it is from these directions that driving rains most frequently come.

There are two possible solutions of this difficult problem. The most common is the attempt to minimize staining by keeping the surfaces as smooth as they can be made so that water will run down them swiftly and will deposit little of its burden of dirt; thus buildings will be rendered as completely self-cleaning as possible. The other solution—the traditional method of the past—is to keep water from the walls by the most careful design of all sills, bands, copings, and so on; to recognize in the design of the detail itself the fact that staining will appear in certain places; and to see that the discoloration will naturally occur in those areas, or in those vertical lines, where it will help rather than harm the eventual effect.

The need of keeping water out of the wall will also affect all sorts of details connected with stone jointing. In good stone detail, for instance, no joint should fall at the exact level of the top of a wash or horizontal projection (Fig. 421); it should come approximately a quarter of an inch above the upper surface of the projecting portion, in order that the slight hesitation in the flow of the water which occurs at the projection shall not be at a place where the water might run back into the body of the wall. Similarly, in rusticated walls the joint should be at the lower side of the projection. Projecting base molds or base courses must be carefully designed with the same principle in view—the avoidance of any points where water resting on a horizontal surface could seep back into a joint. A careful study of the best details of classic or Gothic architecture will be of great assistance in learning these necessary principles and applying them correctly to contemporary design.

The expression of block construction is thus a double matter. One aspect of it results from the major requirements of the construction, such as simplicity, geometric quality, and the like; this might be called the expression of the wall itself. The other aspect results from the very nature of the blocks of which the wall is constructed—their shape and texture, the pattern made by the joints, and so on. In plan, block construction, whether in wood or in stone, will tend toward continuity, toward rectangularity, and toward openings that are relatively narrow when lintels are used but wide and heavily buttressed or abutted when topped by arches. The regular rhythms of colonnades and arcades are frequent factors in the expression of block construction.

On the exterior an expressive effect will result from the development of large and dignified surfaces, from a simple large-scale and reticent treatment, from ornament which either is restrained in character or consists of large blocks of projecting or free-standing sculpture, and from a subtle emphasis of the individual blocks with which the wall is made. Thus the careful jointing of stonework becomes an essential part of the design of any block construction in stone, and problems of the scale and size of the blocks and their relation to openings and to supports will be of first importance. The completed building of block construction should partake of something of the time-defying character of stone itself.

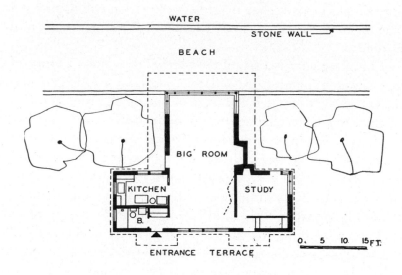

FIGURE 424 (ABOVE AND OPPOSITE). BEACH HOUSE, RICHMOND SHORES, CALIFORNIA. PLAN AND INTERIOR AND EXTERIOR VIEWS

W. W. Wurster, architect

The design of this house is largely conditioned by its site and by the simple construction used: walls of precast concrete block supporting a roof with exposed wood beams. Note the way the uniform sizes of the concrete blocks give rhythm to the exterior and, appearing again on the interior, confer a strong unity on the entire design.

Solid block construction, in which cut stone is carried through the entire thickness of the wall, is now seldom used except in such elements as steps and occasional piers and columns. Most so-called cut-stone buildings have but a comparatively thin facing of the cut stone, and the remainder of the wall (Fig. 425) is built of rubble, concrete, or brick. The question naturally arises, therefore, as to when such walls should be considered block construction and when the mass or framed construction behind the stone should control the design. The use of cut stone for the facing of rough materials or of a filling or backing of brick or concrete is not a uniquely modern technique. It has, in fact, characterized most of the great historical monuments built of stone. It is a natural procedure, the inevitable result of the needs of buildings and the development of structural methods. To cut stone carefully is expensive in labor, and many of the rougher types of construction may be not only as strong as, or even stronger than, cut stone but also more waterproof. From the time of the Romans down to the present it has seemed natural to use rougher materials behind the cut-stone face. The builders and architects of ancient Roman monuments, Gothic cathedrals, and Renaissance palaces found nothing reprehensible in this practice and worked out many ingenious ways of bonding the finished front face to the rougher backing. (See Figs. 423, 425.)

Yet the question of which type of construction should rule will not down. Architects today are generally striving for an architecture more rigidly logical and more ruthlessly expressive than even these great architectures of the past. If stone surfaces are to be used for walls that are composed chiefly of other and cheaper materials, it becomes vitally necessary for the modern architect to make up his mind as to how precisely this mixed construction should be expressed. An answer may perhaps be hazarded, based on the thickness of the

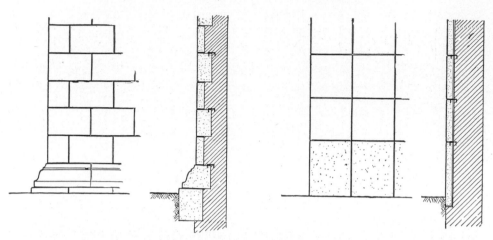

FIGURE 425. STONE WALLS WITH BRICK BACKING

LEFT: Elevation and section of bonded stone wall; RIGHT: Elevation and section of veneered wall. Where the wall is bonded with stones sufficiently thick, the entire wall thickness is integral and structurally valuable. In the veneered wall, only the brick thickness has structural value.

stone and on the way it is attached to its backing: If the stones of the facing have a minimum thickness of one brick or more, and if in addition the depths of the stone vary so that the facing is bonded integrally into the backing and works with it, then the stone is more than a facing; it is an actual working portion of the wall. As such it must be treated as a constructional element; therefore an expression in accordance with the principles of block construction would seem logical and necessary (Fig. 425, left). If, on the other hand, the stone facing is one brick or less in thickness, uniform throughout, and tied to the backing only by metal clamps or anchors, then obviously it is merely a veneer, and the attempt to apply to it the principles of block construction leads only to confusion and a false expression. It is an interesting fact that many building codes recognize this basic difference; in the first case they allow the thickness of the stone to be counted as part of the working thickness of the wall, whereas in the second case the working thickness of the wall is considered to be merely that of the rough construction behind (Fig. 425, right).

Many kinds of stone are easily stained by salts carried by the dampness which may percolate from the mortars or bricks of the backing. For this reason the back of all finished stone is usually protected by a waterproof coating, frequently waterproof cement.

There are other common types of mixed construction in which block construction has a part. There is notably the system in which a wall built generally of brick or rubble or some other kind of mass construction will have, perhaps along the corners and around the openings, trim of finished cut stone. In this type some of the same problems arise as in the case of stone-faced walls, and much the same kind of analysis must be used in deciding on appropriate and expressive treatments. Wherever the stone motif is in blocks of comparatively ample thickness or large size, the principles of good block-construction detail must necessarily control its design. Wherever, on the other hand, it is relatively thin—as, for instance, in the marble lining in the reveal of an important door—it is manifestly a veneer only and should be so considered.

The high cost of skilled stonecutting labor, the large size of many modern structures, and the development of mechanized methods of construction have all combined to make buildings of block construction in stone much less common than they were in many eras of the past. Cut-stone buildings are expensive, and good block construction for the major portions of structures is a luxury which only a few can enjoy. Yet even now it is surprising to realize how much block construction will occur in portions of buildings otherwise of a quite different character—especially in steps, terraces and terrace parapets, occasional porches, retaining walls, and similar elements.

The correct design of steps and of step parapets or cheek walls of stone is a more complicated problem than it seems, because of the danger that frost in the earth or fill below the steps will throw or crack them. For this reason stone steps should always be solidly supported on masonry foundation walls which go well below the frost line. Moreover, each step block should be at least one inch wider than the tread so that there may be a continuous bearing, at least one inch in width, extending the full length of all steps. Only by an adequate bearing for each step can joints be made tight enough to keep water from entering the space below in large quantities. The settling of steps and that of the parapets or cheek walls which flank them will frequently differ. It is therefore good practice to butt the steps against the cheek or parapet walls, instead of attempting to build them in and depending on a well-caulked joint to keep out the water. Stone terrace walls and parapets in monumental structures, then, must receive the same care in detail as any other portion of the structure. And here too, as in the case of other stone details, the truest expression will probably come from that design which recognizes most frankly all the conditions of the problem. (See Vol. I, Chap. 8.)

Although modern economics and modern structural systems have tended to minimize the amount of block construction employed, it is not likely to pass entirely out of use. The strength, the dignity, and the beauty of stone as a building material are too valuable to be forgotten. Moreover, the power which stone buildings exert and the sense of permanence they possess are so deeply enshrined in mankind's emotional background that they are likely to be used for centuries to come wherever men seek to build a structure expressive of their deepest longings and their most powerful dreams.

SUGGESTED ADDITIONAL READING FOR CHAPTER 13

Atkinson, Robert, and Hope Bagenal, *Theory and Elements of Architecture* (New York: McBride [1926]).

Choisy, Auguste, *Histoire de l'architecture*, 2 vols. (Paris: Gauthier-Villars, 1899).

Erixon, Sigurd, "The North-European Technique in Corner Timbering," *Folkliv*, Vol. I, No. 1 (1937).

Guadet, Julien, *Éléments et théorie de l'architecture*, 4 vols. (Paris: Aulanier, n.d.). In general written from the standpoint of block construction.

Reinhard, Ernst (editor), *Stein und Steinwerk*, Vol. III of "Landschaften und Bauten" (Bern, Basel, Olten: Ilionverlag, 1945).

Viollet-le-Duc, Eugène Emmanuel, *Entretiens sur l'architecture*, 2 vols. (Paris: Morel, 1863–72); translated as *Discourses on Architecture . . .* with an introductory essay by Henry Van Brunt, 2 vols. (Boston: Osgood, 1875–81), especially the material dealing with Greek architecture.

Warren, Herbert Langford, *The Foundations of Classic Architecture* (New York and London: Macmillan, 1919).

14

Architectural Design and Structural Methods III: Mass Construction

THE SECOND important structural method is mass construction, so called because the materials which make up the wall are tied together by a binder so strong that the whole becomes a single or monolithic mass. Under this general type there are two main subdivisions. The first comprises mass construction in which the units are separately placed in position in heavy beds of mortar or cement. This class includes rubble and brickwork. The second subdivision comprises construction in which the materials are mixed or homogeneous before they are put in place; these materials are often placed in molds or forms which are removed when the mass is set or hardened. This subdivision includes terre pisé and concrete.

A third and minor subdivision might be formed to include structures built of earth itself, like earth fortifications or temple pyramids (Fig. 426). In nonmilitary architecture, earth construction has been limited to a few types of primitive houses and more recently to semi-temporary dwellings. Various primitive peoples have built houses by excavating holes, generally circular, in the earth to a depth of five to seven feet, and then banking up earth walls to the desired height around the opening. On these a framework of branches is placed, and on this is supported the roof, itself made of layers of earth or sod. The earth lodges of certain tribes of Plains Indians are typical examples. Some of these were of large diameter—up to fifty feet—and were entered by sloping excavated ramps or tunnels. Intermediate wooden posts helped support the heavy weight of the earthen roof. These earth houses had the great advantage of being both warm in winter and cool in summer; they also offered little obstruction to the wind, but they were naturally damp and difficult to drain.

Later, various white settlers in the American plains made shift with two

FIGURE 426. PYRAMID OF THE SUN, TEOTIHUACAN, MEXICO

A sacred pyramid formed of earth, probably with core and lower terrace walls of masonry.

Courtesy Avery Library

FIGURE 427. A KANSAS SOD HOUSE

Early settlers of the great plains of the United States frequently built houses of earth and sod with roofs supported on wooden frames.

Photograph Rev. Alfred Bergin, reproduced from Talbot Hamlin, *The American Spirit in Architecture*, Vol. 13, "The Pageant of America" (copyright Yale University Press)

more highly developed types of earth dwellings—dugouts and sod houses (Fig. 427). With few exceptions, in fact, sod houses were the first dwellings erected by the settlers in parts of Kansas. Like the Indian lodges, they were sunk some feet below the surface, but not so deeply as the Indian type. The walls were built of rectangular sods cut from the surface of the ground; the tough roots of the prairie grass gave them tenacity and strength. The sods were set one on another, like bricks, to the desired wall height, and the wood-framed roof was covered either with wood shingles, if they were available, or with additional layers of sod. Since such sod houses usually had wooden floors and were some-

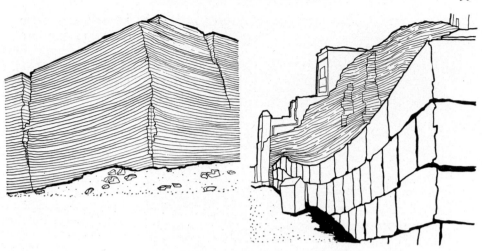

FIGURE 428. EGYPTIAN MASS CONSTRUCTION IN SUN-DRIED BRICK

LEFT: Pan-bed wall, Dimeh; RIGHT: Wall from Philae.

In both cases the bricks have been built in successive blocks, each block with concave courses. In this manner the Egyptians hoped to give longitudinal stability to the walls, despite the weak and fragile nature of the material. In the right-hand example the brick is on a stone foundation built to give the downward concave curve desired.

Redrawn from Petrie, *Egyptian Architecture*

times lined with wood and provided with a wooden door and glazed windows, they formed small dwellings of no little cozy comfort.

Beyond these few types, earth construction has been limited to tomb mounds, or tumuli—which gain their effect from the soft, suave, natural curves of the material itself—to temple pyramids and similar sacred mounds, and to the ramparts and terraces of fortifications. In fortifications a vertical inner wall of timber palisades, logs, or masonry is often banked on the outside with long steep slopes of earth; such a wall is invulnerable to ordinary missiles, since they bury themselves harmlessly in it. And in seventeenth- and eighteenth-century fortifications the appearance of these long geometric planes—often planted with grass—sloping down from polygonal bastions or straight curtain walls is most impressive. Here the architectural use of earth probably reaches its climax.

It was other types of mass construction, however, which were destined for more important architectural roles. Mass construction of stone rubble and rough stone block construction shade into each other so that it is almost impossible to draw a hard-and-fast line between them, although it is a simple matter to differentiate the extreme examples of each type. In general, where the stones are carefully shaped for their position and where the joints between the

FIGURE 429. MUD
CONSTRUCTION IN
PERSIA

TOP: Modern farmhouse
from Shulgistan. The
lower portion is of com-
pacted mud and the vault
and vault end are of mud
brick. BOTTOM: Drying
mud brick near Teheran.
The brick is formed flat
in a mold and partly dried
while flat, then turned on
edge for final curing.

Photographs copyright
M. B. Smith from
*Archive for Islamic
Culture*

stones are relatively thin, as well as in walls built without mortar, the construction is obviously block or gravity construction. Where, on the other hand, the
shape of the stone is unimportant, where the area of exposed joint is relatively
large, and where the construction is to be faced with a more expensive type of
material, then we may say that true mass construction exists; for here it is the
wall or pier as an entire unit which becomes the important element and, by
reason of the strong binder, appears and works as a unit.

Brick construction is itself of two major types. The first consists of unbaked
brick or of compacted clay, like the mud brick of Mesopotamia or the adobe
of our own Southwest; the second consists of burned brick. Construction in
mud brick or adobe is conditioned by the relative weakness of the material, its
porosity, and its sensitiveness to dampness or rain (Fig. 428). Because of the
first condition, walls of unbaked brick have to be relatively thick, with open-

ings relatively small; for openings too wide, even though bridged by lintels of wood or metal, would create high stresses in the piers (Fig. 429). The necessity of protecting unbaked brick from dampness or water tends to produce buildings in which the wall surfaces must be either painted or coated with stucco or cement; it also gives rise to wide overhangs in roofs and to porticos or porches, to protect the walls against driving rain. Examples are common in Arizona, New Mexico, and parts of California.

Baked brick, on the other hand, is a material of relatively great strength, and if laid with proper care it is fairly weatherproof. Since brick clay is widely distributed over the surface of the earth, brick is one of the most common types of building material, found alike in Asia, in Europe, and in America.

The effect of any of these methods of construction on design will inevitably be to stress the basic surfaces and the larger and simpler elements, and the adequate expression of this kind of construction will depend in no small measure on the texture or general appearance of the large planes this kind of structure tends to produce. In good rubblework, for instance, the aim should be a texture as completely homogeneous as possible; the differences between individual units should be minimized, for any accent on individual stones through arbitrary variations in their color or size will make the expression of the building partake more of the nature of block construction than of a unified mass. Many rough stone walls of recent years are less effective than they might well be because of a basic indecision on this very point. Rubble, too crude to be treated as block construction, sometimes is given confusing variety in detail and texture because the builder or architect has chosen stones with different colors, shapes, and amounts of projection. These stones, by reason of the rough nature of the work, cannot be distributed with the care and precision their interest-provoking character demands, and the result will always be a wall which, instead of being attractive in texture and light and shade, looks merely like an ill-built wall with smallpox.

In rough rubble walls of this kind, satisfactory results can be obtained only by building them in as regular and simple a way as possible and allowing the texture to develop, as it were, by itself. The normal variations in the stones and the normal change in the widths of the exposed mortar joints—widths which are dependent upon the stone shapes—will produce ample variety. Any artificial search for additional interest will damage the effect and destroy the unity. This can readily be seen in many thoughtlessly designed suburban communities where the promoter, in an effort to quicken interest, has sprinkled bits of rough

FIGURE 430. WING OF AN OLD CONVENT, SAN ANTONIO, TEXAS

An excellent example of rubble stonework, with the stones more carefully laid at the corners.

Photograph Talbot Hamlin

stone over an otherwise plain wall of concrete or brick or stucco; the result is tawdry and incoherent. If the architect wishes to emphasize the shapes and colors of individual stones, he must go to the additional expense of building a block-construction wall, such as the magnificent quarry-faced walls of which Richardson was so fond or the carefully coursed, ridged rock walls that Frank Lloyd Wright uses so well. The secret of mass construction in rubble will always lie in universal continuity of surface, as, for instance, in Lutyen's superb exterior of the large house "Grey Walls." (See also Fig. 430.)

In walls of baked brick the problem is somewhat similar. Brick is a material of great appeal because of its variations in color and texture. Different clays, different kilns, and different methods of shaping the brick before it is burned can produce all sorts of colors and all sorts of surfaces, from smooth to very rough. Bricks can be glazed so as to present a smooth and glossy surface, they can be pressed to perfect planes, they can be cut smoothly, or they can be shaped with a tool that leaves as rough a ridged surface as that found in so-called tapestry brick. Moreover, the bricks which result from a single firing in one kiln will vary greatly in strength and color. Those on the outside of the kiln may be soft and pale; those close to the fire may be vitrified and black. The outer, pale-colored bricks are too soft for ordinary use, and the inner, over-burned bricks may be twisted out of shape; but in the run of usable bricks from one firing there will generally occur as wide a range of color as any architect is likely to need.

Contemporary architectural taste seeks always for the simplest, the least troubled, and the most serene geometric planes. It therefore becomes all the more necessary for the architect to keep brickwork as quiet and uniform as possible. He must always bear in mind, too, the effect of weathering on the walls he designs. For example, many subtleties of color harmony which show so beautifully in the attractive samples offered by brick salesmen, or even in the sample walls usually called for in a contract for a brick building, will usually disappear entirely in the course of a few months. One cannot be too subtle or too delicate in this matter: smoke and sun, dampness and dirt, will work their will on any wall, and subtle harmonies will often fade to an undistinguished gray; whereas the bolder and more uniform walls where the basic color is defi-nite—red, or brown, or purple, or white—will weather well and look better after years of wear than when they were first built.

One problem that will always arise in the modern brick wall is the problem presented by the tops of openings. In earlier times, brick arches—round, seg-mental, or flat—bridged over the voids and supported the wall areas above. Steel lintels are now well-nigh universal in such places, and the use of an arch be-comes structurally meaningless. Yet to carry the general system of the wall brickwork down to the top of the opening unchanged often gives an unpleasant feeling of weakness and indecision. The human imagination revolts against seeing the same pattern of brick jointing that is used for the continuous walling suddenly stopped at an opening head without meeting any apparent support. The steel angle lintels which support the brick over the openings are usually invisible; yet the eye demands the feeling of strength in what it sees, even when the mind grasps the fact that the actual strength may be present though unseen. Thus some expression of the hidden steel lintel would seem to be desirable. Some designers have continued to use the old arch forms to express this support. Others, and perhaps the greater number of thoughtful architects, feel that this is not an expression but an actual falsification and that some more direct ex-pression is possible and desirable. In such places they have therefore used courses of headers on edge or soldier courses, for they feel that the change in the jointing pattern thus produced, though not in itself structural in nature,

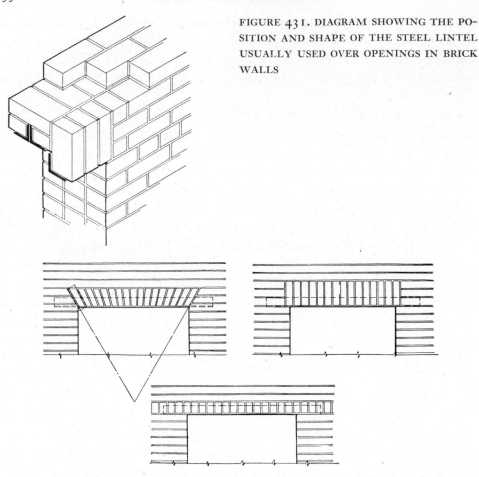

FIGURE 432. TYPICAL WINDOW OR DOOR HEADS IN MODERN BRICKWORK

ABOVE, LEFT: Flat brick arch of rubbed brick—the dotted line of the left-hand arch brick shows
the original size of the brick; ABOVE, RIGHT: A soldier course; BELOW: A rowlock course (headers
or half bricks on edge).

In each case the position of the steel lintel is indicated in dotted lines.

expresses the existence of the supporting lintel hidden by these bricks and
therefore satisfies the requirements of logic as well as the instinctive demands
of the imagination. True expression here, as in other architectural matters, can
be achieved only by an imaginative and sensitive use of the material. Because
of the nature of the construction, it is undesirable—if not impossible—to display the steel itself; its expression, therefore, can be only by suggestion (Figs.
431, 432).

Further interest, if necessary, can be given to brick walls by the use of various

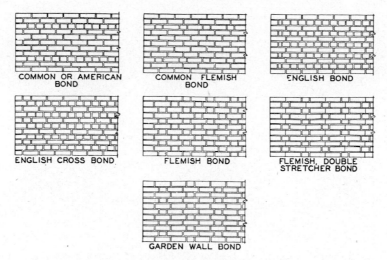

FIGURE 433. BRICK BONDS IN COMMON USE IN THE UNITED STATES. ELEVATION

COMMON OR AMERICAN BOND: One course of headers to each six courses of stretchers; COMMON FLEMISH BOND: One course of alternate stretchers and headers to each six courses; ENGLISH BOND: Alternate courses of headers and stretchers; ENGLISH CROSS BOND: Alternate courses of headers and stretchers, with the joints of the stretchers staggered; FLEMISH BOND: Alternate headers and stretchers in every course; FLEMISH DOUBLE STRETCHER BOND: Two stretchers alternating with one header in every course; GARDEN WALL BOND: Three stretchers alternating with one header in every course.

kinds of bonds in which certain bricks, called *headers*, with their small ends out and their length at right angles to the wall plane, are combined with *stretchers*— bricks laid with their long dimension parallel to the wall plane—in accordance with various specific systems. The headers enable the facing to be bonded to the major body of the wall. The architect must learn at least the most common of those bonds and appreciate the variety of effects which they produce. The bonds in most general use are: *common bond*, with horizontal rows of headers at every seventh course; *Flemish bond*, in which headers and stretchers alternate in each course; *English bond*, where courses of headers and stretchers alternate and the headers and stretchers are aligned one directly over another; and *English cross bond*, which is similar, except that the courses of stretchers break joints. Each bond has its individual aesthetic quality. The use of any of these bonds requires careful study, especially with regard to the exact jointing of the bricks at corners, at openings, and in narrow piers. Here it will probably be necessary to use *closers*, or three-quarter bricks, in addition to the regular headers and stretchers, in order to bring the joints into a regular and uniform arrangement (Figs. 433–435).

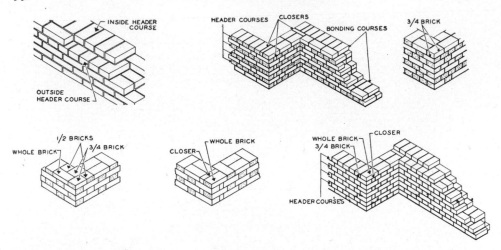

FIGURE 434. BRICK COURSING AT CORNERS (ENGLISH CROSS BOND) AND COURSING OF COMMON BOND

These illustrations show the use of closers and three-quarter bricks occasionally necessary to regularize a bond at interior and exterior corners.

These ordinary bonds, of course, represent only a fraction of the possible ways of laying up expressive brickwork. In Tudor England and in certain parts of Colonial America pleasing lozenge patterns were occasionally made by the use of dark headers. Occasionally vitrified headers give variety to Flemish-bond walls. During the nineteenth century, bricks of unusual length and thickness were occasionally used to produce walls of smooth texture and of stressed horizontality, and such specially designed bricks may still be obtained if their extra expense is not too great a factor. B. G. Goodhue used them with great success in the brick-and-stone walls of St. Bartholomew's Church in New York. It is this wide variety in effect obtainable in simple ways which accounts in part for the popularity of the material. (See Figs. 436–440.)

In the hands of skillful brick masons an even greater freedom is possible. In this development Dutch contemporary architects have been pre-eminent and have made distinctive and original use of the extraordinary skill of Dutch bricklayers. During the early 1920's, especially in housing, this search for variety in brick led to all kinds of eccentric and arbitrary effects; corbelings of various kinds and brick patterns ran riot over some of the apartment houses of this period, particularly in Amsterdam, and balconies and turrets were arbitrarily introduced for purely decorative reasons. This search for novelty led occasionally to an unpleasant confusion of design and destroyed the sense of quiet, orderly strength which is of the essence in good mass construction.

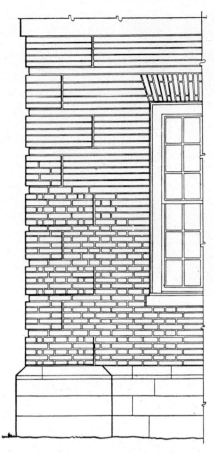

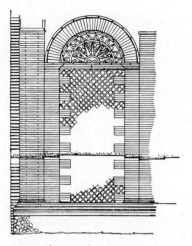

FIGURE 436 (RIGHT). ROMAN BRICK-
WORK FROM A TOMB IN OSTIA, ITALY

Roman architects frequently used exposed brickwork and depended on differing brick colors and shapes to establish interest. Here rubbed brick and tile create a vivid and interesting pattern.

Redrawn from American Face Brick Association, *Brickwork in Italy*

FIGURE 435 (LEFT). GROOMBRIDGE PLACE, KENT, ENGLAND. DETAIL ELEVATION OF PART OF ONE CORNER

This great house is built in Flemish bond, with projecting quoins at the corners. The illustration reveals the care necessary in adjusting pier widths, openings, and other details to the selected bond. Note the bond variation at the bottom of the opening and also the treatment of the brick arch.

Later, in places where brick walls serve merely as screens and support only their own weight, the same bricklaying skill has been put to sounder and more truly expressive tasks. Thus in skeleton buildings the walls are sometimes made of nothing but soldier courses—bricks on end—with horizontal and vertical joints continuous from side to side and from top to bottom. Walls of all header courses, or of headers and half bricks, either on edge or on their sides, are also sometimes used. Dutch architects, in an effort to produce a veneer expression, frequently use light-colored or glazed bricks laid up with the narrowest possible joints and with the pointing mortar colored to match the brick.

FIGURE 437 (LEFT). AN EMPORIUM, OSTIA, ITALY. VIEW IN THE COURT

Carefully detailed brickwork of two colors used to produce expressive and decorative quality.

Photograph Ernest Nash

FIGURE 438 (RIGHT). ISHTAR GATE, BABYLON, AS RECONSTRUCTED IN THE BERLIN MUSEUM

Mass construction in sun-dried brick faced with colored faïence tiles.   Courtesy Avery Library

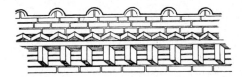
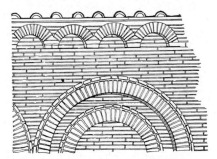

FIGURE 439 (LEFT). BRICK CORNICE, SAN PIER CRISOLOGO, RAVENNA, ITALY

With bricks many interesting varieties of projecting cornices may readily be made. The early medieval builders of Italy depended heavily upon such decorative brick elements.

FIGURE 440 (RIGHT). WALL ARCADES AND ARCADED CORNICE, SAN GIOVANNI EVANGELISTA, RAVENNA, ITALY

Byzantine and Early Romanesque church walls in Italy were frequently arcaded, and arcaded cornices were important features. They furnish much of the exterior effect of many of these brick buildings and also reveal how flexible brick construction is.

Figures 439 and 440 redrawn from American Face Brick Association, *Brickwork in Italy*

FIGURE 441. HOUSING ON SPAARNDAMMERPLANTSOEN, AMSTERDAM, THE NETH-
ERLANDS

M. de Klerk, architect

The arbitrary forms based on amazing brick-laying skill which characterized much early Dutch
housing.   Courtesy Netherlands Information Bureau

A similar search for uniformity and quietness in the appearance of brick walls is becoming more and more apparent in the best architecture. Modern architects have learned that any artificial quest for variety in color and texture—through the use of joints that are too deep, bricks that are too rough, or bricks that project unduly from the wall face—leads only to a restless confusion. Arbitrary changes in the brick bond and any attempt to produce hit-or-miss effects, such as "skintled brick," tend inevitably to destroy that expression of continuity and pleasant surface which is still the nature of good mass construction. The sense of repose and unity expressed in the red brick walls of late Colonial and Classic Revival America, the brick Gothic buildings of the Baltic countries, the seventeenth- and eighteenth-century brick façades of the Netherlands and Belgium, the screne wall surfaces of many English Georgian houses —these all tell the same story. (See Figs. 444, 445.) It is always the quietest and the most uniform brick wall which weathers best, stays cleanest, and expresses most clearly and beautifully the essence of the construction.

FIGURE 442. R. MEES EN ZOONEN BANK, ROTTERDAM, THE NETHERLANDS

Brinkman & Van der Vlugt, architects

Recent Dutch brickwork emphasizes surface by the use of light-colored smooth brick and continuous flush joints. Photograph Kamman, courtesy Avery Library

The problems of expression in terre pisé and concrete are manifestly different since these are essentially cast materials, tamped or poured between forms. Both the shape and the surface of the material will depend on the design and the surface of the formwork. The forms used are in general of wood—either planks or plywood panels—or of metal sheets, held in place by strong bracing. Various attempts have been made to create patterns that will allow standard metal forms of various types to be used over and over again. But the forms,

FIGURE 443. LEFT: JOHN DICKENSON HOUSE. RIGHT: RICHARD SMITH HOUSE. BOTH
NEAR SALEM, NEW JERSEY

The colonial builders of southern New Jersey liked to make elaborate patterns with bricks of
two colors.

Photographs Paul Love from Love, "Colonial Brickwork in the Salem Tenth" (MS.)

whether of wood or of metal, are expensive to build, both as to labor and material, and therefore the real spirit of this type of construction will be expressed
only through the simplicity which results from simple formwork. That will
mean large and uninterrupted areas of wall, concentrated openings, and basic
continuity of surface.

But concrete, since it is a cast material, enjoys also the freedoms which casting makes possible. Thus curves in plan, difficult to erect in block or framed
construction, are easy to produce with cast material and—because of the smallness of the individual bricks—to a lesser degree in brick construction as well.
Similarly, curves of various types in elevation can easily be cast if the cost is not
the controlling factor. Even vertically curved wall sections are possible, pro-

FIGURE 444. LARKIN HOUSE,
PORTSMOUTH, NEW HAMP-
SHIRE

Early nineteenth-century builders
of the United States preferred the
quietest surfaces in brickwork.

Courtesy J. M. Howells and
Metropolitan Museum of Art

FIGURE 445. BUSINESS BLOCK, NANTUCKET, MASSACHUSETTS (CIRCA 1847)
The restrained dignity of Classic Revival brickwork in the United States.

Photograph Talbot Hamlin

vided the general sense of stability and continuity is not thereby destroyed.
Naturally, also, such a system lends itself admirably to various types of domed
and vaulted roof construction. Since this question has already been dealt with
at some length in Volume I, it is not necessary here to go further into it, except

FIGURE 446. SLAVE QUARTERS OF TERRE PISÉ, BREMO PLANTATION, VIRGINIA. GENERAL VIEW AND DETAIL

Terre pisé over a century old. Note the stone foundation, the broad eaves projections, and the signs of erosion where the protecting paint has worn off. The holes were made by mud wasps.

Photographs Leopold Arnaud

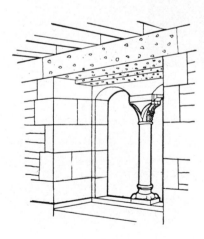

to emphasize the fact that the simplest and most continuous types of curved surface express this special construction method most successfully.

It is the development of steel reinforcement which has made the use of concrete one of the great creative forces in twentieth-century architecture. Con-

FIGURE 447. CHÂTEAU, CARCASSONNE, FRANCE. WINDOW IN THE OLDER PORTION

This window illustrates a rare medieval use of cast concrete to form a lintel.

Redrawn from Viollet-le-Duc, *Dictionnaire raisonné . . .*

FIGURE 448 (ABOVE, BELOW, AND OP-
POSITE). TYPICAL REINFORCED CON-
CRETE BRIDGES IN SWITZERLAND

R. Maillart, engineer

UPPER LEFT: Chatelard Aqueduct; BELOW:
Bridge over the Thur near Felsegg, St. Gall;
OPPOSITE, ABOVE: Lachen Bridge, Canton Zurich; OPPOSITE, BELOW: Footbridge near Wuel-
flingen.

All examples show the flexibility of reinforced concrete in the hands of an imaginative and brilliant designer.

Courtesy Museum of Modern Art

crete, like any good masonry, has tremendous compressive strength; its tensile
strength, however, is relatively small. But by adding steel,[1] designed to take
tensile stresses, reinforced concrete is rendered strong both in compression and
in tension, so that columns, beams, floor slabs, and thin vaults all become
practical. The most cursory glance at any large number of modern structures
will show at once the great fertility of this type of construction.

[1] It was probably a French gardener, J. Monier, who, in 1849, first introduced iron bars into
concrete to strengthen it. A true system of reinforced concrete was patented by F. Hennebique
in France in 1892.

Reinforced concrete can be used in two major ways—either to form monolithic bearing-wall structures or to form a supporting frame on which screen walls are carried. The latter method is the more common and will be treated in Chapter 16. There are also many structures in which elements of both types of treatment are found inextricably combined, for one of the virtues of the method is that it allows a continuity, a oneness, of conception and of execution which no other building method can give. Naturally its true and significant expression will depend largely on the stressing of the unified and continuous character of concrete. It is precisely this that makes the material ideal, both aesthetically and practically, for great dams, docks, sea walls, canal locks, and similar large-scale public works, as well as for stadiums, amphitheaters, grandstands, and so on. It is the perfect expression of that same continuity which constitutes the extraordinary power of the great dirigible hangars at Orly, by Freyssinet, and of the market hall at Rheims by Maigrot or that at Leipzig by

FIGURE 449. NORRIS DAM, TVA

Roland Wank, chief architect

The great scale and simple surfaces admirably express the qualities of mass concrete.

Courtesy TVA

Dischinger & Ritter (Fig. 452), as well as of the many superb concrete bridges that so strongly and gracefully arch over river or valley, railroad or parkway, especially those designed by the Swiss engineer Maillart. If this sense of continuity is constantly in the designer's mind he can hardly fail. On the other hand, where the architect or engineer has broken up the concrete surfaces with rustications, moldings, or cast railings of balusters resembling stone or has attempted to imitate the intricate delicacies of such cut-stone styles as the Renaissance or Gothic (and this is too frequently the case), then both the power and the grace of the material are lost; the only result is an impression of confusion and the sad sense of a lost opportunity.

Because of the wide adaptability of reinforced concrete to all sorts of varied shapes, both curved and straight, and because the steel reinforcement can be designed for tremendous differences in required strength, this material is ideally suited for many types of floor, column, vault, and roof construction (Fig. 453). In many cases, the most efficient shapes follow so closely the stresses they are designed to withstand that they deservedly rank among the most expressive of architectural features. The mushroom column, for instance, carrying a four-way slab without beams, suggests in its very shape the spreading quality of its power, and various other kinds of floor construction based on pan types of form and giving a simple caissoned ceiling express the over-all continuity of the reinforcement (Fig. 454). In the same way, the shapes of vaults in concrete may be

FIGURE 450. HIWASSEE DAM AND POWERHOUSE, TVA
Roland Wank, chief architect
Concrete used with simple and direct power. Courtesy TVA

equally expressive, and, because of the wide adaptability of the construction, they may be day-lighted with vault lights or skylights wherever desirable (Figs. 455–458).

That this wide variety of forms is as yet little developed in the United States results from many causes. The relatively high cost, in this country, of unusual formwork is only one of them. Another is the inertia of the engineering and construction companies, which seek wherever possible to build in routine ways.

FIGURE 451. MARKET HALL, RHEIMS, FRANCE. INTERIOR

M. Maigrot, architect

The parabolic vault is a typical reinforced concrete form.

From Badovici, *Grandes Constructions*

Here, then, is one place where the creative architect endowed with a sure structural sense has an essential role to play. He must never let inertia on the part of engineers or contractors prevent his creation of truly expressive form. His imagination must always be seeking better and more beautifully efficient shapes than those which custom has crystallized, and his technical skill must be sufficient to point the way, at least, in which these expressive forms can be realized in actual construction. Only so could Wright have developed the strong grace of the "lily columns" of the Johnson Wax Company Building at Racine; only so could the Perrets in France have shown the infinite possibilities of design in concrete; only so could Moser have designed the pure, austere lines of pier and vault in St. Antoninus at Basel, or Brinkman & Van der Vlugt have produced the efficient, crystalline clarity of the Van Nelle plant in Rotterdam.

The ubiquitous mushroom column is a case in point. In too many instances, its expressive beauty is lost—merely through carelessness and a lack of struc-

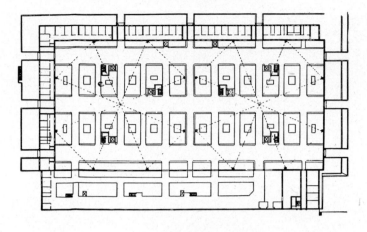

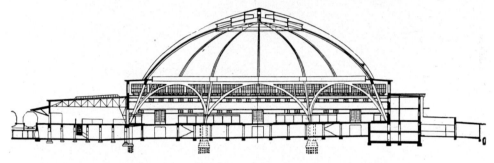

FIGURE 452. MARKET HALL, LEIPZIG, GERMANY. PLAN AND SECTION

Dischinger & Ritter, architects

This vast market hall is roofed with two large octagonal domed roofs. Each dome has a span of nearly 350 feet—one of the largest spans of masonry construction ever built. The domes have light shells between deep ribs, the whole supported on an ingenious braced frame.

tural imagination. A cylinder and a spreading cone built with sloppy formwork to standardized dimensions which express not efficiency but laziness on the part of the designer, the mushroom column becomes an ugly, depressing object good only for cellars and warehouses, where no one is supposed to look at it. Yet, with a little thought and a little care in the study of slope and dimensions, with some consideration of the relation between the column and what it supports, with some feeling for the continuity and the plasticity of the material and some little effort in designing proper forms, the mushroom column might be made into an expressive form of beauty and power. It has been done at times; it can be done again if the architect is determined to do it and is willing to contribute his imagination, his skill, and his time. And, in so doing, he may very well create a form more efficient than the old, ugly, standardized version—a

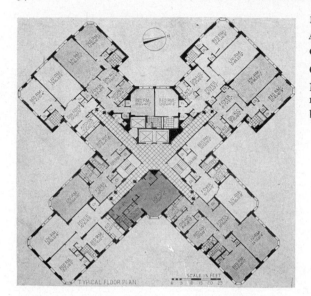

FIGURE 453. CASTLE VILLAGE APARTMENTS, NEW YORK. PLAN OF ONE OF THE FIVE BUILDINGS

George Fred Pelham, Jr., architect

Note the use of columns of long, narrow section to simplify the apartment planning.

form which later engineers and builders will seize upon and perhaps standardize in turn.

Reinforced concrete, therefore, offers the architect a great challenge. Its adaptability—the possibility of its assuming almost any shape the designer may wish—creates for him the opportunity of developing buildings which, outside and in, are both beautiful in their own right, as pure form, and perfectly expressive of the continuity, the strength, and the plastic nature of the material. But to take advantage of this opportunity the architect must possess not only an aesthetic, form-originating imagination but also a deep knowledge of the material; what is even more important, he must have that innate sense of structure which has distinguished the great architects of the past and is still essential if the superb structural systems which science and industry have rendered possible are to be used to create an architecture that shall be worthy of them and shall lead always on to further advances. (See Figs. 459–462.)

The problem of the proper exterior surfacing of mass construction is an important one. Brick, of course, is its own best exterior. Although terre pisé will require a surfacing of stucco or some sort of paint to preserve it from dampness, there is no such requirement in concrete; its exposed surface may therefore be homogeneous with the entire mass. Yet exposed concrete, in the present state of its development and as generally produced, is by no means a perfect and universally applicable material. There will almost always be much stratification and pitting of the surface, caused by differences between the various pours

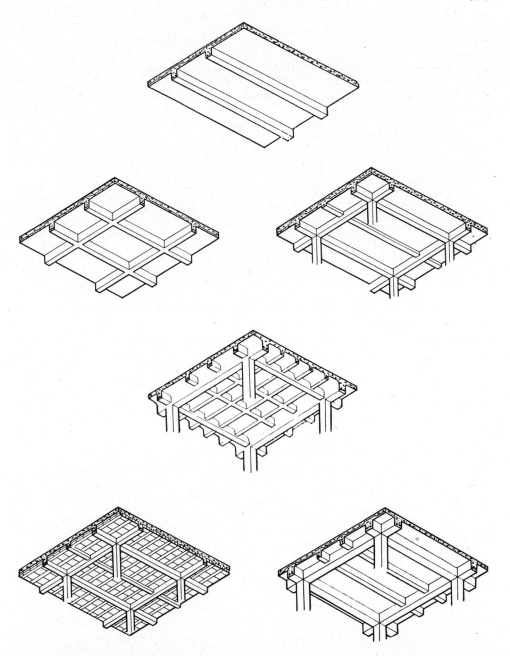

FIGURE 454. TYPICAL CONCRETE CEILING TREATMENTS

These drawings show some of the many varieties of concrete floor construction and the manner in which each creates its own strongly marked visual form. Each is interesting because it is so frankly an expression of structural facts.   Redrawn from *Time-Saver Standards*

FIGURE 455. STORAGE ROOM IN THE FACTORY OF GEBRÜDER ADT, FORBACH, FRANCE

Ways & Freytag, engineers

This top-floor storage room shows a refined and unusual development of simple post, girder, and beam construction in reinforced concrete. Like many German examples, this design is conditioned on the use of the minimum quantity of material, even at the cost of complicated formwork.

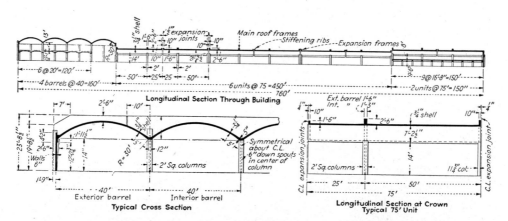

FIGURE 456. TIRE FACTORY, NATCHEZ, MISSISSIPPI. TYPICAL SECTIONS

Roberts and Schaefer Co., engineers; J. T. Canizaro, associated architect

These sections show a brilliant use of thin concrete shell vaults to roof various types of span over spaces for different uses in a large industrial plant.   Courtesy Roberts and Schaefer Co.

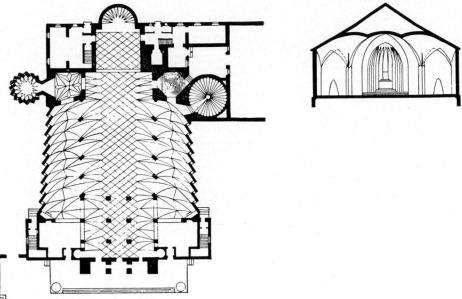

FIGURE 457. CHURCH AT NEU-ULM, GERMANY (1926). PLAN AND SECTION

Dominikus Boehm, architect

This plan and section show the complex concrete vault forms developed by Boehm in the effort to produce an exciting yet honest church interior by means of plastic and dynamic shapes.

used in an entire wall and by the fact that the aggregate may collect against the form and so prevent the cement from filling solidly beneath it or around it. The result will be disfiguring horizontal streaks and numerous ugly holes in the exposed face. Moreover, commercial cements often have a rather drab greenish-gray color, and there may also be considerable color variation even in different bags from the same mill. Furthermore, perfectly smooth areas of concrete will often crack or craze because of unequal shrinking of the material on the surface and in the body of the mass.

The only way to prevent such defects is to prepare the most careful specifications, exercise the most careful supervision, and apply various types of treatment to the wet concrete in the mold in order to insure complete homogeneity. Pittings may be filled after the forms are removed, but such patches will usually show in the finished work. They can be minimized by vibrating the concrete, though that is a relatively expensive operation. Cracking can be directed, if not avoided, by dividing the formwork into panels which furnish natural sinkages where the cracking will be likely to occur.

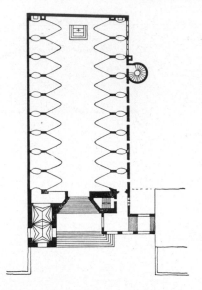

FIGURE 458. CHURCH AT BISCHOFSHEIM, GERMANY. PLAN AND SECTION

Dominikus Boehm, architect

A simpler development of thin vault forms for impressive architectural effect. Both this and the Neu-Ulm church reveal the variety of form possible in mass construction in concrete.

FIGURE 459. STE THÉRÈSE, MONTMAGNY, FRANCE. INTERIOR

A. and G. Perret, architects

A highly developed reinforced concrete interior combining elements cast at the job with elements that are precast.

From Jamot, *A.-G. Perret* . .

FIGURE 460. VAN NELLE TOBACCO FACTORY AND WAREHOUSE, ROTTERDAM, THE NETHERLANDS. EXTERIOR AT NIGHT

Brinkman & Van der Vlugt, architects

A reinforced concrete cantilevered frame allows both strength and openness.

Courtesy Museum of Modern Art

Much of the surface quality of concrete will depend on the nature of the cement and the kind of sand and aggregate used, and also on their proportions. Generally, the richer the mixture—that is, the higher the proportion of cement in it—the better the surface will be. Pitting will be most marked in foundation walls and similar elements in which relatively poor mixtures are used, for there will not be enough sand and cement to fill all the voids around the gravel or broken stone. Rich mixtures, moreover, will produce more impervious and more nearly waterproof walls, so that staining will be minimized. This is often an important matter where the reinforcing is near the surface, for water permeating an ill-mixed mixture—or one that is too poor—will rust the iron and bring rust stains to the surface.

The color of exposed concrete can be modulated in three ways: first, by using special white cements; second, by incorporating in the mixture small amounts of mineral pigments; and, third, by using special aggregates—broken brick or tile, or colored marble—and then scrubbing the wall with a wire brush

FIGURE 461. MUSEUM OF PUBLIC WORKS, PARIS. INTERIOR

Auguste Perret, architect

An interior of monumental, lavish quality that results from the creative handling of logical structural elements.   From *Construction moderne*

so that some of the aggregate is exposed. The first two methods have been used extensively in producing cement stuccos, but in some cases, where the walls are thin and the amounts involved not too great, white cement in the concrete mix itself is preferred. The exposed-aggregate method has been boldly used in several experimental constructions, most notably in the Shrine of the Sacred Heart in Washington, by Murphy & Olmsted. Generally speaking, however, present trends have been against it, for modern designers are seeking methods which require less skilled handwork and by which the effect desired will come naturally from the forms and the materials themselves.

Even when all possible precautions are taken, however, large unbroken areas of concrete will almost always have many imperfections and considerable va-

FIGURE 462. JOHNSON WAX WORKS, ADMINISTRATION BUILDING, RACINE, WIS-
CONSIN. INTERIOR

Frank Lloyd Wright, architect

Uniquely designed concrete columns spread out integrally into the circular slabs that form the
ceiling and the roof.   Photograph courtesy S. C. Johnson & Son, Inc.

riety in color and texture. It becomes the architect's task, therefore, to design
his concrete and his formwork in such a way that these necessary imperfections
do not damage the final and essential effect. In concrete of large scale, like that
found in bridge abutments and major road constructions, it is sometimes sufficient to divide the areas into large panels with deep recesses between the panels;
this has been done with great success by Aymar Embury in many bridge abutments and approaches in the highway network around New York. Another
method for smaller areas is to use wooden formwork of fairly rough texture,
with perhaps appreciable joints or V-grooves between the boards. This will
leave a pleasantly patterned surface of rough, yet systematic, texture, which
will tend to absorb and conceal imperfections in the concrete itself. Thus an
interesting checkerboard effect can be obtained by using forms in which panels
made of horizontal boards alternate with panels of vertical boards. This is excellently shown on the powerhouse vestibule of the Norris Dam of the TVA,

FIGURE 463. NORRIS DAM POWERHOUSE, TVA. ENTRANCE VESTIBULE

Roland Wank, chief architect

Interesting concrete surface achieved by changing the direction of the formwork boards in
alternate panels.   Courtesy TVA

where the contrast between the finished checkerboard surface of the building
and the great horizontal stratified mass of the dam itself is exceedingly striking
(Fig. 463).

Naturally all these methods will add to the cost of the formwork and therefore of the concrete itself. Cheap work in concrete, as in any other material,
will always look cheap and, through increased maintenance costs and the necessity of patching, may perhaps prove in the long run the reverse of economical. Much of the finest untreated smooth concrete work in the United States
can be seen in the dock and canal work of the United States Government engineers, in the work of the TVA, and also in hydraulic constructions by other
governmental agencies. Here the perfection of surface attained is directly related to the high unit costs of construction. Many of these great structures—
locks, dry docks, dams, sea walls, and the like—are examples of untreated concrete at its best.

FIGURE 464. ST. MARK'S, VENICE, ITALY. INTERIOR

Mass construction covered with a veneer, marble below and mosaic above; the mosaic emphasizes the continuity of the mass. Courtesy Ware Library

The beautiful surface quality of this work derives from two sources: the most careful functional design and the richness of the concrete mixture. Frequently mixes of one part cement, one part sand, and two parts of carefully chosen aggregate are used, because rich mixtures are necessary to make the concrete impervious.

In interiors, although concrete ceilings and vault soffits are sometimes left exposed and then painted, wall surfaces and piers in finished areas of the building are usually faced with a finishing material, for the concrete surface is generally too rough and hard for comfort or easy cleaning and it also lacks reflecting quality for illumination. Veneers of stone, marble, or tile are the rule in public or monumental interiors; plaster is the most common surfacing elsewhere. But the architect must always remember that when finished stones or marbles are used they are veneers only; he must always avoid the temptation of detailing them as though they were structural materials. Roman and Byzantine architects realized this to the full; the interior of the Pantheon, with its rich marble-patterned veneer, or the interiors of Santa Sophia in Istanbul and of St. Mark's in Venice (Fig. 464) show the rich yet logical results of such a veneer treatment. The gold-ground mosaics of Byzantine churches are magnificent surfacings for mass construction, and the reflected glints from their myriad surfaces not only give interesting over-all texture but also emphasize the suave continuity of the curving vault surfaces. An excellent example of marble veneering can be seen in the lobby of the International Building at Rockefeller Center, where in the veneer the frank recall of the H-shaped plan of the columns has both expressed the construction and enabled these piers to be used as lighting sources.

We may therefore summarize the directions along which the architect may work in his effort to achieve expressive form in mass-construction buildings somewhat as follows:

For rubble—continuity; large, unbroken surfaces; the avoidance of distracting variations in the shapes, colors, and projections of the component stones.

For brick—plane surfaces, untroubled by excessive projections; quiet, over-all texture and color; careful choosing and handling of the bond; careful study of the tops of linteled openings; regularity of plan; concentration of openings; avoidance of excessively small piers.

For terre pisé—small openings, with adequate piers between them; deep reveals; rounded or splayed edges; projecting roof eaves or protecting porches; stucco or paint waterproofing on all surfaces.

For concrete—the greatest possible continuity of line and surface everywhere; free use of curves in plan where desirable; concentration of supports, walls, and openings into few and large elements; emphasis on the plastic quality of the material; in piers, floor soffits, and vaults the devising of shapes of great interest to express both the material and the function; sensitive and imaginative handling of outside and interior surfaces, by appropriate choice and design of the formwork, by requisite adjustment of the mix and the material, or by the use of veneers.

One axiom in all architecture is that the best buildings express not only their function but also the way in which they are built and the materials of which they are made. In no type of structure is this more true than in buildings of mass construction.

SUGGESTED ADDITIONAL READING FOR CHAPTER 14

FOR BRICKWORK

American Face Brick Association, *Brickwork in Italy, a Brief Review from Ancient to Modern Times* (Chicago: American Face Brick Assn., 1925).

Emerson, William, and Georges Gromort, *The Use of Brick in French Architecture* (New York: Architectural Book Pub. Co. [c1935]).

Hydraulic-Press Brick Company, *Bonds and Mortars in the Wall of Brick . . .* 5th ed. (St. Louis: Hydraulic-Press Brick Co. [c1928]).

Lloyd, Nathaniel, *A History of English Brickwork . . .* (London: Montgomery, 1925).

Stoddard, Ralph P. (editor), *Brick Structures, How to Build Them*, 11th ed. rev. (New York: McGraw-Hill [1948]).

Strack, Heinrich, *Brick Architecture of the Middle Ages and the Renaissance in Italy* (New York: Helburn [c1910]).

FOR CONCRETE

Badovici, Jean, *Grandes Constructions. Béton armé—acier—verre* (Paris: Éditions A. Morancé [1931]).

Crane, Theodore, *Architectural Construction; the Choice of Structural Design* (New York: Wiley; London: Chapman & Hall, 1947).

Fitch, James Marston, *American Building; the Forces That Shape It* (Boston: Houghton Mifflin, 1948).

Giedion, Sigfried, *Space, Time and Architecture* (Cambridge, Mass.: Harvard University Press, 1941), especially pp. 244–255, 372 ff.

Huntington, Whitney Clark, *Building Construction . . .* 2nd ed. (New York: Wiley; London: Chapman & Hall [1944]).

Jamot, Paul, *A.-G. Perret et l'architecture du béton armé* (Paris: Vanoest, 1927).

Peabody, Dean, *The Design of Reinforced Concrete Structures* (New York: Wiley; London: Chapman and Hall [1946]).

Vischer, Julius, and Ludwig Hilberseimer, *Beton als Gestalter* (Stuttgart: Hoffmann [c1928]).

Weidlinger, Paul, "Architecture and Reinforced Concrete," *New Pencil Points* (August, 1943), pp. 58–66.

—— "Cooperation between Architects and Engineers," *Progressive Architecture* (June, 1946), pp. 81–86.

15

Architectural Design and Structural Methods IV: Framed Construction

FRAMED CONSTRUCTION is that type in which the materials that form the shelter and dividing elements—walls, partitions, roofs—are separate from the elements which support the weights. Framed construction is a primitive type developed through the discovery that certain kinds of building material were excellent for carrying weight but had little value in providing shelter and, conversely, that there were many materials, easily available, which were excellent as shelter but had little structural strength. In primitive work the structural material of the frame is universally wood, whereas the shelter materials are extremely varied. Mud plastered on a sort of basket-like interweaving of twigs or reeds, thatch of large leaves or of straw or grass, bark—especially birchbark—and the skins of animals have all served to protect man from wind, rain, and cold.

In these early types of frame building, the wood is used in the simplest possible fashion, and the framing members may consist of simple tree trunks or tree branches, perhaps with the bark removed. Sometimes, as in the case of the tepee of the Plains Indians of America, a number of straight sticks of approximately equal length had their lower ends forced into the ground and the upper ends lashed together to form a cone. Around this, bark or skins were stretched (Fig. 465). In other types of primitive huts, elastic pieces of wood were used, with their lower ends buried in the ground in a roughly circular plan and their upper ends brought together and lashed in place to form a sort of hemispherical dome or, as in certain cases in Africa, a curved pointed conoidal shape. In the African examples, as in those from primitive Europe, the covering is frequently of mud plastered on a lathing of reeds, twigs, or willow withes (Figs. 467, 468). This form of covering, known in England as wattle and daub, was a favorite for half-timbered houses and has continued in common use in parts of Europe

FIGURE 465. NORTH AMERICAN INDIAN DWELLINGS

A: Typical tepee of the Plains Indians, Crow Tribe, showing thunderbird decoration; B: Typical reed-mat and birchbark wigwam of the Forest Indians, Chippewa Tribe.
Most dwellings of the Plains and Forest tribes of the North American Indians are of framed construction with a frame of saplings and branches, covered by skins, bark, or mats and textiles.

From Talbot Hamlin, *Architecture through the Ages*

until comparatively recent years. In other cases the fill between the framing members might be partly of piled stones; many early buildings of northern Europe were constructed with wood-framed roofs, supported on posts that carried down to the ground, but with low walls of rough stone. Sometimes the posts were curved and met together overhead like an arch. Horizontal beams fastened to them carried the roof eaves. This type of construction is known in England as cruck, or crutch, construction (Figs. 469–472).

The advantages of rectangular over circular and oval plans had early been realized, and many of the primitive types of framed building made use of the rectangular shape. This was notably the case in the houses or wigwams of the eastern Indians of North America; in these the posts were brought together in a curve to form a sort of barrel-vaulted roof. In some cases—as, for instance, in the "long houses" of the Iroquois—buildings of this sort were of large size and were divided into bays for separate families.

Growing skill in cutting and shaping timber led inevitably to more highly developed building types in which the frame members were carefully adjusted to the work which they performed. This led to a complete separation between the concepts of posts, of beams or girts, and of roof rafters or roof frames generally. Thus the typical wooden frame came to consist of a series of vertical

FIGURE 466. TWO
THATCHED HUTS

ABOVE: From Mexico; BELOW:
A Nipa hut from the out-
skirts of Manila.

Courtesy Ware Library

posts outlining the plan and tied together at their summits by the horizontal
beams which they supported. On these beams, in turn, were supported the
slanting roof members or, if the roof was flat, the roof boarding and surfacing
itself. Openings for doors and windows could easily be made by inserting horizontal members between the posts at the desired heights, and the remaining
spaces could be filled with wattle and daub or sometimes with brick. In some
primitive examples the posts simply rested on the ground; in others they were
sunk slightly into it or else supported on flat stones. All these methods exposed
the ends of the posts to rot, through alternate states of dampness and drying. A
further step in advance, therefore, was made when the posts themselves came

FIGURE 467. WATTLE AND DAUB FROM A COTTAGE AT WEST BURTON, SUSSEX, ENGLAND

The wattle is a sort of basket-like lathing of sticks (often of willow) or reeds set in between the structural members; on it the daub—mud, clay, or stucco —is applied, usually leaving the structural posts and beams exposed.

Redrawn from Batsford and Fry, *The English Cottage*

to be supported on a horizontal timber, called a sill, which ran around the base of the walls. The sill could be held either on masonry piers or on stone walls.

This type of frame has one marked weakness—extreme susceptibility to lateral racking. Builders struggled with that difficulty for centuries and in many ways. Some tried merely to increase the number of uprights. Others developed the most intricate methods of mortising the frame members together. Still others depended on the strength of the wall fill.

The obvious solution, the use of diagonal brackets or diagonal ties so as to form a sort of truss, was long in coming and in some cultures was never discovered at all. Thus the Chinese, superlative carpenters though they are, make no use of diagonal bracing in their elaborate and monumental wood-framed temple and palace buildings; they depend for rigidity upon carefully mortised connections and upon the heavy brick masonry which partially encloses the exterior posts or columns. Similarly, the Greeks seem to have been ignorant of the principles of the diagonal brace and the truss (see Fig. 332). In primitive work in Asia Minor the indications of the rock-cut tombs give evidence of great skill in purely rectangular framing and also, perhaps, of the general use of solid wooden panels to act as a fill and to give rigidity. The Romans, on the other hand, seem to have thoroughly understood the importance of diagonal bracing; representations on Trajan's Column picture many bridges and other timber buildings which made extensive use of it (see Figs. 349, 475). It is probably from this Roman influence that the diagonal brace became a common feature in later European architecture; the use of such braces is a distinguishing mark of much late medieval half-timber work.

An analysis of the essentials of developed half-timber construction is most

FIGURE 468. WATTLE IN A
BARN FROM WARMINSTER,
GLOUCESTERSHIRE, ENG-
LAND

In this case the wattle is carefully made; it was probably not
intended to be covered, but to
act as a screen against rain that
would, however, permit ventilation.

Redrawn from Batsford and
Fry, *The English Cottage*

FIGURE 469. TYPICAL CRUCK FRAME-
WORK FOR A HOUSE OR BARN ROOF
Redrawn from Innocent, *English Building
Construction*

FIGURE 470 (RIGHT). CRUCK CONSTRUCTION FROM A PARTIALLY RUINED BUILD-
ING AT LANGSETT, YORKSHIRE, ENGLAND
The outer aisle, or "outshot," is probably later than the central, cruck-supported section.
Redrawn from Innocent, *English Building Construction*

enlightening with regard to the quality inherent in framed construction as a
whole. The following features become at once apparent: (1) Regularly spaced
vertical posts. (2) A definitely rectangular plan due to the continuity of the
sills on which the posts rest and of the beams which they support (Fig. 476).

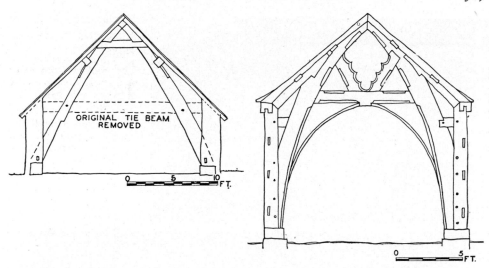

FIGURE 471 (LEFT). DIKE SIDE, MIDHOPE, YORKSHIRE, ENGLAND. SECTION

A cruck-supported roof with the original tie beam removed. This indicates that the masonry walls may be later in date than the cruck framing and they may have replaced earlier walls that carried no weight.   Redrawn from Innocent, *English Building Construction*

FIGURE 472 (RIGHT). LUNTLEY HALL, HEREFORDSHIRE, ENGLAND. SECTION OF HALL FRAMING

Highly developed and carefully finished framing midway between true cruck framing and tie-beam trusses with arched braces. The builder has borrowed from both types and produced a rich, but unnecessarily complicated, system.

Redrawn from Innocent, *English Building Construction*

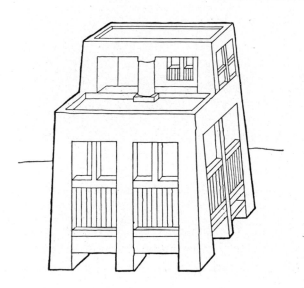

FIGURE 473. AN EGYPTIAN HOUSE MODEL IN THE LOUVRE, PARIS

This ancient Egyptian model of a house shows a building of partial framed character, with wall screens of boards and window openings filling the apertures between the basic structural members.

Redrawn from Perrot and Chipiez, *Histoire de l'art dans l'antiquité*

FIGURE 474. LYCIAN
ROCK-CUT TOMBS AT
TLOS

The rock-cut tombs of
ancient Lycia obviously
represent wood-framed
structures.

From Benndorf and Nie-
mann, *Reisen in Lykien
und Karien*

FIGURE 475. REPRESENTATION OF A WOOD-FRAMED THEATER CARVED ON THE
COLUMN OF TRAJAN, ROME

Important evidence of the application of wooden construction to large ancient Roman buildings.
Note the diagonal bracing.   From Cichorius, *Die Reliefs der Traianssäule*

(3) Existence of a certain number of diagonal braces as a guard against lateral
deformation. (4) Doors and windows placed according to the position of the
structural posts and frequently filling the entire area between adjacent posts;

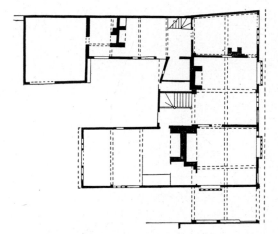

FIGURE 476. PAYCOCKE'S HOUSE, GREAT COGGESHALL, ENGLAND (CIRCA 1500). PLAN

This plan illustrates the basic rhythmical cellular nature of advanced frame construction.

Redrawn from Tipping, *English Homes*

in other words, it is immaterial to the strength of the building whether the space between posts and horizontal framing members is filled with an opaque or with a transparent material or whether it is left open. (5) In multi-story buildings, ease of constructing overhangs, either by projecting horizontal beams beyond the faces of the girts on which they rest or by bracketing out secondary girts beyond the face of the wall below. (6) Gable roofs; considerable complexity in the roof and the use of many gables are easy to produce through the correct shaping and framing of simple straight timbers. (7) Development of rich and varied effects through the decorative enhancement of the major structural members; thus buttress forms and similar decorative elements suggesting support may be carved on posts, brackets may be molded, and horizontal members may be given interesting profiles or panels of surface carving. (8) Basic aesthetic effect achieved through contrast between the frame members and the fill between them and through judicious disposition of framing members and openings. (9) On the interior, frequent expression of the major framing elements—corner posts, girders, or summers—which will reveal the fundamental structural nature of the building.

Many local variations of this basic pattern are found; even in England, different regions develop different types of half-timber composition. In some cases, particularly in the earlier work, the vertical supports are multiplied and the diagonal braces minimized. In others, great curved diagonal braces are an essential part of the design, and it is possible that in their curved shapes there is evidence of influence from shipbuilding techniques (Figs. 477–480). In other cases still, especially in the late sixteenth and early seventeenth centuries, the

FIGURE 477. FRAMING OF A SURREY COTTAGE, ENGLAND

A typical example of English half-timber. Note the overhang at the second-floor level and the ease with which such a motif can be built. Note also the use of curved braces and of roof trusses and purlins.   Redrawn from Batsford and Fry, *The English Cottage*

FIGURE 478. FRAME OF A TYPICAL SUSSEX HALL-TYPE MANOR HOUSE, ENGLAND

The elaborate frame of a large half-timber house. Note the curved and straight braces, the chamfered summer, or girder, in the floor framing, and the framed openings for doors and windows.   Redrawn from Batsford and Fry, *The English Cottage*

diagonal braces are so reduplicated as to form the major element in the decorative effect.

In France, where half-timber work was used widely in close urban building,

FIGURE 479. OLD HOUSES, CHESTER, ENGLAND

Typical English Late Gothic half-timber, with curved and diagonal braces.

Courtesy Ware Library

the desire for maximum light through a narrow façade led to the development of buildings in which the windows on each floor form an almost continuous band from corner to corner. In these the corner posts become very heavy and the intermediate posts are spaced to provide convenient window widths. In order to give lateral stability in a construction of this type the panels between the floor timbers, or girts, and the window sills are all of them crisscrossed with diagonal braces halved together at the centers of the panels (Figs. 481–483).

FIGURE 480. BRAMHALL HALL, CHESHIRE, ENGLAND

Characteristic Early Renaissance half-timber work from northwest England; the timbering is developed into purely decorative patterns.   Courtesy Ware Library

In German towns similar causes gave rise to somewhat similar effects, but German half-timber work is frequently complicated by the use of bracketed-out turrets, bays, and similar forms in which carefully studied diagonal bracing not only assures stability but also creates form (Figs. 484, 485).

One more characteristic of much early half-timber construction deserves to be mentioned—the *bay*. Originally a bay was a space wide enough for the stabling of a yoke of oxen—somewhere in the neighborhood of twelve to sixteen feet. In England, houses were frequently referred to as houses of one, two, or more bays. And long after the time when oxen had been stabled within the house walls this habit of designing in accordance with major bay dimensions continued. Often bays were delimited by the position of major structural girders and posts, and plans were thus developed in terms of basic bay dimensions, with breaks and large partitions occurring naturally at the bay dimension lines.

Half-timber houses, beautiful as they were and susceptible of almost infinite variation, had certain inconveniences. It was difficult, for instance, to make completely tight joints between the timbers and the filling. It is significant that for this reason half-timber work never achieved the popularity in Scandinavia,

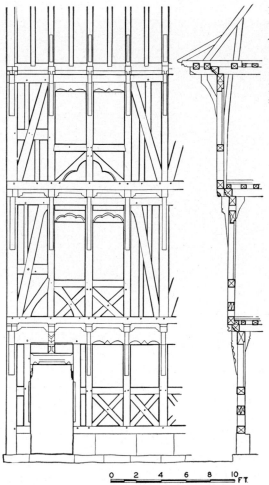

FIGURE 481. FRENCH HALF-TIM-
BER. PARTIAL ELEVATION AND SEC-
TION OF A THIRTEENTH-CENTURY
HOUSE AT CHÂTEAUDUN, FRANCE

This shows the typical clarity of much
French half-timber design. The overhang
at each floor level occurs frequently.

Redrawn from Viollet-le-Duc,
Dictionnaire raisonné . .

where weather conditions are severe, which it did in England and central
Europe, where the climate is more moderate. Even in certain parts of England
itself—the southeast counties, especially Essex and Middlesex—it early became
the custom to cover half-timber work with an exposed protective screen of
weather boards (a kind of clapboard) or with stucco.

In the English colonies in America the severity of the climate rendered such
a covering well-nigh obligatory. Undoubtedly, exposed half-timber was occasionally built in the traditional manner, for a few examples have been found;
but it proved unsatisfactory in the gales and snows of New England winters,
and contracts for alterations are extant which call for the addition of clapboards
or shingles to existing houses. In the greater number of houses built after the

FIGURE 482. HALF-TIMBER HOUSES IN ROUEN, FRANCE
Richly molded Late Gothic half-timbering, with diagonals developed as a decorative pattern.
Courtesy Ware Library

middle of the seventeenth century, this covering became an essential element at the very beginning. The result is known as covered frame construction (Figs. 487–490). It is noteworthy that the most important example of exposed half-timber work in the United States is an eighteenth-century Moravian building in central Pennsylvania, where the winters are less severe than they are farther north (Fig. 491).

The Chinese system of framed construction in wood, with shelter walls of brick and with heavy tile roofs, is one of the most interesting expressions of this kind of building. In China, solid-masonry buildings are exceptional except in fortification walls, bridges, and similar structures. There are a few masonry-vaulted temple halls and a few brick-and-stone or all-stone pagodas. Except for these, all Chinese structures—even the largest temples and palaces—are supported on frames of wood, and the entire decorative effect of Chinese architecture is based on these wooden frames. Halls are surrounded by a row of widely spaced wooden posts of great height and large diameter. Horizontal

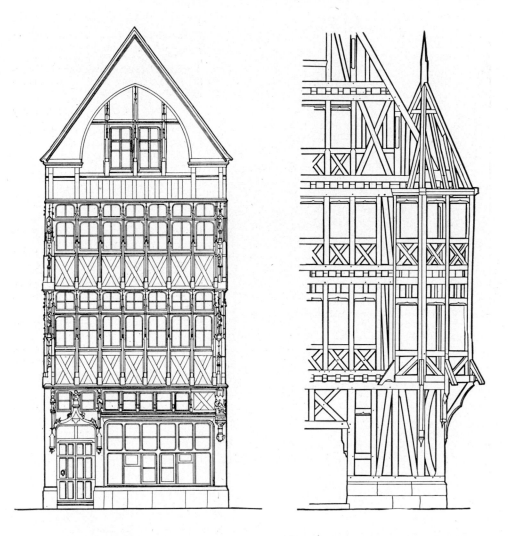

FIGURE 483 (LEFT). A LATE-FIFTEENTH-CENTURY HOUSE AT ROUEN, FRANCE. ELEVATION

This elevation shows the highest type of richly developed French half-timber; it reveals how the most lavish architectural details and effects can arise from the imaginative enhancement of necessary structural members. All the ornament here—moldings, buttress forms, sculpture— is used to emphasize important structural elements.

Redrawn from Viollet-le-Duc, *Dictionnaire raisonné* . . .

FIGURE 484 (RIGHT). CHARACTERISTIC HALF-TIMBER FROM THE RHINELAND

The projecting corner turret and the repeated use of crossed diagonals are typical of much German half-timber. Redrawn from Viollet-le-Duc, *Dictionnaire raisonné* . .

FIGURE 485 (LEFT). HALF-TIM-
BER HOUSE, HILDESHEIM, GER-
MANY

Typical German Renaissance half-timber work, characterized by lavish carving and the projecting bay.

Courtesy Ware Library

FIGURE 486 (BELOW). CHARAC-
TERISTIC EARLY CONNECTICUT
HOUSE PLANS

LOWER LEFT: A typical central-chimney
house showing additions to form a
lean-to; LOWER RIGHT: Lee House, East
Lyme, as originally built and as added
to later.

The influence of the framing determines many elements in plan. The position of major girts (at the wall line)
and girders, or summers, is shown in
dotted lines. Note that the posts project into the rooms. This is a natural
result of covering the frame on the
exterior with clapboards or shingles.

Redrawn from Kelly, *Early Domestic Architecture . . .*

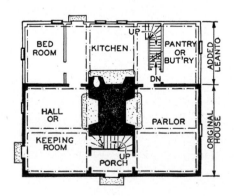

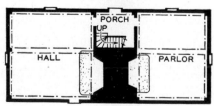

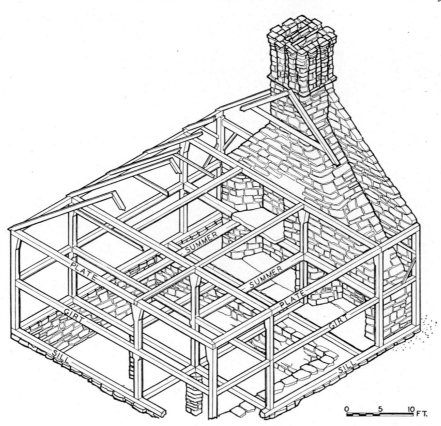

FIGURE 487. VALENTINE WHITMAN HOUSE, LIMEROCK, RHODE ISLAND. FRAME

This frame indicates the simplification of framing forms and of general house form that accompanied the change from half-timber to covered-frame construction.

Redrawn from Isham and Brown, *Early Rhode Island Houses*

architraves or beams are carefully mortised into them and, where spans are wide, these are frequently reduplicated. Sometimes carved brackets or bolster beams are also mortised into the columns under the beams. The upper beams, in turn, carry a series of projecting brackets, frequently of great elaboration and often projecting inside the wall as well as out. On the outer edge of the brackets the roof plate—often a large circular timber—is supported, and this carries the rafters (Fig. 496).

Chinese roof construction is based on heavy transverse timbers carrying from post to post. On these, and mortised into them, are supported one or more vertical columns which carry another higher and shorter transverse timber; this may bear a king-post column at its center. Thus by the use of purely vertical

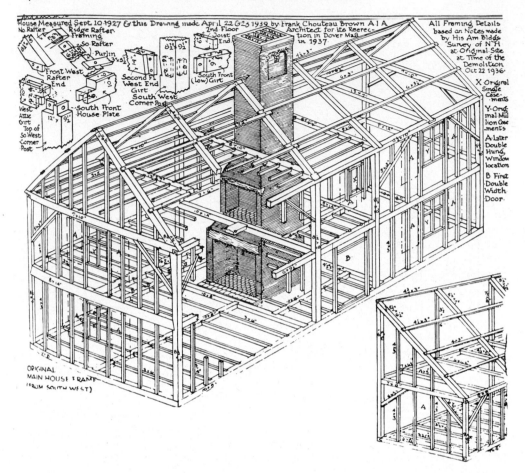

FIGURE 488. PAUL WENTWORTH HOUSE, SALMON FALLS, NEW HAMPSHIRE. PER-
SPECTIVE VIEW, WITH DETAILS, OF THE FRAMING

A highly developed example of the covered braced frame common in early Colonial houses. A
comparison with Figures 477 and 478 reveals the modifications in house framing caused by the
change from exposed half-timber to the covered frame.

Drawn by F. C. Brown, from the *White Pine Series*

and horizontal members the shape of the roof will be formed, and heavy purlins
on the intermediate supports and a ridge purlin over the king posts will form a
basis on which the rafters are supported. Sometimes a framed, wood, paneled
ceiling, supported by the transverse beams, hides the roof construction from
below, but usually in smaller halls and porticos the roof framing is exposed
(Figs. 493–496).

Walls in China are generally of brick—often sun-dried, or unburned, brick.

FIGURE 489. WARD HOUSE, SALEM, MAS-SACHUSETTS. EXTE-RIOR

Covered frame construc-tion of early New Eng-land with traditional half-timber forms faced with clapboards.

Courtesy Essex Institute

FIGURE 490. WARD HOUSE, SALEM, MASSA-CHUSETTS. INTERIOR DETAIL SHOWING CON-STRUCTION

The spaces between the framing members were nogged with unburned brick and clay.

Courtesy Essex Institute

They are of considerable thickness and are built to surround and conceal the outer half of the posts, but the inner half is left to show in the interior. The tops of these walls are sloped off to meet the soffit of the lowest horizontal beam,

and the whole exterior surface is then stuccoed and painted (Fig. 495). Above
the sloping wash at the top of the walls one can always see the horizontal beams
and the tops of the posts into which the beams are mortised; thus, from both

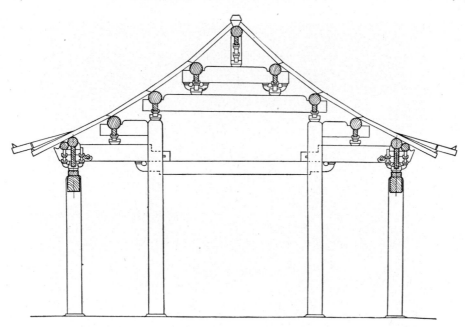

FIGURE 493. TYPICAL SECTION OF CHINESE TEMPLE HALL

The *Ying Tsao Fa Shih*, the great Chinese architectural work of the twelfth century, illustrates many types of roof construction. All of them, like this, are based on simple combinations of horizontal beam and bracketed post carrying longitudinal purlins. No trusses appear. Note that all weight is carried on the posts.   Redrawn from *Ying Tsao Fa Shih*

outside and in, one is always conscious of the supporting wooden frame. This frank expression is emphasized by the fact that in most cases the walls are limited to the north side and the east and west ends of large halls; the south front is enclosed only with wood grilles and paper-covered doors and windows.

All the exposed wood is elaborately painted, the columns usually in oxblood red. The nature of the framing of the beams is suggested by the decorative patterns painted on them and on the column tops. The elaborate bracket work, the plate, and the projecting rafter ends are usually rich with blue, emerald green, white, and gold—colors which give a vivid and lively glow in the shadow of the broad projecting eaves—and the curved roof itself is most frequently constructed of yellow porcelain tiles. The sheltering-wall stucco is stained a rich brown-red, which weathers to colors that vary from pale burnt sienna to a soft orange. The whole forms one of·the richest and most expressive types of architectural polychromy that has ever existed.

The change from exposed half-timber construction to covered frame construction had a tremendous influence on design. No longer could the architect

FIGURE 494. TEMPLE OF THE SUN, PEIPING, CHINA. INTERIOR

Chinese post-and-lintel framing, without diagonals, establishes the complex grandeur of Chinese temple halls.

From Imperial Museum, Tokyo, *Photographs of Palace Buildings of Peking*

depend on the interesting pattern of dark timber and filling of a contrasting color for his effect; it had to be gained by the simple forms of the building as a whole. Yet the influence of the construction hidden behind the covering remained a directing factor in major composition elements. Thus the rectangular and basically cellular type of planning was perpetuated because of the rhythmical spacing of the construction posts (Fig. 486). Openings preserved a similar rhythmical spacing, which again was dependent upon the position of the

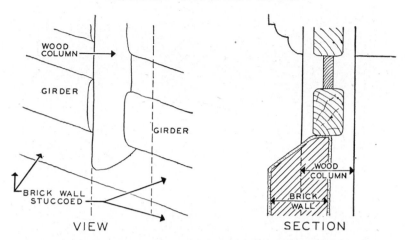

FIGURE 495. DIAGRAM VIEW AND SECTION OF THE TOP OF THE CURTAIN WALL OF
A TYPICAL CHINESE BUILDING

The wall exists for protection only; all roof weights are carried by the columns, which on the
exterior appear above the splayed wall top.

FIGURE 496. TEMPLE OF AGRICULTURE, PEIPING, CHINA. DETAIL OF THE CORNICE

The intricate beauty of the typical Chinese bracketed eaves cornice.

From Imperial Museum, Tokyo, *Photographs of Palace Buildings of Peking*

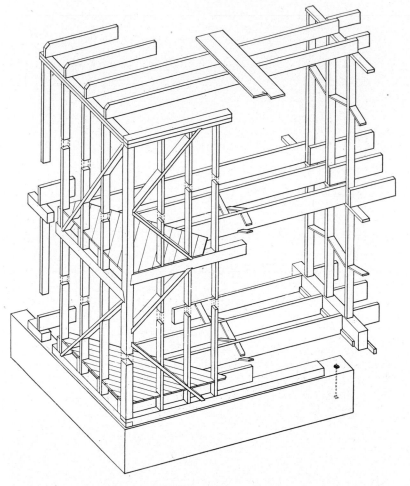

FIGURE 497. MODERN BRACED-FRAME CONSTRUCTION. ISOMETRIC VIEW

Modern braced frames use small-sized, stock timbers for all parts except sills, girts, and corner posts. Studs are regularized at 2″ x 4″; posts and sills are generally 4″ x 6″. Studs and joists are spaced 16″ center to center. This type of construction is essentially a compromise and is but little used today. Based on Ramsey and Sleeper, *Architectural Graphic Standards*

posts or studs, and in many cases even the old overhangs of half-timbered construction continued in use for some time.

Design in covered frame construction tended strongly toward a simplification of the basic composition, for it was manifestly easier to apply a shingle or clapboard covering over a surface that was continuous than over one that was not. Thus, little by little, many-gabled compositions gave way to house roofs

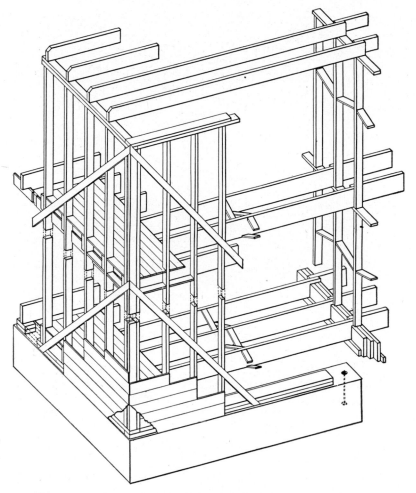

FIGURE 498. BALLOON FRAMING. ISOMETRIC VIEW

The balloon frame was developed gradually from the 1830's on in the effort to obtain a strong, light frame which used only stock, 2″-thick lumber, set at a standard spacing of 16″. Thus all members requiring greater strength are built up of small pieces. Rigidity is given by 1″ diagonal boards let into the studs. Often diagonal sheathing, well-nailed, was used and the diagonal braces were entirely omitted. Rough floors are also often diagonal.

Based on Ramsey and Sleeper, *Architectural Graphic Standards*

with a continuous ridge and continuous slopes, and the old overhangs were replaced by unbroken surfaces.

Covering the frame also affected its design. Once the necessity for producing aesthetic effect by the position of frame members had disappeared, these frame members tended to become more and more regularized and mechanically

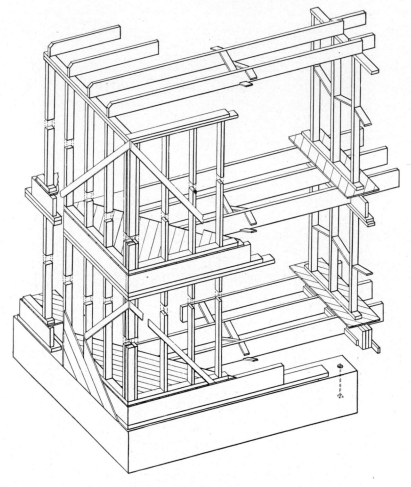

FIGURE 499. WESTERN OR PLATFORM FRAMING. ISOMETRIC VIEW

A variation of balloon framing in which floors are set first, and then studs are supported upon them. Diagonal sheathing and rough flooring are standard.

Based on Ramsey and Sleeper, *Architectural Graphic Standards*

spaced. Eventually the system developed into a continuous wall, with studs placed at fairly close intervals, with somewhat larger corner posts, and with diagonal braces. This type of braced frame controlled the building of houses in the United States, as it did in some parts of northern and western Europe, until almost the end of the nineteenth century (Fig. 488). The typical Colonial frame house and many of the simpler wooden houses of the growing cities of the early nineteenth century in the United States show with extreme clarity the qualities thus produced. Plans of simple rectangularity, wall planes continuous and unbroken (with rhythmically spaced windows pierced through the wall in the simplest manner), delicate cornices of slight projection, decoration reduced to refined wooden moldings at gable end and corners, and a decorated door or porch in which classic forms, somewhat attenuated, frequently appear—this is the almost invariable formula. It is all clear, neat, careful, and untroubled and, by reason of the continuity of its clapboard or shingle surface, produces an effect of serenity and quiet rightness.

The mechanization of building and the gradual standardization of the dimensions in timber members—especially the ubiquitous 2″ by 4″ stud—led eventually to the development of the kind of framing known as *balloon-frame* construction (Fig. 498). Here timber of large dimensions is completely absent; even the corner posts are built up of 2 by 4's. Standard spacings of 16 inches, center to center, are used for both vertical studs and horizontal joists, and no special intricate carpentry is required; a saw, a hammer, and some nails will serve to build the largest frame. Stability against lateral racking is given by sheathing and by under floors laid diagonally, or else by sheathing with large wall boards properly nailed in place.

This type of construction and others closely similar, like the *platform frame*, or *Western frame*, have become almost universal for wood buildings in the twentieth century (Fig. 499). Their popularity is due not only to the fact that little skilled labor is required but also to the lightness of the individual pieces used, any one of which can be handled by one man. It is not, however, economical in material, for the closely spaced studs and joists require a greater amount of lumber than would be necessary under the old carefully designed braced-frame construction; in the braced frame the material is concentrated where it will do the most work, whereas many of the studs in a balloon-frame building carry little or no weight and exist merely as spacers or nailing strips.

There is one other quality in connection with balloon-frame construction which requires comment—the fact that it depends for its lateral stability on the sheathing with which it is covered. In other words, it is actually an unscientific type of what is frequently called *stressed-skin* construction. It is probable, with the looming dearth of wood and the routing of so much of our forest resources into paper manufacture, that there will inevitably be a new attack on the problem of wood building and the scientific development of true stressed-skin construction. Many of the important types of prefabrication in wood depend on a few widely spaced posts with some type of panel between,

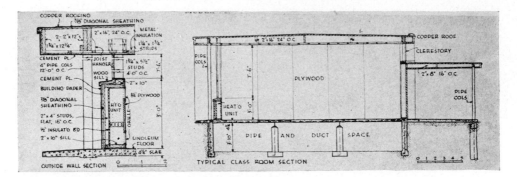

FIGURE 500. ACALANES UNION HIGH SCHOOL, CALIFORNIA. SECTIONS

Franklin & Kump, architects

This section and its details show an ingenious and unconventional type of twentieth-century frame construction.   From the *Architectural Forum*

and to this degree they represent a return to the principles of true braced-frame building. Others may use an actual stressed-skin type of panel composed of sheets of plywood glued to light, thin frames not over an inch thick.

Stressed-skin construction is one in which both lateral and axial stresses are resolved within the limits of a membrane, which in terms of form may have a plane or a curved shape. The stressed-skin principle is related to form; it is "monoplastic." In a sense it may be thought of as a *monocoque* construction— one in which the membrane (veneer) is primarily depended on to carry the stresses. Practical applications of this principle may be found in the egg, the pipe or tube, the new railroad cars, or the sphere; other examples are the pneumatic factory designed by Herbert H. Stevens, Jr.,[1] with its sheet-steel roof held up by air pressure, and the spherical gas tank.

The present-day connotation of the term does include, however, constructions of such form as to preclude the resolving of all stresses of all parts within a single membrane; that is, these constructions are non-monolithic structures. Falling in this category are angular structures of geometric form consisting of a series of planes; in these the membrane of individual parts is stressed. In other words, such structures are composed of a series of individual membranes or stressed skins. In the strictest sense they are corruptions or modifications of the stressed-skin principle. Ribbed structures such as Corwin Wilson's mobile houses, the Tainter lock gates like that used in Mississippi Dam 24,[2] and many

[1] *Architectural Record*, December, 1942, pp. 45–46.
[2] H. D. Phillips, *Stressed Skin Construction*, typescript in the Avery Library, Columbia University, New York, 1939.

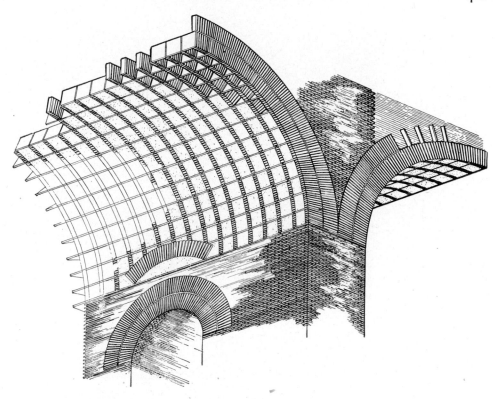

FIGURE 501. TYPICAL ROMAN BRICK-AND-CONCRETE VAULTING

In their efforts to simplify the building of large vaults, the Romans experimented with all sorts of frameworks of brick arching and tiles which both simplified the construction and reinforced and tied together the concrete.   Redrawn from Choisy, *L'Art de bâtir chez les Romains*

proprietary prefabricated panels are examples. Even in light wood-framed buildings the membrane (sheathing) is stressed to a certain degree, especially under lateral pressures.

Framed construction is also possible in masonry. Wherever, in the search for economy, supports have been concentrated in small and heavily stressed areas and tied together by arches or bands of masonry in such a way that stability is produced without the aid of the strength of the exterior sheltering walls, framed construction in a rudimentary form may be considered to exist. Thus colonnades carrying entablatures form a kind of framed construction, and where shelter within the colonnade is desired it is often formed by grilles or panels which have no supporting nature. In the Stoa at Pergamon, for instance, the railing of the upper colonnade consists of thin slabs of marble which are

FIGURE 502 (ABOVE). BASILICA OF CONSTANTINE, ROME. CUTAWAY DIAGRAM
SHOWING CONSTRUCTION

This is a typical example of mixed brick-and-concrete construction, with brick used as facings
for all walls, for the chief arches, and as a sort of network framework for the vaults and the
concrete filled in between.   Redrawn from Choisy, *L'Art de bâtir chez les Romains*

FIGURE 503 (OPPOSITE, TOP). NYMPHAEUM OF THE LICINIAN GARDENS (TEMPLE
OF MINERVA MEDICA), ROME

The refined engineering of late Roman vaults in brick and concrete led to light constructions of
an almost framed nature.   Courtesy Avery Library

FIGURE 504 (OPPOSITE, BOTTOM). VAULTING IN THE PALACE OF SEPTIMIUS SE-
VERUS, PALATINE HILL, ROME

Another example of the Roman method of using ribs and frameworks of brick and tile for
concrete vaults.   Redrawn from Choisy, *L'Art de bâtir chez les Romains*

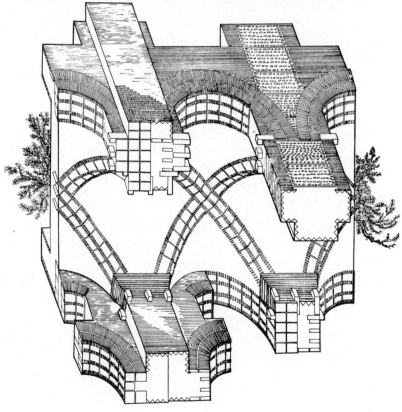

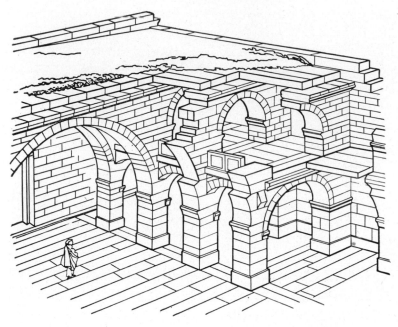

FIGURE 505. BASILICA AT CHAQQA, SYRIA. DIAGRAMMATIC ISOMETRIC VIEW

In the stone-building portions of Syria many attempts were made in the Early Christian period to carry the huge weight of stone floors and roofs on the lightest and most widely spaced supports. Such attempts usually entailed the building of arches carrying web walls on which the roof or floor slabs were laid. Thus weights are concentrated on the arch piers, and external walls have little structural meaning. In highly developed examples such as that shown, this system approaches true framed construction in stone.

Redrawn from Viollet-le-Duc, *Entretiens sur l'architecture*

set between the columns and for their strength depend on being thoroughly anchored to these.

A close approach to framed construction, in its more highly developed sense, occurs in many of the great Roman vaulted buildings (Figs. 501–505). For example, in the central buildings of the Baths of Caracalla and of Diocletian, the structure consists of a network of vaults supported on isolated piers, with powerful buttresses where necessary to resist the thrusts. Here the internal dividing walls and even some of the exterior walls exercise little of the supporting function, and it is immaterial to the strength of the whole whether they are continuous partitions, screens of columns, or great windows. This system is carried to an even higher degree in such late buildings as the Nymphaeum of Maxentius, usually called the Temple of Minerva Medica (Fig. 503).

Even in the construction of the vaults themselves, the Romans occasionally approached the concept of true framed construction. Concrete vaults, for instance, were frequently divided into small areas by a network of ribs of brick. These ribs formed continuous arches independently stable; they were probably built first, and from them the formwork for the concrete could easily be hung.

Nevertheless it was not until nearly the middle of the twelfth century that a more logical system of framed construction in masonry was developed. This was the result of a long series of gradual moves during the Romanesque periods —a story which can be found in any good architectural history and need not concern us here. It is enough to state that the effort to produce a thoroughly fireproof, three-aisled church, vaulted in stone and having large clerestory windows, led inevitably, if slowly, to the full development of the Gothic system, which in its highest forms was a magnificent expression of the two basic ideals of framed construction. These ideals are: first, the concept of structural elements and sheltering elements as completely different architectural features; and, second, the logical and expressive treatment of the structural elements to reveal their nature.

There has been much recent controversy over the details of this long process and especially over the basic purposes which lay behind it. The old constructivism of Viollet-le-Duc is no longer universally accepted. According to him, every form in Gothic architecture developed from the logic of the construction, and the magnificence of the resulting buildings was due to the supremacy of this purely structural basis and to its perfect expression in form. Recent archaeological research has tended to discount the single-minded clarity of this simple theory. Much of the development seems to have been almost accidental —a certain daring builder tried something new and it worked—but some of it, on the contrary, seems to have derived from a purely aesthetic urge. Thus ribs in the vaulting appear to have come into use at first partly as mere attempts to emphasize the often indecisive intersections of groined vaults. Moreover, we now know that medieval architects could have had no such detailed knowledge of the stresses inherent in vaulted construction as that with which Viollet-le-Duc credits them. That they did have a tremendous intuitive structural imagination and a thorough knowledge of the various materials which they used is obvious in the buildings, but we tend to forget the fact that they made many unsuccessful attempts which either were never completed or ignominiously collapsed.

Whatever the history of this development may have been, and whatever were the ultimate structural or aesthetic purposes which lay behind it, the fact

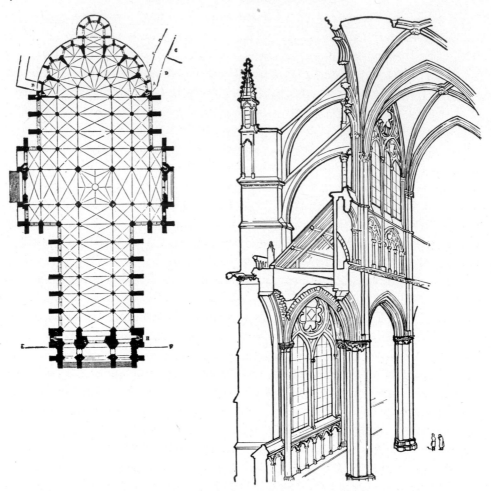

FIGURE 506 (LEFT). CATHEDRAL, AMIENS, FRANCE. PLAN

This plan has all the qualities of frame construction: thin, strong supports, regularly spaced, a basic cellular organization, and the elimination of exterior supporting walls. Although the material is stone, many of the same characteristics appear in framed buildings of other materials. Compare Figure 476 (wood) and Figure 550 (steel).

From Viollet-le-Duc, *Dictionnaire raisonné . . .*

FIGURE 507 (RIGHT). CATHEDRAL, AMIENS, FRANCE. DIAGRAMMATIC CUTAWAY VIEW OF THE NAVE

The Gothic architects of France took the final steps in developing a logical framed construction of stone. All the weights of vaults, roof, and wall are carried upon a framework of stone arches, piers, and buttresses, so that large areas of window are possible and walls become either spandrels, weighting the arch haunches, or mere screens.

Redrawn from Viollet-le-Duc, *Dictionnaire raisonné . . .*

remains that in the cathedrals and even in many of the minor buildings of thirteen-century France we have a magnificent expression of framed construction in stone. Essentially the system is conditioned by the concentration of all weights on isolated supports as small as possible and by the elimination of supporting walls. This has resulted in plans of regularly spaced columns or piers and rhythmical projecting buttresses which take up all the thrusts. These buttresses are naturally spaced on the lines of the columns and arches and thus partake of the same rhythm. The columns and piers support arches which connect them diagonally, transversely, and longitudinally. The outer piers are backed by the buttresses, which abut the thrust inherent in the system. And this frame of piers, buttresses, and a network of arches is thus completely self-supporting and can easily be made strong enough to bear the weights of the vault filling, the spandrel walls, and the roof. The side "walls" thus consist of arched openings running from the ground to the wall arches on the under side of the vault, and these openings can either be filled with skin walls or be left as enormous tracery windows, just as the wish of the architect or the conditions of the problem may require. Such a construction is essentially a cage construction and, in its simplest form, is well shown in the upper chapel of Ste Chapelle in Paris (Fig. 510) or in Ste Chapelle at Germer-de-Fly. In a slightly more complex form many of the three-aisled hall churches of Gothic Germany illustrate the same system.

Where a higher central nave was desired, the nave vault with its ribbing exerted a thrust high in the air, and this thrust was conveyed to the buttresses along the outer side of the side aisles by stone struts—the flying buttresses. This scheme allowed large clerestory windows and in addition, in the space occupied by the sloping side-aisle roof, a triforium gallery, which usually consisted of an open arcade on the nave side and the thinnest of walls between it and the side-aisle roof space. The system is well seen in the section of the nave of Amiens Cathedral (Figs. 506, 507). And through the use of flat or hipped side-aisle roofs, it even became possible to glaze the triforium gallery also, as in the choir of Amiens Cathedral, or even to omit it altogether and simply continue the clerestory windows downward, as in many late Gothic churches.

In this developed cage construction there was a point of weakness where the thrusts were not effectively counterbalanced. This occurred in the nave piers at the level of the side-aisle vaults, for the inward thrust of the latter pressed only against the unbuttressed piers. The Gothic designers evidently felt that the great weight of the nave vault and roof carried by these piers was

FIGURE 508. CATHEDRAL, WINCHESTER, ENGLAND. INTERIOR

Framed construction in masonry with a highly developed architectonic expression in arches, piers, and vault ribs.   Courtesy Ware Library

a sufficient force to withstand such a thrust, and the continued existence through many centuries of the great Gothic buildings proves that in general that assumption was sound. It is nevertheless true that there are many Gothic churches in which the nave piers have taken a slight curve resulting from the outward thrust of the nave vault at the top and the inward thrust of the side-aisle vaults below.

The development and increased use of the pointed arch, of course, was essential to this whole system. It allowed the vault ridges to be brought to ap-

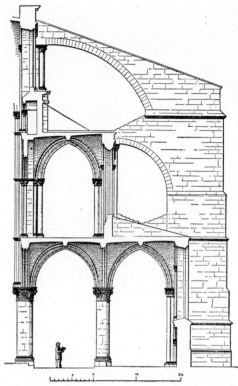

FIGURE 509. ST. REMI, RHEIMS, FRANCE.
SECTION

This section shows the almost complete disap-
pearance of wall which accompanied the full
development of framed construction in the
French Gothic. Masonry masses occur, instead,
in the form of great buttresses to withstand the
vault thrusts.

From King, *The Study-Book of Mediaeval
Architecture and Art*

proximately the same levels, irrespective of the differing spans of cross ribs,
wall ribs, and diagonal ribs. In such construction the diagonal ribs in most cases
are semicircular. The pointed cross ribs rise to approximately the same height,
and the wall ribs over their much narrower openings not only are usually
pointed but spring from levels much higher than the spring line of the other
arches. This naturally develops warped, non-geometric vault-filling surfaces,
but these complicated shapes are easily constructed by merely supporting the
centering at the two ends on the ribs. The existence of the pointed arch allows
complicated warped shapes—such as those which occur in the ambulatory of a
church—to be easily vaulted with shapes which appear simple and logical, for
each half of a pointed arch can be set in any desired plane, provided, of course,
that all the diagonal ribs achieve a basic equilibrium even though they lie in
different planes. Thus the visual center of a warped bay can be established anywhere, and the diagonal arches can be built from the corner of the bay up to
the chosen point. This solution was entirely dependent on the system of
pointed-arch framed construction, and the results achieved could not have been
reached so simply by any other method (Figs. 511, 512).

FIGURE 510. STE CHAPELLE, PARIS. INTERIOR

A most perfect expression of framed construction in masonry; the walls have become mere
screens and are chiefly of glass.   Courtesy Avery Library

There has been much discussion as to the actual structural nature of vault
ribs. Experience seems to prove that, once a ribbed vault has set, it acts as a
unit, and wherever fractures occur they seem to go through both the ribs and
the filling indiscriminately. But, even if in the completed building the vaulted

FIGURE 511. FRENCH ROMANESQUE AMBULATORY VAULTS

A: From Brioude; B: Plan and view from Notre Dame du Port, Clermont-Ferrand; C: Plan and section from Poissy; D: Plan, section, and view from Langres.

These drawings illustrate how the crossing of conical cross vaults with the annular ambulatory vault creates awkward and warped intersections, shown well in A and B. In C, where the groins are straightened, the fact that the span of the pier arch is less than that of the wall arch makes the cross vault slope up and out in an ugly fashion. Even with ribbed vaults difficulties arise if the groin-arch ribs are each in a single plane, D; this brings the intersection at a most unpleasant point in the bay. Only in developed Gothic was this problem finally solved.   Redrawn from Viollet-le-Duc, *Dictionnaire raisonné* . .

ribs do not actually carry the vault filling, they nevertheless serve two important purposes. First, they simplify construction enormously, for they can be built as comparatively light individual arches with a minimum of centering, and when they are complete they can themselves serve to support the centering for the vault fill. In the second place, they allow the easy construction of all kinds of warped vaulting surfaces and the beautiful and efficient construction of vaults over almost any possible shape.

FIGURE 513. NOTRE DAME CATHEDRAL, PARIS. VIEW FROM THE SOUTH

The organized and complex beauty that results from the logical expression of frame construction in masonry.

Much of the compelling and vital beauty of Gothic churches arises from the frank yet imaginative manner in which this construction system is expressed. The typical Gothic plan itself displays the workings of the system at a glance. The rows of slim columns forming regular square or rectangular bays that suggest the arches which connect them, the large windows, the thin walls, and the

FIGURE 514. ST. GERMAIN,
AMIENS, FRANCE. INTERIOR

Characteristic intellectualized expression of the structural logic in
Flamboyant Gothic.

Courtesy Ware Library

strong buttresses which project boldly at the sides—these all exist because of
the structural system used, and in their very relationships they express its workings.

Gothic church exteriors are similarly revealing. The sharp delineation of the
bay divisions by means of the buttress projections marching rhythmically down
the flanks, the tall windows stretching from buttress to buttress, the dynamic
upward thrust of the sloped flying buttresses, and the almost complete elimination of vertical walls except beneath the side-aisle or chapel windows and in
the arched spandrels all tell their tale with graceful vigor. Such exteriors, rich
with tracery, buttress offsets, pinnacles, and gargoyle water spouts, are no mere
stark display of engineering feats. They are rather the true expression of a
system of framed construction developed by keen and sensitive creative artists
who have pondered the construction and realized its spirit as well as its body.
It is the spirit which creates this rhythmical beauty (Fig. 513).

Yet it is in the interiors of these churches that the system finds its most perfect embodiment (Figs. 508, 510). The vertical lines of the piers, the intricate
rising and curving notes of the intersecting vault ribbing, the richness of large
areas of stained glass held in place by strong but graceful tracery, and the triple

division of pier arch, triforium, and clerestory—this all makes a compelling unity, entirely characteristic and expressive of the type of construction which alone makes it possible. Here too, it is the spirit, imaginatively incarnated, rather than the bald brutal fact which has created the effect. It is significant that in many late French Flamboyant Gothic churches, where a more rigid "logic" has eliminated all superfluous elements and a more unclothed display of the structure has dictated the forms, much of the magic and much of the expressiveness have vanished (Fig. 514).

The best Gothic architecture, then, is an architecture which owes its beauty to its expressiveness, but this expressiveness is the result not of the naked exposure of engineering fact but rather of a poetic and creative imagination which, while never denying the fact, ennobles it.

SUGGESTED ADDITIONAL READING FOR CHAPTER 15

Abraham, Pol, *Viollet-le-Duc et le rationalisme médiéval* . . . (Paris: Vincent, Fréal, 1934).

Batsford, Harry, and Charles Fry, *The English Cottage* (London: Batsford [1938]).

Bond, Francis, *Gothic Architecture in England* . . . (London: Batsford, 1905).

Briggs, M. S., *The Homes of the Pilgrim Fathers in England and America* (London, New York, etc.: Oxford University Press, 1932).

Giedion, Sigfried, *Space, Time and Architecture* (Cambridge, Mass.: Harvard University Press, 1941), pp. 268–77.

Harbers, Guido, *Das Holzhausbuch* (Munich. Callwey [c1938]).

Innocent, Charles F., *The Development of English Building Construction* (Cambridge, England: University Press, 1916).

Isham, Norman M., and A. F. Brown, *Early Rhode Island Houses* (Providence: Preston & Rounds, 1895).

Kelly, J. Frederick, *The Early Domestic Architecture of Connecticut* (New Haven: Yale University Press; London: Humphrey Milford, Oxford University Press, 1924).

Kimball, Fiske, *Domestic Architecture of the American Colonies and of the Early Republic* (New York: Scribner's, 1922).

Moore, Charles Herbert, *Development & Character of Gothic Architecture*, 2nd ed., rewritten and enlarged (New York and London: Macmillan, 1899).

Porter, Arthur Kingsley, *The Construction of Lombard and Gothic Vaults* (New Haven: Yale University Press, 1911).

Viollet-le-Duc, Eugène Emmanuel, *Dictionnaire raisonné de l'architecture française du XIe au XVIe siècle* . . . 10 vols. (Paris: Bance and Morel, 1854–68).

—— *Entretiens sur l'architecture*, 2 vols. (Paris: Morel, 1863–72); translated as *Discourses on Architecture* . . . with an introductory essay by Henry Van Brunt, 2 vols. (Boston: Osgood, 1875–81).

16

Architectural Design and Structural Methods V: Framed Construction in Steel and Reinforced Concrete

THE APPLICATION of iron and, later, of steel and reinforced concrete to the construction of buildings offered an extraordinarily efficient new material for the development of strong and rigid frames. Metals had been used for important structural members at least as early as the Pantheon in Rome (A.D. 110 to 115), where bronze trusses were employed to support the portico roof (Fig. 515). The cost and scarcity of the material, however, prevented its widespread application until industrialism and improved systems of mining and refining made it cheaper and more available during the second half of the eighteenth century. From then on, especially in France and England, iron began to play a greater and greater part in large-scale construction. Cast iron was admirably fitted for slim, strong columns and truss members in compression, and wrought iron was equally well fitted for making long-span beams and girders or truss elements in tension. Cast iron was probably used first on a large scale in the interior supports and floor beams of English textile mills toward the end of the eighteenth century, and arched bridges of cast iron, sometimes of considerable span, also were designed and built at about the same time. Yet the manufacture of beams for large-scale use presented great difficulties until the perfecting of the rolling mills in the 1840's. Later still, the invention of methods for the cheap production of steel suited alike for columns and beams gave a new impetus to the structural use of metal.

Thus the development of framed construction in metal was the product of a slow growth, and long before the final emergence of true skeleton construction there were buildings in which all the floors and all the interior supports were framed of metal. This earlier system of framing involved the use of cast-

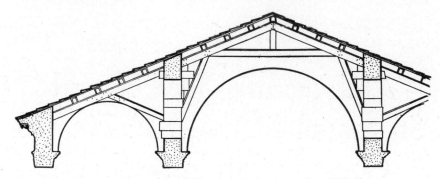

FIGURE 515. BRONZE TRUSSES FROM THE PORTICO OF THE PANTHEON, ROME

These famous bronze beams and trusses were removed during the Renaissance, but they are known from drawings made at the time. They reveal the fact that the Romans understood the great tensile and compressive strength of metal, and they form one of the earliest examples, if not the earliest, of its large-scale structural use.

Redrawn from Choisy, *L'Art de bâtir chez les Romains*

iron columns supporting a network of wrought-iron girders and joists (in the earliest examples these also were cast); between the joists, segmental arches of brick, or occasionally of concrete, were built to form the floors (Fig. 518). Buildings of this type, with exterior walls either of masonry or of cast iron treated like masonry, are common in the older business and industrial sections of many American cities; from shortly before the 1850's to some time after the Civil War this was the almost standard type of construction for loft and office buildings. By eliminating interior bearing partitions, the system allowed great freedom of interior layout. When first introduced, such structures were considered fireproof, but a series of disastrous fires proved how fragile were the exposed columns and beams in the face of high temperatures.

To produce a fully developed skeleton frame required an additional impetus. This was furnished by two factors: first, the development of extremely high land values in the city centers—the result of swift industrial and commercial expansion—which made high buildings desirable; and, second, the invention of the safe passenger elevator which made taller buildings possible. Safe passenger elevators came gradually into use in America after their first appearance in a store on Broome Street in New York in 1857 and the more famous installation in the Fifth Avenue Hotel in 1859. They are said to have been first used for offices in 1871, in the Equitable Life Building on Broadway, designed by Arthur Gilman with George B. Post as consultant.

The construction of high buildings brought with it well-nigh insoluble problems in structures where the exterior walls had to carry their own weight.

FIGURE 516. CRYSTAL PALACE, LONDON, AS RE-ERECTED IN SYDENHAM. INTERIOR

Sir Joseph Paxton, architect

An epoch-making building exemplifying for the first time the utility and beauty of metal and glass as important structural materials.   Courtesy Ware Library

FIGURE 517. BIBLIOTHÈQUE NATIONALE, PARIS. READING ROOM

Henri Labrouste, architect

The most brilliant early use of an iron frame as the chief structural feature in a permanent building.   Courtesy Ware Library

Masonry walls at the bottom of such a building would become tremendously thick, and in addition, since they had to be pierced with the large number of openings required for such a structure, the piers at the bottom became impracticably deep in order to carry the concentrated weights imposed upon them. Twelve stories was almost the limit for height in such a building. The tallest bearing-wall structure was the sixteen-story Monadnock Block in Chicago, designed by Burnham & Root in 1891, and here the piers at the ground floor are seven feet thick (Fig. 519).

Yet already a system had been developed which made possible buildings of almost unlimited height. Before 1865, the court walls of the warehouses at the St. Ouen docks had been supported on iron; the design was published in the *Builder*, of London, on April 29 of that year (Fig. 521). The system there em-

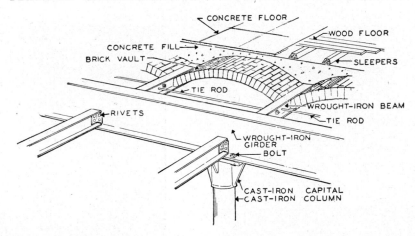

FIGURE 518. TYPICAL IRON-AND-BRICK FLOOR CONSTRUCTION IN VOGUE IN THE UNITED STATES 1860–1890

Wrought-iron connections are riveted; cast-iron connections and those between cast iron and wrought iron are bolted. The tie rods dispose of the brick-vault thrusts. Both cement and wood floor types are shown.

ployed was a sort of half-timber in iron and brick. Cast-iron columns and cast-iron arched beams were used, with iron window frames. The wall fill, of hollow brick, was built between the columns and window frames and was supported on the beams at each floor; the iron columns were exposed both outside and in. And even earlier, in 1857, masonry walls had been carried on metal in connection with shop-front design, as in the Sarl & Sons Building, Cornhill, London, by John Barrett. But the implications of these isolated examples were apparently not realized at the time.[1]

In 1881 George B. Post had carried the court wall of the New York Produce Exchange on a metal frame. The Home Insurance Building in Chicago, 1884–85, by William LeBaron Jenney, was built with metal columns enclosed within its brick supports and with beams so placed that they were integral with the masonry at each floor level; thus both assisted in the support of the exterior walls. Nevertheless the system was not thoroughly worked out, for the iron frame of the exterior was designed as an assistance to the masonry supports rather than as a substitute for them.

The final step was taken in the Tacoma Building in Chicago, by Holabird and Roche, in 1889 (Fig. 522). Here the small amount of masonry necessary and the entire system of spandrel walls and windows which forms the exterior

[1] For a discussion of this problem see Roger Hale Newton. "New Evidence on the Evolution of the Skyscraper." *Art Quarterly*, Winter, 1942.

FIGURE 519 (LEFT). MONADNOCK BLOCK, CHICAGO, ILLINOIS (1891)

Burnham & Root, architects

The highest—and almost the last—tall building to use exterior bearing walls.

Courtesy Museum of Modern Art

FIGURE 520 (RIGHT). A DESIGN FOR A CITY HOUSE IN IRON-FRAMED CONSTRUCTION (1863)

E. E. Viollet-le-Duc, architect

An early attempt to use an iron frame for a wall and to express it frankly.

From Viollet-le-Duc, *Entretiens sur l'architecture*

of the building are actually supported entirely by the metal frame. In 1888, at almost the same time, a Minneapolis architect, Leroy S. Buffington, took out a patent for a metal-framed building. An extensive controversy has arisen with regard to Buffington's priority in the invention of the skeleton structure and its importance at the time. The Chicago developments seem to have occurred quite independently of Buffington, and the evolution of the skyscraper after 1890 was so swift that Buffington's work was rapidly superseded and forgotten.

The essentials of skeleton construction were simple and, in all major matters,

FIGURE 521 (LEFT). ST. OUEN DOCKS, PARIS (1865). TWO PARTIAL ELEVATIONS

M. Prèfontaine, architect and engineer

The left-hand elevation shows the exposed cast-iron framing of columns and connecting girders which carries the weights of both floors and walls. The window frames are also of iron. Thin curtain walls of hollow brick are used merely to fill the spaces between the structural frame and the window frames. The floors are of brick arches supported on wrought-iron I-beams. This is the earliest-known example of pure iron skeleton construction.   From the *Builder*

FIGURE 522 (RIGHT). TACOMA BUILDING, CHICAGO, ILLINOIS (1889)

Holabird & Roche, architects

Generally accepted as the first building with complete iron skeleton framing.

Courtesy Museum of Modern Art

FIGURE 523. FAIR BUILDING, CHICAGO, ILLINOIS (1891)

W. L. B. Jenney, architect

This building illustrates perfectly the broad rectangular bays typical of iron or steel skeleton construction.

Photograph Sigfried Giedion

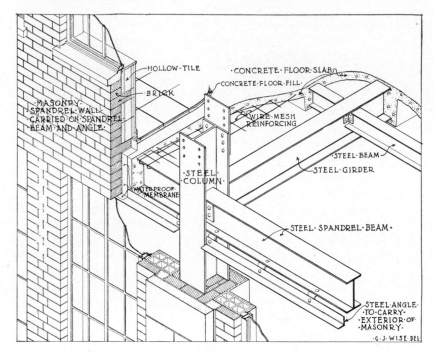

FIGURE 524. CUTAWAY DIAGRAM SHOWING THE CONSTRUCTIONAL ELEMENTS OF
A TYPICAL STEEL SKELETON-FRAMED STRUCTURE

Note that all wall loads are carried by the spandrel beam and its attached angle; these transfer
the weight to the steel column. The floor weights are also borne by the same column.

Drawn by G. J. Wise, from Talbot Hamlin, *Architecture through the Ages*

fairly well perfected before the beginning of the twentieth century. The
change from cast and wrought iron to steel, as well as the development of rolling mills able to turn out beam and column sections ever larger and larger, both
simplified the engineers' problem infinitely and produced eventually a standardization of details and major design elements that was almost universal (Fig.
524).

One problem which arises in connection with the framing of tall buildings is
that of wind bracing. In tall structures the area of side wall is large, and the
pressures upon it during high gales will tend to produce not only a lateral deflection but also an actual overturning moment in the building as a whole. Allowance must be made for both of these contingencies. Deflection is avoided by
the introduction of some kind of bracing to reinforce the connections between
columns and girders. In the earlier skyscrapers this was accomplished by means
of large web plates or even of portal arches. Sometimes diagonal tie rods are

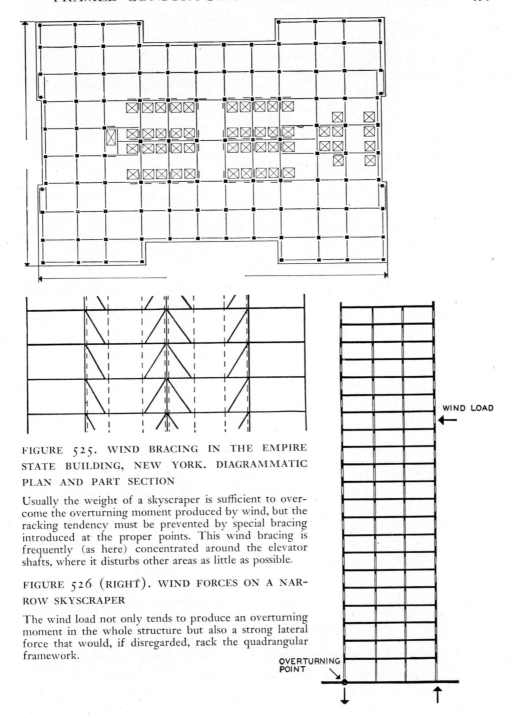

FIGURE 525. WIND BRACING IN THE EMPIRE STATE BUILDING, NEW YORK. DIAGRAMMATIC PLAN AND PART SECTION

Usually the weight of a skyscraper is sufficient to overcome the overturning moment produced by wind, but the racking tendency must be prevented by special bracing introduced at the proper points. This wind bracing is frequently (as here) concentrated around the elevator shafts, where it disturbs other areas as little as possible.

FIGURE 526 (RIGHT). WIND FORCES ON A NARROW SKYSCRAPER

The wind load not only tends to produce an overturning moment in the whole structure but also a strong lateral force that would, if disregarded, rack the quadrangular framework.

WIND LOAD

OVERTURNING POINT

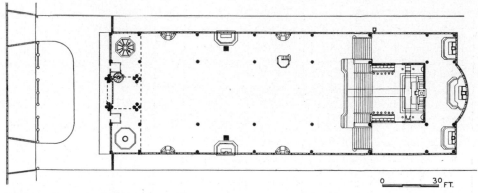

FIGURE 527. NOTRE DAME DE RAINCY, PARIS. PLAN

A. and G. Perret, architects

This famous reinforced concrete church shows the small area required for supports in some types of modern framed construction. The entire exterior wall is a pierced screen of concrete and glass; all weights are carried on a series of slim reinforced concrete columns.

Redrawn from *Architecture vivante*

placed in the panels between the columns of one interior row from top to bottom. In general the tendency in more recent skyscraper design is a maximum simplification of wind bracing and a large dependence both on the strength developed in modern column sections and on rigid connections between the columns and the deep girders (Fig. 525).

The overturning moment of the building as a whole is especially strong in the case of tall, wide, and thin structures (Fig. 526). The nearer the building approaches to a square in plan, the less troublesome this problem will become; but in any case it has to be considered, and the weight of the building must be carefully determined and examined in relation to side pressures under heavy wind stress. In the RCA Building in Rockefeller Center, for example, the masonry piers between windows were kept wide to gain increased weight in the outside walls. Furthermore, it was found necessary to fill at least part of the lower floors to an unusual depth with concrete in order to give a sufficient weight to the building as a whole to resist the overturning moment due to wind pressure. In the case of a light framed building in hurricane latitudes, it is also frequently necessary to work out physical ways in which the frame may be tied down to the foundation so that no side of the building can ever lift from its base.

With the growing use of steel frames for large buildings, it was natural for certain spacings to be developed in accordance with the strength of the material and the use of available steel sizes. Thus the practice has arisen in the normal office or commercial building of using a bay, about 16 feet wide by 24 feet deep, with girders along the long side of the bay and smaller beams between them over the shorter span. The outer row of columns is connected by spandrel beams, which receive the outer edge of the floor, and to these at every floor are attached steel shelf angles to carry the masonry. For reasons of economy, the floor heights are usually no greater than required for the specific use for which the building was designed. Thus in office buildings a general height of approximately 13 feet from floor to floor is common.

Because of the use of straight beams and the desirability of avoiding concentrated weights on beams or girders, it follows that the general pattern of girder and beam division should be as uniform as possible and also that columns should occur at regular spacings in both directions. Where bays of special dimensions exist—such as those that are usually necessary around groups of elevators, exit stairs, and the like—they should be concentrated in order to preserve the continuity of the framing pattern elsewhere (Figs. 546, 550; see also Vol. I, Chap. 6).

There develops necessarily, then, a plan concept of the steel-framed structure that consists of rows of regularly spaced columns supporting a regular network of floor beams and girders. This network, together with the beams which support it, produces, as it were, a series of cells approximately 16 feet wide, 24 to 28 feet deep, and 10 to 13 feet high, running in regular rows and tiers, one above the other. In many industrial buildings, department stores, and other structures with unusual requirements, what is known as long-span construction will create much wider spacings—without, however, affecting the basic cellular quality. Breaks both in plan and in elevation will be produced most economically if developed on the line of one of the cell divisions, for only in this way can the system of columns and beams be kept completely regular. This, of course, is an ideal not always to be achieved in practical buildings, but it is a logical result of the system and should at least be approximated. The result is of necessity a building of strongly rhythmical character, essentially regular and always rectangular in its basis. And the total volume composition may approximate that achieved by piling together, one on another, a series of rectangular boxes.

The exterior design of the steel frame will likewise have a necessarily regular rectangular and rhythmical quality: the structure will tend to present a plaid of vertical columns and horizontal spandrel beams and girders enclosing rectangles, all longer than they are high, for the spacing between the columns is

FIGURE 528. MIDTOWN MANHATTAN, NEW YORK

The wide bay spacing of tall steel-skeleton buildings is gradually superseding the narrower bays of the lower bearing-wall structures.   Photograph Ewing Galloway

FIGURE 529. PRU-
DENTIAL INSURANCE
COMPANY BUILDING,
LOS ANGELES, CALI-
FORNIA. STEEL FRAME

Wurdeman & Becket, ar-
chitects; Murray Erick
Associates, engineers

Here the horizontally ac-
cented plaid and the cel-
lular character established
by steel construction are
obvious; note that the
columns are thinner than
the spandrel beams.

Courtesy American
Institute of Steel
Construction

FIGURE 530. APARTMENT HOUSE, FIFTH AVENUE AND 80TH STREET, NEW YORK

McKim, Mead & White, architects

A palatial masonry skin designed without regard to the steel frame which supports it.

From *A Monograph of the Work of McKim, Mead & White*

greater than the distance between floors. Moreover, the width of the spandrel beams and girders is likely to be considerably greater than the width of the steel columns, so that the horizontality of the rectangles is carried out by the steel work which forms the enclosing lines.

The spirit of steel itself is light, airy, and full of delicate strength. This can be seen in the design of many bridges, cranes, and similar elements (Fig. 529). Yet in actual buildings this delicate slimness cannot be directly expressed because of the need of fireproofing the steel. Steel, men have learned, twists and loses its strength when exposed to a hot fire. The only way of making it fireproof is to cover it with a heavy layer of masonry to prevent its temperature from ever rising to critical heights. In the early years of skeleton construction, tile was often used for this fireproofing, but now tile has almost entirely yielded to solid brick or reinforced concrete. Under such a layer the slim strength of the skeleton, so evident in steel buildings while they are being constructed, necessarily disappears, and the actual forms to which the architect must give an expressive design have therefore a certain heavy and blocky quality which contradicts the character of the steel itself. What, then, should the architect do to establish expressive form in this exterior?

In the fifty years since skeleton-construction buildings have been common, almost every possible answer to this puzzling question has been advanced. Under the impact of early-twentieth-century eclecticism the search for reasoned answers was almost given up, and again and again attempts were made to design skeleton buildings with the completely inappropriate, heavy, masonry expression of an Italian palace—complete with rusticated basement and heavy projecting cornice—or, on the other hand, with the equally inappropriate traceried arches and panels of a Gothic stone building. In structures of moderate height some of these attempts are not without beauty as pure superficial form, particularly when kept as simple as possible within the general style chosen—as, for instance, in the McKim, Mead & White apartment house on the corner of Fifth Avenue and 80th Street, where the palatial quality seems eminently fitted to express the luxury of the enormous apartments which the building contains (Fig. 530). But, in those cases where the height of the building became relatively much greater than that found in the works of past architecture, the basic absurdity of the scheme became at once apparent. What possible meaning can an engaged colonnade twenty-five stories in the air possess? What possibilities are there of achieving human scale when shapes designed for close acquaintance are used in positions where they can only be seen from half a mile away? For when one is close to a high building one never sees its top.

Little by little two general types of high-building composition were developed. One is based on the free-standing tower or campanile, as represented, for example, in the Woolworth Building or the Metropolitan Life Insurance Building in New York or the so-called "Cathedral of Learning" in Pittsburgh. The other system is based on the triple division so common in classic design; it produces a building with richly ornamented lower floors as a base, a central section with windows regularly spaced in an otherwise unstressed wall, and an upper section with a richly applied decoration as a kind of crown. Examples of this type of composition are too frequent to mention.

During the half century of skyscraper development, however, there were many designers who remained basically dissatisfied with this imitative and purely applied kind of treatment and sought for types of design which should have some specific relation to the skeleton frame. Of these the earliest and in many ways the most important was Louis H. Sullivan, who, in such buildings as the Guaranty Building in Buffalo or the Wainwright Building in St. Louis,

FIGURE 531. GUARANTY (PRUDENTIAL) BUILDING, BUFFALO, NEW YORK (1894)
Louis H. Sullivan, architect
Characteristic of Sullivan's bold and logical approach.   Courtesy Ware Library

set a new standard in expressive design. Others naturally followed in his footsteps or worked out independent approaches of their own. Burnham & Root in some of their Chicago buildings and many other structures elsewhere, the Audsley Brothers in the Bowling Green Building in New York, George B. Post in the St. Paul Building in New York, and Harvey Wiley Corbett were all seeking definite expressions of skeleton-building design different from the usual, thoughtless eclecticism.

In this effort, four quite different approaches have led to four differing types

FIGURE 532. BOWLING GREEN BUILDING, NEW YORK

Audsley Brothers, architects

An early New York skyscraper emphasizing verticals.

Courtesy Ware Library

of solution—the vertical treatment, the horizontal treatment, the "stretched skin," and the system of direct expression. The vertical treatment was first used by various designers of the so-called Chicago School in the early years of skyscraper design. Louis Sullivan clarified that approach and brought it to full development in his Guaranty Building at Buffalo in 1894 (Fig. 531). Since it was skeleton construction which made these tall buildings possible and since all the weight is concentrated on the vertical columns, it seemed natural to some designers that this vertical note should dominate the design. Sullivan's analysis went further; to him the essence of the office building lay not only in the verticality of its supports but also in the fact that the offices it contained were presumably much alike and that therefore the most continuous and unified treatment of windows was the one which would be most expressive. To achieve this effect he stressed both the masonry fireproofing over the structural columns and the vertical brick mullions which separated the two windows in each bay, and to these he gave the same weight and emphasis that he accorded to the

FIGURE 533. ROCKEFELLER CENTER, NEW YORK. VIEW FROM THE NORTH

Reinhard & Hofmeister; Corbett, Harrison & MacMurray; and Hood & Fouilhoux, associated architects

Vertical expression used to unify a large and varied group.   Courtesy Rockefeller Center, Inc.

structural columns. On the lower two floors, which presumably were intended for stores, he designed an exceedingly open treatment of large plate-glass windows; behind and above these appear the structural columns, treated as circular columns with wide-spreading foliated capitals.

The vertical nature of the Sullivan treatment has been widely followed, as evidenced by many of the most famous skeleton-constructed buildings—for instance, Cass Gilbert's Woolworth Building, Howells and Hood's Daily News Building (Fig. 191), and more recently the superb structures of Rockefeller Center, all in New York. In some cases these vertically designed skeleton structures follow the lead of Sullivan and give to the vertical mullions in the center of each bay the same value which the structural columns possess. In others, wider vertical piers emphasize the columns and the intermediate piers are narrower. This produces an interesting horizontal rhythm which plays over the basic vertical pattern. The first system, however—as represented by Sullivan's

FIGURE 534. Mc-
GRAW-HILL BUILD-
ING, NEW YORK

Raymond Hood,
architect

A bold attempt to accent
horizontal lines by sup-
pressing the visual importance of the columns.

Courtesy McGraw-Hill
Building Corp.

Guaranty Building and by the magnificent vertical geometry of the New York Daily News Building—has the advantage of giving a basic unity to the structure as a whole and thus emphasizing in the strongest possible way the simple uniformity which the more logical solutions somehow lack.

The second solution, the system of horizontal emphasis, is less common. It is based on the idea that the essential purpose of skeleton construction is the support of many floors and that any large building of this type consists primarily of a series of floor areas, one over the other. Therefore, these designers feel, it is the floors which should be emphasized rather than the columns used to support them. The horizontal solution is found treated in three different ways. In the first, represented by the McGraw-Hill Building in New York, by

FIGURE 535. COLUMBUSHAUS OFFICE BUILDING, BERLIN

Eric Mendelsohn, architect

The use of small struts in each mullion, instead of the conventional widely spaced steel columns, permits the logical development of a horizontal composition.   Courtesy Eric Mendelsohn

Hood & Fouilhoux (Fig. 534), the skeleton is of the normal type, but the spandrel wall treatment is carried unbroken from end to end of the building, and the color of the facing of the columns between the spandrels is merged closely with that of the windows. The columns, moreover, are kept as narrow as possible, so that the whole sense is one of alternate layers of spandrels and of continuous openings. This type of design has one disadvantage: it tends to develop a certain looseness or discontinuity in the over-all envelope of the

FIGURE 536. UNIVERSAL PICTURES BUILDING, PARK AVENUE AND 57TH STREET, NEW YORK

Kahn & Jacobs, architects

Horizontal spandrels accented; the columns in every other mullion made small to emphasize the horizontal movement.

Photograph P. A. Dearborn, courtesy Kahn & Jacobs

structure and consequently may give rise to disturbing optical illusions. Thus the McGraw-Hill Building from many points of view seems to widen from bottom to top because of the contrast of the accented horizontal lines in perspective. In the second type of horizontal treatment, horizontality is developed by treating all the masonry mullions and piers between windows with brick of a different color from that used in the spandrels. This slightly artificial method of obtaining horizontal stress has been used especially on apartment houses and seems to have a quality more domestic than that of other treatments; a good example is the Beaux-Arts Apartments in New York, by Kenneth Murchison and Hood & Fouilhoux. In a slightly different form, in which the projecting edges

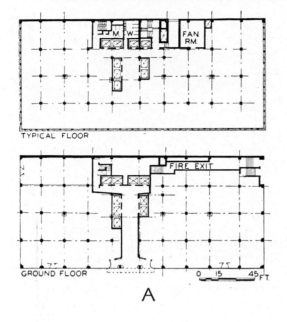

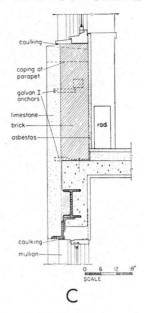

A

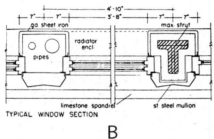

C

B

FIGURE 537. UNIVERSAL PICTURES BUILD-
ING, PARK AVENUE AND 57TH STREET, NEW
YORK. PLANS AND DETAILS

Kahn & Jacobs, architects

A. Plan of typical floor and ground floor; B. Plan
through windows of upper floor; C. Section of typical spandrel.

In this building, the columns in the exterior walls
are placed independently of the rhythm of the interior columns. More of them are used, and they are
lighter; this allows the use of the horizontal bands
of windows that distinguishes the exterior design.

From the *Architectural Forum*

of the concrete slabs and beams at the floor levels are exposed and therefore in
contrast with the red-brick filling elsewhere, the same method has been used in
Williamsburg Houses in New York, by William Lescaze. The third kind of
horizontal expression in skeleton construction arises from the cantilevering out
of the entire exterior from the face of the columns, so that no columns whatsoever will appear and the entire façade will consist of bands of windows separated by horizontal spandrel bands. This has been used with special brilliance
in certain of the works of Eric Mendelsohn, as in the Chemnitz department
store (Fig. 172); it also distinguishes the front of the Philadelphia Saving Fund
Building in Philadelphia, by Howe and Lescaze (Fig. 173).

FIGURE 538. APART-
MENT HOUSE, WEIS-
SENHOF, NEAR STUTT-
GART, GERMANY.
GARDEN FRONT

Ludwig Mies van der
Rohe, architect

Steel construction ex-
pressed by the simple
treatment of the enclosing
skin of stucco and glass.

Courtesy Museum of
Modern Art

FIGURE 539. PETER
JONES STORE, LONDON

Crabtree, Slater &
Moberly, architects

Here the skin of a framed
building is accented by
an interesting combina-
tion of metal and glass.

Courtesy Museum of
Modern Art

FIGURE 540. DAILY EXPRESS BUILDING, LONDON

Ellis & Clarke, architects

An exterior surface entirely of glass—transparent for windows and opaque for spandrels and piers.

From McGrath and Frost, *Glass in Architecture and Decoration*

The stretched-skin expression is essentially a development of the revolutionary architectural movement of the 1920's in Europe. The International School designers reasoned that, since the exterior of a skeleton-framed structure was merely a screen around an enclosed volume, the most logical expression of the system was to express this exterior screen almost as though it were a continuous membrane stretched tight around the frame. In this way, they believed, one would feel more strongly the fact that it was the volume and not the mass of such buildings which was important, and that by this membrane-like type of treatment a strong sense could be given that the exterior walls were merely geometric surfaces enclosing a volume. It was comparatively unimportant, they felt, whether this membrane was of transparent window glass or of some opaque material, provided its non-structural continuity was preserved. With this in mind, every effort was made to eliminate all projections of any kind, to gen-

FIGURE 541. AN APARTMENT-HOUSE PROJECT FOR CHICAGO, ILLINOIS, DESIGNED FOR STEEL-FRAMED CONSTRUCTION

Ludwig Mies van der Rohe, architect

A rhythmic treatment of glass and metal emphasizes the over-all nature of the wall skin.

Photograph Hedrich-Blessing

erate geometric forms as simple as possible, and to give as neutral a character as possible to the skin material. It was this last desire which made them turn more and more to stucco and glass as the only surfaces which had this feeling of undifferentiated and non-structural continuity. Where conditions forced the use of brick, care was taken to use white or light-colored bricks as far as possible and to set them in self-colored joints. This system is seen in much of the work of Walter Gropius and Le Corbusier, and, expressed in a freer way, it has exerted a strong effect on more recent design, as, for instance, in the Daily Express Building in London (Fig. 540)—where the skin is all of glass, part black and part transparent—and in the Bonwit Teller Building in New York, where stone in large, flat, tilelike slabs with continuous joints is used.

The fourth treatment is based on the direct expression of the typical skeleton plaid without attempt to stress either the vertical or the horizontal. It is a system which appears in the central, undecorated portions of many classic skele-

FIGURE 542. THE SAME APARTMENT HOUSE DESIGNED FOR REINFORCED CONCRETE

Ludwig Mies van der Rohe, architect

This design emphasizes the concrete framework.

Photograph Hedrich-Blessing

ton-framed buildings, and in the decorated upper and lower areas it may be present though concealed. Numerous office buildings and department stores by D. H. Burnham, such as the Detroit Dime Savings Bank or 80 Maiden Lane in New York, illustrate this kind of design. These buildings indicate the uniformity of the framing system, but the expressive quality in them seems almost accidental; for few of the early designers seemed to realize that such a direct and simple treatment might furnish an answer to the whole problem of expressing skeleton construction.

One exception to the rule was Louis Sullivan, who with his customary keen analysis and superbly sensitive imagination developed the idea in a magnificent way as the essential element in the design of the Carson-Pirie-Scott department store in Chicago, built between 1899 and 1904. Here expression of the construction is forcefully direct: the details of the large windows that fill the entire area from column to column and from spandrel to spandrel are beautifully handled to accent the horizontal rectangles which form the frame-construction plaid. The proportions throughout are exquisite, and the changing floor heights in the upper administration floors give a subtle and most pleasing rhythm. Only

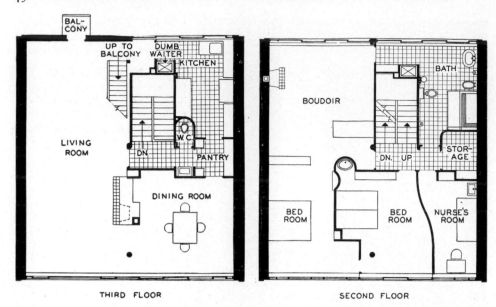

THIRD FLOOR   SECOND FLOOR

FIGURE 543. COOK HOUSE, PASSY, PARIS. SECOND- AND THIRD-FLOOR PLANS

Le Corbusier and P. Jeanneret, architects

A plan of a house between party walls, characteristic of the work of its architects. The structural columns supporting floors and roof are in part exposed, as is the chimney from the fireplace, thus forming definite visual motifs in certain rooms. The garden-side wall is cantilevered to allow continuous glass windows. The rather arbitrary line of the partitions on the second floor is an attempt, among other things, to express the fact that these partitions have no structural meaning; they are simply screens.

at the corner, softened by a rounded pavilion, is the general system interrupted. The two lower floors are characteristic examples of Sullivan's prodigal use of decoration; they are intended to emphasize and to set off the show-window area, and they seem to cut the building into two parts. But the upper portions of the wall, above the show windows, still remain among the most beautiful and the most perfect expressions of steel-frame construction (Figs. 126, 334). This same kind of expression may be found in some comparatively recent work in Finland and in England; it constitutes the major virtue which gives power to the façade of Hunter College in New York. Where buildings are not inhuman in height or size, this is perhaps the most suitable and the most beautiful of all the ways of expressing skeleton-framed construction.

In Chapter 14 it was brought out that reinforced concrete is used more frequently in producing framed structures than in the construction of monolithic buildings. Concrete is especially fitted for the framing of buildings where the floor weights are great and where the height is not excessive. It will often de-

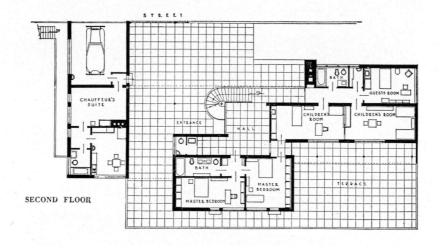

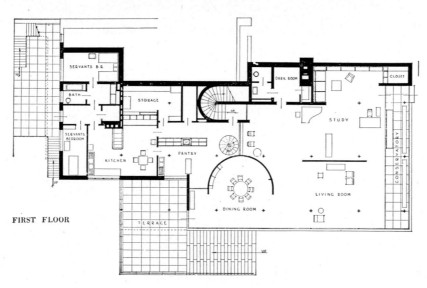

FIGURE 544. TUGENDHAT HOUSE, BRNO, CZECHOSLOVAKIA. PLANS

Ludwig Mies van der Rohe, architect

A plan based on the expression of use pattern and structural pattern as two separate entities, related in a sort of architectural counterpoint. On the chief floor, support is furnished by slim, regularly spaced metal columns. The division between rooms and areas is by means of screens and partitions placed independently of the columns. These columns, sheathed in stainless steel, form an important part of the visual effect of the interiors. A similar rhythmic counterpoint characterizes other work of this architect. See Figure 545.

From Hitchcock and Johnson, *The International Style*

FIGURE 545. HOUSE IN THE BERLIN BUILDING EXPOSITION OF 1930. VIEW FROM TERRACE

Ludwig Mies van der Rohe, architect

Delicacy and openness achieved by the complete separation of surrounding walls and supporting columns. Courtesy Museum of Modern Art

velop column spacings somewhat wider than those found in the standard steel building, and the column widths are likely to exceed the widths of fireproofed steel columns. But except for these few differences the concrete framed building will tend to develop the same kind of exterior plaid that is characteristic of the steel skeleton, and the problems of expression will therefore be similar. In detail, of course, the cast nature of the material will make for many changes; for logical forms in reinforced concrete will always bear a close relationship to the formwork in which it is cast, and economy in form design will tend toward the most simple details. Furthermore, the rather coarse texture of most commercial concrete will discourage the use of detail that is fine in scale or intricate in design.

There is one major difference between steel and concrete frames. The steel frame is formed of separate members put into place and connected on the job, either by riveting or welding, whereas in the true reinforced concrete frame the entire frame is a continuous unit from end to end and from top to bottom. Even when the steel frames are welded, the sense of the construction is still

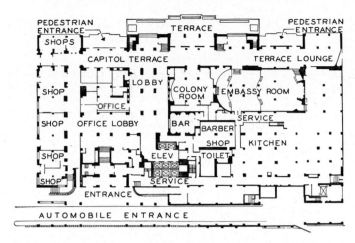

FIGURE 546. STATLER
HOTEL, WASHINGTON.
GROUND-FLOOR PLAN

Holabird & Root,
architects

This plan reveals not only
how the structural col-
umns of the frame form
a generally uniform pat-
tern but also how all the
various functional ele-
ments have to be worked
in and around them,
whenever possible taking
advantage of them to pro-
duce coherent and de-
signed interiors.

that of an assemblage of units, whereas the concrete frame as a whole is a unit.
Furthermore, steel is at its most efficient in tension; concrete, on the contrary,
is strongest in compression. This makes steel the obvious material for all buildings of suspended construction and for buildings of very great height. Concrete, on the other hand, because of the continuity of the structure, can be
much more readily adapted to all kinds of cantilevered construction, and cantilevered frames in reinforced concrete are relatively much simpler than cantilevered frames in steel. Moreover, the sense of continuity which characterizes
reinforced concrete is admirably expressed in the long unbroken horizontal
spandrels of cantilevered construction.

The effects of steel and reinforced concrete skeleton construction on plan
are enormous. Reference has already been made to the general tendency of
framed construction to produce buildings of cellular type and also to the fact
that the natural development of steel and reinforced concrete frames is to give
a regularly spaced grid of structural members, with columns continuous from
the top to the bottom of the building at the grid intersections. These continuous rows of regularly spaced supports are of the essential nature of the construction, and to change this regularity involves inefficiency of structure and a consequent increase in cost. All planning of such buildings must therefore start
out with this strongly rhythmic basis.

But it is an equally dominant feature of twentieth-century planning to seek
always for the most efficient shapes and sizes for all the rooms in a building. The
chief problem then, in planning framed structures, becomes one of relating the
use pattern of a building—that is, the shapes and sizes of the rooms necessary

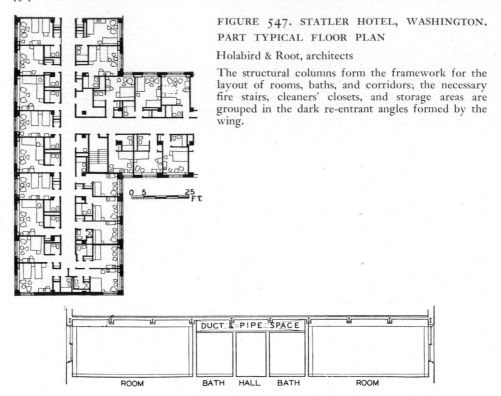

FIGURE 547. STATLER HOTEL, WASHINGTON.
PART TYPICAL FLOOR PLAN

Holabird & Root, architects

The structural columns form the framework for the layout of rooms, baths, and corridors; the necessary fire stairs, cleaners' closets, and storage areas are grouped in the dark re-entrant angles formed by the wing.

FIGURE 548. SECTION THROUGH TYPICAL HOTEL WING

The ceilings in the bedrooms are plastered direct on the under side of slabs, and beams and girders are arranged for pleasant effect. The central bay is furred down to allow duct and pipe space over baths and corridors.

for the activities that will take place there—to this regular grid of structural supports. The problem is rendered more difficult by the fact that the usual partitions in framed structures are much thinner than the diameter or width of the reinforced or fireproofed columns. Everyone knows the unpleasant effect produced by the projection of a column or of furring around a pipe in or near the center of a long wall. Such projections not only are unsightly but also make the furnishing of a room difficult and diminish its possible efficiency.

The problem of relating the use pattern to the structural pattern is thus one of the major tasks which the architect of a framed structure faces. Two entirely different answers have been made to this dilemma. One is based on the complete and separate expression of both the use and the structure patterns, which are considered like two melodies in counterpoint—interwoven and related, but never joined. Partitions are placed where the designer wishes, and columns are set wherever they are structurally necessary. This system is best

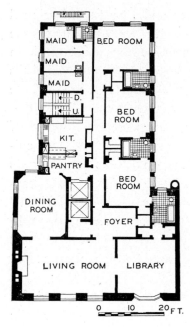

FIGURE 549. APARTMENT HOUSE, EAST 84TH STREET, NEW YORK. TYPICAL FLOOR PLAN

Raymond Hood, architect

An example of the perfect integration of structural pattern and use pattern, achieved by careful study. All rooms are beautiful in proportion and arrangement, and the steel supporting columns are so placed that in no case do they interrupt important walls or dictate awkward shapes.

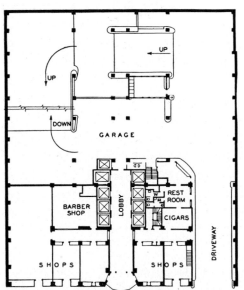

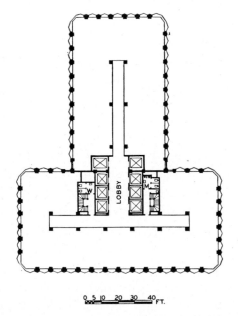

FIGURE 550. 250 SUTTER STREET, SAN FRANCISCO, CALIFORNIA. GROUND-FLOOR AND TYPICAL-FLOOR PLANS

Timothy Pflueger, architect

An unconventional framing plan of great simplicity and interest allows excellent elevator arrangement and an abundance of well-lighted and convenient office space. Note how the garage is worked into the pattern of the columns. In the exterior no attempt is made to treat the structural columns differently from the simple piers between windows.

represented in many of the houses of Le Corbusier, and it has been developed to its highest possible degree in much work by Mies van der Rohe, such as the Tugendhat house at Brno and the German Building at the Barcelona Exposition (Figs. 273, 274, 544, 545). It is shown in a less fantastic manner in the main halls and corridors of the RCA Building of Rockefeller Center (Fig. 224), where the great columns appear almost in the middle of the corridors.

The other system is based on the complete integration of the two systems of use and structure and the planning of the buildings in such a way that the columns will always occur in corners, in closets, or where a definite vertical stress in the interior appearance is sought. This integrated type of planning is characteristic of the best modern hotel and apartment-house work in the United States, and it characterizes the majority of office buildings (Figs. 549, 550). In these integrated structures the rhythms of the rooms are arranged to correspond with the rhythms of the structure itself, and both seem to follow naturally from the concept of the building as a whole.

Which of these systems is best is hardly a question that can be argued, for the choice between them seems to be controlled less by any demonstrable logic than by matters of purely personal taste and feeling. Both have their advantages and their difficulties. In the first of these systems—the separation of structure and use—the difficulty lies in finding the correct contrapuntal relationships and in establishing rooms so designed that the existence of the columns within them becomes no bar to efficiency. The advantages, of course, are in freedom of layout and in the particular character of almost rococo imagination to which the system sometimes gives rise. The advantages of the second scheme—the integration of the two patterns—lie in the basic firmness of the composition as a whole and in the opportunity afforded for the freest possible development of open interiors. The disadvantages involved are the fact that either the room dimensions may have to be made excessively large or small or the column spacings may have to be varied from the theoretically most efficient spans. Sometimes the use of reinforced concrete columns, which can be made long and thin, may assist the integration.

It is perhaps significant that all the great architectures of the past—Greek, Roman, Gothic, Renaissance, and Baroque—have been based on the complete integration of structure and use into one pattern of controlling power. The other system, the separation of structure and use, is therefore one of the most striking innovations which modern architecture has produced. It is, of course, an innovation that opens the doors to an extraordinary variety of expression, but it is also an innovation open to severe abuse and one that often seems to have

FIGURE 551. PROJECT FOR THE FRANZ JOSEF MUSEUM, VIENNA. ENTRANCE LOBBY

Otto Wagner, architect

A design based solely on the surface enrichment of a simple structure in fireproofed steel.   From Wagner, *Einige Skizzen* . . .

something of the purely arbitrary in its solutions. Some architects seem to work best in one of these ways, some in another, and certain problems seem more appropriate to one group than to the other. Beyond that, recommendation is impossible.

Since steel-framed skeleton construction has become standard for all large structures of any considerable height, the importance of the challenge it offers to the architect is tremendous. Not only are large office buildings, apartment houses, and hotels built with a skeleton frame, but increasingly this type of construction is used for important public structures—government buildings, libraries, large railroad stations, and school and college buildings. And it is precisely in the design of these structures, which form the most important commissions an architect can receive, that expression of construction has been least studied and least achieved. Here conventional ideas of character have been supreme, and, in fear of creating public buildings which will look like office buildings or hotels, architects have again and again designed public buildings constructed with skeleton frames as though they were built with solid bearing walls.

This condition cannot long continue. In all the ages of great architecture, a portion of the greatness has come from the imaginative expression of construction methods and materials. A true creative search for a similar imaginative expression of the steel or concrete skeleton frame cannot but result in a similar greatness; our modern methods may well make the same contribution to inspiring architectural beauty in the twentieth century which framed construction in stone made to the cathedrals of France. And in these expressive public buildings of our age we may fear no loss of true character; the creative and sensitive architect will find a hundred ways—through the choice and use of materials, the design of entrances and circulation areas, the adjustment of dimensions, the basic shapes of the enclosing envelope of planes, the use of appropriate sculpture and mural painting to enhance the effect, the relationship to site—in which these structures, built at public expense and for public purposes, shall adequately symbolize their public nature. And they will achieve this union of character and construction with all the more power if their design makes clear —for all to see—the structural system which makes such an expression possible.

SUGGESTED ADDITIONAL READING FOR CHAPTER 16

Fitch, James Marston, *American Building; the Forces That Shape It* (Boston: Houghton Mifflin, 1948).

Giedion, Sigfried, *Space, Time and Architecture* (Cambridge, Mass.: Harvard University Press, 1941).

Gropius, Walter, *The New Architecture and the Bauhaus*, translated by P. Morton Shand, preface by Joseph Hudnut (New York: Museum of Modern Art [1937]).

Hitchcock, Henry Russell, *Modern Architecture; Romanticism and Reintegration* (New York: Payson & Clarke, 1929).

—— and Philip C. Johnson, *The International Style* (New York: Museum of Modern Art, 1931).

Johnson, Philip C., *Mies van der Rohe* (New York: Museum of Modern Art [c1947]).

Le Corbusier (Charles Édouard Jeanneret), *Vers une Architecture* (Paris: Crès, 1923); English ed., *Towards a New Architecture*, translated by Frederick Etchells (New York: Payson & Clarke [1927]).

—— and P. Jeanneret, *Oeuvre complète, 1934–1938* (Zurich: Éditions Dr. H. Girsberger, 1939).

Mendelsohn, Eric, *Three Lectures on Architecture* (Berkeley: University of California Press, 1944).

Mujica, Francisco, *History of the Skyscraper* (Paris: Archaeology & Architecture Press, 1929).

Sullivan, Louis H., *The Autobiography of an Idea*, with a foreword by Claude Bragdon (New York: Norton [c1926]).

Taut, Bruno, *Modern Architecture* (London: Studio [1929]).

17

Architectural Design and Building Materials

A LARGE BUILDING today makes use of an extraordinary variety of building materials—natural materials like stone and wood; manufactured materials like steel, brick, and tile; synthetic materials like glass and plastics. The effect the building makes on the observer depends on the visual impression he receives from these materials as the architect has used them. And, in addition to proportion, to planning, and to structure, the excellence of the total effect will depend to a large degree on the placing, the detailing, and the finishing of these building materials.

In any design problem, the architect is thus faced with a bewildering series of choices. His palette is almost unlimited. He can make buildings lavish in bright color, light or dark in tone, black or white, gray or red; he can produce surfaces which are smooth or rough, shiny or dull. He can design a building in which every material seems to be in the right place and to have the right finish, or he can produce one full of incoherent absurdities. It is by his choice of materials, the way he employs them, and the finish he gives to them that he can control their effective use. What are the criteria on which he may make his choice? How can he produce a building in which all the materials are in their right place and rightly used?

We say that he must use his materials expressively in order to produce a satisfying effect. This, however, hardly answers the question, for how shall we know exactly what is meant by "expressively"? What is implied by the term *expression of materials?* To answer this question it is necessary to examine some of the basic sources of human satisfaction to be gained from observing buildings and to learn something of the way in which materials have been used in buildings of the past. It will not be seriously questioned, we believe, that people in general find an almost instinctive pleasure in seeing all kinds of things well done and neatly executed, nor will it be doubted that the expression of power or strength, where that feeling is appropriate, is a source of enduring satisfaction. People like to see machines at work; they feel the natural rightness inherent in good machine design—the economy of material, the neat meshing of parts, the expression of strength where strength is necessary, the sense of power, and the feeling of the efficient expenditure of power to achieve a purposeful result. Much the same kind of satisfaction lies behind what we call a good expression of materials in architecture.

Men have been building with stone and brick and wood for many centuries. Through trial and error and through imagination and study they have discovered what kinds of materials are best suited for certain purposes and have learned how to use these efficiently and well. They have learned, in other words, what kind of material works and what kind does not work in a given situation. In the case of many materials which have been used over long periods of time, this knowledge of good working solutions is already centuries old. Confronted by building after building in which the result of that knowledge has been embodied, people as a whole have come to recognize and to appreciate this quality. They have developed, in other words, a sense of what they feel as "right."

Thus they realize almost unconsciously the strength of stone in wall or pier; they feel the power in a well-laid wall if its strength and its enduring qualities have been made obvious. They delight in the quiet surfaces of good red brick as they see it in Salem or Portsmouth or in the great houses of Virginia. Similarly, they know many of the qualities of wood and delight in its simple use in the clapboards or shingles of old farmhouses; they have seen wood joists put in place and have no doubt of their ability to carry the floor they bear. They have seen roof rafters and perhaps many wooden trusses in roofs or bridges. In all of these they have felt the strength and elasticity of the timber beams. They have seen, too, the beauty of wood grain in old paneling, the strong pattern of the oak cells in tables or beams, the soft, warm sheen of mahogany in Colonial chests or desks.

These impressions, conditioned by use and design, come to them from all kinds of sources from the time when as children they first became aware of a glimmering aesthetic pleasure. In many cases people know that these qualities they see, these colors and textures and shapes of building materials, are incorporated in structures that have lasted many years and have been relentlessly acted upon by time—they have stood, they have worn well, they still seem to be doing successfully the work for which they were designed. In other words, they seem "right." Thus, in viewing many of these older materials which have been in use for long periods of time, people seem to have developed an innate sense of the qualities of each. They have learned from experience the uses to which each is suited and in which it will satisfy the innate demand of the human mind for neat efficiency, and they have come to realize how the visual nature of these materials may best be brought out.

But people also like to be conscious of how things are made. They love to watch the carpenter busy with his saw and hammer, the stone cutter with his chisel, or the painter with the broad sweeps of his laden brush. This delight in the making of things carries over into the object made, especially when the object shows the process of its manufacture. Thus in ancient timbers the marks made by the adze in smoothing the surfaces often seem added beauties rather than imperfections, and chisel marks in wood carving frequently give rise to this same pleasure. So in stonework the marks of hammer or chisel often increase the richness of the impression which the stone makes, because they recall to the observer the patient labor which shaped the rough mass into the carefully finished block. These evidences of the craft techniques add to our pleasure in the objects that display them.

This delight in the way a thing is made and in the expression of craftsmanship in the completed article runs through almost all building materials. In metal-work, for instance, the sensitive eye finds keen pleasure in the careful differentiation between cast work, wrought work, and repoussé work. The solidity, the weightiness, and the ductile character of the first; the delicacy, the curves, and the weldings of the second; the embossed and incised surfaces of the third—these all add to the enjoyment we derive from those objects which display them fully.

The reasons behind this enjoyment apply to all hand craftsmanship; they lie in the fact that sensitive hand craftsmanship is one of the most pleasantly creative activities in which a normal man can engage. By virtue of his close touch with nature and with natural objects and materials, by his growing knowledge of the qualities and possibilities in the materials with which he works, he somehow seems to become a part of the natural processes of the world, and in this participation he realizes one of the most common of human dreams. Ruskin said that the worth of good architecture and good craft objects was due to the fact that happy workmen produced them, and he saw part of the reason for the decadence of the architecture of his time in the fact that in an industrial culture hand craftsmanship was a rarity and consequently industry was gradually transforming the craftsman into a mindless wage slave. We may not agree with

Ruskin's diagnosis, but we cannot help feeling that in good craftsmanship and in the frank expression of its processes in an object there lies a great source of satisfaction and pleasure for the human spirit. Thus we may say that one way in which we may be sure the expression of materials can be made right or satisfying is by being sure that the finished object furnishes some indication of the tools and the processes which brought it into being.

The nineteenth century brought with it a vast change in the productive mechanisms of mankind. Power-driven machinery began to occupy a large place in the production of goods. Naturally this development affected architecture and immediately brought profound changes in the preparation and use of various building materials. The idea of the machine itself was not a new one, for the increase in productive power which machines made possible had fascinated man for centuries. A machine is merely an advanced kind of tool, and in the course of the ages the building industry had already developed many highly complicated tools of the machine type. Thus derricks and cranes, capstans, and similar devices were common in ancient Rome and during the Middle Ages. Various types of sawmill had come into use, and the application of water power to at least some of these building functions had been accomplished, as the notebook of Villard de Honnecourt indicates. What was new in nineteenth-century industrialism was, first, the application of steam power and water power to the running of machines in ways much more efficient and in amounts infinitely greater than earlier and, second, the growing development of manufacturing processes in which the machine entirely superseded the earlier hand craftsmanship. Articles were produced increasingly in accordance with the inherent nature of the industrialized mechanical process, and more and more materials were brought under the sway of this new industrialized manufacture. Certain of these developments are now so old that we have already built up for them the same kind of innate sense of rightness and wrongness in design which has been noted before in connection with earlier types of traditionally hand-made materials. We have come to realize, for instance, some of the main qualities resulting from machine manufacture—such, for instance, as the indefinite and absolute repetition of units resulting from stamping or casting. We understand the idea of continuity in machine production; for the machine, once set to produce any article, continues to produce it without change or alteration either until it is stopped or until the material runs out. Thus we have come to recognize and to enjoy the perfection and continuity produced by machine planers and molders. On an exposed beam we accept the perfection of plane achieved by mechanical saws and mechanical smoothers with the same pleasure as that with which we accept the adze marks of an earlier period, because we recognize that the exceptional smoothness is just as true an expression of machine craftsmanship as the adze marks are of hand craftsmanship.

It is this principle which makes the imitation of older techniques so fundamentally unpleasant in works produced by newer techniques. People have always built as perfectly as they could; one has only to realize the perfect surfaces of a Greek column flute or the carefully waxed smoothness of a French Renaissance floor to appreciate this. The little irregularities which occur in hand craftsmanship arise inevitably from the technique used. In our eyes they add to the charm of the work because they so well indicate the craftsmanship behind the production. When, on the other hand, a modern tries to imitate these, he is going counter to the whole system of natural expression and architectural development. In cheap wood furniture we all know the absurdities which developed from the attempt to press into the surfaces patterns which in older work had been carved. Any attempt to create an artificial aging, a false impression of antiquity, is merely to spend many unnecessary dollars to make things less good than they otherwise might be. Before such arrant, illogical waste the unbiased human mind recoils in horror. Good craftsmanship, whether by hand or by machine, is always the attempt to realize perfection as far as it can be realized in the particular technique involved. Attempts to imitate the less perfect are therefore by nature bad craftsmanship, bad design, and bad construction. They may be amusing in a stage set; they may even be excusable as conscious works either of a rather perverted humor or of sentimentality in garden structures used only occasionally. But in any serious building designed to be continually before the eyes of users or observers they lead only to tawdry monotony.

One other quality of building materials which the architect must know is of the utmost aesthetic importance, and that is their pure visual quality or nature entirely aside from any scientific concepts of logical use or of expressive manufacture. Walking along a beach one may pick up beach pebbles of great diversity of color—black, gray, pink, red, cream, or white. These illustrate the infinite variety of color in the natural stones and marbles of which our earth is largely formed. The various woods, too, like stone, vary from almost white to almost black, with all kinds of yellows, grays, pinks, browns, and even greens in between. Brick is salmon color, or red, or purple, or gray, or what you will. Thus the architectural designer is faced with an almost unlimited choice. How can he choose the colors which are best?

In addition to such enormous variations in color, the architect must deal with a great range of variations in surface—from rough to glossy smooth—so that his palette is potentially not only one of infinite colors but also one of almost infinite gradations in texture. How in the possible confusion of these many choices can he choose the colors and textures which will be best or, as we call it, most expressive?

Here there will inevitably arise some concept of the organic system in which the materials grew or developed. The crystals and stratifications which embody the life of minerals, the sense of the shaping and of the fire which is inherent in all works in burned clay, the annual rhythmical growth of trees and of tree cell and vein structure which expresses itself in the beautiful veinings of plank or panel—these are all indications of the ways in which materials have become what they are. They are reflections of what one might call the craftsmanship of nature itself. Therefore may we not say that an expressive use of any material will necessarily consider the essential organic nature of the growth or development of the material? It is for this reason that Frank Lloyd Wright so enthusiastically admires the Japanese use of wood. He writes:

Whether pole, beam, plank, board, slat, or rod, the Japanese architect got the forms and treatments of his architecture out of tree nature, wood wise, and heightened the natural beauty of the material by cunning peculiar to himself.

The possibilities of the properties of wood came out richly as he rubbed into it the natural oil of the palm of his hand, ground out the soft parts of the grain to leave the hard fiber standing, an "erosion" like that of the plain where flowing water washes away the sand from the ribs of the stone.

No western people ever used wood with such understanding as the Japanese used it in their construction, where wood always came up and came out as nobly beautiful.

And when we see the bamboo rod in their hands, seeing a whole industrial world interpreting it into articles of use and art that ask only to be *bamboo*, we reverence the scientific art that makes wood *theirs*.

The simple Japanese dwelling with its fences and utensils is the revelation of wood.[1]

We may also say, then, that one of the ways of making the most beautiful use of materials is by emphasizing the uniqueness of each material and by stressing

[1] "In the Cause of Architecture: Wood," *Architectural Record*, May, 1928.

the ways in which each differs from others in its organic nature and in color and texture. Thus we can stress the patterns in veined marbles by seeing that the major lines of the veins emphasize and are coherent with the basic lines of the design as a whole. We can emphasize them still more by matching them— folding out, as it were, adjacent slabs from the same block so that the patterns are accented by reversal at each joint and each slab becomes a reflection of its neighbor. We can do the same thing with wood veneers, by choosing woods— like the walnuts or crotched mahogany—in which the veining patterns are not only exquisitely varied in themselves but also eloquent of the growth of the tree and of the change in direction where the branches start from the trunk. Marble we can polish to any degree of gloss we desire in order to emphasize its color and its pattern, and wood similarly can be finished with oil or wax or glossy varnish to accent the structure of the veins. It is for this reason that stain is frequently used in wood finishes—not to mask or hide the material or to give colors foreign to it but rather, when rightly used, to bring out its underlying natural qualities. Paint finishes, too, are designed primarily for the same purpose. Certain woods are characterized especially by smoothness and perfection of surface, not by interest of vein pattern. Here the correct kind of painted finish accentuates this satin smoothness, this uniformity of texture.

Similarly, the problem of permanence in any material must be solved in accordance with the organic qualities of the material and with the purposes behind the design. Thus the choice of rough or smooth finishes for exterior stonework and the amount of joint emphasis in brickwork pointing are questions to be answered in the light of the particular kind of material involved—its porosity, its water-shedding qualities, its permanence of color.

Thus, too, in choosing textiles for architectural and decorative use, the architect must bear in mind the uniqueness which characterizes textiles—the feeling of the loom, the crisscross of warp and woof, the revealing sheen of silks and satins, or the warm rich shadows and creamy lights on rougher textiles of wool or cotton.

In choosing materials and in specifying their finish, the architect is confronted always with a double problem. He has, first of all, a concept of a building or of an interior as an organic whole, patterned in color and light and shade, where every unit of pattern, every line of shadow, and every change of color is an essential part of the composition. He then has to interpret this pattern in terms of building materials, and in choosing these materials he must work with the organic whole in mind; for the most beautiful and the most expressive result can be effected only when each material is so chosen and so used that its contribution is based on its own distinctive character. Smoothness and roughness, interest of color, and color harmony then are no longer merely the abstract elements of an arbitrarily imposed pattern; they are also the inevitable results of the unique character of each material that adds its voice to the chorus.

How may the architect attain a knowledge of these unique characteristics of building materials? This can come only through an intimate personal acquaintance with them. The architect must himself touch them, lift them, and know whether they are heavy or light, rough or smooth; either he must learn to work them himself and get the feel of the tools and see the result of the action of the tools on the materials, or, if this is impossible, he must at least know how the materials are worked. Only so can he learn the granular or crystalline quality of most stones, the smooth or roughly veined textures of woods, and the way molten metal is shaped, glowing, under the blows of the smith's hammer or fills perfectly the hollows of well-designed molds. He must know at least something of the loom and its rapidly flying shuttle; he must understand how punched cards lift chosen warp threads in the Jacquard loom so that patterns are woven into the web, and how great cylinders are used to print textiles in repeated patterns.

It is manifestly impossible, of course, for one individual to become a skilled craftsman in all the infinite methods of preparing or producing the innumerable materials that go into a modern building, but it is possible for him to gain at least an elementary knowledge of their manufacture and so to understand something of the attributes they acquire in the process. Thus, when confronted with the problem of choosing materials and finishes, he will select only those which result harmoniously from the unique methods by which each is produced.

And the architect must bring to this choice still another quality, one even more important than mere intellectual knowledge. He must approach the problem with a kind of meditative contemplation. He must feel into the nature of materials emotionally and intuitively. Whenever he sees a material used in a building, he must examine it and question its use, its finish, its appearance. He must ask himself: "Is this the really best use of this material? Is this the use which most completely utilizes its peculiar qualities? Is this the appearance which brings out most clearly its essential organic nature?"

It is well, moreover, for the architect to become acquainted with the origins of natural materials so that he learns to feel instinctively, for example, something of the way in which rock ledges have been laid down, cracked, and bent and igneous rocks have been forced up and poured over. He must have some feeling of the way in which minerals have taken shape under the enormous geologic forces that have given form to our present earth. Similarly he should learn something of the growth of trees—the wide spread of the oak, the horizontal branching of the pine, the upward trend of spruce and fir, the wide, firm net of earth-seeking roots, the budding, the flowering, the fruiting. Only thus can he bring to his use of stone a decent sense of its power and permanence and to his use of wood a feeling for its growth and strength. In the case of all materials, of whatever kind, the architect who wishes to find the most expressive treatment must approach them not only with an intellectual grasp of their physical nature and their visual properties but with some deeper, underlying, humble realization of their true place in the hierarchy of nature.

Twentieth-century industrialism has brought with it a flood of new manufactured materials for buildings, and these the architect must evaluate and use rightly, both from the practical and from the aesthetic point of view. They are for the most part new synthetic materials—new types of metal alloy and new kinds of organic synthetic materials called plastics. With them there is as yet only a tiny amount of empirical experience to assist him, and they are too recent for the public to have formed any innate sense of rightness or wrongness in their uses. Yet the necessity for the architect to make the most of these is just as strong as in the case of the older, more traditional materials. They come to the designer and to the observer, as it were, still virgin and without any *a priori* implications as to correct techniques or expressive appearance. How, then, may the architect best use them, how make them most expressive?

The first consideration in this puzzling problem must depend on a careful analysis of the sources of expressive beauty in the use of the older materials. In each of these we have seen that the qualities of satisfaction and of beauty which we sum together under the term "expressive" depend on a feeling of the right and efficient use of the structural possibilities of the material, on the frank acknowledgment of the processes used in its production and preparation, and on some kind of feeling for its organic relation to people and to nature. In the case of new materials, however, since the public has built up no criteria for judging any of these expressive elements, the architect must try to supply this lack. The only way in which he can do this in the case of the many brilliant new materials is *to make the use itself an expression* of the material. In other words, he must so use these materials that their structural nature is self-evident on the surface; it must show at almost the first sight of the material, so that little background of experience is necessary to aid the understanding.

Since the architect cannot depend on innate appreciation on the part of the public, any effect of appropriateness must therefore be made at once and in some striking manner. If the material is structural, its structural function must force itself upon the observer's attention as plainly and simply as do the supporting cables of a suspension bridge. If the material is used as a trim to hold other elements in place or to cover joints, it must be so designed as to show its purpose as a connector or a cover in the most obvious way possible; its nature must be apparent at the first glance. Similarly, if the material is employed as a veneer or a mere surfacing, it must appear so and avoid any shape or treatment which could possibly suggest a structural function.

The desirability of such a frank treatment should reveal at once how stupid and how futile are attempts to imitate, in these newer materials, the appearances of older and more habitual materials, because any such imitation tends at once to fog the clarity of the expression; instead of making the uses and qualities of the new material self-evident, they lead only to confusion and incoherence. They tell the observer not what the material is but what it is not, and any design of this type which expresses nothing of the true use, the true quality, and the true manufacturing processes behind the material cannot, by very definition, be expressive of it.

Yet how frequently this attempt to imitate the old in the new is made! Steel door trims designed like old-fashioned wooden architraves, with profiles and arrises expressive only of wood, are used in all too many office buildings, hotels, and apartment houses. Rubber tile and linoleum are made to resemble marble, and the beautiful simple continuity of plastic sheets is concealed by imprinting on them or incorporating in them the patterns of printed or woven textiles or the simulacra of wood graining. Salesmen and manufacturers seem even more timid than architects and designers in striving to discover the new effects which are especially characteristic of the new materials.

It is not the deception in such imitations which is most disturbing; it is the flagrant waste. The twentieth-century architect and designer have a magnificent new palette of colors and textures. Every new material may become an opportunity for a new kind of beauty that has never existed in the world before. To turn one's back on this new palette, to refuse to make use of the opportunities it offers, seems only a short-sighted defeatism.

To make people understand the use of all these new materials—a use which shall be self-explanatory—the architect must know the material itself, what it consists of, what its properties are, and how it is made. For this knowledge he must not depend alone on the optimistic promises of advertisements or of salesmen; he must also take advantage of the best technical information obtainable and observe closely and critically the material itself and any previous uses of it which he can discover. Only so can he discern its actual and positive qualities—strength, texture, color, ductility, and so on—and, building upon these known facts, develop that use which will be most self-explanatory, will take the most perfect advantage of the visual qualities of the material, and will thus achieve an effect that is directly and obviously expressive.

And almost universal in these new materials are two distinctive qualities which are due to the machines by which they are manufactured. The first is perfection of surface; with metal dies or stamping elements, or with metal or plastic molds which themselves are machine-produced, the resulting surfaces will have a quality of geometrical perfection unobtainable by any hand craftsmanship. The second quality is continuity or perfect rhythmical repetition. These two qualities, the inevitable results of good industrial production, create specific effects and allow a perfection in building materials that is almost Platonic. Thus by using these machine-produced materials the architect may achieve effects unknown before and possessing a special and characteristic beauty. How silly, then, to attempt to imitate the old with the new and to seek in modern industrial products the inequalities and accidental effects which hand craftsmanship necessarily engendered, when by creating them in accordance with their own nature we can give to buildings in which they are used a new definition and a new geometrical perfection.

Thus the architect who is confronted with the problem of selecting and using a new material will ask himself many questions about it in order to clarify in his mind its special characteristics. He will ask himself: "How strong is it in compression and in tension? How flexible or how brittle? Is it easily dented? Is it resistant to blows? Is it thick or thin? Is its color permanent and non-staining? Is it washable? Can it be easily worked at the job, or does it require complete plant fabrication? What is its modulus of expansion in relation to temperature? in relation to moisture content? Is it impervious and resistant to damp, or porous and absorbent? Is it best screwed in place, nailed in place, or held between moldings or in a rebate? Is it shaped by casting, by pressing, by stamping, by planing, by polishing, or by extrusion?" The answers to these questions will show him how to use the material rightly in accordance with the specific purpose to be achieved. Once this matter of practicality and functional use is solved, the answers to the questions will also enable him to use it in ways that are self-explanatory and therefore expressive of its nature.

But this is not all; the architect must with similar care consider the purely visual qualities of the material. He must ask himself: "Is it flat in color, mottled, striated? Is its color right for the proposed location? What is its reflecting quality, high or low? Does it give perfect mirrorlike reflections, or are they mat or diffused? Is its surface polished, rough, hard, or soft?" On the answers to these questions the architect can base his use of the material not only from the aesthetic but also from the functional point of view, for colors and surfaces have definite functional qualities as well as definite visual effects. One thinks of the problem of cleaning; common sense dictates the use of hard, smooth, or even polished surfaces where cleaning is of the first importance, as in bathrooms and around kitchen sinks. One thinks, too, of the fact that colors must be chosen in relation to the purposes of rooms and building spaces and of the necessity of avoiding visual disturbance where concentration is necessary or excessive visual stimulus where repose is desired.

Thus in the choice of materials and their treatment, as in all other matters, architecture is an integrated art in which use, structure, and aesthetic effect are intimately related.

On such a general basis, therefore, we may develop a set of fairly comprehensive criteria for judging the expressive use of materials, both old and new. These criteria fall into two classes, the first dealing with the use of materials as affected by their essential nature, and the second dealing with the use of materials as affected by their function. Under the first class we may list the following requirements:

1. Materials should be used in ways that are in keeping with their individual character and not in ways which imitate other materials.
2. Materials should be used in economical ways, not in ways that are wasteful.
3. Materials should be used in ways that emphasize their unique qualities, both structural and visual.
4. Materials should be used in ways that explain as explicitly as possible the function they play.

Under the second class we may list two simple standards:

1. Materials wherever used should be so chosen that they will be appropriate in nature to the specific purposes they are to serve.

2. Materials should be used in ways that are appropriate to the specific purpose involved.

If the architect learns to bear in mind these simple requirements, and if in addition he will take the time and make the effort to learn thoroughly the qualities of any material he considers using, he cannot go far wrong. Only in this way and by virtue of this knowledge can materials be made expressive and thus enabled to yield, each one, its own unique contribution to the beauty of a building and to a sense of satisfaction in those who see it.

18

The Building and the Community

BY FAR the greater number of buildings which architects design form parts of a community. Except for individual country houses and a few institutions located far from towns, the average architect's practice is concerned with structures in towns or villages or cities. As such, these buildings exist not for themselves alone; they partake of the life and of the fortunes of the community in which they stand. They are subject to its laws and regulations, taxes on their value do much to support the town services, and their economic future is bound up with that of their locality.

Aesthetically, also, the buildings in a community are subject to all kinds of community influence. Many communities have a long-established tradition of building type; what is the architect's duty in the relation of a new building to this tradition? Some communities—notably many English towns and local authorities and such American towns as La Jolla, California—demand that, from the standpoint of aesthetic design, all plans for new buildings be approved by a board or committee; what, then, should the architect's attitude be toward such a board? And even in towns where there is no community control over design and no long-standing tradition, the architect is faced with the fact that his proposed new building will have neighbors—perhaps close neighbors—and that these existing structures will inevitably affect the impression which his building is going to make.

Thus legally, economically, and aesthetically all new buildings in a community are unavoidably influenced by the regulations, the mores, and the character of that community. Furthermore, as additions to the community, they will just as surely affect its future. They will add to its value, its permanence, and its beauty; or they will assist its blight and add to its incoherent ugliness. And, since the question of which of these fortunes will eventuate rests largely in the architect's hands, it behooves him to consider these matters seriously.

FIGURE 552. THE HADWEN AND CHAMBLISS HOUSES, NANTUCKET, MASSACHUSETTS

Greek Revival grandeur and individuality harmonized.

Photograph
Talbot Hamlin

Many of an architect's most serious professional responsibilities and most challenging opportunities are involved in the relation of a building to its community; it may be well, therefore, to go into some of the problems in more detail.

Legal Problems. The architect, in designing a building in most cities and many smaller towns, is directly concerned with two types of law—building codes and zoning regulations. *Building codes* deal with the safety of the building itself and usually regulate such matters as the allowable stresses in structural materials, the thicknesses of walls, the definition and requirements of fireproof construction, the size and disposition of exits, the proportions of stairs, the amount of outside light required by various types of rooms, elevator-safety re-

FIGURE 553. UNITARIAN CHURCH AND PARSONAGE, NANTUCKET, MASSACHUSETTS

Note that the church has forms which harmonize with the houses.

Photograph Talbot Hamlin

quirements, plumbing standards, and standards of heating and ventilation. The question of utilities—sewers, water supply, gas, and electricity—has already been covered in Volume I, Chapter 17; the local building codes may specify many details regarding these. *Zoning regulations*, on the other hand, deal with the relation of the building to its site and specify allowable building uses, heights, bulk, and sometimes setbacks and reserved areas for any given lot. Society no longer gives absolute freedom to the owner of a lot to build on it anything he pleases, nor does it permit that owner's architect complete freedom in design. A first requirement, therefore, in the design of any town or city building is a thorough knowledge of the local building code and zoning regulations.

The problem of building codes is a thorny one. It is a truism that laws lag behind customs, and nowhere is this more true than in the average building code. Current codes usually embody the building science of a generation earlier, and there are always vested interests intent on avoiding changes—materials

FIGURE 554. BANK
(CIRCA 1860) AND
BUSINESS BLOCK
(1850), WICKFORD,
RHODE ISLAND

Two buildings of different dates and styles harmonized by materials, lines, and color.

Photograph
Talbot Hamlin

dealers handling older types of building material, real-estate owners who fear the obsolescence of their buildings, and even certain groups of organized labor which are afraid of unemployment as a result of changed building practices.

Yet the architect desires to make use of the best that science and industry have to offer. He is always looking for economies. He is—or should be—alert to the possibilities, both structural and aesthetic, of new materials and new building methods. He knows that research over the past few decades has cast floods of new light over such problems as insulation and fireproofing, and he is anxious to make use of this knowledge for his client's best interests. Sometimes—in fact, frequently—local building codes will not permit him to do so. What is he to do then?

His problem may be complicated, too, by the over-eager owner—perhaps with political connections—and by chiseling contractors. There is always the temptation to "beat the law," to "get by" with all sorts of violations in the effort to save pennies. Here the architect's responsibility is plain; he has, of course, a responsibility to the owner, but as a professional man he has a superior responsibility to society. He must realize that building codes are for the protection of society, and he must never wink at or countenance a willful violation of them, however onerous they may be.

But this does not mean that he cannot work for the acceptance, by local authorities, of building methods newer and better than those of which an obsolete code takes cognizance. Indeed, his duty to society is to do precisely this. Building codes are human creations and, as such, always imperfect; many municipal building departments are well aware of these imperfections and are willing

FIGURE 555. A PART OF QUEENS, NEW YORK. AIR VIEW
Thoughtless planning and monotonous repetition destroy community values.

Courtesy *Daily News*

to make reasonable exceptions and approve unconventional construction where adequate tests prove to them its efficiency and strength. By all means let the architect exert all the pressure he can to bring building codes and building departments up to date and to make the authorities flexible and open-minded in accepting new materials and methods (such, for instance, as the newer types of thinner and lighter curtain walls in fireproof structures). But what he must never countenance or permit is an underhand violation—showing one thing on the drawings to obtain approval and then building something quite different,

FIGURE 556. HIGHWAY VIEW, LOS ANGELES, CALIFORNIA

Thoughtless planning and greedy, unsightly development effectively prevent community feeling.

Photograph Talbot Hamlin

for instance, or giving a present to a building inspector to make him close his eyes to something not quite up to standard. There have been, alas, all too many examples of such practices.

The architect, then, must always remember that building codes are part of the law of the land and therefore deserving of respect and obedience. He must keep in mind that they exist to protect the public health and safety. When, by open means and fair tests, he can win acceptance for materials and types of construction that are not covered by the code, so much the better. But, when he knowingly permits code violations by owner or contractor, he is acting contrary to his duty both as architect and as citizen.

The basic professional problems which confront an architect in the matter of zoning and city planning regulations are somewhat similar to building-code problems in general character, though different in application. The architect, from the moment a job is brought to him, must consider the relationship of the proposed structure to the community as a whole. He must advise the owner as to the desirability of the site for the proposed type of building. If he is wise, he will not only learn the zoning regulations which apply to the lot in question but also gain at least a general knowledge of the comprehensive city plan as well as of the relation of that lot to its street or streets and of those streets to the basic traffic pattern of the city. He will learn why the particular lot is zoned in the way it is. Only with this knowledge will he be able to advise his client

FIGURE 557. WOLFORD HOUSE, HAMPSTEAD, LONDON

Connell, Ward & Lucas, architects

A twentieth-century house that seems completely at home in an eclectic development.

Courtesy Basil Ward

intelligently. And to give this advice is one of the architect's important tasks.

But there is one great difference between building codes and most zoning acts—the comparative flexibility of the latter. Most towns which are zoned have a City Plan Commission or a Board of Standards and Appeals, whose function it is to pass on all kinds of applications for exceptions and for basic changes in the zoning regulations. Such boards realize that communities are living, growing, dynamic entities and that no purely *a priori* zoning pattern can be considered as a permanent, changeless law. They know that there may be many individual cases where changing conditions make exceptions to the law necessary in the public interest, and by public hearings and the views of neighboring lot owners they seek to determine the just and forward-looking decision.[1]

[1] Notable examples of the effect of changing conditions and changing attitudes on zoning can be seen in two typical problems—the placing of garages and service stations and the placing of small non-nuisance (noiseless, smell-less, smokeless) industrial plants or laboratory buildings in

It is this flexibility that is both the architect's danger and his opportunity. His client may wish to build a structure that is not in accordance with the present zoning limitations. For an architect to determine whether or not he should advise the client to try to get an exception, whether he should urge him to abandon the project, or whether he should suggest that he obtain another piece of property where such a structure is permitted by the regulations requires much more from the architect than a knowledge of the owner's wishes. Weighing all the facts, he must decide whether or not the proposed structure on the proposed lot will actually make for a better or a worse community. Will it spoil a neighborhood or improve it? Will it be a note that is new but harmonious in the city pattern, or will it be a shrieking discord? To answer such questions honestly the architect must know something of the entire city pattern, he must understand sympathetically the *raison d'être* behind the zoning, and he must be able to form some judgment as to the city's probable development and growth. Then he will be able to be true to his responsibilities both to his client and to society.

If the architect's reasoned judgment tells him that the projected building will be a true addition to the community even though it may not conform to the present regulations, he will advise the owner to fight for an exception and will himself do his utmost to help. If, on the other hand, he believes that the proposed but non-conforming structure would be a civic detriment, he is bound to urge his client to abandon the project, or change its nature, or else seek another, more suitable site. And, if under the circumstances he succeeds in changing the owner's original purpose, he not only will have saved his client from later disappointment and loss but also will have benefited the community. For the good building well placed is as much of an asset to the community as it is to its owner, and the good architect sometimes is the one man who can protect a town from the detrimental purposes of a wily, exploiting owner.

Economic Problems. Any building project usually represents a heavy investment on the part of its owner; it may entail the expenditure of the savings of many years. The architect must always bear this in mind; it is his responsibility to see not only that the owner's investment is well spent—that the building is worth what it costs—but also that it is well protected, that the value represented in the building will have at least a certain permanence. Part of this value

---

residential areas. Until recently, such establishments were usually banned there, but the more progressive opinion now considers that better, more integrated, more efficient and livable neighborhoods will result if such buildings—in reasonable moderation, of course—are permitted.

FIGURE 558. A VIEW IN GREENBELT, MARYLAND

Ellington & Wadsworth, architects; Hale Walker, town planner

Here variety in unit design is no bar to community harmony.   Courtesy Library of Congress

and much of its permanence will be the direct result of the place of the project in the community.

A building on a specific site is definitely a part of the community where it stands—economically as well as sociologically. If the values of that community decline, the value of the owner's investment will decline with them; if they increase, the owner's investment will generally increase proportionately. Clients usually know this, and one of the reasons why they consult an architect is their confidence in his ability to advise them on the suitability of a proposed site. Thus one of the necessary qualifications of a good architect is the ability to judge a site intelligently.

This is true of all kinds of buildings. It is obvious that buildings which exist to earn income, whether shops, apartments, hotels, or industrial plants, must be located where they can do so. Shops must be placed where shoppers congregate or where newly developed residential areas create a fresh demand for shops and stores. Apartment houses must be where people are eager to live. Office buildings must in general be situated where commercial facilities abound and must be conveniently placed for the transaction of business. And factories must be located where means of transport are excellent, where there are people to do the work, and where raw materials may be easily obtained. Common sense

FIGURE 559. HILLSIDE STREET, SAN FRANCISCO, CALIFORNIA

A group of apartment houses harmonized by their close adjustment to the site and their similar geometric character.   Photograph Talbot Hamlin

will serve to make lists of factors equally compelling for any type of structure.

Even the placing of an individual house has its economic aspects—the relation of cost of house to cost of lot, for instance. It is generally unwise to build an expensive house on a cheap lot, and vice versa. Usually cheapness of residential property in a community indicates some kind of undesirability; the manner of living in the neighborhood may not be consonant with that desirable in a large and expensive residence—its "social position" is different. And, conversely, if a client with little to spend puts too large a proportion into lot cost, his house will naturally suffer; moreover, his taxes, based on the total value of lot and improvement, will be out of proportion to the size of the dwelling and too large an annual drain on the owner's income.

There is no fixed rule for the relative costs of house and lot; the proportion varies greatly from community to community. Land which would be relatively excessive in cost in a community newly developed might, for the same house, be relatively inexpensive or even cheap in an old, established community which society—in the cant sense—had accepted as desirable. In respect to the relation of the economic cost of land to cost of house one may pay extravagantly for the good address. The only way the architect can arrive at the correct relative cost in any specific case is by assaying as well as he can the kind, age, and costs of

FIGURE 560. QUINCY MAR-
KET, BOSTON, MASSACHU-
SETTS

Alexander Parris, architect

Harmony, community feeling, and
efficient planning in business buildings.   Photograph Talbot Hamlin

houses already in the community. Any projected house markedly larger and
more expensive, or markedly smaller and cheaper, than its neighbors is likely to
be an economic and social misfit.

There are, of course, all sorts of exceptions to this general rule. Clients may
have their own good and sufficient reasons for violating it—attachment to the
neighborhood, sentiment, or what not. Generally speaking, most of the good
reasons are on the side of the smaller, less expensive house on the larger, more
expensive lot, rather than the other way round. There may be many reasons
why what seems an excessive price for property, considering the size of the
house desired, may in the long run be justified; beauty of the property as a
future home, plenty of space for a growing family, and protection of privacy
are some of these good reasons.

Yet it is nevertheless the architect's task to make his client aware of any unbalance—to advise against careless and unwarranted extravagance or to point
out the undesirable features of the cheap lot. The final decision, of course, is the
owner's. But the architect should see to it that the owner makes his choice while
aware of all the facts; only so can the architect be true to his trust and protect
his reputation. To do this, he must learn to assess communities with a clear eye.
He must learn to recognize the first signs of blight—to know when neighborhoods are on the upgrade or the downgrade. He must be able to judge how contemplated city improvements are likely to affect a given piece of property and
thus be able to make at least intelligent guesses as to the lines of probable community development or decay.

But there are other economic factors involved—factors of which the architect must have some knowledge if he is to give sound advice. In buildings for
income, he must be able to make a reliable preliminary financial statement—
a sort of income and outgo table—showing the possible profits (or losses). To

FIGURE 561. BELMAWR HOUSING, NEAR CAMDEN, NEW JERSEY. COMMUNITY
BUILDING AND PLAYGROUND

Mayer & Whittlesey, architects

The long, inviting horizontals of the building and the careful preservation of old trees create a
winning atmosphere that both expresses and welcomes community use.

Photograph A. Chelouche

do this, he must know the rental levels in the community for structures of a
given type and he must understand the maintenance and carrying charges involved—salaries, heating, water, electricity, taxes, insurance, interest rates, and
so on. A sound and reliable tentative statement of this sort will do much to win
a client's respect. For some of the information he may have to depend on the
client himself, particularly in specialized buildings for industrial purposes or
in proposed shop or store projects; yet the information the owner gives must
be examined critically by the architect, who should be prepared to protect his
client against a dangerously enthusiastic optimism or to enhearten him if he is
unduly pessimistic.

In domestic work there is the additional problem of resale value. In the case
of a well-to-do client of established reputation in a stable occupation this may
be a matter of minor importance, but in the case of younger people beginning
a career and building with a high proportion of mortgage money it should be a
major consideration. The client may later obtain a more advantageous position
in another town; he may encounter financial reverses; his family may be subject
to expensive illnesses; the family may be broken up by divorce—and in all these
cases and many more a quick sale of the house may be necessary. Where a

FIGURE 562. BALDWIN HILLS VILLAGE, LOS ANGELES, CALIFORNIA. DETAIL
R. D. Johnson and Wilson, Merrill & Alexander, associated architects; Clarence Stein, consultant
Outdoor living in private patios excellently combined with over-all community feeling.

Photograph Margaret Lowe

family is living close to the margin of its income and a house represents the
major part of its savings, the resale value should be relatively as high as possible.

   These are all problems which have much to do with the position of a building in a community and the quality of the neighborhood. Though they seem
sometimes to have little to do with the design of beautiful buildings, nevertheless they will all play a part in the decisions a client makes on the basis of the
architect's advice, will form integral parts of the building program, and will

intimately affect a thousand matters of planning, general aspect, and detail. Thus no architect worthy of the name can neglect, or be ignorant of, the economic aspects of his work—the myriad ways in which it is woven into the economic texture of modern life.

Intangibles in Community and Site Relations. The legal regulations and the economic facts and probabilities are definite enough; they are things that anyone with intelligent application can master. But there are a host of other factors that tie up a building with community life—factors much more subtle, which are matters of feeling and imagination rather than of fact.

There is, for instance, what one might call, for want of better words, the spirit of a place or a neighborhood. There are towns, or neighborhoods in towns, which somehow charm and delight the sensitive person. Intuitively he wants to live in them; he will be willing to sacrifice convenience or undergo extra expense for the privilege. An architect, of all people, must be most sensitive to such an atmosphere. In his advice to a client regarding a site he must be able and willing to give expression to this feeling; he must be prepared to say that one place is delightful and attractive or that another, despite high values, somehow seems all wrong.

The basis of this spirit in communities seems to be composed of three chief elements: the social milieu (that is, the quality of the people who live and work in the neighborhood); the sense of permanence or historic continuity; and the purely aesthetic factor, a matter of harmony, individual building design (whether new or old), and site planning. The quality of one's neighbors is important, even if the newcomer has his own circle and plans to know his neighbors but slightly. A community that seems permanent and shows continuity in its habits and in its old buildings adds somehow to the sense of human dignity. And a community that has real beauty is a cause of abiding delight, an ever-present source of emotional serenity and of deep, half-unconscious satisfaction. When all three factors are present, the power and the worth-whileness of these intangible elements make a spirit that is overpoweringly attractive and more valuable than any mere economic analysis could ever indicate.

In these intangibles the architect's function does not cease with advice to his client on the desirability of a certain site for a certain structure. Nor does his responsibility end with making a design which his client approves; he has the same kind of responsibility to this intangible spirit of a community that he has to its legal restrictions. He must not willfully sanction or design a structure that will destroy its social amenities, its historical tradition, or its existing beauty.

The first and last of these precepts are self-evident and undisputed. But the second, the question of historical tradition, is more controversial. The really alert and imaginative modern designer no more wants to parrot the details or copy the motifs of a past style than the cathedral builder of the Middle Ages wished to copy the temples of ancient Rome. Yet this does not mean that he is insensitive to the beauty of ancient structures or blind to the harmonies which the architectural past has produced. Being ourselves does not mean that we must necessarily hate and vilify the works or the persons of our ancestors. The trained architect should, above all other men, be conscious of the perfection of Gothic cathedrals or Colonial houses or Classic Revival towns, for he understands better than others not only *what* they are but *why* their forms developed as they did. Confronted by the problem of designing a new structure for an old town rich in beautiful old buildings, the modern architect finds himself in what at first seems to be a dilemma: Shall he design in the traditional style, or shall he forget the surroundings entirely? Both alternatives are sterile and absurd. There is but one escape from them—to design in an inner harmony with the existing tradition.

More will be said about this harmony in Chapter 20; here the necessity for it is mentioned because it is so intimately wrapped up in the problem of the building and the community. Whatever the architect's credo may be, his minimal duty is clear: He should absorb so completely the spirit of the site on which he is to build, make it so completely a part of the background of his mind, that he can never think of the proposed building without being conscious of that spirit, can never imagine its appearance without seeing it in its actual relationship to its surroundings, whatever they may be. The good building will be a new, yet harmonious, note and will itself enrich the spirit of the community it adorns. The bad building will be always discordant, always an excrescence.

Thus it can be seen how in every way—legally, economically, sociologically, and aesthetically—every new building is bound up with, and forms part of, the community in which it stands. The architect must use all his influence with his client, in addition to all his knowledge, his technical skill, and his imagination, to see that this part is a constructive one. For the building in which an owner can feel a deep satisfaction and of which the architect can be proud is one that is as much an asset to its community in every way as it is a delight to its owner; it will be one in connection with which the architect has been not only a brilliant designer but a good citizen as well.

SUGGESTED ADDITIONAL READING FOR CHAPTER 18

Churchill, Henry S., *The City Is the People* (New York: Reynal & Hitchcock [1945]).

Hegemann, Werner, *City Planning, Housing* . . . Vol. III, *A Graphic Review of Civic Art, 1922–1937*, edited by W. W. Forster and R. C. Weinberg, with a foreword by Sir Raymond Unwin (New York: Architectural Book Pub. Co., 1938).

—— and Elbert Peets, *The American Vitruvius: an Architect's Handbook of Civic Art* (New York: Architectural Book Pub. Co., 1922).

Mumford, Lewis, *City Development; Studies in Disintegration and Renewal* (New York: Harcourt, Brace [1945]).

National Housing Agency, Federal Public Housing Authority, *Public Housing Design; a Review of Experience in Low-Rent Housing* (Washington: Government Printing Office, 1946).

Also, publications of the Federal Housing Administration, the American Society of Planning Officials, the National Association of Housing Officials, and the Committee on the Hygiene of Housing of the American Public Health Association.

19

Process of Architectural Planning

ARCHITECTURE has always reflected the qualities and the ideals of the people who have produced it. And, since the art and science of planning, as we have seen, is at the very heart of architecture, it is logical that the architectural planning of a people may be used as an index to their characters and aspirations.

The art of planning today, therefore, is bound to have a different character from the planning of the past—even a past as recent as the middle of the nineteenth century. Profound changes which have overtaken the human race in the last century have revolutionized its thinking; they have changed both its needs and its techniques in satisfying those needs. Two outstanding features of nineteenth-century thinking have had great influence on architecture and especially on architectural planning: first, the growth and gradual clarification of the scientific attitude, which has come to be employed with growing frequency in fields of life originally considered outside the realm of science; and, second, a growing insistence on the economic basis of life, as forced by savage competition and by a vast increase in population.

The scientific attitude is characterized by the concepts that nothing happens arbitrarily and that, in the physical world at least, every occurrence has a measurable and physical cause. The application of these concepts to architecture—both in cases where they manifestly applied and in others where their application may now be seen as definitely questionable—had astounding effects. It tended inevitably to limit and to channel the architect's creative imagination. It also tended to discount architectural elements and features which existed only for aesthetic reasons, because the basic causes underlying aesthetics were considered too tenuous and too individual to be susceptible of scientific statement.

The effect of the tightening of economic bonds was even more influential in

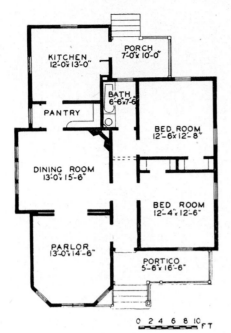

FIGURE 563. "SAN JOSE COTTAGE" (1891)

This is a minimum house of its time, designed to cost $1200. Even here the combined parlor and dining-room space is large, and the kitchen and bedrooms are far more extensive than at the present day.

Redrawn from *National Builder's Album of Beautiful Homes*

design. J. L. Garvin, the editor of the fourteenth edition of the Encyclopaedia Britannica remarks, in the editor's preface (page xviii), "We have entered upon an age when economics, whether we wholly like it or not, are preponderant as never before in politics and in all existence." It is said that the population of the Western world doubled during the nineteenth century. This meant an unprecedented demand for new construction, a demand with which the world has not yet caught up. And it meant not only an unprecedented bulk of construction but also construction of new types of building which resulted from the crowding together of the growing population in towns and cities. Moreover, the very development of these cities brought in an era of uncontrolled real-estate speculation and consequently inflated and absurd land values, and this means that, if the total investment for land and building is assumed as a constant, less money is available for the construction of the building than when land was less costly.

With the conventional idea, then universal, that all buildings for residence and for trade, commerce, and industry must pay their way by means of rentals or sale price, the problem of their design assumed a new shape; the rigid elimination of so-called waste spaces became an absolute necessity, and areas for human use were forced by high costs and competition into a continually smaller

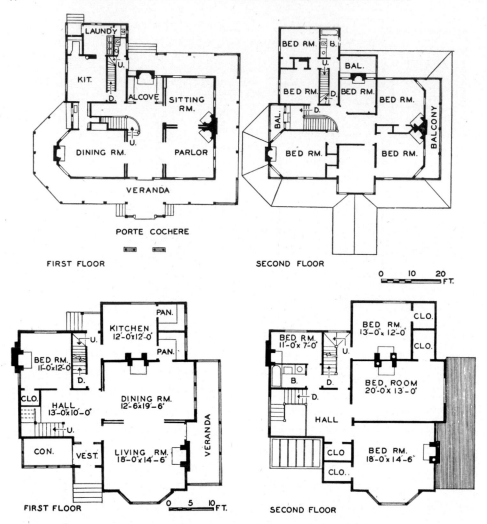

FIGURE 564. NINETEENTH-CENTURY HOUSE PLANS (1887)

ABOVE: A house to cost $7500; BELOW: A house to cost $4800.

Both plans show the large rooms, the ample halls, the connected open spaces for large social functions, and the small amount of plumbing characteristic of the house design—even the inexpensive house design—of their day.

Redrawn from Palliser and Palliser, *New Cottage Homes and Details*

compass. (See Figs. 563–567.) The development of the so-called efficiency apartment—one room with kitchenette and bath—is a case in point. Architects, builders, and real-estate operators began to study the problem of required space not in terms of "What is the just or optimum area for a given human activity?" but, rather, "What is the minimum size in which these human activities can be

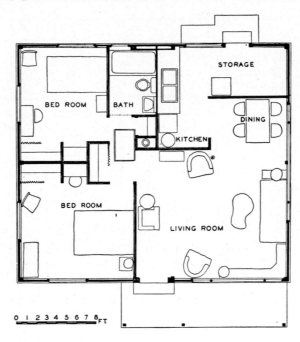

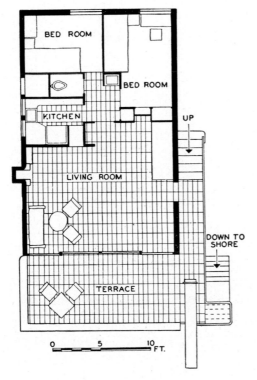

FIGURE 565. TWO TWENTIETH-CEN-
TURY MINIMUM HOUSES. PLANS

ABOVE: Cemesto house; Pierce Foundation
and Robert Davison, architects; BELOW: A
shore house, Zurich, Switzerland; Hubacher
& Steiger, architects.

The Cemesto house is designed for all-year
living; the Zurich house, only for vacations
and week ends. In both, the shrinkage of area
for kitchens, bedrooms, and living rooms and
the elimination of the hall space are obvious.

FIGURE 566. HARLEM RIVER HOUSES, NEW YORK. UNIT PLANS

Archibald Brown, chief architect

This low-rent housing project shows the room sizes accepted as standard at the time of construction. Later, United States Housing Authority standards were even further reduced. Compare with the sizes shown in Figure 564. From *Pencil Points*

carried on?" The coming of the twentieth century brought an increase in this trend and a more careful and a more factual study of these minimal requirements; this study is still progressing. Generally accepted standards were based on the smallest areas compatible with decency or with some imagined mechanical efficiency, not on a consideration of what was best or most humanly useful.

Naturally in this process so-called human values have definitely suffered. Under this system only families in the upper ten per cent income levels can expect to obtain, in new structures, really adequate areas for residence—that is, areas which will permit real privacy, thorough comfort, and the mental relaxation and even the inspiration that seem to derive from space itself. The same process has inevitably been at work in any structure built for investment or for commerce and industry. Always the demand for minimal costs and minimal areas is a dominating factor in the program. A century or more ago a man constructing a building for rent would ask himself: "Is this going to be profitable?" Today he thinks that is not enough. Today he asks himself: "Is the profit from this building just as large as it can possibly be made? Will it bring me the last possible one-tenth of one per cent of revenue?" In other words, just as scientific thought progressed from qualitative to purely quantitative analysis, so economic thought similarly stressed the quantitative.

In architectural planning the effects of these two developments—the scientific attitude and the economic imperative—have been momentous. In the first place, an architectural plan must have in it nothing arbitrary. It must be the

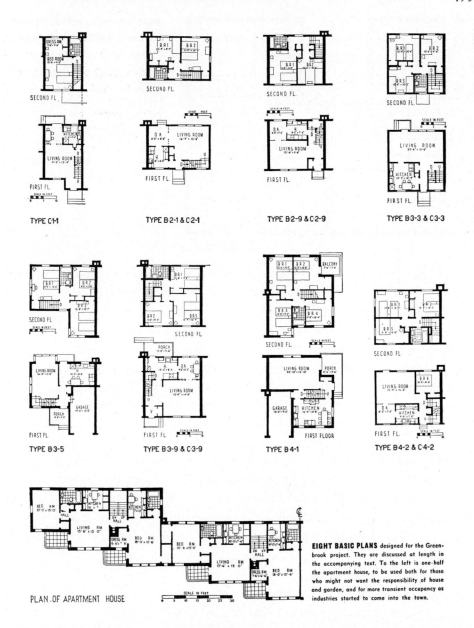

EIGHT BASIC PLANS designed for the Green-brook project. They are discussed at length in the accompanying text. To the left is one-half the apartment house, to be used both for those who might not want the responsibility of house and garden, and for more transient occupancy as industries started to come into the town.

FIGURE 567. DWELLING UNITS PROPOSED FOR THE GREENBROOK DEVELOPMENT, NEAR RARITAN, NEW JERSEY, FOR THE RURAL RESETTLEMENT ADMINISTRATION

Henry Wright, Allan Kamstra, Albert Mayer, Henry Churchill, Carl Vollmer, architects

This development was never built. Its carefully studied unit plans show the sizes and amenities current in the best modern middle-income dwellings.   From the *Architectural Forum*

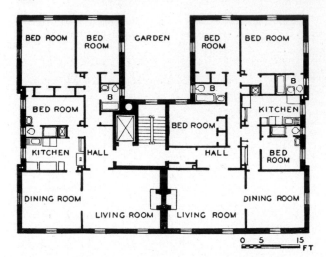

FIGURE 568. APARTMENT HOUSE, JACKSON HEIGHTS, NEW YORK. TYPICAL PLAN

Andrew J. Thomas, architect

Even in those areas in a city where land is less expensive than in the center, the utmost efficiency and economy are necessary to bring apartments of this character within the means of prosperous professional people or the upper middle class.

result of a careful analysis of all the requirements, and these requirements themselves must determine the essential nature of the plan. One should not design a rectangular building merely because he likes rectangular buildings; a rectangular building should be designed only when the required areas and the demands of building economy give rise to a rectangular building as the natural result. Secondly, in any architectural plan, economy of construction costs and efficiency in arrangement must be primary. Even in buildings constructed for public purposes and with public funds, an economy of design almost as stringent as that required in buildings for investment is frequently sought, partly as the result of mental inertia and the carry-over of a controlling thought pattern from the field of investment, and partly because of the real necessity for economy that comes from limited public resources (Figs. 570, 571).

Primarily, of course, economy in architectural planning means economy of area in the plan and of volume in the construction. It means that no room or activity center should be larger than its purpose requires. It means a rigid avoidance of waste space. It means economy of construction material and labor through the choice of room sizes or column spacings which can be economically spanned, and it means also economy of time from the user's point of view.

The amount of waste space in a building is a thorny problem. To the builder for investment any space seems waste which does not bring in an immediate rental of so much a foot. But the problem cannot be solved on that basis alone. There are necessary circulation areas (for getting from place to place in a structure) which do not return immediate and recognizable rentals but nevertheless are absolutely essential if the building is to function. There are many other types of area which, although not direct sources of income, add incalculably to the real usefulness of a structure—storage areas, areas for rest and recreation, and so forth. Furthermore, there is the problem of what might be called the competitive position of the building; a structure built for income in a given locality cannot, if there is a free market, compete with a near-by structure that is more beautiful, more attractive, more human, and less cramped. If a free-market economy really existed in buildings, this fact of competitive position would guarantee a certain level of human usefulness and attractiveness. But a true free market in buildings has never really existed since the Industrial Revolution and the consequent and subsequent increase in population, except spasmodically and, as it were, accidentally. There have been times, of course, of overbuilding in certain types of structure; but, taking the construction field as a whole, the real needs of the entire population have never been adequately filled. Especially in residence structures, particularly those for families of low and medium income, people by and large have had to take what they could get; here the choice between the better and the less good has seldom been able to operate except in occasional localities and at very occasional periods.

This places a tremendous burden upon the architect. As a professional man, he has a responsibility to society as well as an individual responsibility to his client. His creative imagination again and again points out to him solutions which would be of great benefit to the people as a whole and yet from the standpoint of income would be impossible. As a professional man, the architect must always search for solutions in which these two paradoxical requirements are reconciled as far as possible. He is the guardian of the good of society as well as of the pocketbook of his client, and there are times when he must stand, undaunted, as a bastion protecting society from the greed or thoughtlessness of exploiting investors.

Not only economy but also efficiency in design is an inevitable part of the ideals of twentieth-century architectural planning. Indeed, a study of true efficiency, in many cases, can resolve the demands of economy and small areas into benefits to humanity. This has been the case, for instance, notably in the design of kitchens, for the really well-planned and efficient small modern kitchen is a pleasanter and an easier place in which to work than the old type. (See Vol. I, Chaps. 3, 4.) This is but one example of many in which an architect's study of efficiency can make a true contribution to human living. It is a matter of the utmost importance, therefore, to define efficiency in a building plan.

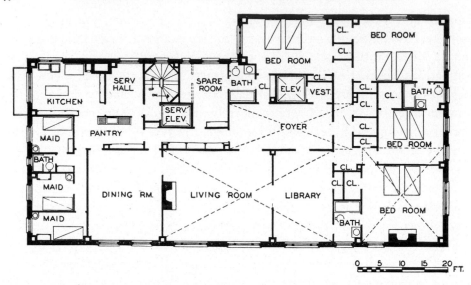

FIGURE 569 (ABOVE AND OPPOSITE). TWO EXAMPLES OF HIGH-COST APARTMENT
PLANNING OF THE ERA PRIOR TO 1930

ABOVE: 141 East 79th Street, New York; Rouse & Goldstone, architects; OPPOSITE: 16 Park Avenue,
New York; Fred F. French Co., architects.

Rooms of large size, but a rigid reduction of hall and waste-space area. Rentals of such apartments
limit their use to a small, wealthy portion of the population.

Efficiency in planning involves, first of all, a logical relating of parts so that
areas which belong together in the functions of a building are closely related
in the structure. In domestic work, for example, it is manifest that an English
house plan of the older type, in which the kitchen was separated from the
dining room by vast distances—the kind of house in which, it has been said,
one needs a bicycle in order to serve a dinner—is preposterously inefficient. The
logical relation of parts will require the development of a natural flow of materials or people—for instance, a natural sequence from a delivery area to a
storage or preparation area and from there to a use or consumption area—a flow
without break or interruption. It will mean that, as far as possible, there will
be no crossing of two types of traffic, because every crossing of traffic lines,
whether of people or of material, produces hesitation, delay, and even accident.

Efficiency in planning means, secondly, that the required distances traversed
in any operation shall be minimum distances. Materials must be carried or
moved as short a distance as possible in their natural progress through a building, and the plan must be so arranged that the human activities in it can be
carried out with a minimum of steps and of wasted time.

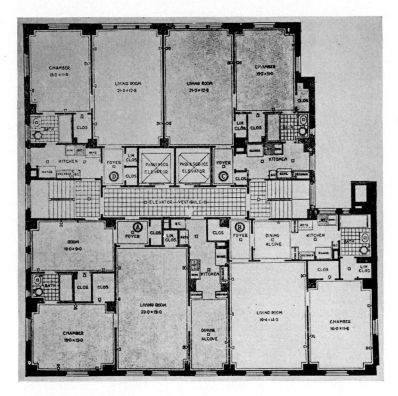

Thirdly, efficiency in planning requires not only that important activities be logically related and the necessary distances of travel minimized but also that each activity be located in the part of the building most appropriate for it. Here outside daylight, ventilation, whether natural or artificial, and distance from the entrances are important considerations. Much thought is necessary in analyzing each activity, determining the conditions under which it is best performed, and seeing to it that in the space designated for that activity the plan will provide these optimum conditions.

This concept of efficiency is not merely a problem of mechanical relationships. In order to consider any human activity architecturally, it is necessary to consider many human needs and desires that are hardly susceptible of mechanical or mathematical analysis. There is the psychological demand for space and the need to avoid any stimulation of claustrophobia; there is the emotional lift to be obtained from the connection of the building with the outdoors; there is the consideration of what people will do in this structure during the many periods, whether short or long, when they are not actively engaged in further-

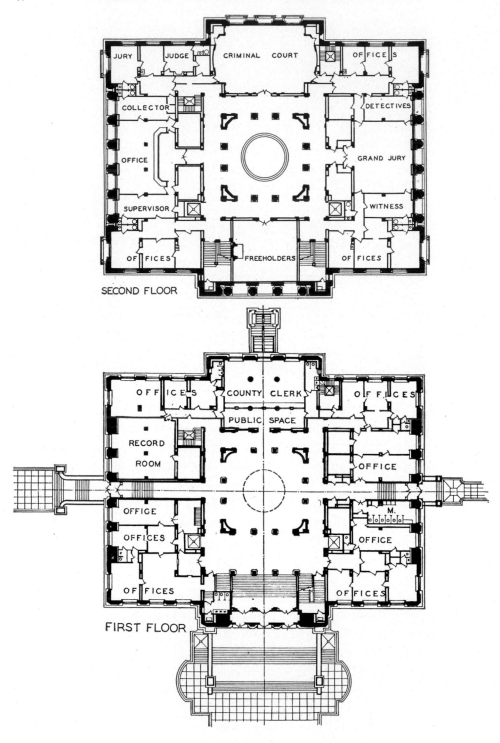

ing the purposes for which the building was built; and, lastly, there is the inestimable importance from the human standpoint of an environment that is good to look at, is composed of shapes and colors which harmonize both with the person and with the activity, and does not clash or distract.

In order to make a good plan, therefore, the architect must develop a deep sense of what people are and how they react. He must become a dramatist; he must be able to see his projected building with the eyes of all the various people who will enter it. He must be able, as it were, to become the cook preparing a meal, the housewife with small children to watch, the worker at a machine in the factory, the stenographer in an office, the janitor, the elevator boy, the clerk, the waiter, the chef. With equal vividness he must enter the minds of the hotel guest, the spectator at the theater, the home owner or renter coming into his abode after a tiring day at work or after spending a lazy Sunday outdoors and in, the office manager, the boss, the customer, the visitor who enters merely to observe or admire. . . . On all these people, whether they are conscious of it or not, the building which the architect plans will exert its influence—an influence making for human enrichment, happy relaxation, pleasure in work, and a true enlargement of the spirit or an influence leading to racked nerves and frustration. Only by the exercise of this kind of creative imagination can the architect be sure as to which of these influences his building will exert.

With such an imaginative approach, architects will no longer start the process of planning by thinking principally in terms of rooms. Instead they will think of areas for human activities—areas which may or may not be enclosed by walls. They will conceive of a building as a logical arrangement of ideally planned activity centers and as a controlling pattern in creating the perfect environment for these activities.

So far, we have been speaking not of building materials or building appearance but merely of human activities and their efficient fulfillment. This, of course, does not give the whole picture of the architect's mental processes in making a design; for, as was stated in the beginning, architecture is an integrated art, and in approaching any problem or considering any side of the

FIGURE 570 (OPPOSITE). HUDSON COUNTY COURTHOUSE, JERSEY CITY, NEW JERSEY. PLANS

Hugh Roberts, architect

Here is a typical eclectic plan showing the imposition of monumental axial symmetry upon a program and a structural system essentially foreign to it. This entails a great use of furred areas to conceal the steel columns and to create the effect of a non-existent heavy masonry construction. Such a plan is bound to be somewhat wasteful.

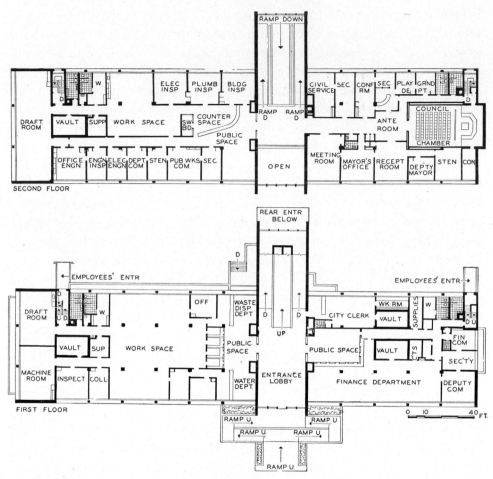

FIGURE 571. CITY HALL, FRESNO, CALIFORNIA. PLANS

Franklin & Kump and associates, architects

BELOW: First floor; ABOVE: Second floor.

This typical plan of a modern public building should be compared with that of the typical eclectic public building shown in Figure 570. Efficiency and economy dictate the excellent planning of the Fresno structure; not only cubage but also wear and tear and footsteps are saved, and convenience is gained as well. Note the relation of entrance lobby to the most used public spaces. A convenient ramp leads to the upper floor and the council chamber. The open hall with its great windows achieves true monumentality.

process of design the trained architect cannot help thinking almost automatically of all three sides of architecture—use, construction, and effect. No choice is possible in any single field of design without the other two fields being influenced as well. Naturally, with the use factor dominant, the architect's preliminary study of the human activities to be carried on in a building results not in an actual architectural plan but merely in an abstract diagram which may or may not eventually find expression in a good building. But almost unconsciously, as it were, the trained architect continually criticizes and controls the use pattern which such an analysis of activities will produce; from the outset, at least in an elementary way, he thinks of this pattern as incorporated into a structure that is buildable, structurally sensible, and beautifully composed.

THE PROGRAM

A program is essential to any architectural planning, even when a building is to be of the simplest type or is to exist for purely decorative or memorial purposes. It consists of a list of requirements and purposes, and it must take definite shape either on paper or in the mind before the design can be created. In this sense a program becomes virtually the first stage in the process of design. Buildings are erected to serve mankind either practically or emotionally, or both, and in its broadest terms a program is merely a statement of this purpose. Not only is the existence of a program a condition of the creative act, but its preparation is also in a very real sense a part of the creative act. The clarity and completeness of a building are often the results of a straightforward program, carefully thought out; conversely, confused and incoherent buildings tend to arise from confused and incoherent programs.

The quality of the program pervades the whole field of architecture. Although in one sense a great solution is possible for almost any program—and in this sense architecture of any kind and for any purpose may be great—in the larger sense and from the point of view of the sum total of the human benefits produced, the greatest architecture can only arise from the greatest program. The greatest programs are those in which the noblest purposes and the highest aspirations of mankind find voice. In general, they bring in superpersonal elements; they are the programs of buildings for governments, for religious or memorial purposes, and for wide social usefulness. Buildings which adequately solve these significant and supremely useful programs necessarily have in them qualities quite different from those of buildings which result from programs which exist merely to satisfy human greed or thoughts of personal aggrandizement. The White House is great largely because of its public and symbolic character and not merely because of its quality as a luxurious residence. And it is the communal and social purpose behind the programs of the TVA buildings which creates their special kind of nobility, not merely the fact of their mechanical efficiency.

Nevertheless almost any well-considered program, however limited in scope, can give rise to solutions that are architecturally adequate; moreover, since almost every building will have certain points of contact or relationship with the larger social world, the architect, by emphasizing these points of contact, may give to his program a value—and to his building an authority—which they would not otherwise possess. Not all architects will be asked to design buildings that have programs of an essentially noble character; but all architects, whatever the program, can see that as far as possible the social factors which create nobility are stressed.

In the ordinary run of architectural practice, the client will usually come to the architect with a program of some definiteness already prepared. He has dreamed about the building he is going to build; he knows which of his purposes it is supposed to satisfy, and with a little assistance from the architect he can usually set down his requirements in considerable detail. These ideas of the client will generally include the sizes, purposes, and numbers of rooms. They may also include definite notions with regard to the relation of the building to the site and the appearance and materials of the structure.

Included in the client's first program there may be various kinds of illustrative material clipped from magazines or predilections conveyed in the statement, "I want a building like so-and-so's." In other words, the client's program not only may list the purposes and conditioning factors of the building design but also may include definite ideas as to the type of design the solution should embody. It is just here that the first difficulty frequently arises; for the purposes the client wishes to satisfy may not, and often do not, lend themselves to the kind of solution he has dreamed. The usual client, not being trained in architectural thinking, will not at first realize that there may be essential contradictions between the purposes he has in mind and the solution he hopes to achieve, and his program may thus become a barrier to logical design instead of an assistance to it.

Here the architect must exercise all his tact, his human imagination, and his powers of persuasion. He must bring out the reasons which exist in the client's mind for his decisions. He must try to give his client's desires a most sympathetic examination and thus build up a feeling of confidence and co-operation. Once this feeling has been established, the architect's battle is half won. For on such a basis of mutual trust and understanding he can enter upon a course of education for the client. He can show him little by little the contradictions inherent in his ideas and desires; he can gradually uncover the real needs and separate them from purely accidental prejudices. If the architect can find the true reasons for the client's preferences, he can frequently show him how, if followed out logically, they will produce an effect quite different from what was first conceived. Then, since the dealings between the two have been on a logical basis, the client will be more willing to realize the force of the reasons which an architect may adduce in support of his final and different solution. As this process is carried on, sensitively and gradually, the client will have the sense, quite rightly, that he is actually partaking in the process of the design of his own building, and his final program will no longer be full of contradictions and hampering limitations.

When this difficulty has been ironed out, the program should be carefully set down and incorporated in a document which the client should sign. In that way the possibility of future controversy is largely eliminated, and the process of design can continue on the basis of mutual good will.

Two troublesome problems will frequently come up during the preliminary discussions. The first of these is the architect's professional responsibility to the community and to society; this has already been considered at greater length in Chapter 18. The client's program must always be examined and criticized from the standpoint of the impact the building will make upon the community. This is not usually a serious difficulty, for most clients sincerely wish to add to the value of the community in which they build. There are occasions, however, when it becomes the basis of an inevitable clash, and some in which the professional architect's only recourse is to resign if he wishes to preserve his professional integrity.

An outstanding example of such an impasse may be seen in the early history of the Union Station in Washington. At the beginning of the twentieth century and before the final plan of Washington had been adopted, the Pennsylvania Railroad tracks crossed the Mall just at the foot of Capitol Hill. It was there on this most important main axis that the company wished to build a railroad station, and the commission was offered to D. H. Burnham. Burnham absolutely refused the commission under those circumstances and, despite continued efforts on the part of the railroad company to make him change his mind, he remained adamant in his decision. His refusal was in no small part responsible for the fact that the railroad finally accepted the proposed (now the present) site. The company then relocated its tracks and entered wholeheartedly into the plans for the new and final station. Burnham's example in this controversy was one which should be followed more often than it is.[1]

[1] Charles Moore, *Daniel H. Burnham, Architect and Planner of Cities* (Boston: Houghton Mifflin Co., 1921).

The second problem in these preliminaries arises much more frequently—the problem of cost. One architect who was once asked how he handled this question remarked that when hopeful clients came to him, listed their requirements, and asked breathlessly, "How much will this cost?" he always answered, "Twice as much," even before they had announced any figure whatsoever. In this way he was able to break the ice with a certain humor and to indicate to the client that he must cut his coat to fit the cloth. Human psychology being what it is, people always think hopefully that they can obtain more for their money than is physically or economically possible. It is the question of cost which has probably caused more controversy between architects and clients than any other single factor. This in many cases is unnecessary, and it usually arises through the architect's failure to be completely honest and candid with a hopeful client.

When an architect is handed a list of requirements which cannot possibly be satisfied within the cost set, it is his duty to say so and to find out which of two factors is dominant: Does the list of requirements contain only absolute essentials, or does the cost figure represent the absolute maximum? Either the list or the figure may have to yield, and it is the architect's duty to find out which of them should control. Once this matter has been cleared up beyond any possibility of misunderstanding, the architect can then proceed with confidence, and the worth-while client will have only gratitude and an increased respect for the architect because of his honesty. If clients are lost to the architect because of such honesty they are usually well lost, for the jobs they would bring in would produce continual headaches in his office and might even end up in a lawsuit. It is well to have any decisions on cost written down as part of the program, or at least covered in correspondence, so that they will be on record.

This developed client's program is only the beginning of the process of program making; for the final program of a building must contain all the factors which may condition its design and the client's list of requirements is only one of them. The final program must consider the orientation of the proposed structure, its relation to its surroundings and to the community in so far as that may affect the design, as well as whatever observations the architect has made with regard to materials and similar practical necessities. It should be a definite, terse statement of *all* the facts that will influence or determine the design—and especially the plan. It will thus include the answers to almost all the questions the designer is likely to ask during the process of design. A typical program might be outlined as follows:

(residence, or what not)

FOR . . . . (*client*) AT . . . . (*town*)

A. General Purpose of Building (manufacture, residence, business, public, religious, etc.)

B. Site

General description

Orientation (winds, views, sun)

Foundation and soil characteristics

Drainage and sewers

Water supply

Utilities (gas, electricity, telephone)

Outstanding characteristics (trees or foliage to be preserved, rock ledges, etc.)

Relation to means of approach

Neighborhood characteristics

Zoning or other regulations that control or limit placing and extent of buildings

C. Required Spaces and Minimum Areas

Major spaces

Minor spaces

Service spaces

D. General Construction Elements

Type of construction

Type of materials: available; commonly used in locality; preferred

Type and extent of mechanical equipment desired

E. Special Requirements

Any special and unusual circumstances or wishes that will help determine design: special client preferences, local prejudices, unusual arrangements desired, etc.

F. Cost

A general tentative statement of the desired expenditure (if expenditure is rigidly limited to a definite figure, this should be stated)

In cases where a building is to be an investment for rental, another section containing a tentative preliminary financial statement of projected income and expenses may form part of the program. This, however, is usually a separate document (see Chap. 18).

Such a program is, of course, the joint product of the architect and the client, and in most cases it should go to the client for his approval and signature. Here again a complete understanding at the beginning will obviate any misunderstandings and controversies.

In addition to this explicit program which the architect is called upon to lay out, there may also be an implicit program which, although never set down definitely, is nevertheless an essential part of the program as a whole. The implicit program may embrace the architect's emotional reaction to the project as a whole—his judgment of the client's needs and dependability, his own feeling for general types of composition, or his own decision to use certain types of construction or certain kinds of building material. It may also contain many minor technical requirements which the client would not understand but which are implicit in the proposed building.

In order to obtain a smooth development of the planning process, it is important for the designer to realize fully all the implications of the two programs, written and unwritten. If he is a different individual from the architect, the architect should convey to him as fully and clearly as possible the sum total of the reactions, imagination, and thoughts which compose the second program, the implicit, that he may work effectively in the process of planning.

A program for an architectural competition, whether for students or for those in actual practice, often is by no means a complete one. It lists only the most definite and specific requirements of a building and frequently leaves to the architect many unsettled questions. Thus the first task of a designer in such a case is to complete the list of detailed and specified requirements, to realize what elements left unmentioned are necessary to the elements that are mentioned, and to decide on any additional spaces that will make for a better solution. Then, using these analyses, he should prepare a revised program, on the basis of which the design can go ahead with confidence. Frequently this revision will take form only as random notes.

From this explanation it should be evident that program making, like program revising, is definitely a work of the creative imagination. Occasionally, in fact, a program for a structure will grow as the design itself grows; the design will establish requirements or opportunities which themselves become parts of the future program of the building just as much as though they had been in the program from the beginning. In general, however, it may be said that the more complete—the more carefully and imaginatively thought out—a building program is, the easier will be the process of design and the more satisfactory will be the building which results.

PREPARING THE PLAN

Analysis. The first step in the process of planning, after the program has been made, is a careful study and analysis of that program with all its requirements and implications. Now at once it becomes necessary to make one or more classifications of the required areas so that we may know how to relate them to one another and to the building as a whole. We may classify them, for instance, according to whether they are public areas, private areas, service areas, or circulation areas. Such a systematic classification will tell us at once where to place certain important elements in the plan; we know, for instance, that public areas need to be close to public entrances. The terms "public" and "private" both indicate definite kinds of space and definite relationships to entrances, exits, and the outdoors. Circulation areas similarly demand directness, simplicity, and, as far as possible, straight-line passage. Thus this first general classification will be of inestimable help in forming the final arrangement of the required spaces.

A second classification, made according to the importance of the areas, may also be drawn up, and a third in accordance with the required sizes. Both classifications are essential, because it is not always the largest area in a plan which is its most effective and vital feature or, for that matter, the feature which is always to be stressed. Very large areas by their brute size will frequently determine large portions of the plan arrangement; but, if certain smaller areas are more important, special emphasis must be given to them in plan position, both from the standpoint of interior arrangement and from that of exterior form. When these preliminary classifications have been thoroughly studied and mastered, many questions which arise in the process of planning will be automatically answered.

Still one more classification of the required areas—this time according to their uses—should then be made in order that spaces which belong together in function may be placed together in the building. The program, both explicit and implicit, must be examined imaginatively to discover these necessary relationships, these necessary collocations of similar activities or of activities that are integrally related to one another. Examples of such relationships may be seen, for instance, in the necessity of placing coatrooms by entrances and in the need of having receiving and shipping rooms close to service and trucking rooms on the one hand and close to storage or finishing areas on the other. Similarly, locker rooms should normally be placed between an entrance and the work space or exercising space which they serve. In houses, essential relationships exist between cooking and eating areas, between food-storage and cooking spaces, between bedrooms, bathrooms, and clothes-storage areas, and so on. This classification according to use will determine many details in the final plan,

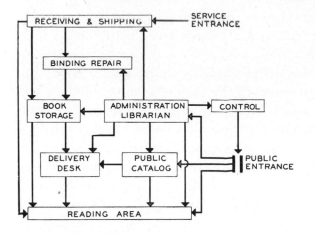

FIGURE 572. DIAGRAM OF THE FUNCTIONAL RELATIONSHIPS OF A PUBLIC LIBRARY

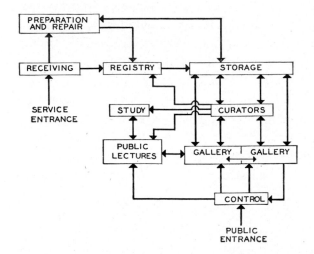

FIGURE 573. DIAGRAM OF THE FUNCTIONAL RELATIONSHIPS OF AN ART MUSEUM

just as the earlier classifications—according to the nature, importance, and size of the various areas—will determine many major plan relationships.

It is often a great help, especially in buildings of complicated functions, to set down the results of this fourth classification in a loose diagram; in this all the areas, not necessarily drawn to scale, are arranged and connected by lines indicating their functional relationships. Arrows may indicate the direction of the flow of activities; if it is in both directions, arrowheads will occur at both ends of these connecting lines. Such a diagram is of great importance, for it can be checked against the final plan more quickly and more surely than can a list or a written outline. Furthermore, in some cases the diagram arrangement itself may suggest possible *partis* [2] for the actual plan relationships. Ideally, there should be no crossing of circulation or connecting lines, and, where it is impossible to make a diagram without much crisscrossing of these functional connections, it may be an indication of the necessity of multi-storied or broken-level arrangements.

We are showing use diagrams of two types of building as examples (Figs. 572, 573). One is that of a medium-sized public library, the other that of an art museum. The first diagram makes clear at once the necessity for the close relationship of catalogue, delivery desk, reading room, and stack area. It shows, too, that the librarian's work area must be easily reached from the service entrance and also from the receiving room and that at the same time it must have close connections with the stack as well as with the catalogue. The librarian's office should be approachable both from the public area and from the librarian's work area, but this work area itself should be private, and the public entrances and exits should be easily controlled.

The second diagram is based on an attempt to relate logically the educational function of the museum, its exhibition function, and the large storage and work areas which modern museum practice makes necessary; it also shows the close relationship of the curators and the administration staff with all these functions. Furthermore, it demonstrates that, in the modern art museum, visitors should be able to circulate through all the galleries in succession or go from the entrance to any one of them.

The preparation of such use diagrams is in no sense merely a mechanical task; they do not necessarily follow easily and inevitably from the reading of the program. Into them must go that penetrating exercise of the imagination mentioned earlier in this chapter. The true lines of functional connection are seldom stated in a program; they are almost always implicit, and only that designer who has both the knowledge of the way building types operate and the imagination to pierce through the list of rooms to the actual human activities they house can make a diagram of the necessary soundness. Thus not only is a program of the utmost clarity needed in order to achieve a true picture of the possibilities inherent in it but also a considerable knowledge of building types and, even more, of human actions and activities. (See also the function diagrams in Vol. I, Chaps. 3, 4.)

[2] The term *parti* is used in architecture for a general preliminary arrangement of a building, in both plan and elevation.

There is one danger in these use diagrams—the fact that the designer may consider them as elementary architectural plans and not merely as diagrams. As we have said, such diagrams sometimes do suggest *partis* for a plan, but they can never resemble more than one of all the possible *partis;* sometimes, too, their arrangement, if it suggests a *parti* at all, will suggest one that is hampered and impossible of development. These diagrams, therefore, are nothing more than tools. They are simply graphic ways of presenting a complex set of relationships and should assist, not hamper, design. Their fundamental purpose is double: first, to act as aids in clarifying the necessary functional relationships that exist within a structure; and, second, as a diagram of these relationships, to serve as a quick check against any proposed plan.

Research. It was stated above that some knowledge of building types is necessary in order to analyze a program thoroughly and to present the analysis clearly. It is here that the problem of the use and abuse of research arises. A building for complex modern use cannot be designed out of an intellectual vacuum. The greatest architects, to be sure, have an extraordinary power of intuition in the workings of the kind of building they happen to be designing, but even they will usually check their intuitions by careful investigation and research.

Research in connection with architectural design can be both used and misused. Essentially the constructive purpose of such research is to gain as exact a knowledge as possible of the activities that go on in buildings of a given type and to find out the kinds of building relationship which naturally result from these activities. The true purpose of this kind of research is never that of obtaining a ready-made solution of the problem at hand; a search for ready-made solutions, if undertaken, can lead only to confusion and disappointment. Every architectural problem differs in some respect from every other architectural problem—where the requirements are similar, the sites may be different; where the sites resemble each other, the climate may vary. Thus any search for ready-made solutions leads to a completely wrong emphasis, and, if by chance the plan of a past building is found which seems on superficial examination to solve all the problems of a new program and if it is adopted *in toto*, the result will almost always be a building that is not the most perfect possible solution for the problems under consideration.

This does not mean that one can forget or ignore what has already been accomplished toward solutions of difficult building problems. The designer, in duty to his client, is bound to look up many published examples of similar buildings. He is supposed to furnish not only his own creative skill but also a thorough technical knowledge. Each of the plans which research will bring to light should be studied as critically as possible. One must not believe that, just because a building has found publication, its solutions of the planning problems involved are the best, or even good ones. It may be more valuable to the designer to discover what is *wrong* with an existing building, and why it is wrong, than it is to search out and reproduce what seems to be a satisfactory solution of his problem.

Naturally the sources for such a study will be largely the files of past and current architectural magazines. These may have been clipped and arranged according to building types in a clipping file; many architects and numerous libraries have developed such files. It may be well for the student designer to start one of his own. If carefully expanded and edited, it will come to contain an immense amount of valuable material. The advantage of a clipping file is that it enables the designer with ease and dispatch to select a large series of plans, spread them out in front of him, and study them comparatively. In addition to the architectural magazines, technical books on the subject are of great importance; even histories and general handbooks, too, may offer material of considerable value, for a knowledge of the way mankind has met various problems in the past may be of great help in attacking the problems of today.

But the most valuable kind of research in connection with architectural planning lies not in the examination of published examples but in the study of actual buildings. The designer should make a point of visiting as many structures as he can of the type he is planning. He should watch people at work in these buildings. He should see how they come and go and what they do with their time and energy. Only by such vital and firsthand knowledge of the activities for which a given building is being designed can the best solution be reached. Here again, as in the case of the published plans, it may be more valuable to discover what is wrong with the buildings observed—where human energy is wasted in them, where the spaces are too large or too small—than to discover the elements which are obviously right.

Thus research of the right kind, undertaken with the right attitude, will clarify most profitably the special planning problems raised by any proposed building and should lead to solutions even better than any of those which have been studied. In this way research may become an integral part of progress and improvement in building design and construction. On the other hand, if the purpose of research is merely to find a ready-made solution to copy, its result

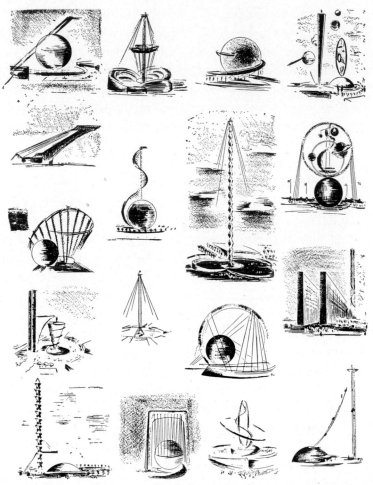

FIGURE 574. STUDIES FOR CENTRAL FEATURE, THE THEME BUILDING, NEW YORK WORLD'S FAIR OF 1939, BY THE OFFICE OF HARRISON & FOUILHOUX

In many cases, numberless sketches of all conceivable solutions will be required before an acceptable idea is reached. These studies show all sorts of ideas, some almost purely fantastic; out of them the concept of sphere and tower gradually emerged.   From the *Architectural Forum*

will inevitably be the crystallization of past accomplishments and the perpetuation of outdated standards.

Search for a Parti. The designer, we may assume, has by now mastered the program in its various classifications and, by means of research, has obtained an insight into the actual workings of a building and into the ways in which designers of the past have sought to shelter these functions best. He should now begin the actual search for his own solution.

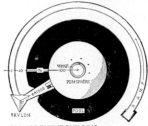

PLAN OF THEME BUILDING

FIGURE 575. STUDIES FOR THEME BUILDING, NEW YORK WORLD'S FAIR OF 1939

Harrison & Fouilhoux, architects

This study shows the final idea adapted and clarified, with tower, sphere, and ramp. The design was then checked for scale by comparing its silhouette with those of various well-known buildings—the Great Pyramid, Parthenon, Pantheon, Santa Sophia, St. Mark's, Chartres Cathedral, and St. Peter's.

From the *Architectural Forum*

This can be done only by trying out all the possible schemes. The designer should jot down every arrangement of the required activity spaces which occurs to him, without thinking much at the beginning about their relative merits. In this study it is necessary to have some sense of the relative size of the different parts to be included, even if the first sketches are not made to exact scale. To help in the development of this sense, it may be wise at the outset to lay out, to scale, block rectangles of each of the required areas, although the proportions of the individual areas in the sketches may in no sense agree with the final shapes developed in the plan. They will at least enable the designer to gain a definite

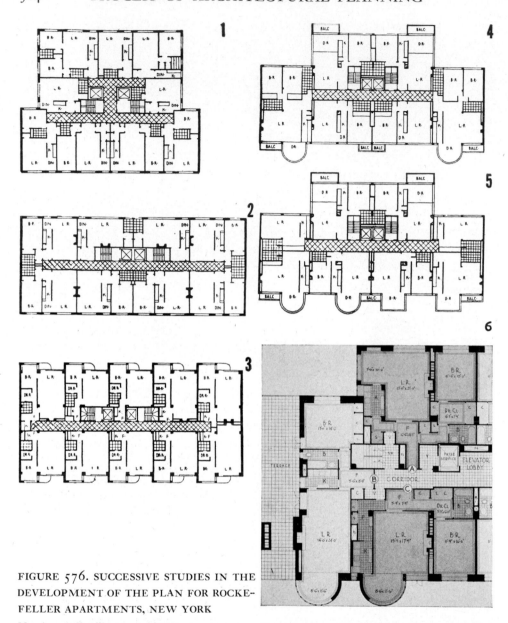

FIGURE 576. SUCCESSIVE STUDIES IN THE
DEVELOPMENT OF THE PLAN FOR ROCKE-
FELLER APARTMENTS, NEW YORK

Harrison & Fouilhoux, architects

(1) A conventional plan, abandoned because of the undesirable apartments at the corridor ends;
(2) A study with all apartments facing street or court, but with little variety; (3) A variation of
No. 2, adopting certain ideas taken from apartments in Sweden, but it was felt that these did not
meet the New York demand; (4) A plan for fewer and larger apartments to meet the special
demands this site suggested, with cross ventilation in most apartments; (5) Approaching the
final solution; (6) The final solution.　　　　Courtesy the architects and *Architectural Forum*

sense of the relative sizes of the areas which he must arrange. These preliminary jottings should be of approximately equal sizes and sketched in a similar manner as far as possible, so that later no differences in perfection of drawing or in scale will prejudice the designer in favor of one or another and therefore prevent a candid evaluation.

In such jottings the importance of circulation must always be foremost in the designer's mind; for good and simple circulation, designed in relation to the numbers of people who use it and in harmony with the building's purpose, should be the major consideration both functionally and aesthetically. If the building is to consist of two or more stories, the position of vertical circulations —stairs, elevators, ramps, and escalators—may be a determining factor in the design. Since these vertical circulations will run through all the floors, they will develop important circulation centers on the upper floors, and, since they are fixed in relation to one another, it is most important to see that they are in the best possible position. These preliminary sketches, or rather jottings of ideas, will indicate primarily the relation of activity centers to one another and their position in the building as a whole. Detailed problems are best ignored in this study, and such questions as which activity centers need to be enclosed by partitions or made into rooms should also be, for the time being, forgotten. What the designer is after at this stage in the process of planning is merely a presentation of all the possible arrangements of the required areas which his imagination can conceive of.

Out of this group of jottings a few will, even on the most cursory study, appear to be better than others. The designer should go over them all, bearing in mind the program and his knowledge of the building and examining them for straightforwardness, for economy, and for possibilities of creating from them expressive and coherent volumes. Arrangements which do not stand up under this preliminary examination can be eliminated from further consideration.

There will remain a number of possible arrangements—it may vary from two or three to as many as ten or a dozen, depending on the building and the flexibility of the program. In order to judge these remaining schemes one must study them further. From here on, plans to scale are absolutely necessary, but the scale should be kept as small as possible without losing intelligibility in the drawing. For small buildings, a scale of $1/16'' = 1'-0''$ is good; if the building is larger, a scale of $1/32'' = 1'-0''$ is better; for the largest type of complicated structure and for group plans, scales of $1/64'' = 1'-0''$ or even $1/100'' = 1'-0''$

FIGURE 577. A SKETCH BY BRAMANTE FOR ST. PETER'S, ROME

Note how Bramante is thinking in terms of space; the plan conceptions are paralleled by thumb-nail perspectives to indicate the actual forms which the plan generates.

From H. von Geymüller, *Die ursprünglichen Entwürfe für Sanct Peter in Rom*

or $1/128'' = 1'-0''$ should be used. The use of small scale will have two advantages: first, it will allow the designer to get an over-all picture of the plan in the most simple and direct fashion; and, second, it will prevent such waste of time and confusion of mind as may arise through a premature study of minor details which tend to distract the attention from larger and more important relationships.

These plan studies incorporating the arrangements which, among the preliminary jottings, have been found best should be drawn with sufficient clarity and definiteness so that one can examine them intelligently; also, as in the case of the earlier jottings, it is well to keep them similar in presentation so that each may have an equal chance in the final selection.

The preparation of these preliminary plan studies will entail much more than mere mechanical enlargement or drawing up of the earlier jottings, for their somewhat larger scale and more careful presentation will at once bring to light

FIGURE 578. AN ARCHITECTURAL SKETCH BY RAPHAEL, UFFIZI GALLERY, FLOR-
ENCE, ITALY

A typical Renaissance preliminary sketch: elevations, details, and perspective view all studied
together. Courtesy Ware Library

many conditioning relationships which the earlier examination did not make
clear. Furthermore, as the designer spends more and more time at his problem,
he will find that many requirements which appeared to him vague at the beginning will almost automatically begin to clarify themselves. Moreover, at this
second stage of the study, if the designer is possessed of a true architectural
mind, questions of appearance and of possible construction will begin to gain
an ever increasing importance as he ponders the plans. Sketches of possible
volume composition, perhaps in rough perspective like those which Renaissance
architects so often used, are frequently of value (Figs. 577, 578). Rough elevations and sections will be necessary, not only to assure a plan that will develop
into an effective structure but sometimes also to clarify the plan relationships
themselves. This of course will be especially true in buildings where the required heights of different parts vary. Problems of lighting and natural ventilation in a plan can often be clarified only by such rough elevation and section

studies. Thus behind each of these final preliminary plan studies there will be dozens of rough sketches—and the designer should always bear in mind that tracing paper is relatively inexpensive!

Perhaps no two individuals will go through this process of developing preliminary small-scale plans in the same way (see Figs. 579–585). Architectural minds seem to belong to two basic types—those who work best from the small to the large and those who work best from the large to the small. The first type of designer will tend to favor the more detailed relationships first; when these have been solved, he will make various arrangements of the details in as organic a way as he can, thus creating larger volumes from the small elements that make them up. If the problem of organizing these comparatively detailed elements has been correctly solved and if the program is a coherent one, the eventual solution of the whole plan is likely to be coherent. The other type of designer will see the major relationships and major volumes as the first problems to be attacked, and when these have been solved he will arrange in each the details which go to make it up.

Both approaches have their dangers and their advantages. The danger in the first—designing from small to big—is that, in the fascinating study of the smaller relationships and details, the questions of major importance may be overlooked and the final building may become not an organic and unified whole but the mere sum of many efficient details strung together with no controlling pattern. Such a building will have no unity; each part, instead of helping the other portions and existing in relation to them, will be a separate and distinct entity. The danger inherent in the other approach is the fact that the designer, in his eagerness to find the best over-all relationships, may slight and forget important details or may produce major shapes into which the component details can be forced only by compromising their efficiency or their effect.

Geniuses in architecture seem to partake of both natures equally, and in their planning they tend to work in both ways almost at the same time, so that the detailed solutions are always being checked against the larger pattern and the larger pattern is always being criticized from the standpoint of the detailed solutions which it permits. This, of course, is the ideal planning approach, and every designer, whatever his primary tendency, should strive to achieve it and to train his own imagination along the lines in which it is weakest.

It is in this stage of the study that the concept of areas as activity centers will begin to translate itself into the concept of rooms or enclosed or open spaces, and the purely abstract concept of arrangements with which the study started

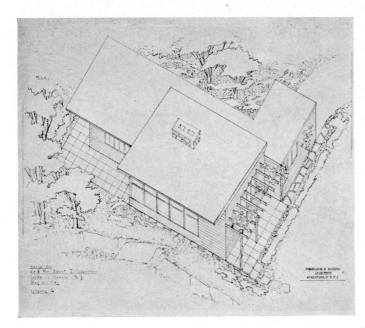

FIGURE 579. A HOUSE IN CROTON, NEW YORK. PRELIMINARY STUDY

Pomerance & Breines, architects

ABOVE: Bird's-eye view; BELOW: The plan.

Courtesy Pomerance & Breines

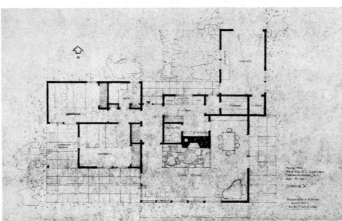

will now take form as a possible building; it will clothe itself with walls and supports and roofs.

The final result of this stage of the study will be a series of plans, usually accompanied by block elevations and sections; each set will represent a possible building, and each will be sufficiently worked out so that the designer is assured of at least its constructibility. Naturally in this study some of the earlier arrangements will reveal fundamental contradictions and impossibilities and can now

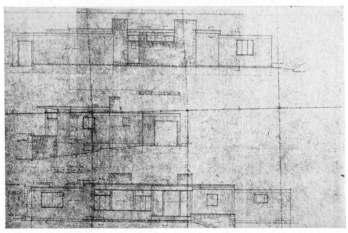

FIGURE 580 (ABOVE AND OPPOSITE). A HOUSE IN CROTON, NEW YORK. PLAN AND
ELEVATION SKETCHES

Pomerance & Breines, architects

Further study to give a better position for the dining space and greater privacy and better
arrangement for the bedrooms resulted in a plan quite different from Scheme A (Fig. 579).
This solution was the basis for the working drawings. Note that the changed plan necessitated a
completely different exterior. In execution, the stone in wall and chimney shown on these drawings was changed to concrete block.   Courtesy Pomerance & Breines

be eliminated. The ones that remain and seem possible of development should
be drawn up with considerable care, in similar technique, and then put away
and, if there is time, forgotten by the conscious mind for a day or two. During
this period the designer's subconscious mind will undoubtedly be working for

VIEW FROM NORTH

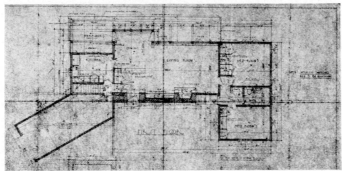

him, a process which will be doubly helpful if the whole problem has just previously been reviewed carefully. Both the popular saying, "Sleep on it," and the universal acceptance of the benefits of a "fresh eye" are acknowledgments of the power of the subconscious mind to bring new light upon a problem or to furnish a sudden solution which seems, as it were, to spring from nowhere. The history of creative and scientific activity is full of such happenings.

A careful study of the different preliminary schemes undertaken after, and with the benefit of, this period of rest will probably enable the designer to pick from them readily the one which seems definitely the best. This should now be criticized relentlessly for imperfections. It may be well to draw on it circulation lines for both people and materials in order to check its efficiency, and it should be examined carefully to make sure that it fulfills in the best possible way all the requirements of the program. If it stands up under such an analy-

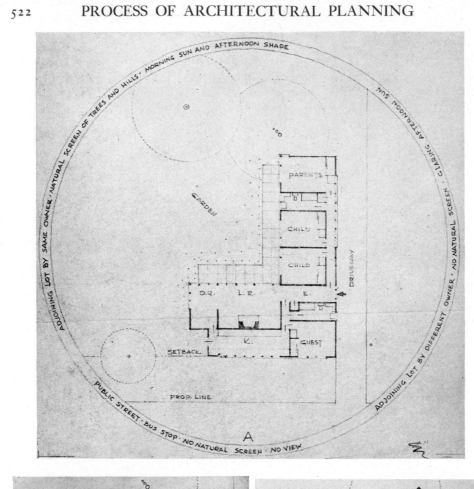

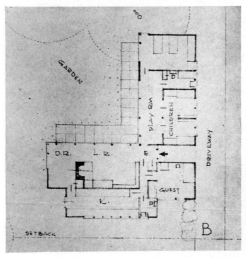

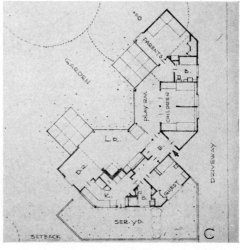

sis, it may be accepted as the *parti* for further development. If it fails, the scheme which appears next best should be similarly examined and criticized, for it is possible that the first judgment was faulty. In the end, one of the preliminary schemes will probably prove acceptable as a basis for further study.

Developing the Parti. To develop a *parti* means much more than merely drawing up the scheme carefully at a larger scale. New factors will be bound to enter as a study of the details continues. Each room or space in the plan must now be scrutinized as carefully as the whole general arrangement, and in this examination of rooms and spaces the amount and the placing of furniture and equipment must play an essential part. Frequently the difference between a well- and an ill-studied house plan, for example, will lie in the fact that the rooms of the former can be furnished easily and with a certain flexibility, whereas furniture in the latter can be installed only with difficulty and awkwardly.

Now is the time, too, for the study of all sorts of details in connection with the plan—the kind and quality of illumination, the positions and sizes of doors and windows, the ease of approach, and so forth. Now is the time also to think of all the possible difficulties which may be inherent in the arrangement. Are the room shapes and arrangements appropriate to the type of construction? Are they the best shapes for the use? Will the natural position or size of necessary structural columns interfere with interior arrangements? Is there ample space for taking care of all the mechanical equipment? If these important questions are in the designer's mind during this study and if satisfactory answers to

FIGURE 581 (OPPOSITE). THREE PROGRESSIVE STUDIES FOR A HOUSE IN CALIFORNIA

Harwell Harris, architect

A: The first study, which merely distributes the areas required in the necessary positions. The architect's criticisms are: living room looks into children's bedrooms; entrance hall and bedroom hall are wastefully long; kitchen is bad in shape; there is no room for service yard on the street side; paved areas separate all major rooms from the exterior planting. As a result, the study was revised.

B: The second study, developed from the first to overcome some of its difficulties. This was criticized for: narrow approach to entrance; length of kitchen hall; lack of space for service yard; relation of paved terrace to all interiors. Other difficulties in Plan A, however, have been removed.

C: The final scheme. The change to a 45° angle in the dining room and parents' room shortens the house, makes the kitchen smaller and more efficient, gives greater privacy to the parents' room, improves the entrance, and permits two paved terraces with planting between them to be carried right through to the house wall. The revised plan also permits a continuous glass wall through which all the chief rooms look out on the garden. The partition between living room and playroom is a sliding one of glass, so that the two rooms may be used as one when necessary; it also permits easy supervision of the children. This scheme was approved and served as the basis of the house erected.   Courtesy Harwell Harris

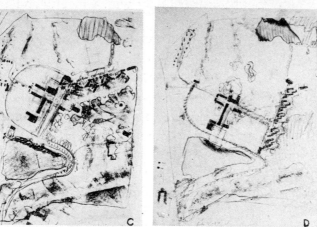

FIGURE 582. COM-
PETITION GENERAL-
PLAN STUDIES FOR
GOUCHER COLLEGE,
BALTIMORE, MARY-
LAND, I

Moore & Hutchins,
architects

Studies A to F show how
the architects, in designing a complex group for a
steeply sloping site, gradually departed from the
formal *parti* (A,B) because
a closer study of desirable
orientation and views, as
well as a realization of the
character of the site, revealed that freer solutions
were more efficient (C,D).
The whole was then re-
studied for better utiliza-
tion of the site (E,F).

From *Pencil Points*

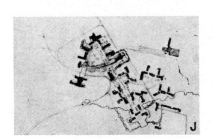

FIGURE 583. COMPETITION GENERAL-PLAN STUDIES FOR GOUCHER COLLEGE, BALTIMORE, MARYLAND, II

Moore & Hutchins, architects

Gradually the concept of an academic group evolved, coherently but freely planned at the left, with dormitories arranged around informal intimate courts at the right (G,H). With this conception established, attention was concentrated on the building groups in detail (I–K). Out of this study grew the final clarification of the triangular academic group, with the library at the apex, the curved terrace walk leading to the chapel, and the dormitories grouped around the dining and social centers. The final winning competition plan was drawn on this basis. Only a small selection of the sketches made is shown here.　　From *Pencil Points*

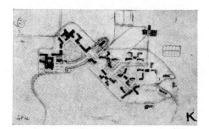

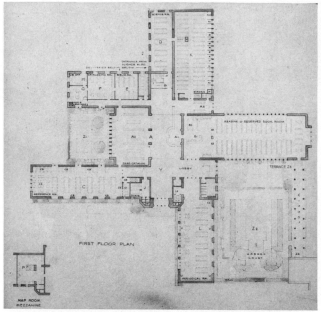

FIRST FLOOR PLAN

MAP ROOM
MEZZANINE

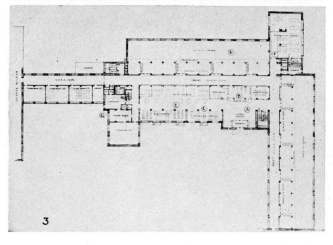

3

FIGURE 584 (LEFT AND OPPOSITE). LIBRARY, GOUCHER COLLEGE, BALTIMORE, MARYLAND. PROGRESSIVE PRELIMINARY SKETCHES

Moore & Hutchins, architects

(1) and (2) Competition drawings for the library. The building shown is of the conventional library type with three reading rooms and a stack area in four wings. Subsequently a revised program was prepared calling for a radically different library type, in which the books were to be as close as possible to the readers, with large shelf areas in the reading rooms and the utmost flexibility in arrangement. (3) Scheme 2, the first developed study showing the revised requirements. (4) Scheme 3, a further development with greater compactness. (5) Scheme 4, with a rearrangement of the position of the administration area and reduced width in the reference room. (6) Scheme 5, a return to the earlier position of the administration offices but with greatly increased economy.

In Schemes 3–6, A: Lobby; B: Circulation desk; C: Catalogue; D: Reading room; E: Reference room; F: Periodical room; G: Librarian and administration.

Courtesy Moore & Hutchins

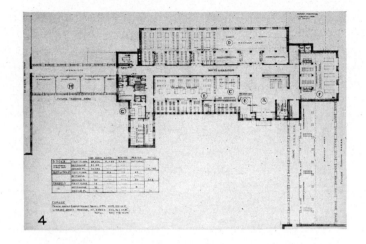

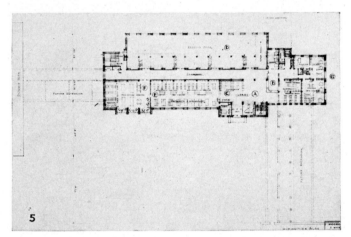

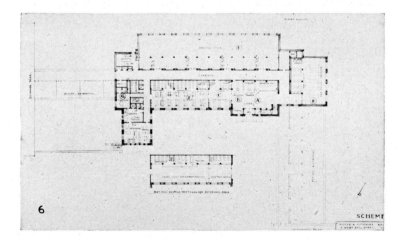

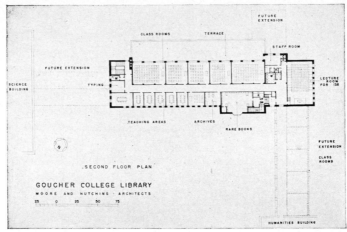

SECOND FLOOR PLAN

GOUCHER COLLEGE LIBRARY

MOORE AND HUTCHINS · ARCHITECTS

25 0 25 50 75

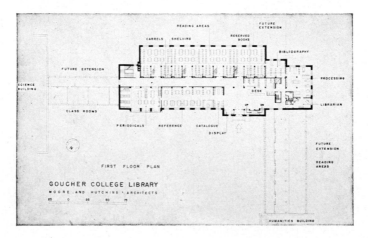

FIRST FLOOR PLAN

GOUCHER COLLEGE LIBRARY

MOORE AND HUTCHINS · ARCHITECTS

25 0 25 50 75

them can be determined at this early stage of the process, the making of working drawings and the actual construction of the building will proceed simply and with the least possible difficulty; furthermore, the client will not be bothered with extras caused by the sudden discovery of unforeseen difficulties or by the necessity of furring to conceal pipes or equipment.

If this study in detail shows that the *parti* chosen will not work, or will work only with difficulty and by forcing its arrangement into unnatural forms, it is best to abandon it at once and, on the basis of the new knowledge gained, to find a new *parti* that will work. This is seldom necessary, for, if the primary schemes have been prepared with sufficient care and criticized with sufficient stringency, the *parti* selected will usually serve and will incorporate the necessary details without strain. It is sometimes the case, however, that an architect's stubbornness in trying to force necessary details into an ill-considered *parti* will not only occasion expensive and unnecessary work in the office but also produce a building that is at best a series of compromises.

In this detailed study, the position, size, and arrangement of such vertical elements as stairs, chimneys, elevators, and the risers for mechanical equipment must be considered with especial care. Nothing can cause more difficulties in later stages of the work than a failure to clarify such elements at this time. If stairs are of importance, it is well to draw a careful preliminary section through them so that the number and size of risers and treads, the widths and position of landings, and the headroom and the lengths of the required flights may be determined; for in sketches, especially plan sketches, the designer is almost always tempted to underestimate the space required for a stairway.

A truism which should be accepted by every architect holds that no plan can be studied to this point without a concomitant development of elevations and sections, to be checked by many sketch perspectives. Inherent in every plan

FIGURE 585 (OPPOSITE). LIBRARY, GOUCHER COLLEGE, BALTIMORE, MARYLAND. FINAL APPROVED SCHEME (6)

Moore & Hutchins, architects

TOP: Perspective; CENTER: Second-floor plan; BOTTOM: First-floor plan.

The approved scheme returned to the basic arrangement shown on Scheme 4 but with additional clarification of the lobby and administration area. The lobby is more open, spacious, and inviting, and the offices are more efficient and airy, with a more logical relation. There is a mezzanine over the inner half of the reading room; additional stack space, with small reading areas, is located in the basement. All reading areas may be subdivided at will by movable book shelves. The final scheme produces an exterior that preserves the spirit of the original design but has greater simplicity and quietness because of its longer horizontals.   Courtesy Moore & Hutchins

shape there is an appearance of some definite type. Almost every plan detail, especially the position of doors and windows, will profoundly affect the appearance of a building, so that both in general composition of volume and mass and in details of light and shade, outside and in, plan shapes and arrangements are of vital concern. Therefore an intelligent or successful development of a *parti* into a final plan can no more be made without a consideration of the structure's appearance than without a consideration of structural systems and building materials. One affects the other, and every change in one will mean some changes, large or small, in both of the others. The development of a *parti* into a finished plan, therefore, must be accompanied by the creation of the exterior and interior forms and by a consideration of the structural systems necessary to bring these forms into being.

It was one of the false assumptions of the eclectic tradition of design, further stimulated by artificial systems of elaborate plan presentation, that a beautiful plan would necessarily produce a beautiful building. Thomas Hastings, in his Scammon Lectures at the University of Chicago in 1915, gave eloquent expression to this idea.[3] The fact, of course, is that a beautiful building has a beautiful plan—which is a very different statement. And mere beauty of plan, except as it may reveal some basic, fruitful, and harmonious system of volumes, is no guarantee whatsoever of the beauty of the building which results from it. Thus the designer must never allow himself to be seduced by the beauty of a plan; he must always in his study keep in mind the actual appearance of the structure which will arise upon it.

It is in this further and detailed study, so necessary in the development of the plan *parti* into the final plan, that the architect must apply all that he knows of the general principles of composition—balance, rhythm, preparation, and climax. He must make sure that the sequences of experience which confront the visitor to the building, or its inhabitants, shall have meaning, both practical and aesthetic. And in details he should be aware of that architectural ideal which Trystan Edwards terms "inflexion," [4] the fact that every part of a building necessarily has a definite connection with and an effect upon all the adjoining parts.

Here, in addition, the visualizing power of the architect's imagination is most necessary. The ideal architect can never draw a line in a plan without having

[3] Ralph Adams Cram, Thomas Hastings, and Claude Bragdon, *Six Lectures on Architecture* (Chicago: University of Chicago Press [c1917]).
[4] Trystan Edwards, *Style and Composition in Architecture* (London: John Tiranti, Ltd., 1944).

its meaning in the appearance and in the structure rise automatically in his mind. When he draws a plan for a flight of stairs, for instance, he is conscious of the sloping plane of the flights, the size and appearance of the open well above, the shape of the floor space which the stairs leave free, and the direction and quality of the light which may pour down them. He sees doors not simply as white interruptions of black wall lines, and even not merely as ways of getting in and out of a space, but also as shapes of a definite geometric size in definite relation to the shapes of the wall around. He will not depend entirely on his imagination, however; he will check it by making sections and perspectives. It is an interesting fact that many of the architects who seem to have been most highly gifted with this ability to visualize have also been those who made the greatest number of sketches during the course of their designs. This is notably true of most of the best architects of the Italian Renaissance and, among more recent designers, of such men as Charles A. Platt, B. G. Goodhue, and Frank Lloyd Wright.

Nearly five hundred years ago, Leone Battista Alberti wrote of the process of design:

In a word, you ought to make such Models [preliminary designs] and consider them by yourself and with others so diligently, and examine them over and over so often, that there shall not be a single Part in your whole Structure, but what you are thoroughly acquainted with, and know what place and how much room it is to possess, and what use applied.[5]

Only by constant study can this end be achieved. Only by the expenditure of many feet of tracing paper can a building be developed out of a preliminary idea. And only by a constant checking back from plan to exterior and interior effect and by the continual correlation of all with the construction can a true plan, and consequently a good building, finally arrive. This final plan, together with the design of the exterior which it indicates and the interiors which result from it, will be the definite preliminary plan of the building and the foundation for all the working drawings and the myriad details which are to follow it.

But even at this stage the architect should not be in too much of a hurry to proceed at once with the next stages of his professional service. Time for careful consideration is necessary here; unless there is an absolutely compelling practical reason for hurry, a few days should elapse before any further work is

[5] *The Architecture of Leone Battista Alberti* . . . translated by James Leoni (London: Thomas Edlin, 1726).

done. As Alberti writes at the end of the first chapter of Book II in the same work:

To conclude, when the whole Model and Contrivance of all the Parts greatly pleases both yourself and others of good Experience, so that you have not the least doubt remaining within yourself, and do not know of any thing that wants the least Reexamination: even then I wou'd advise you not to run furiously to the Execution out of a Passion for Building . . . which rash and inconsiderate men are apt to do; but if you will hearken to me, lay the thoughts of it aside for some time, till this favorite Invention grow old. Then take a fresh Review of everything, when not being guided by a fondness for your Invention, but by the Truth and Reason of things you will be capable of judging more clearly. Because in many cases Time will discover a great many things to you, worth Consideration and Reflection, which, be you ever so accurate, might before escape you.

SUGGESTED ADDITIONAL READING FOR CHAPTER 19

BOOKS OF STANDARDS, OR DRAFTSMEN'S MANUALS

Neufert, Ernst, *Bau-entwurfslehre* . . . (Berlin: Bauwelt-verlag, 1936).

Ramsey, Charles George, and Harold Reeve Sleeper, *Architectural Graphic Standards* . . . 3rd ed. (New York: Wiley; London: Chapman & Hall [1944]).

Time-Saver Standards, a Manual of Essential Architectural Data (New York: Dodge [c1946]).

GENERAL WORKS

Clute, Eugene, *The Practical Requirements of Modern Building* (New York: Pencil Points Press, 1928).

Curtis, Nathaniel Cortlandt, *Architectural Composition*, 3rd ed. rev. (Cleveland: Jansen, 1935).

Fletcher, Donald Atkinson, *Introduction to Architectural Design* (New York [the author], 1947).

Gromort, Georges, *Essai sur la théorie de l'architecture* . . . (Paris: Vincent, Fréal, 1942).

Guadet, Julien, *Éléments et théorie de l'architecture*, 4 vols. (Paris: Aulanier, n.d.).

Hamlin, Talbot [Faulkner], *Architecture, an Art for All Men* (New York: Columbia University Press, 1947), Chap. 3.

Haneman, John Theodore, *A Manual of Architectural Compositions* (New York: Architectural Book Pub. Co., Paul Wenzel & Maurice Krakow [c1923]).

Harbeson, John Frederick, *The Study of Architectural Design* . . . with a foreword by Lloyd Warren (New York: Pencil Points Press, 1927).

Marks, Percy L., *The Principles of Planning Buildings* . . . 3rd rev. ed. of *The Principles of Planning* (London: Batsford, 1911). Written from the English point of view and illustrated with English examples; the text has much valuable material.

Nobbs, Percy Erskine, *Design; a Treatise on the Discovery of Form* (London, New York, etc.: Oxford University Press, 1937), Chap. 19.

WORKS DEALING WITH BUILDING TYPES

Few books on this subject are of contemporary value; in addition to the series listed below, the reader is referred to Volumes III and IV of the present work.

"Progressive Architecture Library," a series of books dealing with building types (New York: Reinhold).

   Abel, Joseph Henry, and Fred N. Severud, *Apartment Houses* [c1947].

   Burris-Meyer, Harold, and Edward C. Cole, *Theatres and Auditoriums* (1949).

   Ketchum, Morris, *Shops and Stores* (1948).

   Rosenfield, Isadore, *Hospitals, Integrated Design* . . . [c1947].

   (Others in preparation.)

20

Group Planning I: General
Considerations

THE ART of architecture has never achieved its greatest values for society by the design of individual buildings, however grand. It is only
when buildings become part of a group or a community that their true
values can make their strongest appeal. This is as true of aesthetic content as it
is of sociological purposes, and it is therefore most important to lay considerable
emphasis on the problems of composition which arise in the design of groups of
buildings. It is the building as part of a group and the design of building groups
as a whole which present architects with the most inspiring challenge and offer
them opportunities for their most valuable achievements.

In *Towards a New Architecture*, [1] in the chapter entitled "The Illusion of
Plans," Le Corbusier says, "The exterior is always an interior." By that he means
that the eye of an observer anywhere commands a view which, as he turns,
embraces the entire 360 degrees of the surrounding picture; nowhere does his
view or his attention close itself automatically at the corner of a building. He
writes: "The human eye, in its investigations, is always on the move and the
beholder himself is always turning right and left, and shifting about. He is interested in everything and is attracted towards the centre of gravity of the
whole site. At once the problem spreads to the surroundings. The houses near
by, the distant or neighbouring mountains, the horizon low or high, make for-
midable masses which exercise the force of their cubic volume."

Thus everything in the immediate vicinity of an architectural work becomes
a factor in the aesthetic effect of that work. In group planning alone can the
architect control this complete circuit of a building's surroundings; in group
planning alone can he make the building count for its utmost value, because all
of its surroundings are part of the larger composition he has produced.

Group planning has a special importance for architects in the present world,

[1] Translated by Frederick Etchells (New York: Payson & Clarke [c1927]).

because both economical and sociological factors have combined to bring problems of large-scale group design more and more to the fore. We are inevitably learning economies of many kinds that arise from large-scale multiple-unit construction. The complex organization of modern living more and more forces upon us the need for the existence of careful and systematic mutual relationships between buildings of many different kinds, and, just as growing functional study tends toward differentiating individual buildings according to their multiple uses, so the systematic relation of separate buildings to one another becomes more and more important. We are learning that cities themselves must be planned with system and organization. We develop groups of industrial buildings, of commercial buildings; great schools and universities bring with them increasingly difficult problems of group planning; and even in dwellings we are more and more confronted with the fact that it is only through the carefully articulated group plan, comprising many features, that human beings can be most efficiently and pleasantly housed.

In large measure this growing demand for skill in group planning has found the American architectural profession comparatively unprepared. Trained almost entirely through their professional schools—and later through their practice—in the design of individual buildings, architects confronted with the problem of planning a coherent and effective group all too frequently seem to have been at a loss and, consequently, their designs have relapsed into unimaginative and barrack-like regularity or else into an incoherent confusion.

The present preference for informality in architecture has occasionally increased the difficulty of this problem. Under its influence modern architects seem sometimes even to have been afraid of system and order; they have apparently had no guiding principles and possessed no ideals of design which would produce a coherent and effective ensemble even in informal groups.

Yet there are principles and ideals in group planning as powerful and as comprehensible as those which control the design of individual structures. The problems, to be sure, are more complex—one has, for instance, to think constantly of the question of traffic—yet, both as functional and working entities and as visual compositions which can give pleasure or pain, even the most complex groups will reveal the working of these principles and will show inevitably whether or not the designer has realized their implications.

Moreover, the principles that underlie group planning have many resemblances to those at the basis of good design in single buildings. It is only a question of carrying them further, of realizing the compositional values in group

FIGURE 586. HILDESHEIM,
GERMANY. STREET VIEW

The typical harmony of late-medie-
val architectural forms.

Courtesy Ware Library

plans by dealing with entire buildings as units instead of merely with masses or rooms or enclosures. First of all, there is the cardinal demand for unity in a group. The whole must appear a unit; however large it may be, however long it may take to progress through its complexities, the sense of underlying unity must everywhere be apparent. This unity is the secret of the beauty we find in many towns throughout the world; in them every street leads naturally into others, every building seems to benefit rather than to fight its neighbor, and every part seems related in some preordained way with every other. Such unity would probably be accepted by almost everyone as a necessary quality in a good group; the difficulties and the perplexities arise in studying the ways in which this unity may be achieved. In general, it would appear that the basic methods of achieving unity arise from the following qualities: harmony, continuity, balance, and climax.

Harmony. Harmony does not mean identity. It does not require every building in a group to resemble every other one; it in no sense implies monotony in design (Figs. 586–588). Nor does harmony necessarily signify harmony of style. If one is planning a new building in an old college or a new dwelling in an old historical town, harmony does not demand that he design in the Gothic or Colonial manner of the older buildings in the college or in the Gothic or Classic Revival manner which characterizes the old town. What it does imply, in such a case as this, is the realization, first, that the qualities of the buildings already existing are *inevitably parts of the final effect which the new building will make in the group* and, second, that the sensitive architect must so absorb their quality—of color, material, shape, or what not—that they become part

FIGURE 587. WICKFORD, RHODE ISLAND. VIEW ON MAIN STREET

Harmony resulting from the simple development of a single constructional system and from similar colors and basic shapes.   Photograph Talbot Hamlin

FIGURE 588. LOUISBURG SQUARE, BOSTON, MASSACHUSETTS

Greek Revival harmony in New England.   Photograph Cousins, courtesy Essex Institute

FIGURE 589. TALIESIN, SPRING GREEN, WISCONSIN. VIEW OF CORNER
Frank Lloyd Wright, architect
Harmony with the landscape through sensitively designed shapes and carefully chosen materials.
Photograph Ezra Stoller

of the background of his mind while he is designing the new building and thus help, rather than hinder, the effect.

There are many possible bases for harmony besides harmony of style. There is harmony of scale, of materials, and of basic intellectual and imaginative approach, as well as harmony of color and harmony of general shape. Just as the sensitive abstract painter can harmonize, in one canvas, forms as diverse as angles and circles, so the sensitive architect can harmonize buildings just as modern as you please with an ancient town or a confused nineteenth-century college campus. The women's dormitory at the University of California, by Wurster & Bernardi and Harvey Corbett, associated, is a perfect example of this inner harmony between a modern building and a classic group; many of the most modern buildings in the Netherlands, too, seem perfectly at home

FIGURE 590. TALIESIN WEST, NEAR PHOENIX, ARIZONA
Frank Lloyd Wright, architect
The shapes and materials harmonize the building with the desert and the distant mountains.

Photograph P. Guerrero

among the rich brick fronts of seventeenth- and eighteenth-century buildings because of deep inner harmonies, in materials (brick and glass), in rich color, and in basic design attitude.

Harmony with the site also is a primary consideration in the case both of buildings and of the group as a whole. The relation of a building to contours, to views, and to existing vegetation does much to affect its appearance. The great natural factors of earth and water are among the most powerful visual elements in the world; if the designer follows with implicit sympathy the suggestions which they may give, earth and water themselves will do much to confer harmony upon otherwise diverse structures. For example, in both the Chicago Exposition of 1893 and the Paris Exposition of 1937 water served as the great binding and harmonizing element. In Paris especially this was true; not only did the river—the strong thread on which were strung the many separate and widely different exhibition buildings—lead inevitably from one

VIEW OF THE DANUBE

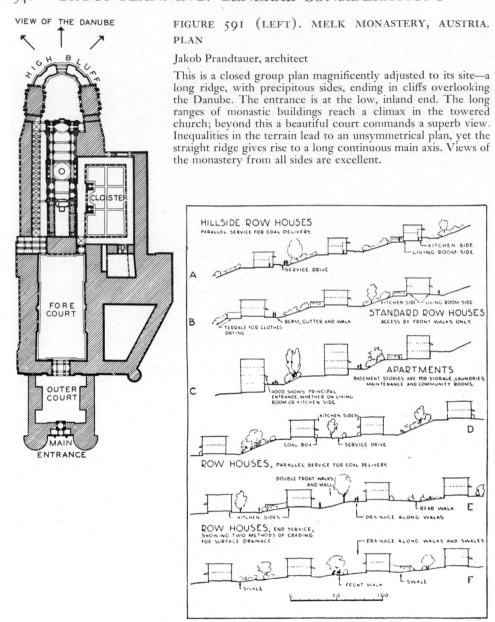

FIGURE 591 (LEFT). MELK MONASTERY, AUSTRIA. PLAN

Jakob Prandtauer, architect

This is a closed group plan magnificently adjusted to its site—a long ridge, with precipitous sides, ending in cliffs overlooking the Danube. The entrance is at the low, inland end. The long ranges of monastic buildings reach a climax in the towered church; beyond this a beautiful court commands a superb view. Inequalities in the terrain lead to an unsymmetrical plan, yet the straight ridge gives rise to a long continuous main axis. Views of the monastery from all sides are excellent.

FIGURE 592. VARIOUS ARRANGEMENTS FOR HOUSING UNITS ON A SLOPE

Difficult terrain frequently gives opportunities for solutions which, both practically and aesthetically, are even more successful than solutions for simpler problems. These studies by the Federal Public Housing Authority reveal ways of utilizing a hillside site.

From FPHA, *Public Housing Design*

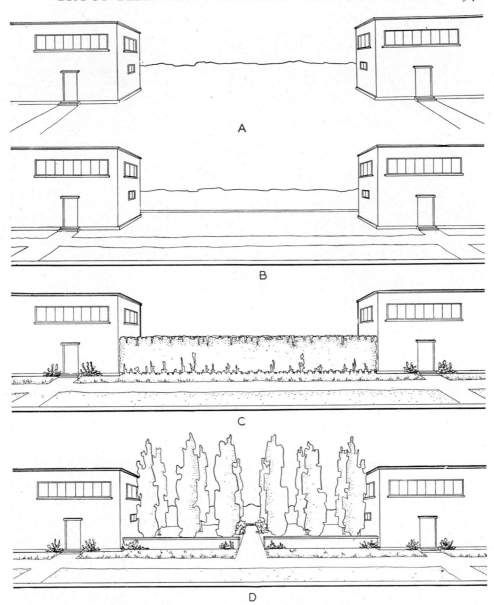

FIGURE 593. A FEW WAYS OF PRODUCING CONTINUITY

A: Despite the similarity of the two structures, there is little sense of continuity. B: The addition of paths, curb, and road, by stressing the sense of direction, assists the feeling of continuity. C: The use of a hedge gives an actual visual connection between the two structures, thus still further emphasizing continuity. D: A wall, with two rows of tall, narrow trees, emphasizes the continuity. In addition the path in the center, by giving a logical and visual reason for the wide separation of the structures, adds to, rather than subtracts from, the sense of continuity between them.

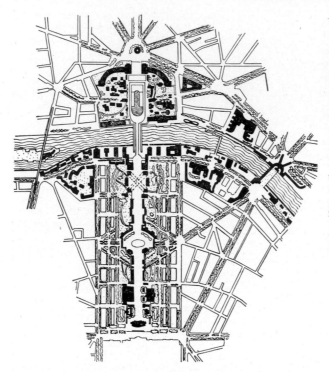

FIGURE 594. PARIS EXPOSI-
TION OF 1937. PART PLAN

This plan shows a skillful combination of formal and non-for-
mal qualities. The great axis
across the Seine through the
Trocadéro site and the Eiffel
Tower is strongly formal, emphasized by the great fountain
and basin, the bridge, and the
balanced national buildings. The
smaller, lower national buildings
that flank the basin are, however,
informally placed. Most of the
great exhibition buildings are informally stretched along the two
banks of the Seine but the river
forms a strong unifying tie between them.

building to the next, but also the sense of it seemed somehow to pervade all the
buildings and give them a basic and pleasant harmony. In much the same way,
strongly accented changes in grade—bluffs or cliff edges—or the undulating
lines of a curving valley may be used to bind together into an enduring harmony
a group of buildings which follows them simply and truly (Fig. 591). Many
river-valley towns in the Alps or in New England give proof of this, and the
hill towns of central Italy rising sheer from bluff or cliff teach the same lesson.
What may at first seem to be difficulties in the terrain for a proposed group may
well become one of the major sources of its harmony and its total effect; success depends only on the architect's ability to realize the opportunities which
rough and broken sites present to him (Fig. 592).

Harmony, then, is the first requirement for effectiveness in group planning.
It is a twofold quality and implies both the harmony of building with building
and the harmony between all the buildings and the site they occupy. Yet harmony by itself is not enough, as many real-estate developments of similar houses
indicate. Without other qualities, harmony alone may produce a stultifying
monotony.

Continuity. The principle of continuity is plainly a logical conclusion to be

FIGURE 595. PARIS EXPOSITION OF 1937. VIEW ON THE CROSS AXIS

The strong formal axis through the Eiffel Tower intersects the informal axis made by the river Seine.
Courtesy Avery Library

FIGURE 596. PARIS EXPOSITION OF 1937. VIEW ACROSS THE SEINE

The river acts as a powerful connecting feature between the structures that border it.

Courtesy Avery Library

drawn from Le Corbusier's dictum that every exterior is an interior. This is a recognition of the fact that the eye as it swings from position to position is continuously alert; it brings its message to the brain continuously, no matter what

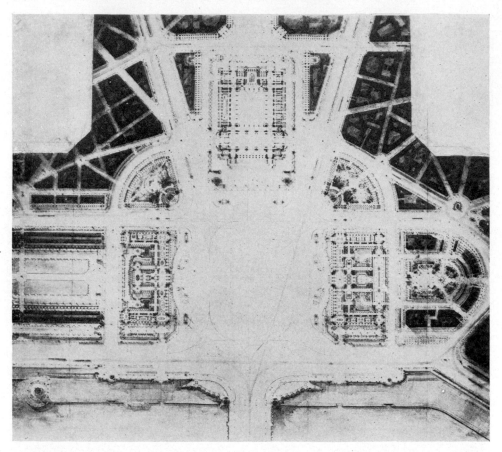

FIGURE 597. A GRANDE PLACE, COMPETITION PLAN FOR THE GRAND PRIX DE ROME
OF THE PARIS ÉCOLE DES BEAUX ARTS

L. Jaussely, architect

Pure paper planning, with unrealistic enrichments which in actuality would be meaningless if
not impossible.   From *Les Grands Prix* . . .

that message may be. In the well-planned group what happens between buildings is as inevitable a part of the composition as is the placing and the design of
the buildings themselves; moreover, the design of the group will be such, and
the relationship of its parts will be so close, that each building will seem to lead
to the next and no shock will result when the eye passes from building to space
and from space to building.

Here we must recall what was said in the chapter on sequence planning regarding both the time element in design and the fact that what one has seen
builds up expectations of what is still before him—expectations which must be

FIGURE 598. CIVIC CENTER, ST. LOUIS, MISSOURI. GENERAL VIEW
A grand plan, with unity frustrated by the volume of traffic pouring across it.

Courtesy St. Louis City Plan Commission

fulfilled to avoid frustration and unpleasantness. In group planning the time element is of even greater importance than in the planning of a building's interior because greater distances and more complex elements are involved. Greater distances to traverse mean a longer time expended in traversing them; if the units in a group are too distant from each other or too unrelated, one forgets what has come before and the relationships of the units become tenuous or invisible.

This is one of the points where a paper plan or even an air-view photograph may be most deceptive. One may arrange units on a plan into a pattern which has definite coherence and beauty, yet the group indicated by that plan may be completely ineffective because of the actual distances between its parts. Much group planning of the nineteenth-century eclectic type, like many of the group plans developed in those days in the major competitions of the Paris École des Beaux Arts, illustrates this quality. Jaussely's *Place Publique projet* is an excellent example (Fig. 597). As a paper plan it is a superb composition, rich, interesting, and coherent; as an actual construction it would be completely with-

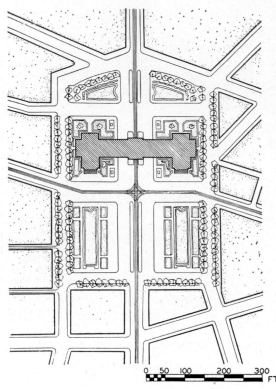

0 50 100   200   300
FT.

FIGURE 599. A CIVIC CENTER ONCE
PROPOSED FOR AN IMPORTANT
EASTERN CITY

A. W. Brunner, F. L. Olmsted,
B. J. Arnold, architects

This is an excellent example of the unfortunate result of the confusion resulting
from the attempt to put a civic center at
a point of traffic congestion. Here one of
the major transit intersections of the entire
city is at the center of the plan. Cross traffic would effectually disconnect the city
hall from the parked spaces in front of it,
and pedestrian approach would be difficult
and dangerous.

Redrawn from Gurlitt, *Handbuch des
Städtebaues*

out group effect. The little side buildings are so far away from the central and
climax building that any connection between them would be lost. With the
great open space in front of them filled with the hurly-burly of busy city traffic,
with automobiles charging in and out of the radial avenues and swinging madly
around the ends of the side buildings, one would be conscious only of danger
and of confusion. Each building would be a completely separate visual unit,
an island in the traffic; it would seem merely a fortunate accident, as one looked
across the public place in a quiet moment, that the building opposite was of
similar design. In actuality, buildings like these would appear to be separate and
distinct, and all the careful relationships of the three main elements so richly
indicated on the paper plan would be visually without effect. Such a plan, then,
lacks the quality of continuity and necessarily falls into pieces. The same difficulty has spoiled the potential effect of several modern civic centers—notably
that of St. Louis (Fig. 598), where a long plaza of monumental proportions is
chewed into separate fragments, each counting for itself and by itself because
of the traffic streets which cross it. (See also Fig. 599.)

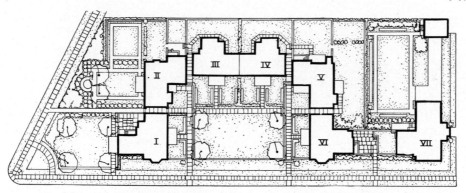

FIGURE 600. LINDEN COURT, ST. MARTIN'S, PHILADELPHIA. PLAN

Edmund B. Gilchrist, architect

Harmony of materials and a carefully stressed continuity make this suburban group of seven houses a most effective composition. Yet the whole is so arranged as to allow for a desirable individuality and privacy for each house and its garden. This is an imaginative answer to the difficult problem of suburban group planning.

To achieve continuity, therefore, we must think not only in terms of buildings, sidewalks, trees, and so on, but also in terms of their use. We must realize that types of continuity effectively achieved by units set in quiet and untraveled green might be completely ineffective if major traffic routes separated the buildings.

Once this fact is realized, the problem resolves itself largely into one of achieving continuity between adjacent buildings. Here we may suggest a natural corollary—the more dissimilar the adjacent buildings are in design, the closer they must be to each other in order to produce continuity. Where a building strikes one definite note with great power and the building beside it has the same general characteristics, the distances between them may be considerable, for each reminds one of the other and a psychological connection will thus be created between them. It ought to be obvious, too, that horizontal lines in the buildings will assist the feeling of continuity and make possible greater spaces between them than if a strongly vertical accent is present. It is noteworthy, for instance, that where gabled buildings have their eaves parallel to the street, as in the greater number of New England towns, continuity exists even though the distances between the buildings may be considerable. In the towns of northern and northwestern Europe, on the other hand, where the gabled ends face the street, continuity is assured only by having the units very close together.

It is a lack of continuity which accounts for the unpleasant character of

FIGURE 601. WASH-
INGTON SQUARE, NEW
YORK. NORTH SIDE

Continuity and harmony
give repose.

Photograph Bérénice
Abbott, courtesy Mu-
seum of the City
of New York

many American suburbs, even where the individual houses are large and expensive. In such localities the houses are often on lots of considerable size and
each house is designed as a completely separate entity. Here the buildings are
too far away from one another to count as a group, yet they are too close to
allow each to be judged on its own merits. In many cases each will be of a completely different character and style, although the houses may be close enough
to the street they face to become unavoidably parts of the same street picture.
Moreover, the gardening of each lot is usually handled in as individual a way as
is the design of the house. Thus there is absolutely no continuity between each
one and its neighbor, and the result is a feeling of aesthetic confusion and dis-
satisfaction. In certain suburbs of Philadelphia where all the houses use the same
basic materials—local stone and slate—the general effect is much more pleasant
because the harmony of material and color and the basic similarity of design
create a feeling of continuity, despite the distances between the units (Fig. 600).

Fortunately there are many methods of creating the feeling of continuity
in a group besides the design of the individual buildings (Fig. 593). Paths or
roads, if well designed, will do much to carry the feeling of continuity from
one unit to the next, and the material and color of these connections may also
become an important part of the group design. Long, unbroken motifs, such
as hedges, walls, and fences, may help enormously; the white picket fences of
New England bordering the tree-shadowed streets do much to produce the

FIGURE 602. A STREET IN NANTUCKET, MASSACHUSETTS

Harmony of form, materials, color, and function; continuity furnished by parallel eaves and roof lines, by curb and sidewalk, by closeness of buildings to street, and by picket fences and garden planting.

Drawn from a photograph by Talbot Hamlin

FIGURE 603. A STREET VIEW, NANTUCKET, MASSACHUSETTS

The continuity results from the horizontal ridges and the lines of sidewalk and fence.

Photograph Talbot Hamlin

FIGURE 604. CHESTNUT STREET, SALEM, MASSACHUSETTS

The arching elms help produce an inviting harmony and unity.

Photograph Cousins, courtesy Essex Institute

FIGURE 605. ROCKEFELLER CENTER, NEW YORK. AIR VIEW

Reinhard & Hofmeister; Corbett, Harrison & MacMurray; and Hood & Fouilhoux, associated architects

Close spacing and vertical emphasis produce harmony and continuity; the height of the RCA Building gives climax.   Photograph Thomas Airviews, courtesy Rockefeller Center, Inc.

feeling of harmonious continuity that one feels so strongly in many beautiful villages (Figs. 602–604).

Planting of other types is also of the utmost importance. The aesthetic purpose of planting in a group is not only to relate the building to the ground on which it stands and to produce some kind of over-all pleasantness but also to achieve a connection between adjacent elements within a group. It is here that

FIGURE 606. CHURCH ON THE COMMON, IPSWICH, MASSACHUSETTS
A powerful climax developed by position, color, and height.

Courtesy School of Architecture, Columbia University

American landscape designers, as a whole, seem to have been egregiously lacking; trained chiefly in the art of planting for individual buildings, they have failed to realize that in the art of planting for a group it is the group design which must always predominate. Architects, too, have frequently failed to make clear to their landscape-design collaborators the importance of this problem. That is the reason why the planting of so many recent housing developments in the United States is artistically wasteful. Trees are regularly spaced along streets or scattered freely over open areas, and bushes are banked around dwelling entrances; yet frequently this purely conventional pattern obscures views which should be open and leaves open some connections which should be closed. In group plans, trees and masses of shrubbery are as definitely a part of the over-all composition as are the buildings themselves, and their placing must be as carefully studied in relation to the desired effect as is the general arrangement and relationship of the architectural structures. Building groups in which the distance between units endangers continuity can frequently be welded into a powerful group unity by placing the correct planting between the buildings. Sidewalk trees are not the answer to every problem of landscape architecture, especially in the case of housing groups.

In using planting as an aid to continuity, it is well to remember that regularly spaced vertical elements, like poplars, are stronger than rounder or flatter types of trees. They seem to have a stronger architectural quality; they become, so

FIGURE 607. BELFRY AT
BRUGES, BELGIUM

In many European city squares the
town belfry acts as the climax.

Courtesy Avery Library

to speak, natural colonnades. In tropical countries, lines of royal palms have
the same quality; in the north, the tall trunks of the American elm, which spread
high up into arching foliage, seem to form, as it were, a sort of natural Gothic,
as strongly architectural as is the natural classic of the poplar or the cedar (Fig.
604).

It is for these reasons that the closest possible collaboration between architect and landscape architect should be sought in every group plan. The architect knows the basic visual patterns which his plan is aimed to produce, and
he must make absolutely sure that the landscape architect also understands them
and uses all the means of which he is in command to assist and not destroy the
basic concept of the group.

Climax. The problem of climax is complicated by the fact that group plans
fall naturally into two basic types. The first consists of those groups—usually
rather tightly knit, like town squares—in which the climax is of great importance and is highly stressed. The second type consists of groups in which all
the buildings have almost equal importance and the composition is likely to

FIGURE 608. HARLEM RIVER HOUSES, NEW YORK. ENTRANCE PASSAGE

Archibald Brown, chief architect; Heinz Warneke, Richmond Barthé, Theodore Barbarossa, sculptors

The climax value of this entrance pavilion is charmingly emphasized and humanized by the sculptures.

Photographs Charles Pierce

be loose and open, as, for instance, in a suburban housing subdivision or an urban housing group. Yet even here, if the group is to be aesthetically successful, some kind of climax or some succession of climaxes will occur.

The first type of group climax may be easily attained in one of various ways. The simplest is by mere size and bulk. Thus, in a group consisting of a number of similar buildings having more or less the same shape and the same treatment, if there occurs a building manifestly larger than the others, a feeling of climax will inevitably arise, and this accent must be considered both in the placing of the larger building and in its design. The second method is by height. As we saw in Chapter 3, on balance, high elements always possess a strong attention-compelling quality. If, therefore, it is necessary to make a climax of one of the smaller elements in a group, this can frequently be achieved by making that

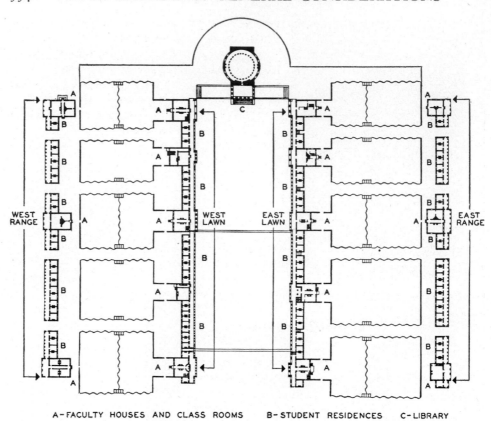

A—FACULTY HOUSES AND CLASS ROOMS   B—STUDENT RESIDENCES   C—LIBRARY

FIGURE 609. UNIVERSITY OF VIRGINIA, CHARLOTTESVILLE. ORIGINAL GENERAL PLAN

Thomas Jefferson, architect

A superb general plan, closely organized, and expressing Jefferson's theory of education. The library forms the climax because of position (at the end of a court) and shape (circular and domed); it is also placed higher than other buildings. The professors' houses, while similar in general shape, differ in detail and give variety. Close to them the students' rooms are placed behind connecting arcades; thus continuity is established. The lawn slopes gradually up towards the library with two banks to assist the rise. Behind the professors' houses lie their gardens, surrounded by serpentine brick walls but one brick thick, and the students' privies flank the walks between them. The Ranges are less continuous and less rich in detail than the Lawns; in this way the climax quality of the central area is stressed. Great trees on the lawns give richness and shadow, and the green of vegetation composes well with the red brick and white stone and wood trim. The whole forms one of the most beautiful of American groups for any purpose, and it contains many lessons for success in group composition.

building taller than the others and by emphasizing its vertical nature, or by the use of a definite tower. The use of towers as climaxes is common and, if well handled, almost always effective. The white steeples of early American towns, the city belfries in medieval communities, and the parish church spires of Eng-

FIGURE 610. UNIVERSITY OF VIRGINIA, CHARLOTTESVILLE. VIEW OF THE ROTUNDA

Thomas Jefferson, architect

The compelling interest of the dome form makes it admirably adapted to serve as a climax element.   Courtesy Professor Edmund Campbell

land all furnish strong and beautiful climaxes not only for the squares or open spaces on which they are placed but also for the communities as a whole (Fig. 606).

There is also a climax through position. The first climax position is naturally that at the end of any long vista or axis. The second is the climax achieved by placing the climax structure or object in advance of the general plane of the rest of the composition, as by using a projecting pavilion on a main building. The third climax position is attained by recessing the climax element behind the general plane of the composition. This is perhaps the strongest climax position possible, and it is the secret of the success of many types of successful group planning in almost all cultures. Thus the town hall or cathedral in a city, the main building of a college, or the community building in a housing group may be at the far end of a sort of court and will receive a strong accent because of its position (Fig. 610; also Fig. 72). The reason for this is twofold: first, the vanishing points of all the buildings along the sides of that court focus necessarily on a point behind them and in the center; and, second, a view into such a court suggests progression through it, and such a progression inevitably creates an expectation of some climax at the end. Yet this method of obtaining climax needs to be used with caution, for the simple reason that distant things appear smaller than near things; in designing the climax itself, therefore, one must always bear in mind the diminutions which result from perspective. (See Figs. 609, 610.)

The importance of framing a climax by some sort of flanking verticals has also been referred to in Chapter 3 (Fig. 70). It is well to keep the tremendous importance of this so-called gate-post principle in mind in complex group plans and to realize that, in many powerful groups of superb effect, not one but many methods of stressing the climax are used. The Governor's Palace at Williamsburg illustrates a powerful stressed climax in a small group (Fig. 72). Climax of position through recessing of the main building; climax of size because of the dominant mass which the main house possesses; climax through verticality because of the height of the main building and its cupola, with the whole reinforced and strengthened by the fence and the gate posts—these all combine to produce an effect of dignified and satisfying power, reposeful through its balance, pleasing in the way it fulfills all the expectations it creates. It is a simple group but one that contains lessons which may be applied to groups of almost any kind or complexity.

Just as in sequence planning, so even more in group planning, there may exist not one but many climaxes all related into one harmonious and meaningful pattern. In a community or a town, each changing view down street or walk will have its own climax; parks, public open spaces, and stretches where distant views may be enjoyed all offer climax points of varying degrees of importance. But in the really great community plan there will be some one climax stronger than any other. There will be one place in the group where the observer will instinctively think, "Here is the reason for it all. Here is the place where the community life is centered." As Albert Mayer said in his article, "What's the Matter with Our Site Plans," in *Pencil Points*, May, 1942:

Unity of Project and Dramatic Interest: The whole community must be the basis of design. We must get the sense of the build-up of individual homes into a community. We must avoid the endless, pointless, sterile rows of houses that don't reach a focus anywhere; but we must equally avoid the developer's overindividuality of interest which chops up his development into quarreling atoms, which is tawdry and meaningless, and which by violently avoiding monotony actually achieves a restless super-monotony.

We can achieve the unity and the drama which a community requires, in two ways. The community as a whole requires *some focus impressive in itself*, and heightened by a site plan which inevitably leads into it. This focus may be a community house, or a playground, or a fine grove of old trees, or a group of two-story houses in a one-story community.

Balance. When one walks through any group of buildings he receives a complex sequence of visual stimuli. He looks from side to side, he looks ahead. He is bombarded from all directions by a series of views which have varying degrees of interest. If he is free to wander, what line of passage will he naturally follow? He will inevitably take the path in which the amount of interest on either side of his passage is equal. In other words, the natural line of progress through any group is the line characterized by artistic balance. Thus it can be seen that balance is one of the most important factors in the design of the group, and one should, therefore, make sure that the progress from the normal entrance of the group to the center or climax is along an axis which has a balance of interest on either side.

In the consideration of sequence planning in Chapter 7, it was shown that an axis considered in these terms is neither a mere line on paper nor a convention of architectural drawing; rather it is the simple expression of two related concepts—the general sum of visual impressions and the natural line of progress. In group planning the considerations resulting from this definition of an axis are merely further developments of the same idea. As Le Corbusier states, the exterior is an interior. The group plan must therefore consider the relation of building, of trees, of masses, and of views in much the same manner in which the planner of the individual building considers the shapes and sizes of enclosing walls and the openings in them.

In the well-designed group, the balance anywhere, free or formal, will be such as to assist the functional connections and the desirable progress through the group. It will frequently be a dynamic balance which suggests and aids motion either straight ahead or to one side or the other. An equilibrium of balance in all directions will never be used except at the climax point, or points, or where the architect wishes the observer to stop or to rest. Just as in the complex building, so in many groups there will be many minor climaxes along the way—interesting views through to the outside of the group, fascinating glimpses down minor courts, or definite places for relaxation and rest by fountain or park or in front of a building door. In these places the balance will necessarily be more perfect, the sense of equilibrium more developed, than in other portions of the plan. Yet in the most successful group these minor points of balance will be subsidiary to the perfect sense of equilibrium developed in the major climax area.

The visual elements which constitute the aesthetic balance in the planning of groups are of great variety, and it requires a sensitive imagination to control them, to understand and evaluate properly their relative importance. This is perhaps the reason why many designers who are capable of creating individual buildings of interest and beauty sometimes fail in designing groups. They have been trained too much to think in terms of walls and windows, of glass and masonry; their imagination is limited to the comparatively dim scale of illumination found in the interiors of buildings and, as it were, stops at the edge of the actually constructed areas. The good group planner, on the other hand, realizes the importance of hill and tree, of skies and distant horizons. He knows where views beyond a property must be closed to hide that which is unpleasant or destructive of the feeling of the group; but he realizes equally well when the group must be opened to include the wider world, when a distant view may become itself a part of the architectural composition.

Here careful topographic models, as a basis for the study of group planning, may be both helpful and deceptive—helpful when they enable the designer to gain a truer and more real appreciation of the visual qualities of the group on its site; deceptive when the mere beauty of the model itself is accepted as the only criterion of the success of the executed work.

And it is especially in the problem of internal balance that group models are of the least help, for it is difficult if not impossible to gain from a miniature representation the actual visual impression which a person standing in the middle of a group will receive. His eye is seldom over five feet above the level of the ground, and it is his eye level which will control the position of all the vanishing points of what he sees and the resultant perspective angles, which, in turn, will have much to do with the sense of balance. Moreover, if the terrain is steep, it is difficult from a model to find out how much of the upper areas will be hidden from an observer below by the slope of the ground itself; only sections can check this most important quality.

Visual balance, whether formal or informal, can be achieved only by an imaginative study which makes use of all the means at the architect's disposal—models, sections, elevations, and perspective sketches. As an architect becomes more and more experienced in group planning, his imagination will become habituated to an almost intuitive appreciation of many of the desirable qualities. Naturally, he will need to check his imagination less by drawings than will the beginner; but even the most polished and experienced architect will usually make many rough perspectives and thumbnail sketches of bits here and there through the group in order to confirm and to reinforce his idea of what his imagination has created.

Functional Considerations. Group planning entails much more than the aes-

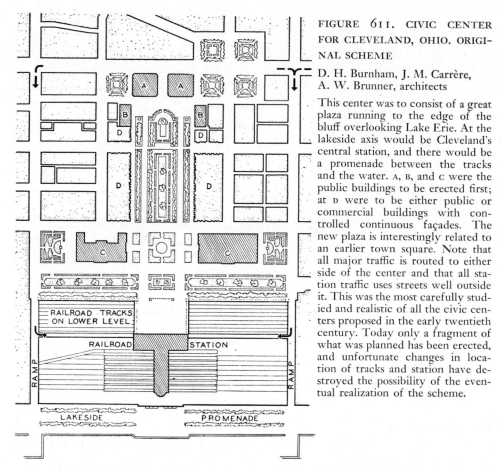

FIGURE 611. CIVIC CENTER FOR CLEVELAND, OHIO. ORIGINAL SCHEME

D. H. Burnham, J. M. Carrère, A. W. Brunner, architects

This center was to consist of a great plaza running to the edge of the bluff overlooking Lake Erie. At the lakeside axis would be Cleveland's central station, and there would be a promenade between the tracks and the water. A, B, and C were the public buildings to be erected first; at D were to be either public or commercial buildings with controlled continuous façades. The new plaza is interestingly related to an earlier town square. Note that all major traffic is routed to either side of the center and that all station traffic uses streets well outside it. This was the most carefully studied and realistic of all the civic centers proposed in the early twentieth century. Today only a fragment of what was planned has been erected, and unfortunate changes in location of tracks and station have destroyed the possibility of the eventual realization of the scheme.

thetic relationship of necessary structures. Just as the ideal toward which building design today is aiming is a structure designed for a specific purpose and achieving its aesthetic effect through the logical and imaginative relationship of its necessary parts, so in group planning the first purpose of the plan must be to achieve a group which performs its work efficiently and develops its aesthetic effect from the required relationship of its units. This functional consideration will affect group planning chiefly in two ways: first, in the relation of buildings to each other and to the lot; and, second, in the design of the means of communication between them.

The first of these—functional relationship of buildings—should be comparatively easy to determine. In a college group, for instance, common sense will tell the designer that dormitory and eating areas must be close together and

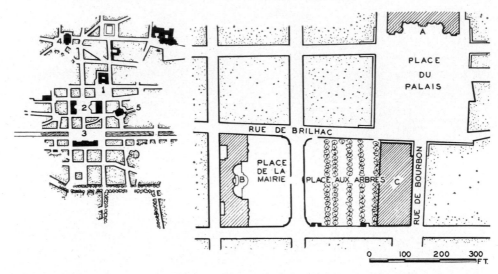

FIGURE 612. PLAN OF THE CENTRAL PART OF RENNES, FRANCE, AND A DETAIL OF TWO OF ITS MANY PUBLIC SQUARES

For the general plan: (1) Place du Palais; (2) Place de la Mairie and Place aux Arbres; (3) Place before the Palais de Commerce; (4) Church. Note how all the important public buildings have been given impressive climax sites, either at the head of streets or avenues or recessed back of open squares, or both; note, too, how at 5 a street intersection has been widened to furnish a site for a structure which is axially related to all the streets that approach it.

In the detail plan, the Place du Palais communicates at the corner with the Place de la Mairie and the Place aux Arbres. A is the Palais de Justice, B the Mairie, and C a theater. Surrounding buildings of uniform height enframe both open areas, and both have important public buildings as climaxes. The different views as one progresses through the streets and squares are rich and varied, yet coherent.

Redrawn from Hegemann and Peets, *The American Vitruvius* . . .

that kitchens will require greater service facilities than will the dormitories. Common sense may also indicate that the library might well serve as a kind of link between residential portions and those which are purely academic, such as classroom buildings or laboratories. Again, common sense will tell the designer that if there is to be a stadium seating many thousand people, to be used for spectacular public sports events, it would be silly to place it in such a position that approach to it was only through residential quadrangles. In industrial groups, shipping and receiving rooms must necessarily be closely related to main traffic facilities. Raw material must arrive at its final storage areas with the least possible carry from railroad, trucks, or ships. Finishing and assembly areas will normally be closer to the shipping room, just as the space for the first manufacturing process will be more closely related to the raw-materials

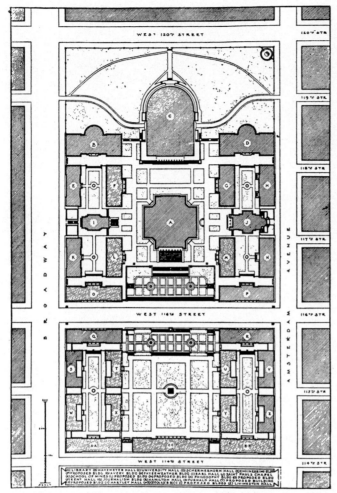

FIGURE 613. COLUMBIA UNIVERSITY, NEW YORK. PROPOSED GENERAL PLAN

McKim, Mead & White, architects

This plan, in large measure executed, is based on grouping the chief educational buildings north of 116th Street around the university library, A, and the gymnasium and proposed alumni hall, C; the chapel, J, and the social and religious center, I, are on the cross axis. South of 116th Street this plan called for a group of ten dormitories with a central dining hall and students' building, CC. A plan of strict formality was adopted as best expressing the impersonal, almost civic character of the university and its position in a rectangularly plotted city; yet the whole was so planned as to produce a number of small enclosed courts of human scale. This plan was predicated on removing athletic facilities to a distance. One minor criticism is the undefined and entirely open character of the axes formed by the broad walks at the sides of the library.

Courtesy Avery Library

storage areas. In Chapter 19, on the process of architectural planning, the general steps of functional analyses have been set down. These apply to group planning even more compellingly than they do to the planning of individual buildings. The correct functional relationship of buildings in a group will often have more than a merely practical value. For the greatest success, the arrangement must be functionally logical in order to be aesthetically logical. (See Figs. 609, 611, 614.)

Moreover, the users of any group feel the importance of the functional relationship of the buildings continually; hence any conflict between functional continuity and aesthetic pattern is bound to produce confusion and incoher-

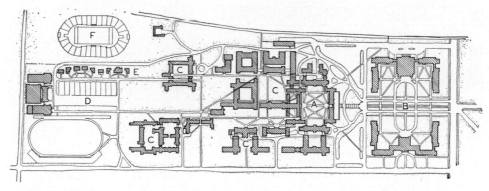

FIGURE 614. WASHINGTON UNIVERSITY, ST. LOUIS, MISSOURI. ORIGINAL GENERAL
DEVELOPMENT PLAN

Cope & Stewardson and Jamieson & Spearl, architects

A: Chief academic group; B: Public quadrangle; C: Student residential quadrangles; D: Athletic
group: gymnasium, tennis courts, and track; E: Fraternity houses; F: Athletic field.

This plan shows excellent handling of both functional relationships and traffic and pedestrian
circulation. Approach by automobile is easy to both the public quadrangle and the academic
group; service roads, using some underpasses, serve the residential areas, and a road encircles
the major group to give access to the athletic facilities at the rear. In general, pedestrian circulation within the group is entirely separated from automobile circulation. The group plan also
has marked qualities of harmony, continuity, and human scale.

Redrawn from Klauder and Wise, *College Architecture in America*

ence. Thus the climax of a group should be in some way the functional as well
as the aesthetic center. It might be the group element which serves more people
than any other single structure, or the one which is used more hours of the day
or more continuously. In a housing group, for instance, community buildings
might well form the climax, just as in many educational groups the library—
because of its importance to all types of education and because it is designed to
serve all the students—is frequently the climax. Functional characteristics of
buildings, therefore, are of major importance in the development of any group
plan, and the designer must see to it that the functional pattern and the aesthetic
pattern run parallel and do not conflict (Fig. 615).

The second way in which function affects group planning results from the
importance of communication and traffic, both within the group and between
the group and the outside world. This means that a careful study of traffic is an
essential part of the process of group planning. Such a study generally consists
of two major parts: first, the study of pedestrian circulation; and, second, the
study of automobile and truck circulation. In occasional, special groups—port
groups, piers, large-scale wholesale markets, and the like—railroad circulation
may also play an important part.

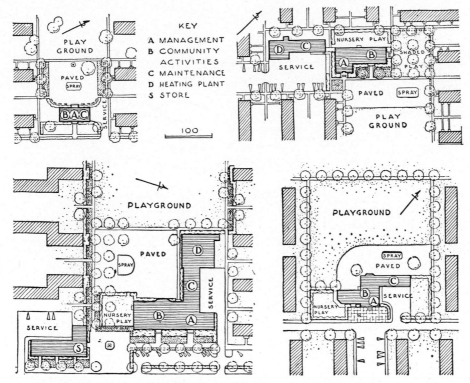

FIGURE 615. STUDIES FOR THE ARRANGEMENT OF COMMUNITY BUILDINGS

The complexities facing the designer of groups are well illustrated in housing design where problems of recreation, service, parking, and pedestrian safety must all be considered in the placing of every building. These studies by the Federal Public Housing Authority illustrate how they affect the shape and location of community buildings in housing groups.

From FPHA, *Public Housing Design*

The study of pedestrian circulation is comparatively simple. The designer must know how great a portion of the group inhabitants will proceed from place to place on foot; on this basis, the general widths of paths may be approximated. He must also know what communications between what buildings are desirable and which of these are used the most. He must also realize that people hate to lose time in circulating within a group; they hate to go around corners or to swing wide curves if it can possibly be avoided. Hence the designer will furnish straight-line communication from door to door so far as this is feasible, and he will not hesitate to use diagonal paths when they are necessary (Fig. 614). As a result, no time will be lost and the maintenance of the grounds will be made easier and cheaper. The most complete separation possible between pedestrian and automobile traffic is also of major importance. This may involve

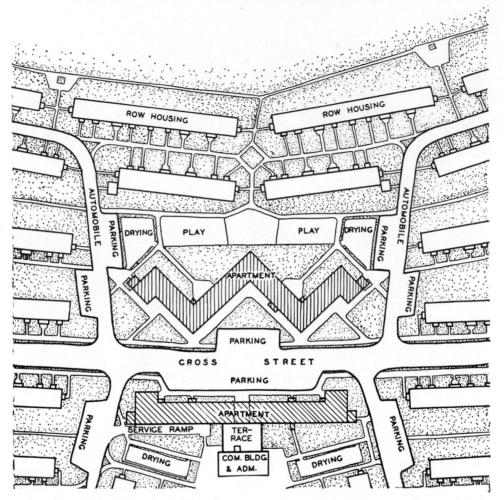

FIGURE 616. ELM HAVEN HOUSING, NEW HAVEN, CONNECTICUT. DETAIL PLAN OF THE CENTRAL PORTION

Orr & Foote, architects; Albert Mayer, consultant

This arrangement shows the importance of carefully planned circulation elements in the design of housing groups. Automobile traffic and parking, pedestrian circulation, drying areas convenient to apartment houses, and children's playgrounds are here all efficiently related, without confusion. The resultant visual effects are excellent.

two-level schemes, with overpasses or underpasses. But in the good group any pedestrian can go from place to place in it as he needs with a minimal crossing of roads or streets (Figs. 616, 617).

The problem of automobile circulation is itself a double one, comprising an adequate road arrangement both for the general public and for service. In some cases, separation of these two types will hardly be necessary—as, for instance,

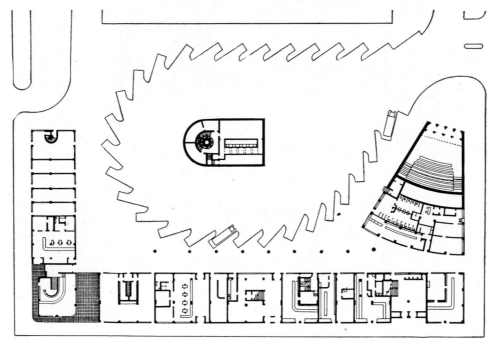

FIGURE 617. BUS STATION WITH SHOPS, HELSINKI

A successful group for commercial and transportation purposes. Automobile approach is along the exterior; the central area is reserved for busses, with a central service island. A cinema, shops, ticket offices, lunchrooms, and administration offices occupy the low surrounding structures.   Redrawn from Hegemann, *City Planning, Housing* . . . (Vol. III)

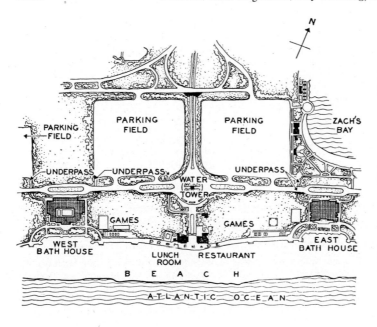

FIGURE 618. JONES BEACH, LONG IS-LAND, NEW YORK. PART GENERAL PLAN

H. A. Magoon, architect

Groups for mass recreation distant from cities require extensive parking areas. The two central parking fields are shown; note that there is underpass pedestrian circulation from them to the recreation areas. The whole is brilliantly arranged.

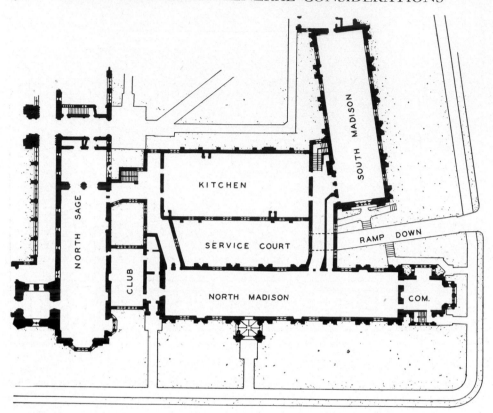

FIGURE 619. KITCHEN AND DINING HALLS, PRINCETON UNIVERSITY, PRINCETON, NEW JERSEY. PLAN

Day Brothers & Klauder, architects

A plan which enables a central kitchen building to serve four dining halls. Note the large service court reached by a driveway ramp. The service court is completely concealed from the exterior and the students' quadrangles, yet it is ample in size and airy.

FIGURE 620 (OPPOSITE, TOP). VALENCIA GARDENS, A PUBLIC HOUSING APARTMENT DEVELOPMENT, SAN FRANCISCO, CALIFORNIA

Wurster & Bernardi, architects

The small size of the lot, plus the necessary congestion, has forced the most careful segregation of uses and thus suggested a formal plan. Note the alternation between the garden courts and those devoted to service, laundry drying, and play and the way the service is concealed from the streets.

FIGURE 621 (OPPOSITE, BOTTOM). UNIVERSITY OF ROCHESTER, ROCHESTER, NEW YORK. PROPOSED PLAN

Gordon and Kaelber, architects; Charles A. Platt and Olmsted Brothers, consultants

A formal plan of great brilliance. There are separate, carefully studied circulation patterns for pedestrians, passenger cars, and service, with railroad approach to the Engineering School. Underpasses or overpasses keep the pedestrian traffic separate. The plan also allows for a future enlargement more than doubling the capacity, though the buildings first constructed form a definite composition.   From Klauder and Wise, *College Architecture in America*

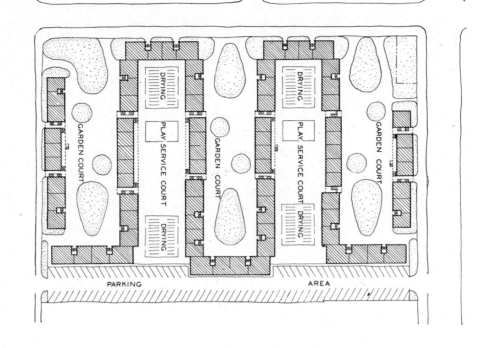

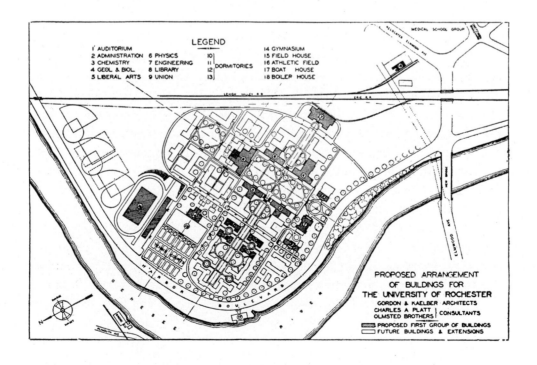

PROPOSED ARRANGEMENT
OF BUILDINGS FOR
THE UNIVERSITY OF ROCHESTER
GORDON & KAELBER ARCHITECTS
CHARLES A PLATT
OLMSTED BROTHERS } CONSULTANTS

LEGEND

1 AUDITORIUM
2 ADMINISTRATION   6 PHYSICS
3 CHEMISTRY   7 ENGINEERING
4 GEOL & BIOL.   8 LIBRARY
5 LIBERAL ARTS   9 UNION

10 }
11 } DORMITORIES
12 }
13 }

14 GYMNASIUM
15 FIELD HOUSE
16 ATHLETIC FIELD
17 BOAT HOUSE
18 BOILER HOUSE

in the normal house group. But in school and college groups it is desirable to have the two systems completely independent, and in many types of group planning—such as shopping centers—the most complete separation between ordinary automobile and service traffic is indispensable. Ordinary automobile traffic requirements not only necessitate a careful study of the placing and arrangement of roads, so that each element can be approached safely with the least effort, but also demand a careful consideration of essential parking areas. Here the specific uses of individual buildings will be the deciding factor. Some buildings, like auditoriums, places for large public assemblies, factories, or industrial groups of various kinds situated in the country, will require very large parking areas. Other buildings that are used by only a few people will require less. In some cases parking will hardly be necessary at all. Parking is a matter of ever growing importance, and, since it requires large areas of easy gradient, the placing and design of parking spaces may exert a tremendously strong influence on the entire layout of a group (Figs. 617, 618).

Separate service circulations are especially needed where the delivery of large quantities of supplies is an essential part of the group function. In the design of these service circulations, the planning of adequate loading and unloading areas and of service courts or truck parking areas is frequently as important a question as the layout of the service drives. Such areas are necessary for large kitchens, shops, factories, laboratory buildings, institutions, and so on. Since they are usually unprepossessing and often noisy, they must be placed with care and, if possible, screened from the general view (Fig. 619).

Still another traffic consideration which profoundly affects many group plans is the relation of the group to outside transportation facilities—to railroads, main highways, bus routes, and the like (Figs. 621, 668). The designer must ask himself: "Where do the people who visit or use the group come from? How do they get there? Will they come all at once or in smaller numbers over a long period?" The answers to these questions will frequently determine the position of the main entrance to a group, the minor entrances or exits, the desirable aspect of the buildings for public use, and the basic road and path patterns of the entire scheme.

It will thus be seen that group planning is an imaginative exercise of the greatest complexity. There are numerous factors to control, both practical and aesthetic. There are the topographic peculiarities of the site to transform into aids to effective group planning, instead of accepting them as barriers or limitations. There is the establishment of a correct and logical and functional order throughout the composition, in addition to the necessity of tying it all together by safe, simple, and efficient means of communication. There is the study of harmony in the group as a whole and of continuity between its varied parts. There is the problem of achieving the correct and dynamic balance and of the creation of adequate climaxes. Yet, however complex, these problems must be solved. All of them are under the designer's control, and it is through his careful exercise of this control and the play of his creative imagination, through which he is able to visualize the advantages and disadvantages of various possible schemes, that the successful group will eventually arrive—a group not only efficient and economical but orderly and beautiful as well.

SUGGESTED ADDITIONAL READING FOR CHAPTERS 20, 21, AND 22

The problems of group planning frequently interweave with those of town and city planning. Since there are but few works dealing specifically with the former, the list that follows is necessarily overweighted with books on town and city planning. Those of special interest from the viewpoint of group planning are distinguished by an asterisk.

Ackerman, Frederick L., and Wm. F. R. Ballard, *A Note on Site and Unit Planning* (New York: New York City Housing Authority, Technical Division, 1937).

Adams, Thomas, *The Design of Residential Areas* . . . Vol. VI of "Harvard City Planning Studies" (Cambridge, Mass.: Harvard University Press, 1934).

Curtis, Nathaniel Cortlandt, *Architectural Composition*, 3rd ed. rev. (Cleveland: Jansen, 1935), pp. 210–29.

Federal Housing Administration, *Architectural Planning and Procedure for Rental Housing* (Washington: Government Printing Office, 1939), pp. 21–25.

* Gromort, Georges, *Choix de plans de grandes compositions exécutées* . . . (Paris, Vincent, 1910), for examples of executed groups.

—— *Essai sur la théorie de l'architecture* (Paris: Vincent, Fréal, 1942), pp. 59–63.

Guadet, Julien, *Éléments et théorie de l'architecture*, 4 vols. (Paris: Aulanier, n.d.), Vol. I, Liv. III, Chaps. 3 and 4.

Harbeson, John Frederick, *The Study of Architectural Design* . . . with a foreword by Lloyd Warren (New York: Pencil Points Press, 1927), Chap. 28. From the Beaux Arts standpoint.

* Hegemann, Werner, *City Planning, Housing* . . . Vol. III, *A Graphic Review of Civic Art, 1922–1937*, edited by W. W. Forster and R. C. Weinberg, with a foreword by Sir Raymond Unwin (New York: Architectural Book Pub. Co., 1938).

* —— and Elbert Peets, *The American Vitruvius: an Architect's Handbook of Civic Art* (New York: Architectural Book Pub. Co., 1922).

Klauder, Charles Z., and Herbert C. Wise, *College Architecture in America* . . . (New York: Scribner's, 1929). For college group planning.

* Lanchester, Henry Vaughan, *The Art of Town Planning* (New York: Scribner's, 1925).

* Larson, Jens Fredrick, and Archie MacInnes Palmer, *Architectural Planning of the American College* (New York: McGraw-Hill, 1933). For college group planning.

Mawson, Thomas H., *Civic Art* . . . (London: Batsford, 1911).

Miller, James Marshall, "Site Planning . . ." [New York], 1941, typewritten manuscript in Avery Library, Columbia University.

National Housing Agency, Federal Public Housing Authority, *Public Housing Design; a Review of Experience in Low-Rent Housing* (Washington: Government Printing Office, 1946).

* Ponten, Josef, Heinz Rosemann, and Hedwig Schmelz, *Architektur die nicht gebaut würde,* 2 vols. (Stuttgart: Deutsche Verlagsanstalt, 1925). For examples of unexecuted projects.

Sitte, Camillo, *Der Städte-bau nach seinen künstlerischen Grundsätzen* (Vienna: Grasser, 1901); English ed., *The Art of Building Cities* . . . translated by Charles T. Stewart (New York: Reinhold, 1945).

Thompson, Francis Longstreth, *Site Planning in Practice* . . . "Oxford Technical Publications" (London: Henry Frowde and Hodder & Stoughton [1923]).

United States Federal Emergency Administration of Public Works, Housing Division, *Unit Plans* (Washington: Housing Division [1935]), Sec. III, "Site Plans."

* Unwin, Sir Raymond, *Town Planning in Practice* . . . (London: Unwin, 1909).

See also, in the present work, Vol. III, Chaps, 2, 4, 5, 6, 18; Vol. IV, Chaps. 48, 50, 51.

21

Group Planning II: Formal and Informal Groups

OF ALL the many classifications of building groups that seem especially fruitful, the first is their division into formal and informal groups; the second is their differentiation into open and closed groups. No extensive definition of formality or of informality in group planning is necessary here. The problem has been sufficiently considered in the discussion of sequences in Chapter 8. It ought to be obvious that many great groups, such as the imperial palace—the Forbidden City—at Peiping (Fig. 622) or the incomparable series of squares with which Héré de Corny decorated the city of Nancy (Fig. 623), are groups of the strictest formality, whereas other groups of equal beauty, like many of the market squares and cathedral places of medieval cities which Camillo Sitte illustrates,[1] are just as definitely informal. We therefore cannot judge the excellence of a group on the sole basis of whether it is formal or informal. At the present time the informal trend dominates. Formality, in fact, is at a slight discount among us. We have become so thoroughly imbued with the idea that organic forms based essentially on natural functions are unsymmetrical that we are often blinded to the equally valid truth that some problems are formal in their very nature. In order, then, to decide whether or not a given group should be formal or informal we must consider the problem with an open mind and from many different points of view. We must find out without prejudice whether the nature of a program will direct us to the symmetrical or unsymmetrical scheme, and in this consideration we must realize that the effect to be produced—an emotional effect that harmonizes with the essential purpose of the building—may itself be a part of the program.

First of all, then, our analysis must be based on questions of pure function, as outlined in the previous chapter. If, for instance, the program should call for an uneven number of buildings, where all but one are comparatively similar

[1] *The Art of Building Cities* . . . translated by Charles T. Stewart (New York: Reinhold Publishing Corp., 1945).

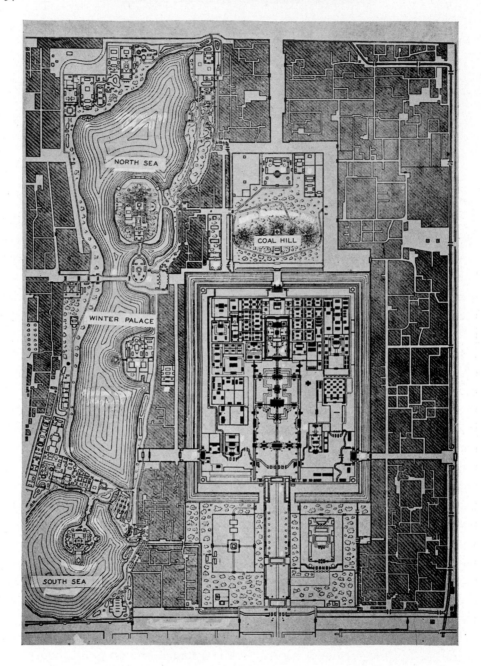

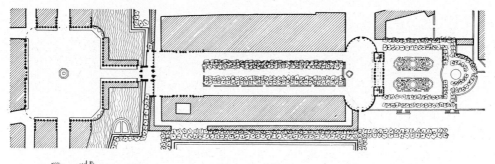

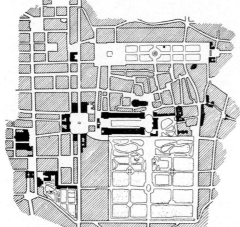

FIGURE 623. THE OPEN SPACES OF NANCY, FRANCE

ABOVE: Places Stanislas, de la Carrière, and du Gouvernement as originally planned; Héré de Corny, architect; BELOW: Center of Nancy today, showing the relationships of its many open squares.

The three squares in the upper plan form one of the richest and most satisfactory of formal European group plans. The Place Stanislas at the left is almost enclosed, with iron grilles at the corners and iron gates at all street entrances. The great Hôtel de Ville at its head (left) forms a strong climax; the L-shaped shops opposite are kept low and simple and act as a forecourt for the Triumphal Arch gate. Originally a moat flowed behind the shop buildings; this has since been filled. The long, narrow Place de la Carrière (center) is kept rigidly simple, and its clipped trees and quiet houses emphasize its connecting function. The hemicycles and Governor's Palace of the Place du Gouvernement (right) are smaller and more intimate in scale than the buildings of the Place Stanislas but rich enough to furnish a strong end climax to the entire group. This group is equally satisfactory in both directions and shows the power of exquisitely modulated formal planning.

FIGURE 622 (OPPOSITE). CENTRAL PART OF PEIPING, WITH THE FORBIDDEN CITY AND THE WINTER PALACE

One of the most effective group-planning compositions in the world. Note how informal lanes (*hutungs*) lead into larger streets of rectangular type and how the many little courts and squares give variety. Note also how the Forbidden City and Coal Hill are placed on the chief axial avenue that runs through the entire city from south (at the bottom of the plan) to north. The artificial lakes (North and South Seas), with gardened banks, surround peninsulas and islands on which are grouped the Winter Palace buildings; each group is strongly axial, but with a perfect adjustment to the site. In the Forbidden City two long entrance courts make a magnificent preparation for the lavish beauty of the palace to which they lead. As in most Chinese planning all the Great Gate buildings and halls are placed across the axis, an arrangement which gives climax importance to the one exception, the square imperial pavilion in the center. Even seen from a distance the great yellow roofs, one behind another, make obvious the line of the axis and form a powerful climax for the entire city. The contrast between the absolute geometry of the Forbidden City and the informal-formality of the Winter Palace increases the effect of both.

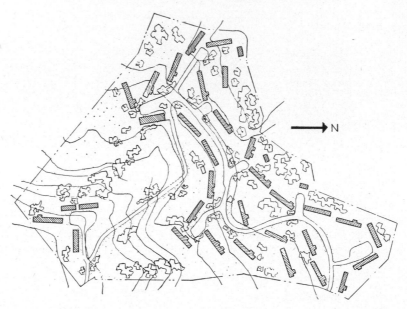

FIGURE 624. NEW KENSINGTON, PITTSBURGH (PENNSYLVANIA) HOUSING AUTHORITY. BLOCK PLAN

Walter Gropius, architect

Informal planning; row houses placed as the contours suggest, thus emphasizing the close relation of building and site. The houses at the bottom of the slope (left) have but slight relation to the rest of the group but compose with the steep slope behind them. The necessity of achieving a certain density has caused occasional congestion.

in function and size and where that one is more important and perhaps larger than the others, some kind of a symmetrical arrangement might well prove to be the only solution that would satisfy the functional needs. If, on the other hand, a site is broken and confused, with contours running diagonally across it or parallel to the line of entrance, the quality of the site itself might make any group of pure axial symmetry absurd (Fig. 624). Similarly, in a group where many buildings for completely different purposes are involved and where their sequence and relationship to one another are fixed by different practical needs— as, for instance, in the buildings of an industrial or manufacturing group—the practical necessities of arrangement must always dominate any attempt to impose a formal scheme. Such a group is likely to be informal in its very essence (Fig. 691). Another consideration which may affect the choice between formal and informal sequence lies in the intensity with which the group is to be used. A congestion of people on any site and for any purpose is likely to force a certain formality in layout in order to concentrate the usable areas and to make

FIGURE 625. NEW
KENSINGTON, PITTS-
BURGH (PENNSYL-
VANIA) HOUSING AU-
THORITY. GENERAL
VIEW AND DETAIL OF
AN ENTRANCE COURT

Walter Gropius, architect

An informal layout
closely adapted to a steep
and broken site.

Photographs Gottscho-
Schleisner

as definite and straightforward as possible the desired lines of progress through
the group. It may almost be stated that the greater the number of people who
use a given area the greater becomes the pressure toward formality of layout.

An excellent example of this relation of formality to intensity of usage may
be seen in the history of Bryant Park in New York, at the rear of the Public
Library, which has already been discussed in Chapter 8 (Figs. 241, 242, 626).
Although strictly rectangular in basic area, this park was originally a characteristic piece of informal, romantic, nineteenth-century park planning, with curving walks, trees spotted here and there, and shrubbery placed in picturesque
clumps. With the growth of the city, Bryant Park became the one green spot
in the middle of a heavily populated region of great shops and office buildings;
instead of the hundreds of an earlier period thousands now used it. And it be-

FIGURE 626. BRYANT PARK, NEW YORK. AIR VIEW

The repose and dignity which result from a direct treatment of logical formality.

Courtesy New York City Parks Department

came a center to which all sorts of vagrants came to enjoy its benches and its touch of green. With this increase in use, Bryant Park became impossible to maintain in its earlier form. People hurrying across it cut corners, and beaten paths destroyed the lawns. Vagrants and mischievous children plowed through the shrubbery, and bush after bush died. Little by little the old romantic park became a dreary waste of beaten earth, a few half-dead trees, and long rows of crowded benches that offered neither shade nor view nor comfort.

A new design became a necessity. What could be done to increase the usefulness of this area and yet make it a city beauty spot? The design adopted, based on the competition design by J. H. Freedlander, has proved supremely successful both aesthetically and practically. It is a design of the most forceful and symmetrical formality. Seating areas are arranged along three paths which border the site on three sides as well as on the old terrace next to the Public Library. This seating arrangement is formally planted with four rows of plane trees, which shade the benches excellently and form a strong green wall that shuts in the park from the surrounding confusion. Instead of grass, all the unpaved portions of the seating areas have a ground cover of almost indestructible

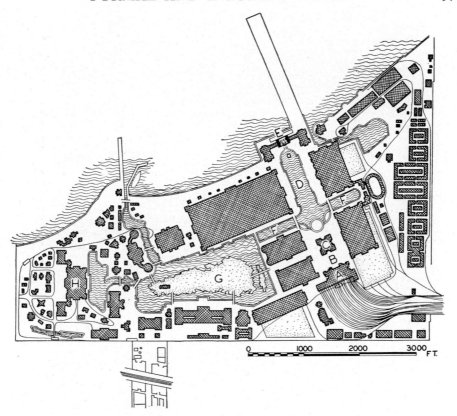

FIGURE 627. CHICAGO EXPOSITION OF 1893. GENERAL PLAN

A: Railroad station; B: Forecourt; C: Administration Building; D: Lagoon; E: Colonnade and Triumphal Arch; F: Waterway; G: Informal, wooded island; H: Museum of Fine Arts.

The basic division between formal and informal groupings is noteworthy, as is the use of water to bind the various parts together.

ivy. The sunken area in the middle is a green lawn; though there are steps down to it, they are so placed as to discourage any idea of there being short cuts across the park. By these means the seating area has been vastly enlarged and the satisfaction given by the sheltered feeling of the park increased. There is no traffic across the grass lawn, and there are unobstructed views from side to side and from end to end. The maintenance problem has been solved; what was originally a sore spot in the city has become an area of true beauty and greatly heightened usefulness. In this case only a formal scheme could solve the problems occasioned by the park's intensive use.

Formal groups inevitably will stress order, balance, and climax, for these qualities are inherent in the concept of formality itself. An examination of a series of outstanding formal groups should make this clear.

FIGURE 628. CHICAGO EXPOSITION OF 1893. DIAGRAMMATIC VIEWS

TOP: Looking at the Administration Building and the end of the water axis, F–F. Note the dominant height of the Administration Building and the minor climax element at the end of the cross water axis. CENTER: View looking from across the lagoon toward the open end of the water axis, F–F, showing how it serves to tie together the formal part of the exposition in the foreground and the informal portion in the background. BOTTOM: View along the main axis toward the chief climax, the Administration Building, from a point near E on the plan. Note the importance of the Statue of the Republic in the foreground as a preparatory minor climax and also the free balance across the main axis.

The phenomenal popularity of the Chicago World's Columbian Exposition of 1893 is evidenced by the influence it had upon the architecture which followed it (Figs. 627–632). It was the compelling effect of its formal plan, rather than the accident of its superficial style, which was largely responsible for this

FIGURE 629. CHICAGO EXPOSITION OF 1893. ADMINISTRATION BUILDING

Richard Hunt, architect

Courtesy Avery Library

FIGURE 630. CHICAGO EXPOSITION OF 1893. VIEW TOWARD COLONNADE AND LAKE

A. Atwood, architect of the Colonnade and Triumphal Arch

Courtesy Metropolitan Museum of Art

popularity. For the first time, hundreds of thousands of Americans saw a large group of buildings harmoniously and powerfully arranged in a plan of great variety, perfect balance, and strong climax effect. This vision of harmonious power was such a contrast to the typical confusion of the average American town of that era that the visitors were almost stunned, and the enthusiasm of their admiration bore witness to the success of the plan.

One entered through a railroad station, A, into a sort of vestibule court, B, a preparation for the grandeur that lay beyond. From there, one either progressed through the Administration Building, C, or passed by it on one side or the other into the great court; here the lagoon, D, filled most of the area; build-

FIGURE 631. CHICAGO EXPOSI-
TION OF 1893. VIEW UP THE
WATER CROSS AXIS TOWARD
THE UPPER BASIN

Courtesy Avery Library

FIGURE 632. CHICAGO EXPOSI-
TION OF 1893. VIEW DOWN
THE WATER CROSS AXIS
TOWARD THE INFORMAL LAKE

Courtesy Avery Library

ings which balanced, although they were not symmetrical, were ranged on each
side; an open colonnade stretched across the far end, E, and between its columns one was conscious of the level horizon of Lake Michigan beyond. Part
way down the length of this major court an axis at right angles to it opened
up, FF; at the end of that axis, on the right, was a building of great richness and,
on the left, an open view over an informal inner lake, with its green shores and
the white mass of the Fine Arts Building, H, as a minor climax. This connecting
of the more informal part of the Exposition with the more formal by means
of the waterway between the lagoon and the inner lake was most brilliantly
handled and gave a needed variety to the whole impression. The way in which
the waters of Lake Michigan itself were woven into the whole composition
—their broad sweep made an integral part of the Exposition—was also a stroke
of genius and an extraordinary contrast to the treatment of the Chicago fair
of forty years later, when a confused and incoherent collection of enormous

FIGURE 633. PLACE STANIS-
LAS, NANCY, FRANCE. VIEW
TOWARD THE CITY HALL

Héré de Corny, architect

Courtesy Metropolitan Museum
of Art

FIGURE 634. PLACE STANIS-
LAS, NANCY, FRANCE. VIEW
TOWARD THE TRIUMPHAL
ARCH

Héré de Corny, architect

Courtesy Metropolitan Museum
of Art

buildings turned their back doors to Lake Michigan and its beauty was all but ignored.

All through the Chicago Exposition of 1893 the handling of climaxes, both major and minor, was outstanding. From a distant view in one direction the dome of the Administration Building, c, formed a climax (Fig. 629). But within the central court more intimate and human climaxes were furnished by the great fountain at the inshore end of the lagoon and by the colossal figure of the Republic, backed by the Triumphal Arch, E, on the axis at the end toward the lake (Fig. 630). Everywhere the visitor found views, intimate or distant, which were satisfactorily balanced, with climaxes proportionate to their importance and with the balance so arranged as to suggest the correct progress through the Exposition. The whole formed a group plan of superb general composition.

Another extraordinarily successful piece of formal group planning is the succession of open spaces which Héré de Corny designed in front of the Nancy City Hall (Figs. 633–637). Here the City Hall, by Héré or Boffrand, faces a

FIGURE 635. PLACE STANIS-
LAS, NANCY, FRANCE. VIEW
OF CORNER GRILLE AND THE
FLANKING BUILDINGS

Héré de Corny, architect

Courtesy Metropolitan Museum
of Art

FIGURE 636. PLACE DE LA CAR-
RIÈRE, NANCY, FRANCE. VIEW
TOWARD THE TRIUMPHAL
ARCH

Héré de Corny, architect

Courtesy Metropolitan Museum
of Art

FIGURE 637. PLACE DU GOU-
VERNEMENT AND HEMICY-
CLES, NANCY, FRANCE

Héré de Corny, architect

Courtesy Metropolitan Museum
of Art

square—the Place Stanislas. On each side lie two buildings similar to each other,
with a street of approach between them; other important entrances come in
at the corners on each side of the City Hall. The side buildings have been kept
somewhat characterless in order not to detract from the importance of the City

Hall (Fig. 633). Their design would have no meaning whatsoever were these simply isolated individual buildings, yet it is superb in relation to the square which they flank. Opposite the City Hall are two L-shaped, arcaded shop buildings, one on either side of a wide avenue on the axis (Fig. 634). We thus get a continual stepping up from the low shop buildings, through the four flanking structures, to the climax of size, height, and richness to be found in the City Hall. A minor interior climax is furnished by the statue in the center of the square.

Since the streets leading into the square at the corners and at the center of the sides were wide, the designer thought it necessary to stress as strongly as possible the feeling of continuity across these openings. This he did by the use of lavish ironwork grilles and of lamp and gate posts (Fig. 635). In the corners by the shop buildings, where the new constructions originally faced a canal or moat, these grilles took the form of great quadrants with fountains in the center of each.

But this square is only the beginning. The avenue between the shops leads to the Triumphal Arch, and through this one enters the second of the open spaces, the Place de la Carrière (Fig. 636). In contrast, the Place de la Carrière is a long widened avenue, with formally planted and clipped trees in four rows down the center and a road on each side. Here again the architecture of the buildings has been made completely subservient to the desired group effect, for the rows of houses which border the Place and form part of the original design are kept completely simple, with nothing in them to disturb the sense of direction along the axis. Touches of rich ironwork here and there recall, or act as preparations for, the richness of the ironwork in the Place Stanislas.

The Place de la Carrière opens at its farther end into the entirely different Place du Gouvernement (Fig. 637). This has its long axis at right angles to the direction of the Place de la Carrière and is closed at either end by two beautiful hemicycle arcades tying in with the houses that border the Carrière. Its climax on the main axis of the whole composition is the exquisite Palais designed originally for the military governor of the area. The building is monumental and symmetrical though it possesses domestic scale, and it is tied in closely with the delicate design of the hemicycles. The central part of the ground floor is an open loggia, through which the palace garden can be approached; thus is formed a sort of coda—a pleasant diminuendo—to the whole composition.

These three squares taken together have a true symphonic quality—each is beautiful in itself but still subservient to the entire composition. The whole is

FIGURE 638. PLACE DE LA CONCORDE, PARIS. TWO GENERAL VIEWS

Jacques-Ange Gabriel, architect

Admirably designed both to separate traffic and to point up the intersection of two important axes.
Courtesy Avery Library

a formal scheme which can be entered at either end with almost equal satisfaction; it works both ways, and the terminal climaxes of the City Hall and the Palais are in beautiful contrast to each other—quite different in scale and treatment but perfectly adjusted to their respective positions. This is a formal piece of city beautification of striking variety and interest.

Many other important city squares that show the possible power and beauty of formal order in city design might be mentioned; only a few will be noted here. In the Place Vendôme in Paris there is almost a complete sense of enclosure, with minor climaxes in the pedimented buildings at the corners and the major climax in the center. Originally this larger climax was an equestrian statue; the present column, although a more powerful climax, is too heavy in scale for the size of the square and therefore oppressive in its relation to the surrounding buildings.

The Place de la Concorde (Figs. 638, 684, 685) owes its effect not so much to its buildings as to the general plan and the firm design of its balustrades, fountains, and enframing greenery. These, however, give still more emphasis to the two buildings at the head of the Place, and they in turn act as framing elements for the Madeleine beyond them. At the other end the main axis is now closed by the great portico of the Chambre des Députés. The whole, in its breadth of conception and its magnificence of detail, has sometimes been called the most beautiful city square in the world. The one adverse criticism that can be made is that the Madeleine was placed too far back from the plane of the flanking buildings, and consequently its climax effect is somewhat reduced.

A third of these outstanding formal squares is a group of related open areas in Copenhagen called the Amalienborg (Figs. 639, 640). Here on a much smaller scale is some of the same kind of rich symphonic composition to be found in Nancy. Especially rewarding is the handling of the octagonal *place* with its "gate post" buildings framing the axial views; equally satisfying is the balance between the two views along the main axis—one over the harbor and the other up a wide avenue to a domical church, the Frederiks-Kirke.

The Chinese have always been devoted to superbly formal group plans. The entire city of Peiping, built on a great main axis seven miles long, reveals how the formality of the conception can give both form and meaning to an entire metropolis; this is the reason why many people have considered the old Chinese capital one of the greatest, if not the greatest, architectural city in the world. Peiping, like the Chicago Exposition of 1893, shows the richness to be obtained from a combination of formal and informal elements related to each other by a controlling scheme in which formality is dominant. The old houses are formal

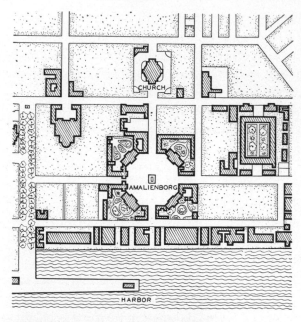

FIGURE 639. AMALIENBORG
PLACE, COPENHAGEN. PLAN

A closely knit, beautifully detailed element in the city plan, of a type useful only in residential districts where there is little traffic. Four streets approach the octagon and enter it between buildings that serve as gates; a statue is in the center. At the end of one of these streets is a domed church, set in its own little square; opposite it is a view of the harbor. The whole is formal but gracious, with an inviting human scale—formality that is not oppressive.

FIGURE 640. AMALIENBORG PLACE, COPEN-
HAGEN. AIR VIEW

Gracious formality at human scale for the residential portion of a city.

Courtesy School of Architecture,
Columbia University

in general plan, and through them all runs the harmony of the Chinese planning ideal, already referred to (page 199). Gardens, on the other hand—big and

FIGURE 641. IMPERIAL PALACE (THE FORBIDDEN CITY), PEIPING, CHINA. CHIEF GATEWAY

The impressive formality prepares one for the grandeur within.

From Imperial Museum, Tokyo, *Photographs of Palace Buildings of Peking*

FIGURE 642. IMPERIAL PALACE, PEIPING, CHINA. A COURT

Axial formality controls the impressive effect.

From Imperial Museum, Tokyo, *Photographs of Palace Buildings of Peking*

little, from the smallest house garden to the great park of the palace—are carefully and exquisitely informal. The tiny streets which lead to most of the houses are often curving and informal also, but they all lead out to wide straight ave-

FIGURE 643 (ABOVE). IMPE-
RIAL PALACE, PEIPING, CHINA.
GENERAL VIEW

The existence of one great axis is
expressed by the roofs of the larger
halls which cross it.

From Sirén, *The Imperial Palaces
of Peking*

FIGURE 644 (LEFT). BELL
TOWER, PEIPING, CHINA

Like the Drum Tower, the similar
Bell Tower is astride the main axis
of the city.

From White, *Peking the Beautiful*

FIGURE 645. WINTER PALACE, PEIPING, CHINA. VIEW ACROSS THE LAKE TOWARD THE ISLE OF JEWELS

Small formal groups informally related on a picturesque site.

From H. von Perckhammer, *Peking*

nues and in that way relate to the strong pattern of the who!e. The central avenue, the axis of balance, is emphasized by the height of the towers and the size of the buildings upon it. At its southern end it is flanked by two great temples balancing each other, the Temple of the Sun and the Temple of Agriculture. Just north of the center of the axis is the Forbidden City, the great imperial palace, gorgeous with burnt-sienna walls, dark red columns, and yellow tile roofs. Behind the palace the central axis climbs to a secondary climax on the artificial Coal Hill, crowned by five pavilions; behind this, again, there are still two more minor climaxes, the Drum Tower and the Bell Tower.

It is noteworthy—and one of the reasons for the richness of Peiping—that one is not allowed to progress along this main axis throughout its length; he is forced continually to the side by buildings across it, yet the visual impression of the axis is always present. This arrangement gives a great variety as well as a certain sense of mystery to the whole. Everywhere, important axes are crossed by ridge after ridge of the roofs of the buildings that intersect them, and this

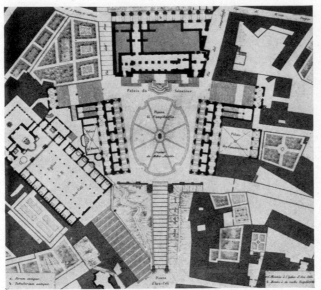

FIGURE 646. CAMPIDOGLIO, ROME. PLAN AND BIRD'S-EYE VIEW

Michelangelo, architect

A formal group of great yet subtle power. The Senatorial Palace door at the head of the group is raised above grade to count strongly. The central climax is accented by the sculptured groups at the top of the ramp, by the ends of the flanking museums, and by the old campanile. Inside the square, the fountain and the step walls of the Senatorial Palace form a dramatic climax; a minor interior climax is furnished by the equestrian statue. The contrast between the architectural treatment of the climax building and that of the flanking structures helps the effect.

From Letarouilly, *Les Édifices de Rome moderne*

bold stress of the axes by these definite stopping elements is one of the secrets of Chinese formal planning (Figs. 622, 641–645).

Formal group planning, in its stress on order, on balance, on climax, and on

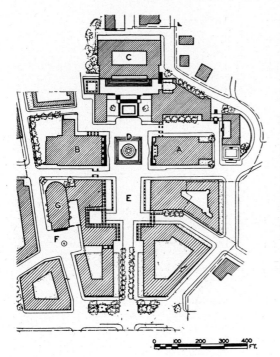

FIGURE 647. CENTRAL SQUARE AND CIVIC CENTER, GÖTEBORG, SWEDEN

A formal composition of great richness. The museum, c, is at the end of the main axis; in front of it the rich Milles fountain, D, acts as an interior climax and also ties the museum to the theater, B, and the concert hall, A. The forecourt, E, with its bordering façades, acts as a strong preparation for the whole. An earlier church, G, has its own little square, F, in the traditional medieval manner. All heavy traffic is routed outside the main group, but cross streets and courts allow ample automobile approach to all buildings without disturbing the quiet of the central square, which is largely pedestrian. The whole forms one of the most successful of modern civic centers because of its visual harmony and continuity, its strong climaxes, and its basic plan.

conscious design, necessarily establishes a feeling of something greater in scope than individual charm. Through careful balance it produces many areas of repose. It arouses occasionally a sense of exhilaration and of inspiration, because it reveals the power of human beings working together to impose dignity and order on the chaos of existence. A formal scheme is to be used, therefore, where such feelings are appropriate. (See also Figs. 627–648.)

The basis of informal group planning lies in the absence of symmetry, in the frequent use of changing or curving axes, in the variety of structures forming the group, and in the more informal and less definitely stressed quality of climax (Fig. 651). Just as formal groups almost necessarily have in them something of the impersonal, so good informal groups are likely to be more personal, more closely related to the individual. They seek for intimate charm. They may be full of minor climax elements—places for quiet rest or view—and thus they frequently possess a greater variety of visual aspect than do formal groups (Fig. 691).

In this quality of variety and the accompanying feeling of change and motion lies one great danger in informal group design—the danger of lack of unity, of incoherence. One cannot sprinkle buildings over a lot merely in accordance with considerations of convenience of approach or of fitness to site and expect

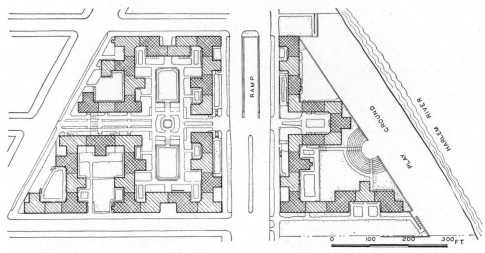

FIGURE 648. HARLEM RIVER HOUSES, NEW YORK. PLAN

Archibald Brown, chief architect

This group has one of the most successful group plans of any of the urban housing developments. It is formal but not forbidding, and its scale is reduced to intimate and human proportions
by the rhythmically projecting wings. Seventh Avenue divides it into two almost separate portions, and only the strong axis of 152nd Street ties them together. Pedestrian circulation throughout is well arranged and visually attractive, and the planting is unusually carefully designed for
good architectural effect and easy maintenance. The whole forms a charming environment for
living and is a definite addition to New York's beauty.

to create a good informal group plan. It is, in fact, much more difficult to produce a really effective informal group plan than it is to design a good formal
one, because there are many more elements to be controlled and, furthermore,
a higher order of visual imagination is needed to control them satisfactorily.
Just because of the variety involved, the quality of order must be stressed as
strongly as possible (Figs. 654, 655). Harmony and continuity are also of
primary importance in informal groups. The monotonous and confused ugliness of many suburban developments laid out on an informal basis is most often
caused by a lack of harmony between adjacent buildings and an almost complete lack of continuity.

But this stress on unity, harmony, and continuity is only the beginning of
good informal group planning. Even more complex is the problem of achieving that kind of dynamic balance throughout which will confer upon the
whole a pleasant feeling of rightness. As has already been shown in the study
of sequence planning, the sense of balance within a plan has much to do with
the direction of progress through the whole design. In informal group plans this
problem is one of prime importance. Where the axes are curved, the balance

FIGURE 649. TOWN
SQUARE, SIENA, ITALY

Informal plan with strong climax.

Courtesy Avery Library

FIGURE 650. PIAZZA
DELL' ERBE, PADUA,
ITALY

Informality of outline and differences in the enclosing buildings do not interfere with unity and coherence.

Courtesy Ware Library

across an axis must be a dynamic balance, which aids the circulation around the curve. Everywhere through the plan this problem of free balance must be in the designer's mind. In group plans of this type the elements which establish balance will also be complicated. One may, for instance, achieve a certain balance between buildings close together on one side of an axis and open views on the other. One may have a balance between a hillside rising on one side of a road or path and a retaining wall or slope falling away on the other side. Positions of tree groups and shrubbery demand the most careful consideration in creating the desired balance. In climax treatment, also, the problem in informal

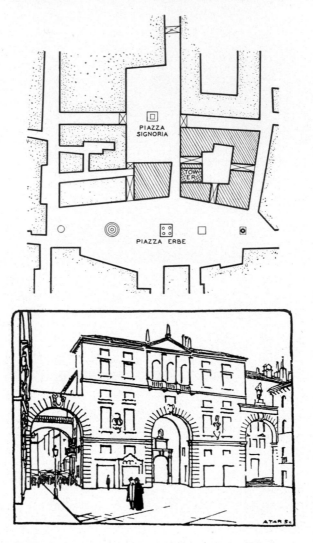

group planning is likely to prove more difficult than it is in the case of more formal groups. The informal group will frequently have many small elements of minor climax, yet the perfect group will be so designed that these minor climaxes are merely rests on the way and in no sense destroy the final and dominating climax.

The best examples of this type of treatment are undoubtedly to be found in many medieval towns and small cities, especially in hilly country. In almost all of them there are little open spaces (where streets have been widened) or smaller squares which offer minor climax points; there may be open places be-

FIGURE 651 (OPPOSITE AND ABOVE). PIAZZA DELL' ERBE, VERONA, ITALY

A characteristic informal Italian *piazza*, with close relationship to a second open space, the Piazza della Signoria. There is informality in the lack of symmetry and in the variety in the surrounding buildings, but the composition is firm; the tower is a visible climax to both squares.

Plan redrawn from Sitte, *The Art of Building Cities*
Views from Hegemann and Peets, *The American Vitruvius . . .*

fore small parish churches. Yet all of these will be subordinate to either the market square or the cathedral square, which becomes the true climax in the true town center.

English architects and city planners have been generally more skillful in this kind of informal planning than have the designers of the United States. Such compositions as Hampstead Garden Suburb in London (Figs. 654, 656) or Wellhall in Greenwich are characteristic. Here the houses are ranged along the streets with a complete naturalness. They have personality and charm in their groups; there is in the composition nothing of the obviously imposed or the formal. Nevertheless, in them all one will find pleasure in balanced views; the ends of streets and vistas are always composed with subtle and definite minor climax elements. Street intersections are handled with a conscious regard for their appearance from any point of view. The result is unusual satisfaction to anyone who walks around such developments; there is no strain.

This careful thought of the English for informal street composition in a group-plan problem has had a wide influence, especially on many of the best architects and town planners in pre-Hitler Germany. The suburbs built around Frankfurt am Main under the general direction of Ernst May, for instance, are almost all of them outstanding examples of carefully designed informal group

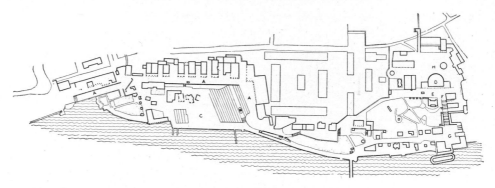

FIGURE 652. STOCKHOLM EXPOSITION OF 1930. GENERAL PLAN

E. G. Asplund, architect

A revolutionary exposition plan laid out along the edge of a lake. The general public circulation, A–A, leads by the exposition buildings, commanding a view over the lake and the lower-level terrace, c, which was used for dramatic and dance presentations. At the head of this circulation, overlooking the informal terraced seats, was a restaurant. All buildings were obviously temporary, with the lightest possible posts and a great use of textiles and bright colors. Smaller buildings were grouped along the shore and on a higher terrace, H. Note that here there is slightly greater formality and a careful placing of buildings (G, F, E, D). In even the most informal parts of the group, however, there is never incoherence; continuity is stressed, as well as the harmony of type and general form, and the views presented to one following the walks are all exciting and composed.

FIGURE 653. MINISTRY OF SUPPLY WAR HOUSING (JELLICOE SCHEME), ENGLAND

Quiet formality in plan with careful placing of units to achieve visual coherence.

Courtesy British Information Service

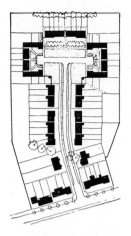

FIGURE 654 (LEFT). A CUL-DE-SAC ON ASMUNS PLACE, HAMPSTEAD GARDEN SUBURB, LONDON

Parker & Unwin, architects

Informal approach to a quiet and symmetrical interior group. The curved road gives changing views climaxed at the end by balance and repose.

Redrawn from Unwin, *Town Planning in Practice*

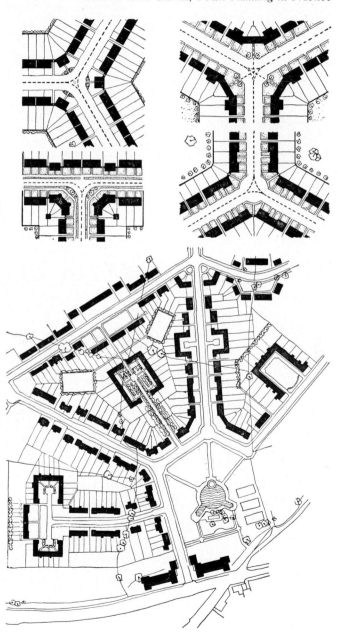

FIGURE 655 (RIGHT). ROAD INTERSECTIONS

Sir Raymond Unwin, architect

Studies to show how variety, interest, and axial climax can be produced where roads come together.

Redrawn from Unwin, *Town Planning in Practice*

FIGURE 656. CENTRAL PORTION OF HAMPSTEAD GARDEN SUBURB, LONDON

Parker & Unwin, architects

This is one of the most skillful subdivisions ever planned. Pleasantness and variety of well-composed views are obvious. Interior and public open spaces and buildings are well balanced, and cul-de-sacs are used to make large superblocks economical, yet traffic is simple and direct. There is a most interesting combination of formality and informality.

Redrawn from Unwin, *Town Planning in Practice*

FIGURE 657. VIEW IN
EDGARTOWN, MASSA-
CHUSETTS

Informal placing of
houses at an angle to the
street gives variety without destroying harmony
or coherence.

Photograph
Talbot Hamlin

FIGURE 658. ST. HELIER HOUSING ESTATE, LONDON
London County Council Architectural Office, architects
The pleasant, inviting, and harmonious grouping typical of many English housing developments.
Courtesy British Information Service

planning, and May was a disciple of Unwin. The famous housing group of Römerstadt (Fig. 659) has great human charm in the handling of its curving streets on a hillside and in its careful consideration of free balance between buildings and of wide views across the Nidda Valley. The best American example is probably the town of Greenbelt in Maryland (Figs. 660, 661). Here there is a beautiful sense of informal order and a charming balance between

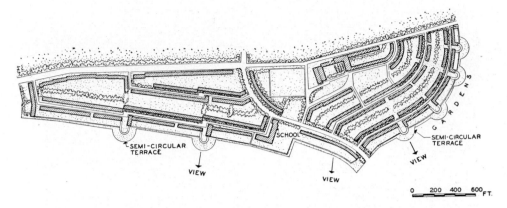

FIGURE 659. RÖMERSTADT, NIDDA VALLEY, NEAR FRANKFURT AM MAIN, GERMANY. PLAN

Ernst May, chief planner

This housing development built on the sloping sides of the Nidda Valley follows the contours closely. Its curved streets and the breaks in the building frontage give great interest, and there are many places where the view across the valley is used to furnish minor climaxes.

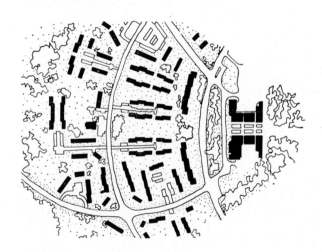

FIGURE 660. CENTRAL PORTION OF GREENBELT, MARYLAND

This plan shows the strong axis developed through the center of Greenbelt and running through the open court between community buildings at the right. Here the axis is not closed, and there is not sufficient visual climax. For this reason the actual effect is less satisfactory than it might have been had a climax been furnished.

building and vegetation. Good earlier examples can be seen in some of the suburbs of Philadelphia, where the widespread use of local stone gives harmony of color and of material to the houses, and general similarities of basic form help the feeling of continuity. Some of the residential groups in this region designed by Edmund Gilchrist are especially worthy of note (Fig. 600).

Certain housing groups erected in fairly recent years, either under government auspices or with government assistance, have also achieved true informal

FIGURE 661. GREENBELT, MARYLAND. AIR VIEW AND DETAIL OF ONE COURT
Ellington & Wadsworth, architects; Hale Walker, town planner
An excellent example of the pleasant spacing of buildings   Courtesy Library of Congress

beauty (Figs. 662, 666). The Elm Haven housing development in New Haven (Figs. 616, 663) has many elements of charm in its row-housing sections, and the handling of the curved walk at one end of the project is especially good.

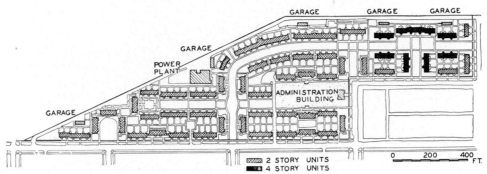

FIGURE 662. TRUMBULL PARK HOMES, CHICAGO, ILLINOIS. PLAN

William Holabird, chief architect

This is one of the best of the earlier Federal housing developments, distinguished in its combination of straight and curved lines and in the subtle climaxes furnished by the administration building and the four-story apartments. Formality of detail gives occasional accent to a charmingly free and natural arrangement.

The housing group at Coatesville, Pennsylvania, is also interesting. Yet the greater number of good examples in the United States seem to be in the western part of the country. The Channel Heights development in California is an unusual and successful example of the solution of a difficult site problem, and among the more expensive groups Wyvernwood and Baldwin Hills Village, both in Los Angeles (Figs. 665, 666), are outstanding. In a slightly different class the Buhl Foundation housing development in Pittsburgh (Fig. 667) is a remarkable small group, of real charm and human quality, where harmony, continuity, and balance have all been handled with unusual sensitiveness.

How, then, is one to choose between formality and informality in any given problem of group planning? The decision must be made on at least two, and possibly on three, bases. The first is the basis of pure functional logic. That is, in any group plan, every building must first of all be in the correct and logical position which its use indicates. Any attempt to violate this first principle for the sake of imposed effect is doomed to destroy the effectiveness of a group (Fig. 671). Some groups fall naturally and logically into formal patterns; in others the function of the buildings is such that informality inevitably follows. We must not allow any merely personal preferences for one type over the other to confuse our decision in this matter of functional logic. Such an arbitrary choice of either formality or informality leads to the development of false formalities or false axes which get nowhere, or, on the other hand, it leads to false informalities, because as our taste changes we tend arbitrarily to like

☐ ROW HOUSES   ▓ APARTMENT HOUSES

FIGURE 663. ELM HAVEN HOUSING, NEW HAVEN, CONNECTICUT. PLAN

Orr & Foote, architects; Albert Mayer, consultant

One of the most interesting of United States Housing Authority projects, limited in plan by the necessity of carrying a city street through the center of the area. On this the community center is placed. There are apartment houses here, and also on the exterior street; row houses elsewhere. Specially interesting elements are the following: subtle changes in the angle of the rows; the two passages through house rows; the long curved "street," with the central third of its length reserved for pedestrian traffic, at the left end of the plan; the general closing of vistas; the careful preservation of existing trees; the closely knit integration; and the occasional touches of slight formality which give definiteness to the whole. Views almost everywhere within the project are varied yet coherent, and the whole gives a pleasant feeling of repose. The concentrated open areas create a deceptive feeling of spaciousness. See also Figure 616.

the free patterns of abstract art rather than the more normal patterns of the classic.

The second great basis of choice is the type of emotional effect which is appropriate to the purposes of the group. Wherever we wish to achieve an ex-

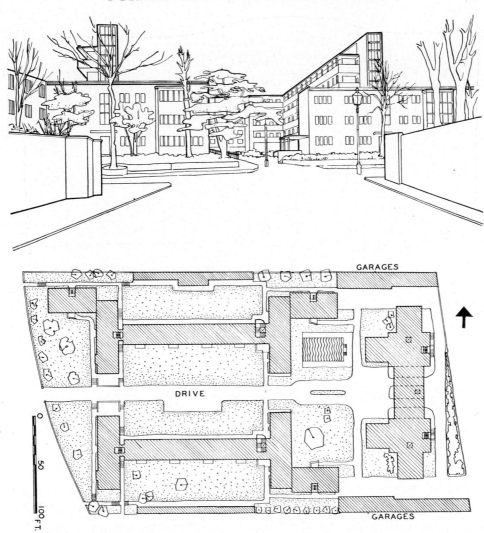

FIGURE 664. PULLMAN COURT APARTMENTS, STREATHAM, LONDON. VIEW AND PLAN

Frederick Gibberd, architect

Here is a most interesting example of flexible formality in group arrangement. The formality allows the most efficient use of the site. Flexibility is achieved by keeping all the units carefully oriented, so that the symmetry is of mass only, details and fenestration differing on the two sides of the main axis. The effect is both coherent and full of interest.

pression of the collective mind of people and of more-than-personal activities, wherever we wish to place the major emphasis on the expression of some impersonal ideal, there we may naturally expect formality (Figs. 613, 623). On

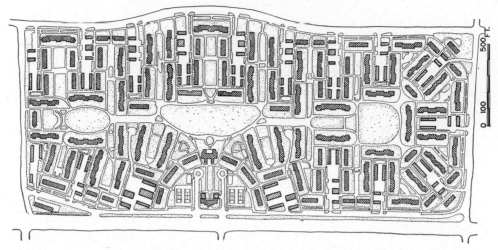

FIGURE 665. BALDWIN HILLS VILLAGE, LOS ANGELES, CALIFORNIA. PLAN

R. D. Johnson and Wilson, Merrill & Alexander, associated architects; Clarence Stein, consultant

Up to 1948 the best of the government-assisted "private industry" housing projects. The block plan is distinguished by great variety—which prevents the similarity of units from being regimented or institutional in feeling—by the concentration of open area in three large connected parks, by the successful placing of garage courts between pairs of rows and around the perimeter, and by the rich and always well-composed views which the plan creates for those who live in it or walk through it.

the other hand, in groups where the individual is dominant and every effort must be made to emphasize the primacy of *persons* in the conception—wherever one seeks for what is usually called "charm" rather than what is usually called "impressiveness"—there an informal group as a rule will prove better. (See Figs. 668, 669.)

The third basis which may affect the choice is the question of the intensity of usage which any group will receive. The greater the congestion in the group —the greater the number of people who use it—the more necessary do straight-line patterns become and the more likely is it that a certain formality will result.

In this choice one must remember that many of the greatest of group plans of the past have combined informal and formal features. The plan basically informal will almost always be made more effective by little touches of formality here and there, little elements of minor climax where a delicate touch of pure formality will give a pleasant sense of repose and balance. Similarly, great formal plans are frequently improved if they are varied by occasional touches of informality, of dynamic balance, which, as minor elements, will serve to enhance still further the richness of the entire experience.

FIGURE 666. BALDWIN HILLS VILLAGE, LOS ANGELES, CALIFORNIA. TWO VIEWS
R. D. Johnson and Wilson, Merrill & Alexander, associated architects; Clarence Stein, consultant
A brilliant combination of formal and informal planning creates a livable and likable environment.   Photographs Margaret Lowe

FIGURE 667. BUHL FOUNDATION HOMES, CHATHAM VILLAGE, PITTSBURGH, PENN-
SYLVANIA. TWO VIEWS

Ingham & Boyd, architects; Robert Griswold, landscape architect; Henry Wright and
Clarence Stein, consultants

A compact and coherent plan flexibly arranged to suit a sloping terrain.

Photographs S. J. Link, courtesy Buhl Foundation

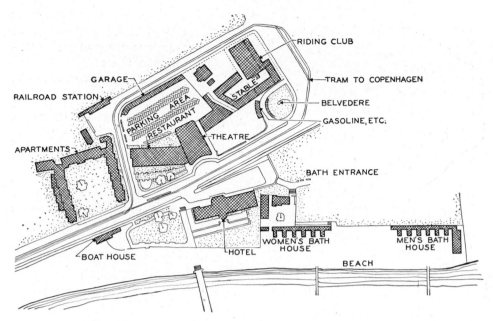

FIGURE 668. BELLEVUE, A COASTAL RESORT AND RECREATION CENTER NEAR CO-PENHAGEN. PLAN

Arne Jacobsen, architect

Informal planning to emphasize rural quality despite the close spacing of elements. There is careful functional division of elements, yet all are carefully placed to make the most of the sea view and sea air; the apartments are at one side to be close to bathing, boating, and restaurant, but away from noise and crowds. The visual relationships established are also attractive.

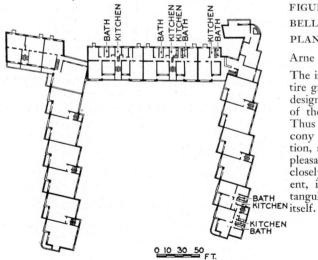

FIGURE 669. APARTMENTS AT BELLEVUE, NEAR COPENHAGEN. PLAN

Arne Jacobsen, architect

The informality of the plan of the entire group allows an apartment layout designed to take the utmost advantage of the site in views and orientation. Thus every apartment has a sunny balcony with a sea view, cross ventilation, and living rooms with the most pleasant aspect. The result, though closely organized and visually coherent, is neither symmetrical nor rectangular; the true climax is the view itself.

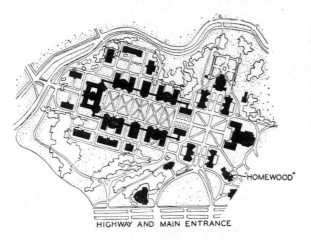

HIGHWAY AND MAIN ENTRANCE

FIGURE 670. JOHNS HOPKINS UNIVERSITY, BALTIMORE, MARYLAND. GENERAL DEVELOPMENT PLAN

A formal building scheme of two related quadrangles, with climax buildings at the ends. The pedestrian and automobile circulations are difficult, with much crossing, and the automobile circulation is confused by many turns and dead-end elements, with little real study of delivery courts or parking areas.

Redrawn from Klauder and Wise, *College Architecture in America*

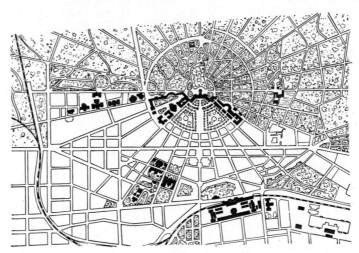

FIGURE 671. KARLSRUHE, GERMANY. GENERAL PLAN

The most extreme actual example of imposed artificial formal pattern over an entire city. Radial streets focus on the palace, but this is in actuality too small and distant to count as a climax; the result is merely blocks with angles that seem forced and without meaning. Here is paper planning carried to the point of absurdity.

22

Group Planning III: Open Groups and Closed Groups

ONE of the most important choices the designer of a group of buildings has to face is whether the group shall be completely enclosed or, instead, a systematic arrangement of structures at some distance from one another—in other words, whether it shall be an open or a closed group. By a closed group one does not necessarily mean that all the buildings must be continuous and that the approaches to the group shall be only through buildings. It does mean, however, that the group shall appear closed from most points of view, that is, that the approaches shall be indirect or so placed as, in general, to be visually closed. Thus a closed group may frequently have many changes of plane in the buildings which surround it. They may be stepped back behind one another with openings between, yet so located that from the greater part of the group there appears to be a continuous enclosure. An ingenious use of this method of concealed entrances characterized the gates of the San Francisco Exposition in 1939 (Fig. 672). Where the approaches are thus concealed, the group may rightly be called an enclosed group. If, on the other hand, the buildings of a group, however formally arranged, are so placed as to leave large areas between them, then the group is an open group. Camillo Sitte in *The Art of Building Cities* [1] devotes a chapter, "The Enclosed Character of the Public Square," to the advantages that were gained in the almost complete enclosure of public squares in the ancient, medieval, and Renaissance periods and describes various methods by which the approach was so arranged as to permit almost complete visual enclosure. The cathedral square at Ravenna (Fig. 675) and the piazzas at Parma (Fig. 674) are particularly interesting from this point of view. (See also Figs. 676, 677, 680.)

One thing that must be borne in mind in connection with those early squares

[1] Translated by Charles T. Stewart (New York: Reinhold Publishing Corp., 1945).

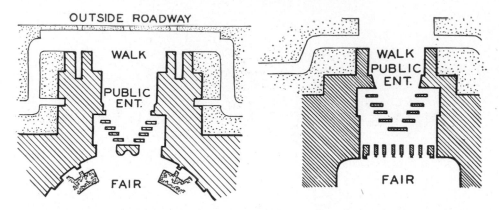

FIGURE 672. MAIN GATES OF THE SAN FRANCISCO EXPOSITION OF 1939. PLANS

These gates were designed to keep the fierce winds of the San Francisco area out of the Exposition courts. They served another important function, however—they furnished complete visual enclosure although permitting the free flow of people entering or leaving. Once inside them, the outer world seemed entirely excluded; one could give one's self up to the beauty of the gardened courts without distraction.

FIGURE 673. SAN FRANCISCO EXPOSITION OF 1939. AIR VIEW OF MODEL

The chief buildings form an enclosed court, open only on the leeward side (right). The main gates are at center and left, below.   Photograph Ewing Galloway

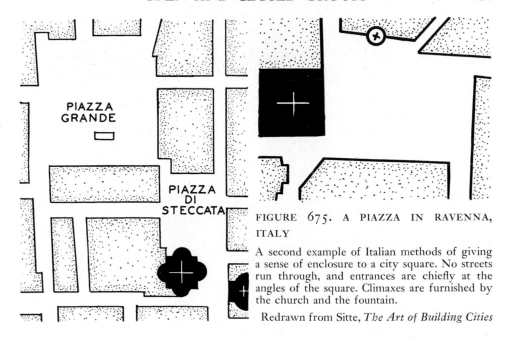

FIGURE 675. A PIAZZA IN RAVENNA, ITALY

A second example of Italian methods of giving a sense of enclosure to a city square. No streets run through, and entrances are chiefly at the angles of the square. Climaxes are furnished by the church and the fountain.

Redrawn from Sitte, *The Art of Building Cities*

FIGURE 674. CITY SQUARES OF PARMA, ITALY

Two related squares so designed as to be from most points of view completely closed; note the interesting corner connection between them.   Redrawn from Sitte, *The Art of Building Cities*

is the fact that the traffic in and through them was chiefly pedestrian. It is obvious, for instance, that the forums of Roman cities (Figs. 681, 682) were never designed for wheeled traffic. It is equally obvious that the people who came to the market places or the cathedral squares of medieval and Renaissance times came chiefly on foot. Within these spaces there was little possibility of canalizing traffic. The enclosed areas were more like great unroofed halls than like the open traffic places of a later era.

Wheeled traffic, we are told, did not become an important problem in city layout until the Baroque period, when the use of the coach became common. And it is precisely with the coming of the Baroque that we begin to find the open group achieving dominance. This was the period also of the spectacular development of standing armies and of military panoply, when military parades became a familiar type of popular amusement and an almost universal accompaniment of court functions.

Both the extensive use of wheeled traffic and the demands of military parades made the existence of wide, straight streets and avenues necessary. And, since

FIGURE 676. PIAZZA DELL' ERBE, VE-
RONA, ITALY

The intimacy of an enclosed group.

Courtesy Ware Library

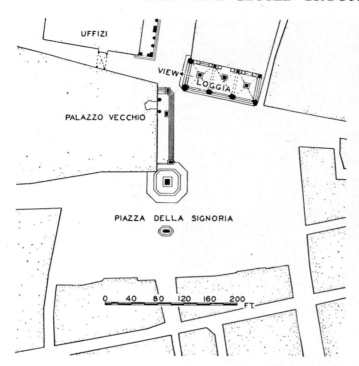

UFFIZI

VIEW

LOGGIA

PALAZZO VECCHIO

PIAZZA DELLA SIGNORIA

0   40   80   120 160 200
                              FT.

FIGURE 677. PIAZZA DELLA SIGNORIA, FLORENCE, ITALY. PLAN

One of the most beautiful of Italian squares, it owes its effect to its enclosure, to the great scale of the Palazzo Vecchio, and to the minor climaxes— all subtly related to one another and to entrances —furnished by fountain, sculpture, and the Loggia dei Lanzi. The placing of this loggia is masterly; it not only furnishes a sense of connection between the Piazza and the streets on each side but even more serves as a visual climax to one of these streets. This is subtle and effective planning.

most of this traffic and almost all the parades would focus at the ruler's palace or at the city's center, the open spaces which developed there were entered by many wide, straight avenues. Necessarily the squares became open groups like the Grande Place in front of the palace at Versailles (Fig. 683). Later still, the use of artillery and the fear of revolution encouraged this tendency, for a small amount of artillery could command all approaches through wide straight avenues whereas it would be almost powerless if the streets were narrow and crooked.[2]

Thus open groups became as characteristic of Baroque and nineteenth-century city planning as closed groups had been during the earlier periods. The Place de la Concorde in Paris (Figs. 684, 685) is a typical example of the new type of traffic square which the new type of city made necessary. It is, in a way, the parent of all modern bridge plazas, rotary traffic centers, and the like. The intensive wheeled traffic of the twentieth-century community has had a

[2] This consideration reached its climax in the layout of the British garrison city of Khartoum in the Sudan, where the garrison was placed in the exact center of the town and was approached only by eight straight radiating streets, equally spaced like the spokes of a wheel. Here the Governor General set eight machine guns; one for each street could almost certainly repel any local revolutionary attack.

FIGURE 678. LOGGIA DEI
LANZI, FLORENCE, ITALY

This loggia serves not only to
beautify the Piazza but also to
connect it subtly to the streets
outside.

Courtesy Avery Library

further interesting development which has affected the planning of open spaces;
in the effort to prevent accidents, it has worked for a much stricter type of
traffic canalization than was usual even as late as the end of the nineteenth century. We now aim at the complete separation of automobile and pedestrian
traffic and, as far as possible, the avoidance of pedestrian passages across automobile traffic. Thus purely pedestrian areas have been brought into being again;
where these occur, the old type of closed group represented by the Greek
agora, the Roman forum, or the medieval town square again becomes logical
and practical. The basic confusion arising from the thoughtless mixture of
pedestrian and wheeled traffic areas shows in the incoherence and lack of effect

FIGURE 679. CATHEDRAL PLAZA, HAVANA, CUBA

Visual enclosure in a Renaissance city square; the cathedral front forms the climax.

Courtesy Avery Library

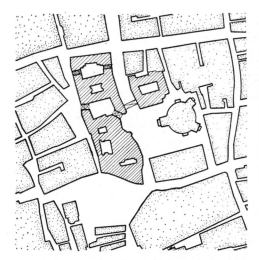

FIGURE 680. RÖMER AND ADJACENT SQUARES, FRANKFURT AM MAIN, GERMANY. PLAN

The two closely related public squares are typical of much medieval German town form. Note that both squares are visually closed compositions, with no distant views from them possible. Note also that the outline is much broken and irregular; nevertheless the close connection of all parts gives unity and visual repose. The hatched section forms the Römer—the old Frankfurt city hall.

in many attempted monumental public squares of early twentieth-century town plans, such as the ambitious civic center project at St. Louis (Figs. 598, 686, 695, 700).

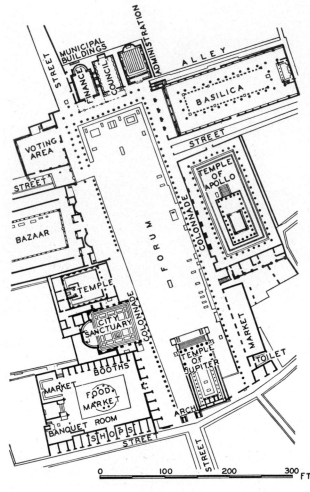

FIGURE 681. FORUM, POM-
PEII, ITALY. PLAN

A characteristic Roman enclosed forum; colonnades surround it and unify the buildings,
though there is variety in the arrangement of the buildings and
the width of the colonnades. At
one end the governmental buildings are grouped. The chief climax, the Temple of Jupiter, is
within the forum limits. Streets
lead to the forum but approach
it only through arched gates or
beneath the colonnade; the
whole is inward turning.

Today, then, the scientific canalization of wheeled traffic has again made the
closed group for essentially pedestrian use not only possible but also in many
cases the only logical solution. This is true, for instance, in the residential portions of schools and colleges, and it is true also of portions of the shopping
groups and community centers in housing developments. The modern group
planner enjoys much greater freedom in this respect than was the case at the
turn of the century; again we may have the relative quiet, the pleasant restful
sense of enclosure, the charming and human scale that governed many small
public spaces in the past. The problem of choosing between closed and open
groups, therefore, becomes one of the first tasks of the architect faced with the
designing of a group plan.

FIGURE 682. FORUM, POMPEII, ITALY. RESTORED

A formal enclosed square for pedestrians.   From Weichardt, *Pompeii vor der Zerstoerung*

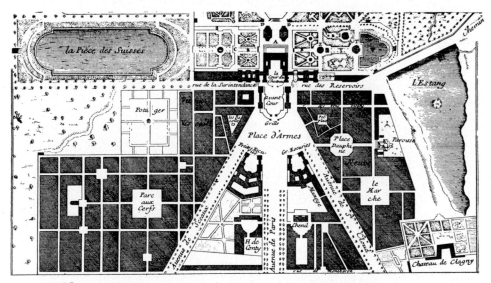

FIGURE 683. CENTRAL PART OF VERSAILLES, FRANCE. PLAN

This composition shows the vast scale of many Baroque city improvements. The scale is based on a pageantry requiring hundreds or thousands of troops. Architecturally it is ineffective because of the great distances between the buildings and because there is no visual climax for the radiating avenues. The enormous open spaces dwarf the huge structures; at ordinary times these *places* seem mere huge, bleak areas of useless pavement.

From De Mortain, *Versailles*

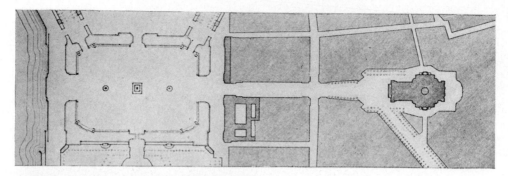

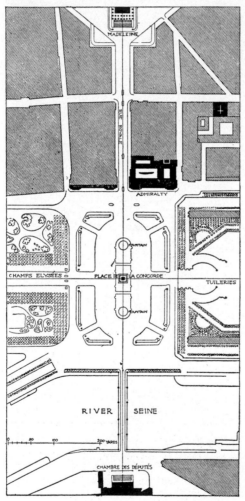

FIGURE 684. PLACE DE LA CONCORDE, PARIS. ORIGINAL PLAN

Jacques-Ange Gabriel, architect

The Place de la Concorde marks the intersection of two important axes of the Paris plan and, in addition, serves as a traffic distribution point. It is therefore an open group, gaining its effects not only by the relation of two similar buildings that flank the street leading to the Madeleine but also by carefully planned balustraded traffic islands, by carefully placed sculpture, and by the central group of fountains and statue.

From Patte, *Monumens érigés* . . .

FIGURE 685. PLACE DE LA CONCORDE, PARIS. PLAN IN THE TWENTIETH CENTURY

The modern Place preserves the old scheme almost intact, adding, however, wide pedestrian sidewalks and street lighting. The Madeleine axis has been further emphasized by the Seine bridge and the portico of the Chambre des Députés, and the Champ Élysées axis by the Arc de l'Étoile. This additional axial power has required strengthening of the central climax by the use of an obelisk at this point instead of a statue. Yet all changes have emphasized the qualities of the original plan and point up rather than destroy its original brilliant conception.

From Triggs, *Town Planning* . . .

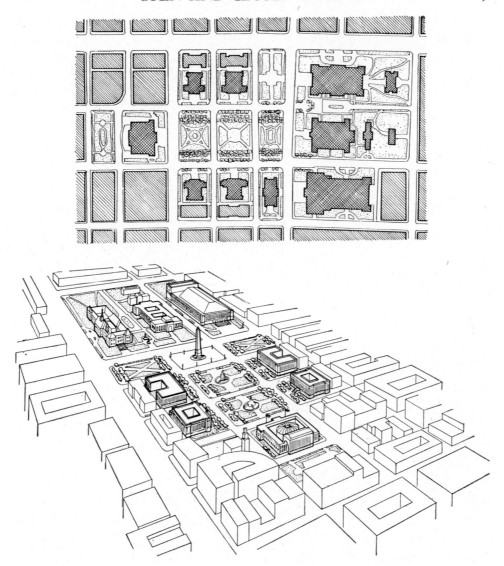

FIGURE 686. ORIGINAL DESIGN FOR THE CIVIC CENTER, ST. LOUIS, MISSOURI. PLAN
AND AIR VIEW

A characteristic piece of so-called "city beautiful" civic design, which groups large public
buildings around a central gardened plaza. In reality heavy traffic through the four cross streets
within the group effectively destroys the scale and the unity of the composition.

On what basis may this choice be made? As in the case of formal and informal
groups, the designer must analyze his problems down to their essentials. He
must first of all consider the function both of the group as a whole and of the

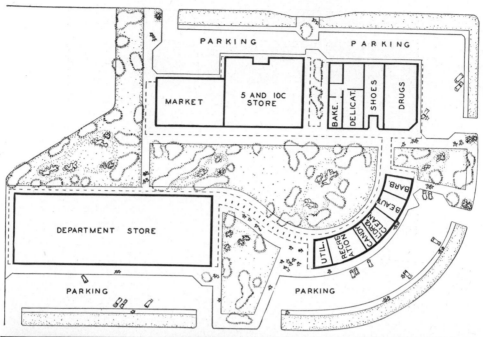

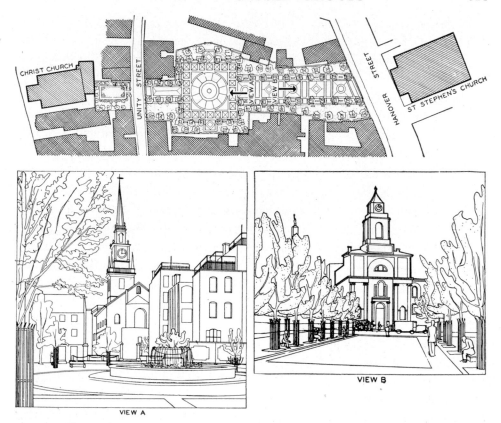

FIGURE 689. THE PRADO, BOSTON, MASSACHUSETTS. PLAN AND TWO VIEWS

Arthur Shurcliff, landscape architect; H. R. Shepley, architectural consultant

The Prado is an open square for pedestrian use carved out of a blighted slum district in Boston's congested North End. It is enclosed on the sides by brick walls, with planting to emphasize this enclosure, but at the ends it opens on two old churches, which furnish beautiful visual climaxes. A fountain acts as an interior climax. Many benches give it great usefulness as an outdoor sitting area for the neighborhood. Its formal composition suits both its congested use and its position, while the pavement design, brick walls, trees, and planting not only make it a beautiful oasis but also add to the importance, beauty, and accessibility of two important architectural monuments of old Boston.

FIGURE 687 (OPPOSITE, TOP). SHOPPING CENTER, LINDA VISTA, CALIFORNIA. PLAN

Earl F. Giberson and Whitney R. Smith, architects; H. Dankworth, landscape architect

A closed group as a shopping center, with the interior reserved for pedestrians. Covered ways connect the units, and there is an admirable arrangement of parking spaces.

FIGURE 688 (OPPOSITE, BOTTOM). SHOPPING CENTER, LINDA VISTA, CALIFORNIA

Earl F. Giberson and Whitney R. Smith, architects; H. Dankworth, landscape architect

Groups of an almost closed character are well fitted for use as shopping centers.

Courtesy Museum of Modern Art

individual units it comprises. How will people come to the buildings? How much service by truck or car will each building require? Is privacy an essential part of the problem? What do people do within the group? Realistic analysis of these points will often reveal that automobile traffic to certain parts of the group is much less important than would at first appear, or that in many cases it can be brought to one side of the buildings only, leaving the other sides clear for pedestrians; this is often the case in shopping centers (Figs. 687, 688). It has been a convention in much contemporary group planning to sacrifice pedestrian interests to the interests of those who drive or use automobiles. Yet if a true analysis shows that by far the larger number of people who use a certain building come to it on foot, either from other parts of the group or from outside the group, would it not be the democratic—and logical—thing to have the automobile traffic make the sacrifice? On the other hand, in the case of a railroad-station plaza—where usually (except in some commuting stations) the automobile problem is much the more important of the two—a group open in character, with traffic circulation as its main element, might be absolutely necessary.

Other things being equal, the closed group has certain definite functional advantages over the open group. If the group is large, closing it reduces the distances between units and permits a more tightly woven, and sometimes more logical, arrangement.

But a second type of analysis of a more imaginative character is also necessary —an aesthetic analysis of the coherence between the buildings, which may be of many different sizes and types. Here the designer will remember that coherence is frequently a matter of continuity and that continuity is sometimes easier to obtain in a closed group than in an open one. Naturally this does not mean that there can be no breaks in the series of enclosing buildings. What it does mean is merely that the feeling of a visitor will be one of enclosure. That feeling can be obtained in all sorts of ways—by offsetting or curving the approach walks or roads, by using corner entrances, or by some similar method. Often, however, approaches to groups, particularly the smaller groups, by means of arcades or passages under and through buildings may also be extremely effective. (See Fig. 663.) They have been brilliantly used in many housing developments and are frequent in dormitory groups; as one passes through such a covered approach there is a dramatic effectiveness in the sudden opening out of space and the sudden appearance of the sky which can be gained in no other way.

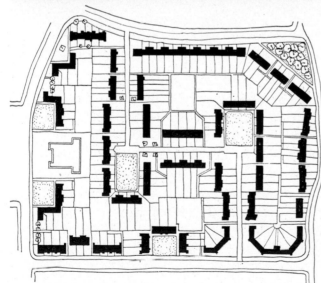

FIGURE 690 (ABOVE).
TRAFFIC SEPARATION, RAN-
DALL'S ISLAND, TRIBOR-
OUGH BRIDGE, NEW YORK

Modern traffic requires sweeping curves, great sizes, and visually open arrangements.

Courtesy Triborough Bridge
and Tunnel Authority

FIGURE 691 (LEFT). PLAN
OF A SUPERBLOCK AT
LETCHWORTH, ENGLAND

Parker & Unwin, architects

An ingenious method of developing an interior service circulation to all houses which at the
same time creates pleasant intimate lawns and courts. This is
a beautiful example of combined
closed and open group planning. Note that no one would be likely to mistake the cross circulation for a major traffic road.   Redrawn from Unwin, *Town Planning in Practice*

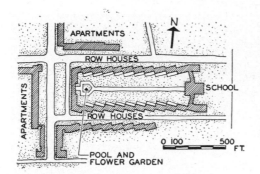

FIGURE 692. BRUCHFELDSTRASSE HOUSING GROUP ("ZIGZAG HOUSES"), FRANKFURT AM MAIN, GERMANY. BLOCK PLAN AND VIEW IN THE GARDEN

Ernst May, architect

This scheme is an excellent example of the intimacy and quiet effect of an enclosed housing group. A community building—which houses a nursery school—serves as a climax at one end of the group; at the other a pool surrounded by gardened terraces acts as a minor climax.

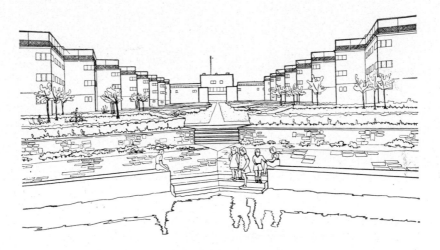

Another quality possible in closed groups is an extremely varied and often subtle handling of climax (Fig. 692). Because of the continuity of the sense of enclosure, anything which interrupts it—such as a high tower or a sudden change in building treatment—will produce at once a sense of climax. This can be seen in many medieval town squares, like those at Bruges or some of the old squares of Frankfurt am Main (Fig. 680), where either a church tower, a town belfry, or the suddenly increased scale of a town hall produces a most effective climax. In an enclosed group, because of its very nature, the placing of the climax is also much easier than it is in an open group; in a closed square the climax can take the form of a building set entirely within the square, or it may even be as small an element as a town fountain or an important statue. In Brunswick, Germany, the town hall is an L-shaped building in the corner of the square, yet its richly decorated arcade is a brilliant climax feature; in Halle

FIGURE 693. MILL HOUSING, SOMERS-WORTH, NEW HAMP-SHIRE

Open grouping typical of the early nineteenth-century village tradition in the United States.

Photograph
John Coolidge

a town belfry and market hall furnish another type, an interior climax. Many of the most interesting of these town squares owe their particular richness of aesthetic effect to the fact that, small as they are, each may contain several climaxes—statues, monuments, fountains—all leading up to some larger, more compelling climax element such as a church, a belfry, or a town hall.

A third type of analysis in group planning must concern itself with the quality of emotional character which the group should embody and express. A closed group has a restfulness which the open group usually lacks; it will have a kind of free balance which is reposeful. Above all else, the closed group is definitely inward turning; it will seem to be the heart of something. It will be a place one comes to, rather than an open space through which one passes. Closed groups would therefore seem to be best fitted for certain types of residential or of school or college groups, as well as for many community and neighborhood centers (Figs. 687, 692).

Open groups, on the other hand, are outward turning. They emphasize a relationship to that which is beyond and outside. Thus the Place de la Concorde in Paris is not a place one comes *to*, but rather a beautiful incident in one's passage to some place or object beyond its borders—from the Louvre to the Arc de l'Étoile, or from the Seine to the Madeleine. Bridge plazas and such traffic areas all have this quality of relationship to something beyond themselves, and thus for them the open group is the only logical plan. Open groups almost always suggest motion, dynamic progress. But they offer many difficulties. Because of their very openness, the distances between their component buildings will make continuity and coherence sometimes difficult to attain; for this

FIGURE 694. MAGDALEN COLLEGE, OXFORD, ENGLAND. THE QUADRANGLE

The closed grouping typical of the English collegiate tradition.   Courtesy Ware Library

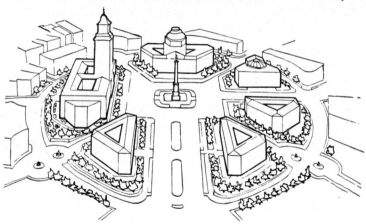

FIGURE 695. SCHEME FOR A PROPOSED CIVIC CENTER OF A CITY IN THE UNITED STATES (CIRCA 1915)

This project illustrates the old concept of the civic center as a traffic intersection, with all streets radiating from it. Functionally dangerous and designed to produce only traffic confusion, such a scheme is doomed to aesthetic failure because of the distances between buildings, the narrowness of their ends towards the center, and the separation between them inherent in hurrying traffic. Since most traffic between such buildings is on foot, it is easy to see the illogicality of separating them by wide streets full of vehicular traffic.

Redrawn from Hegemann and Peets, *The American Vitruvius* . . .

FIGURE 696. CIVIC CENTER, NEW YORK

An open plan, incoherent because of differences in building quality and heavy cross traffic.

Photograph Ewing Galloway

reason the climax of open groups must be more powerful, more dominantly stressed, in order to hold the whole spreading network together. In the Place de l'Étoile in Paris, the climax, the great Triumphal Arch, is the only bit of its architecture which has meaning, for the narrow façades of the enclosing buildings are so distant from one another across the circle, and so separated from their neighbors by great radiating avenues, that they become meaningless as parts of the group. A similar difficulty will account for the basic ineffectiveness of many American civic centers (Figs. 695, 700), where buildings intended to count as a group are separated by the rushing traffic of great avenues and, because of the radiating plan, can present to the group center only their narrow ends. Here human scale is entirely lost, and the buildings exist only as so many individual units.

But in open-group plans there is another type of relationship to the outside

FIGURE 697. TYPICAL NEW ENGLAND VILLAGE GREEN. PLAN, SIDE ELEVATION, AND VIEW OF ONE END

This diagram is typical only and is composed of elements taken from many sources. It illustrates, however, characteristics true of many examples. The houses that border it are harmonious in color and material. Continuity is given by the fences and the overarching trees, as well as by the views of meadow and hill seen between the buildings. The church portico and spire form a powerful climax at the end.

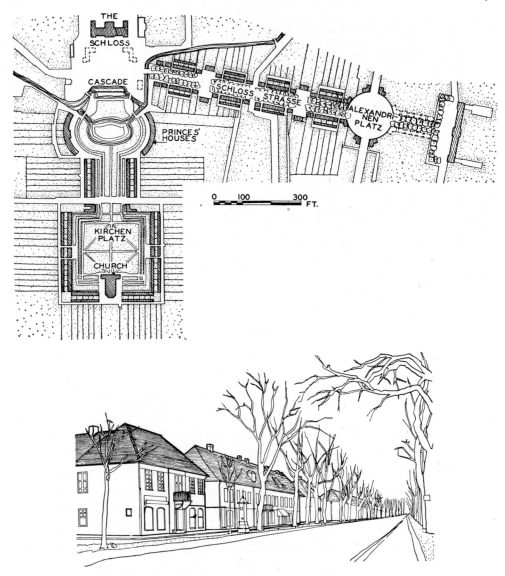

FIGURE 698. LUDWIGSLUST, GERMANY. PLAN AND VIEW IN THE SCHLOSS STRASSE

This village is a charming combination of formality and informality, of open and closed planning. The rhythmic platting of the houses on the Schloss Strasse, the simple Kirchenplatz, with
its climax church, the curves offered by the princes' houses and the pool between them and by
the Alexandrinenplatz, all combine felicitously to give variety and yet perfect unity.

Redrawn from Hegemann and Peets, *The American Vitruvius* . . .

of an entirely different nature—the relationship of an open group to the surrounding landscape. The enclosed group definitely shuts this out; it thus has

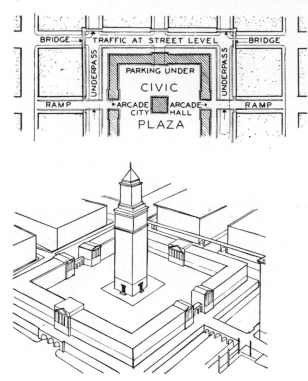

FIGURE 699. PLAN AND PERSPECTIVE OF A TWO-LEVEL CIVIC CENTER AS PROPOSED BY HEGEMANN AND PEETS

Automobiles are restricted to the lower level, which furnishes ample parking space and permits under-cover approach to all portions of the group. The upper level is reserved for pedestrians and forms an enclosed group with a central tower climax.

Redrawn from Hegemann and Peets, *The American Vitruvius* . . .

necessarily a certain urban character. Where, therefore, the desire is to produce a really rural feeling in a group, and to relate buildings in the strongest possible way to the surrounding country, the open group is the obvious choice.

Once this choice is made, it becomes the architect's duty to realize all the more that by his choice he is making himself definitely responsible for the views between buildings (see Figs. 689, 697). These must be meaningful and must in some way be brought into the group—by planting, by the furnishing of view areas, or by various tricks of enframement. For instance, the major error in the group planning of Greenbelt, otherwise so successful, lies in the completely open and characterless axis which pierces through the community center (Fig. 660). Everything in the plan establishes this as the climax point; by the simplest kind of terrace or shelter treatment, which would at once have reinforced the view and yet tied in with the buildings on either side, this climax could have been beautifully stated. As it is, the wide view, pleasant though it be, seems a completely unrelated element; the important axis peters out, and there is an instant feeling of disappointment.

One of the best examples of an open group which still preserves continuity,

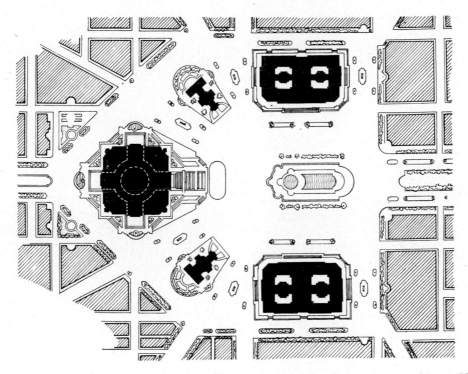

FIGURE 700. CIVIC CENTER PROPOSED IN THE CHICAGO, ILLINOIS, PLAN BY D. H. BURNHAM

This plan reveals the complete unreality of certain proposals to combine a civic center with a traffic intersection. One can only imagine the extraordinary confusion that would result from any attempt to route traffic through this vast plaza, and the impossibility of arranging for safe pedestrian approach to any of the public buildings is obvious. The city hall, on the main axis, was supposed to have a dome nearly a thousand feet high. Visually, the effect would be far less than the plan indicates because of the great distances between the buildings and also because of the complete lack of human scale. An individual would seem dwarfed and lost in these gigantic areas.

coherence, and a pleasant and relaxed sense of balance is the typical New England village common or green. Figure 697 shows the plan and the elevation of one of the sides of such a group. These illustrations are purely diagrammatic and contain qualities that have been abstracted from many examples. It will be noticed that along the sides of the green the houses, although they are widely spaced, have main roofs which always parallel the street, cornice lines of approximately the same height, and a general harmony of material and form. More definite continuity is given to them by the fences which line the street, punctuated by the vertical notes of higher posts at gates and corners. The tall trunks of wineglass elms spaced with some regularity along the road act as

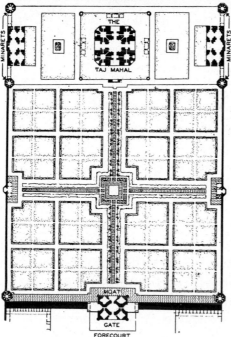

FIGURE 701 (ABOVE). TAJ MAHAL, AGRA, INDIA. GENERAL VIEW

Courtesy Metropolitan Museum of Art

FIGURE 702 (LEFT). TAJ MAHAL, AGRA, INDIA. PLAN

Much of the breath-taking beauty of this great tomb comes from its superb planning. It is simple in scheme but complex in the variety of its units—water basins, fountains, trees, terrace walls, tanks, and marble structures. The tomb itself stands at the intersection of two important axes, and the four slim minarets, by framing it from every point of view, emphasize its climax character. Note that the minarets themselves are on the minor axes formed by the paths through the formal garden beds—this is symptomatic of the close organization of the entire plan. The preparation for the climax given by the gate and the long progress up the central walk past rhythmic pointed trees, around the pool, and then up to the terrace steps adds enormously to the emotional aesthetic impact of the tomb.

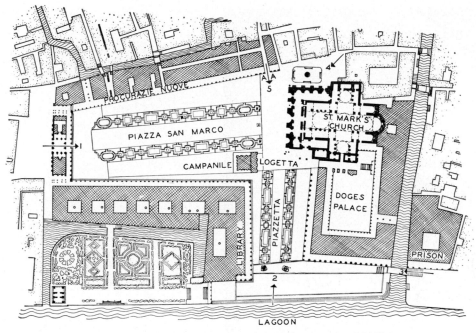

FIGURE 703. PIAZZA AND PIAZZETTA AT VENICE, ITALY. PLAN

This is one of the most successful pieces of building arrangement in the world. It is reserved for pedestrian use. St. Mark's climaxes the Piazza; the view across the lagoon, enframed by the columns, B, climaxes the Piazzetta; the Campanile connects the two, and its height is great enough to command both. The main entrance is at 1; but any approach—from the city at 4 or 5, from boats at 2, or from along the lagoon and over the bridge at 3—gives exciting views and leads one inevitably into the great square. No absolute symmetry exists, but all views are superbly balanced; furthermore, minor view balances are all of a dynamic nature to suggest and assist the "correct" progress through to the center. A is the relatively low clock tower that not only acts as a full stop to the march of the arches of the Procurazie Nuove but also helps balance the view toward St Mark's from the Piazza. The architects of the buildings flanking the Piazza have had the sense and humility to keep them absolutely continuous, with no accents to disturb the major effect.

strong connecting elements, and the fact that many of the houses have twin trees at the sides of the entrance also helps. Moreover, the landscape is important, and the undulating lines of meadow and hill seen between the houses become definite, though unconsciously felt, elements in the composition. The barns, often set behind the houses or at one side of them, serve as transitional elements between the more formal placing of the houses and the informal natural background of meadow, woods, or hill. The treatment of the ground between the houses also often helps to bring the feeling of outside nature into the group itself. Such an example as this should be most instructive in the design of many types of open groups, particularly groups of houses. Especially inter-

FIGURE 704. ST. MARK'S, VENICE, ITALY. VIEW FROM ACROSS THE PIAZZA

Courtesy Avery Library

FIGURE 705 (BELOW). VIEW ACROSS THE PIAZZA FROM ST. MARK'S, VENICE, ITALY

Courtesy Ware Library

FIGURE 706. THE PIAZZETTA, VENICE, ITALY. VIEW OUT ACROSS THE LAGOON
Courtesy Avery Library

esting is the way the side yards, rhythmically repeated, create contrasting notes of greenery which tie into the background.

Another important element in these compositions is the existence of the strong climax furnished by the white spire and the portico of the village church. The open nature of the group planning renders this powerful climax necessary to give unity to the whole.

In the design of any open group, and particularly one in which traffic plays an important part, the problem of the exact relationship of the traffic to the group must always remain as a dominant factor. Subtleties of design, delicate notes, and elements which call too much attention to themselves—and thus suggest delay or stopping—have no place in a traffic circle, a bridge plaza, or a cloverleaf intersection. To people in automobiles, the landscape and the buildings immediately on either side become mere blurs; the only definite visual impression is given by what is ahead and particularly what can be seen from some distance away. Group planning for this type of automobile traffic, therefore, must always consider primarily the view ahead; if there are no pedestrian

FIGURE 707. THE PI-
AZZETTA, VENICE, IT-
ALY. VIEW ACROSS
THE ENTRANCE
Courtesy Ware Library

paths to consider, it can almost ignore the buildings at the sides of a group, except as they are related to the more distant views ahead.

If a traffic intersection is in a city and is controlled by signal lights, the auto-mobilist's attention should be concentrated on these signals and not be drawn aside constantly by elements that are too interesting. This should prove the complete impossibility of developing, for instance, an effective and beautiful civic center at any point of major traffic intersection. Architectural beauty in the ordinary sense is largely wasted at such points, and in the middle of an area noisy with the roar of automobiles there is never a possibility for that type of quiet, reposeful balance which such civic centers should have. Yet again and again the problem of combining the needs of an automobile approach with an adequate sense of civic dignity and beauty will come up. Again and again there will be public buildings which have to be in close touch with major traffic thoroughfares and yet also demand convenient and quiet pedestrian approach. The only solution in cases of this kind is the absolute separation of automobile and pedestrian traffic, either through by-passing the automobile traffic around the buildings or group or by means of some kind of two-level scheme. Werner Hegemann and Elbert Peets were the first, we believe, to call attention to this fact in *The American Vitruvius, an Architect's Handbook of Civic Art*,[3] where the illogical nature of any attempt to design a civic center as a sort of magni-fied street intersection is cogently pointed out. (See Fig. 699.)

[3] New York: Architectural Book Publishing Co., 1922, p. 138.

FIGURE 708. THE PI-
AZZETTA, VENICE, IT-
ALY. VIEW TOWARD
THE PIAZZA
Courtesy Ware Library

It is in the design of open groups that the danger of the paper plan is most acute. Again and again projects for civic centers or for universities, like many of the *projets* of the École des Beaux Arts, make magnificent paper drawings. If built, they would be either completely without effect or horrible violations of human scale. Can anything be imagined that would be more terrifying in actuality, more murderous under modern traffic conditions, or more utterly a waste and misapplication of money than the Gargantuan city hall on its vast traffic intersection shown in the Burnham plan for Chicago (Fig. 700)?

Many of the greatest groups are combinations of open- and closed-group elements. In Nancy, for instance, the Place Stanislas is open, the Place de la Carrière partly open, the Place du Gouvernement closed (Fig. 637). In Venice, the Piazza, facing St. Mark's, is entirely closed; but the Piazzetta, which opens out from it, has one end entirely open to the blue waters of the lagoon (Figs. 703–709). Notice, however, the tremendous importance in the Piazzetta of the two Byzantine columns which act as frames for the distant view across the lagoon and make one design of the whole.

Since many travelers have thought that the Piazza and the Piazzetta combined represent the most beautiful of all European public areas, some of the qualities which produce this effectiveness may well be studied. We cannot build such a civic square today, but we may be able to apply to our own architecture some of the lessons to be learned from its perfect rightness. It is formal, yet informal; it is enclosed, yet through the Piazzetta it is wide open to the distant view. The climax of the Piazza is the superb church of St. Mark's, yet the Campanile

FIGURE 709. THE PIAZZA AND PIAZZETTA, VENICE, ITALY. AIR VIEW

Courtesy Avery Library

forms another climax which suggests the opening of the smaller square beyond it. However one approaches this group of buildings, whether through the loggia opposite St. Mark's, or through the side court under the clock tower, or along the quay past the prison, or by gondola from the Piazzetta steps, the visitor will always be faced by a series of experiences of extraordinary coherence—rich, yet not confused; balanced, but never stolid. And everywhere the balance is such that it suggests and assists one in taking the right turns as he proceeds through these rich areas. Perhaps nowhere else in the world has the problem of dynamic balance in group planning been so exquisitely handled.

It is in group-planning problems that the architect finds a challenge to his greatest and his noblest efforts. It is in group plans themselves that the quality of a community's or a nation's life is most inspiringly expressed. By means of group planning the architect can do much more to enrich the social life of the world than in the designing of individual buildings. It is therefore to problems of group planning that he must bring the very summit of his powers of analysis and the full scope of his creative imagination.

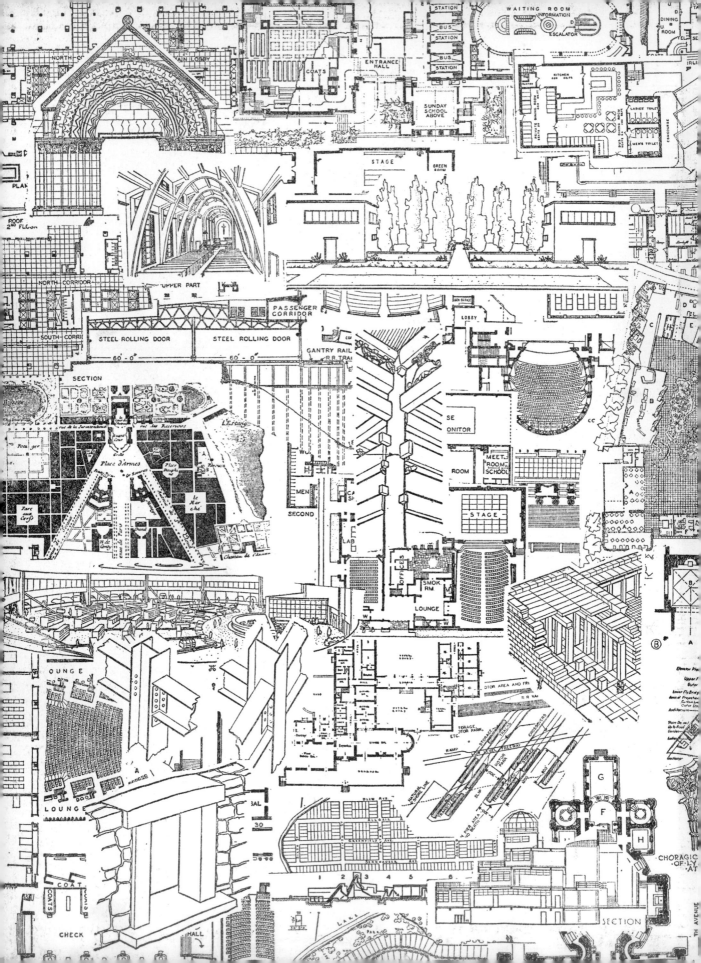